D1572262

*John
Laurens*
and the
*American
Revolution*

Portrait of John Laurens

John Laurens

and the

American Revolution

Gregory D. Massey

University of South Carolina Press

Frontispiece: *Portrait of John Laurens,* a miniature painted by Charles Willson Peale in 1780, watercolor on ivory. Privately owned. On deposit at Gibbes Museum of Art/Carolina Art Association, Charleston.

© 2000 University of South Carolina

Published in Columbia, South Carolina, by the University of South Carolina Press

Manufactured in the United States of America

04 03 02 01 00   5 4 3 2 1

Library of Congress Cataloging-in-Publication Data

Massey, Gregory De Van.
  John Laurens and the American Revolution / Gregory D. Massey.
    p. cm.
  Includes bibliographical references and index.
  ISBN 1-57003-330-7 (alk. paper)
    1. Laurens, John, 1754–1782. 2. United States—History—Revolution,
  1775–1783. 3. Soldiers—United States—Biography. 4. United States.
  Continental Army—Biography. I. Title.
  E207.L37 M38 2000
  973.3'092—dc21   99-050753

For Van S. Massey,
and in memory of
Helen P. Massey

Contents

Illustrations

Family Line of John Laurens

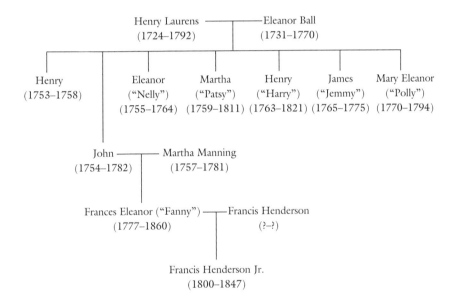

Henry Laurens ——————— Eleanor Ball
(1724–1792)   (1731–1770)

Henry
(1753–1758)

Eleanor
("Nelly")
(1755–1764)

Martha
("Patsy")
(1759–1811)

Henry
("Harry")
(1763–1821)

James
("Jemmy")
(1765–1775)

Mary Eleanor
("Polly")
(1770–1794)

John ——————— Martha Manning
(1754–1782)   (1757–1781)

Frances Eleanor ("Fanny") ——— Francis Henderson
(1777–1860)   (?–?)

Francis Henderson Jr.
(1800–1847)

Acknowledgments

Much of the historian's craft involves long hours of individual labor. On occasion, fortunately, the moments of solitude are punctuated by collaboration with others. It is a pleasure to extend appreciation to the people who helped me bring this project to completion.

Robert M. Weir directed this study in its original form as a doctoral dissertation. His historical imagination and resourceful intellect focused my attention on questions I otherwise might have overlooked. It is a testimony to Professor Weir's talents as a scholar that after extensive research, involving repeated efforts to find holes in his own essay on John Laurens—I wanted to avoid the appearance of merely parroting that work—that this book corroborates the principal conclusions in his exploratory essay. I would like to thank other scholars at the University of South Carolina: Owen Connelly, who commented on the dissertation; Ronald Maris, who provided insights into self-destructive behavior; Kendrick Clements, who read the sections on revolutionary diplomacy; and Samuel Smith, who allowed me to cite his unpublished work on Henry Laurens's religious views.

Without the assistance of the staff of the Papers of Henry Laurens, this study would not have been possible. I owe more than I can express to David Chesnutt, Jim Taylor, and Peggy Clark, who provided me access to their archives—and coffee room—and read an earlier draft of the manuscript and saved me from numerous errors. Two people I met at the Laurens Papers project deserve special mention. The late George C. Rogers Jr. allowed me to use his extensive research files and library; in addition, he read and commented on multiple drafts of the manuscript. George's civility and generosity, his enthusiasm for history and zest for life, will ever inspire those who were fortunate enough to have known him. Martha King read more drafts of this study than anyone else. On several occasions she directed me to John Laurens documents that I had not previously uncovered. Martha's editorial pen and historical sensitivity immeasurably improved the quality of this book and made me a better historian.

Several individuals helped turn an unwieldy dissertation into a book. My colleagues at the Naval Historical Center's Early History Branch, where I spent ten months as a National Historical Publications and Records Commission fellow, read the dissertation and offered useful suggestions for revision. Special thanks is owed to Michael Crawford, who went beyond the call of duty and provided translations of French documents. More recently, Daphene Kennedy, professor emeritus at Freed-Hardeman University, has translated several French texts. A succession of librarians at Freed-Hardeman University—Jane Miller, Hope Shull, and Shirley Eaton—procured materials for me on interlibrary loan. Jeffrey Watt allowed me to read his unpublished work on Geneva and provided insights into John Laurens's enigmatic reference to suicide. Joyce Chaplin and Don Higginbotham gave the manuscript a critical reading when it was most needed. Professor Chaplin, in particular, posed questions that led me in new, profitable directions. Dr. Charlton de Saussure Sr. and Mary de Saussure showed me the meaning of Charleston hospitality during a research trip to that loveliest of historical cities. Robert Calhoon has encouraged my work for nearly a decade. As the study neared completion, Loren Schweninger kindly sent me a copy of a petition from his edited microfilm collection of black petitions to state legislatures. At the University of South Carolina Press, Alex Moore has been unfailingly helpful.

Because the Laurens Papers project has amassed an extensive collection of photocopied manuscripts, I was able to conduct much of the research in South Carolina, though the bibliography appears to reflect extensive travel. Still, I had to obtain manuscripts from other sources, and would like to thank the following people and institutions: David Fowler of the David Library of the American Revolution; the late Richard Showman and Senior Associate Editor Roger Parks of the Papers of General Nathanael Greene; and staff members at the New York Public Library; the New-York Historical Society; and the Clements Library, University of Michigan.

I am grateful to the following institutions that granted me permission to quote from their collections: the Adams Manuscript Trust; American Philosophical Society; the Trustees of the Boston Public Library; the Charleston Museum, Charleston, South Carolina; Chicago Historical Society; Special Collections, Tutt Library, the Colorado College, Colorado Springs; the Connecticut Historical Society, Hartford; the David Library of the American Revolution; Rare Book, Manuscript, and Special Collections Library, Duke University; the Historical Society of Pennsylvania, Philadelphia; the Huntington Library, San Marino, California; the Houghton Library, Harvard University; the Kendall Whaling Museum, Sharon, Massachusetts; the Maryland Historical Society, Baltimore; Massachusetts Historical Society, Boston; Clements Library, University of Michigan; Morristown National Historical Park; the New-York Historical Society; the New York Public Library, Astor, Lenox and Tilden Foundations; Princeton University Library; the Controller of Her Britannic Majesty's Stationery Office for permission to reproduce Crown copyright material in the Public Record Office; the Trustees of the Rt. Hon. Olive Countess Fitzwilliam's Chattels Settlement, the City Librarian, Sheffield Libraries and Information; the South Carolina Historical Society, Charleston; the South Caroliniana Library, University of South Carolina; and Yale University Library. I thank the editors of the *Journal of Southern History* for permission to use portions of my article, "The Limits of Antislavery Thought in the Revolutionary Lower South: John Laurens and Henry Laurens," vol. 63 (August 1997): 495–530.

Rick and Elaine Massey provided computer access when I completed the first draft of the manuscript. Rick, more than he knows, inspired my love of learning. Danae Massey commented on the first page, which was revised accordingly; Vanessa Massey frowned at the book's size, which prompted me to purge extraneous material.

The final debt is difficult to convey and impossible to repay. From the beginning, I thought of my parents as this book's primary readers. I am pleased finally to present the finished product to my dad, but deeply saddened that my mom did not live to see it completed. Their grace and fortitude remain my example; their deep and abiding love is, and always will be, my inspiration.

Abbreviations

Note on the Text

Some matters of usage deserve mention. During the colonial and revolutionary period, South Carolina's principal city was known as Charles Town. Upon incorporation in 1783, the city's name was changed to Charleston, which is the form used in this book. The words of the historical characters are presented as written, including capitalizations and spellings, with two exceptions: the baseline dash, commonly used in the eighteenth century, is here rendered as either a comma or a period, depending on which form of punctuation appears more appropriate; superscript letters are brought down to the line.

*John
Laurens*
and the

*American
Revolution*

Introduction

In early 1782 the long war between Great Britain and the rebellious American colonies neared its end. The British held only the strategic seaports of New York, Charleston, and Savannah. In South Carolina the American army under the command of Major General Nathanael Greene warily watched the British garrison at Charleston. A vital part of Greene's force was a celebrated legion of light horse and infantry that had been commanded by Lieutenant Colonel Henry Lee. Physically and emotionally exhausted, Lee retired from the army and returned to his home in Virginia. Rather than promote one of Lee's subordinates to command the Legion, Greene appointed Lieutenant Colonel John Laurens, a native Carolinian. Though Laurens had served in many of the important engagements of the war as an aide-de-camp to General George Washington, he had never held a permanent command.

Laurens proved an unpopular choice. The Legion officers, who wanted one of their own to replace Lee, did not accept his leadership. The transition of authority was made even more difficult by Laurens's impulsiveness, his tendency to confront the enemy without weighing the potential danger to his own men.[1]

His recklessness was most conspicuous on one occasion. A sentry posted at Ashley River near Dorchester noticed a red coat moving in the underbrush on the opposite bank. Concluding that a British party was near, he promptly relayed the information to Laurens, who ordered troops to cross the river to investigate. Because the current was rapid, Captain Ferdinand O'Neal, commander of the detachment, requested a boat to convey the soldiers to the other side.

Learning of the delay, Laurens rode to the site and demanded an explanation: "Why this halt, Captain? Were not orders given to cross?"

When O'Neal pointed to the dangerous current, Laurens replied impatiently, "This is no time for argument. You who are brave men, follow me!"

At that point Laurens plunged into the river. Forced by the swift waters to dismount, he barely made his way to the other side. Watching his commander fight the rapids, O'Neal called out, "You shall see, sir, that there are men here as brave as yourself." He led the remainder of the troops into the river.

The chaotic mass of struggling men and frightened horses made their way across the river with great difficulty. Amazingly, no one drowned, though they were exhausted by the ordeal. The infantry, using a plank and doors removed from a nearby warehouse, crossed with less trouble.

Upon reaching shore, Laurens, accompanied by his aides, searched for the red coat. To their surprise and chagrin, they discovered that the coat had been hung in a tree by a British soldier who had been drummed out of his regiment for drunkenness. Having endured a flogging, his "lacerated back would admit of no covering." There was no party of redcoats. Because Laurens hastened to cross the river without waiting to obtain more accurate intelligence, he endangered his men unnecessarily.[2]

This account, perhaps apocryphal, appeared in Alexander Garden's *Anecdotes of the Revolutionary War,* which was published in 1822, a period when South Carolinians began to perceive that their cultural system, based on slave labor, was threatened by actions of the federal government. Garden's avowed purpose was to honor Revolutionary heroes and to encourage their descendants—the current generation of Carolinians—to imitate their ancestors's example of virtue. Like their Revolutionary forebears who resisted British tyranny, Carolinians would stand united against external threats to their social order. Thus, although Garden deplored Laurens's recklessness, he extolled the hero's "chivalric gallantry." Had Laurens not been killed in August 1782 at the age of twenty-seven, Garden concluded, "he would have proved a model, both of civil and military virtue, 'a mirror by which our youth might dress themselves.'"[3]

It is an irony of history that Laurens became a model for Carolina youths to emulate as they endeavored to defend their slaveholding way of life, for he had opposed slavery and formulated a plan to free slaves in return for their service in the Continental Army, an aspect of his career Garden conveniently omitted from the book. Yet whatever Garden thought of these views on slavery, he correctly recognized in Laurens a heroic life, one devoted to virtuous self-sacrifice for the public good.

In the 170 years since Garden published his work, other authors and historians have examined the life of John Laurens with varying success.[4] To date, however, Laurens has not received the comprehensive study his exciting and diverse career merits. Because Laurens played a secondary role in many important events of the American war for independence, historians have largely over-looked him. They may quote him to make a particular argument or mention his convictions on slavery in the broader context of antislavery thought, but otherwise they reserve their focus for the major players in the Revolution. This biography aims to fill the gap. Laurens plays the leading role, but his status as an ancillary participant in larger events necessitates a life-and-times approach that illuminates the period in which he lived as well as explains the meaning of his life. For example, this study will examine in detail the character of the person to whom John was closest, his father, Henry. To understand the son one must also know the father. So, on occasion John will assume a place on the sidelines, but more frequently he will occupy center stage, for his life illustrates a central facet of the Revolutionary period, one that still informs public life today: the divergence between image and reality.

John Laurens packed a great deal into twenty-seven years. His life contains elements of triumph and tragedy that will interest general readers: his privi-leged adolescence as the son of one of South Carolina's most respected public figures; his mother's death when he was sixteen years old; more than two years of schooling in Geneva, Switzerland, followed by legal studies at the Inns of Court in London; the death of his youngest brother in an accident while under his care; a relationship with a young English woman that led to her pregnancy and a precipitate marriage; his hasty departure from England to enlist in the American war for independence; service as Washington's aide-de-camp, which brought him in contact with the prominent political and military figures of the Revolution; conspicuous conduct in a succession of major battles and sieges—Brandywine, Germantown, Monmouth, Newport, Charleston, Savannah, and Yorktown—resulting in four wounds and six months spent as a British prisoner of war; a diplomatic mission to France in 1781 that procured needed money and supplies for the American war effort but left a triangular trail of contro-versy stretching from Europe to the West Indies and then to the United States; and finally his appointment as commander of Lee's celebrated Legion.

On one hand, therefore, this biography is written for the general reader, a person interested in the drama of the past, how other people have shaped historical events by making choices that often produced unexpected results. The scholarly apparatus one associates with books authored by historians—disagreements with other scholars, lengthy historiographical commentaries—has been kept to a minimum and does not encroach on the narrative. On the other hand, Laurens's life touches on subjects of interest to scholars: the con-struction of identity and masculinity in the Anglo-American world; the meaning and importance of virtue in Revolutionary America; and the future of slavery and the distribution of wealth in the American republic. So this biography is constructed as a chronological narrative designed to appeal to a wider audience, but organized along analytical themes that invite the attention of historians as well.

People who have heard of John Laurens at all know him primarily for his views on slavery. John and his more famous father, who served as president of the Continental Congress, were the only prominent native South Carolinians who consistently expressed misgivings about the institution of slavery. Their dialogue on slavery has been cited by numerous historians, and some scholars have briefly surveyed John's attempt to form a black regiment.[5] In general these studies have allotted the Laurenses a small part in a larger framework. What is missing is an examination of individual motive and context. This biography will explore the personal, social, and cultural factors that prompted father and son to pursue a divergent course on the slavery issue. Their separate paths and ultimate fates suggest the limits of antislavery thought in the Revolutionary lower South.[6]

Laurens's life illuminates several aspects of the aristocratic experience in eighteenth-century Anglo-America. The richest inhabitants in the North American colonies possessed wealth that was comparable to that of members of the middle-class in England. But the colonial elite, or gentry, tried to imitate the English aristocracy, often failing in the attempt. John Laurens exemplified the tension many American gentlemen encountered as they attempted to establish their place in a peculiar world, where their models of behavior were inherited from England but the provincial arena in which they operated failed to approximate the English paradigm.[7] In his career choices—forsaking his first love, medicine, to study law, and then abandoning his education for military service—he demonstrated the difficulties young men experienced in constructing a public identity. In his personal credo—devoting his life to assisting oppressed people in society—he embodied the man of feeling, a symbol of eighteenth-century Britain's celebration of sensibility. In his relationships with other men, particularly with his closest friend, Alexander Hamilton, he illustrated how the man of feeling constructed sentimental attachments that tended to restrict women to the marginal role of spectators exhorting their men to virtuous accomplishments in the public realm.

Thus far the different studies of Laurens have shared a common focus: their recognition of his reckless behavior. Though in many respects Laurens's behavior resembled that of other Continental Army officers, his contemporaries believed that his daring went beyond socially acceptable limits. To explain Laurens's conduct, this book will examine closely the tension he encountered in constructing his identity,[8] a process that compelled him to confront eighteenth-century notions of private and public virtue, and on occasion supplement that approach by utilizing the empirical findings of psychological and sociological investigations of self-destructive behavior.[9] There are dangers inherent in such an approach. Several historians have criticized biographers who explore their subject's psyche in order to uncover the unconscious motivations behind his or her actions. Indeed, some scholars question whether conclusions derived from the social scientists of the twentieth century can be used to explain the actions of eighteenth-century Americans. John Laurens was decidedly an eighteenth-century man. Imperatives that seem remote today—virtue and honor, fame and sensibility—informed his conduct his entire adult life. Despite the cultural and societal differences between his time and today, one can still presume that fundamental human behavior maintains consistent patterns.[10]

More often than not, Laurens's self-fashioning involved personal decisions that produced costly, unintentional consequences. He ultimately bore responsibility for his own choices, but specific cultural and historical contingencies delineated his range of options.[11] The political culture of his native South Carolina placed great demands on members of its patrician class, who were expected to be virtuous, actively involved in promoting the common good. And the American Revolution, the historical contingency that most affected his life, provided opportunities for virtuous self-sacrifice on the grandest possible scale.

John Laurens devoted almost his entire adult life to winning his country's freedom from Great Britain. He and his father pledged their lives and fortunes to secure American independence. American revolutionaries like the Laurenses fought to establish a republican form of government. They realized the historic import of the moment, that their labors, if successful, would win the acclaim of posterity. In a real sense their efforts dangled on a thread. For they considered republics inherently fragile, dependent on the virtue of the people, both in terms of moral purity and the willingness to sacrifice private gain for the public good. Yet theology and experience told them that man's nature was more corrupt than virtuous, more avaricious than sacrificing. It was a revolution, therefore, fraught with tension, a conflict between dreams and realities.[12]

For John Laurens this tension proved arduous and enduring. He accomplished much in a short time, yet he sensed a dichotomy between his private ambitions and his public achievements. As the son of a prominent leader in South Carolina society, he was expected to be a model of moral virtue and to make a positive contribution to the community at large. His father put pressure on him, and he put pressure on himself. From his perspective, he literally lived on stage, observed by a demanding father and an audience of contemporaries who expected his performance to meet their high expectations. His life starkly demonstrates a crisis of confidence many Americans of his generation faced: the contrast between their aspirations as republican citizens and their accomplishments as individuals. How John Laurens responded to this dilemma will be observed in the story that follows.

Chapter 1

"An ornament to his country"
Early Life in Charleston

Less than a century before the American Revolution, the Laurens family migrated to the New World. Arriving first in New York before moving to Charleston, South Carolina, the Laurenses, over the course of three generations, achieved a prominent place in provincial society. André Laurens, his son Jean, and grandson Henry adhered to the Huguenot tradition of industriousness and enterprise that had produced so many important businessmen in their native, Catholic France. John Laurens's hardworking and public-spirited ancestors laid the groundwork for him to play a conspicuous role in the Revolution.

Like other Huguenots, the Laurenses left France in the wake of Louis XIV's efforts to stamp out Protestantism. André Laurens first moved to England, before deciding to try his fortunes in America. He and his wife Marie emigrated to New York, where many Huguenots had already settled. On 30 March 1697 Marie gave birth to the third of their five children, Jean Samuel. While in New York, the Laurenses befriended another family of Huguenot refugees, the Grassets. Jean Laurens married Esther Grasset shortly before André Laurens decided to uproot his family again. In 1715 the Laurenses, for a second time following in the footsteps of other Huguenots, sailed to Charleston, South Carolina. Charleston served both as provincial capital and center of economic life in the low country, the swampy coastal region of tall oaks, scrub pines, and rice plantations. The South Carolina low country's economy stood on the verge of an expansion, fueled by the demand for rice and, in later years, indigo, that eventually made some of its white residents among the wealthiest people in the British North American colonies. Industrious and enterprising individuals could prosper in this setting.[1]

Portrait of Henry Laurens as president of the Continental Congress.
Painted by John Singleton Copley in 1782. National Portrait Gallery, Smithsonian Institution, Washington, D.C.

André Laurens died soon after arriving in Charleston. He "had Saved So much Money as enabled him" to provide his five children "with Such portions as put them above low dependance." As Henry Laurens, the son of Jean Laurens, later recalled, "Some of them retained the French pride of Family, & were content to die poor. My Father was of different Sentiments, he learned a Trade, & by great Industry acquired an Estate with a good Character & Reestablished the Name of his Family."[2]

Jean Laurens, or John, as he was called, became a saddler. Over time he prospered in his trade and invested in real estate. Like most Huguenots, he quickly assimilated into Charleston society, the Anglicization of his name being one step in the process. He also joined the colony's established Anglican church, where he served as warden of St. Philip's Parish, and he owned at least five slaves. Yet he remained ambivalent toward the institution that formed the basis of South Carolina's prosperity. On one occasion, he made a cryptic prediction that slavery would eventually collapse.[3]

John and Esther Laurens had five children who lived to maturity: Mary, Martha, Henry, Lydia, and James. Their eldest son, Henry, was born on 6 March 1724. Little is known of Henry's early years. His closest friend was Christopher Gadsden, who was eight days older. The two companions "encourage[d] each other in every virtuous pursuit, to shun every path of vice and folly, to leave company whenever it tended to licentiousness. . . . By an honorable observance of a few concerted rules, they mutually strengthened virtuous habits."[4] Their behavior was a model of moral virtue; Henry Laurens adhered to these rules his entire life.

On 3 April 1742, less than a month after Henry's eighteenth birthday, his mother died. Three months later his father married Elizabeth Wicking, a native of England. Henry's reaction to his father's precipitate remarriage was not documented. Shortly before the wedding, John announced his retirement.[5]

John Laurens "gave his Children the best Education" available in Charleston. Like other parents throughout history, John hoped his children would advance beyond the foundation he established for them. He decided that Henry, who was destined to be a merchant, should journey overseas to receive further training. About 1744 John sent Henry to London to work in the counting house of the respected merchant James Crokatt. In 1747 Henry finished his apprenticeship and returned to South Carolina.[6]

When Henry landed at Charleston on 3 June 1747, he learned that three days earlier his father had died. In language typical of the dutiful oldest son whose closest tie was to the family patriarch, he lamented the death of "my best friend my dear Father. . . . As he was a tender & affectionate Parent I am under great concern for my Loss." Named coexecutor of the will along with his stepmother, Henry spent the next three months settling his father's estate. Both

Henry and James received property, while their three married sisters were each granted fifty pounds in current money.[7]

Henry decided to settle in Charleston and in 1748 he formed a partnership with George Austin, a native of Shropshire, England. Austin & Laurens, joined in 1759 by Austin's nephew George Appleby, became one of the leading merchant firms in Charleston and brought extensive wealth to the partners. They traded in rice, indigo, and deerskins, the primary commodities in South Carolina, and profited greatly from their involvement in the slave trade. The firm also invested in ships that operated in the West Indies. Laurens's methodical work habits proved a major factor in the firm's success. Requiring less sleep than most people, he often wrote letters by candlelight during the early hours of the morning. Indeed, he "frequently had the business of the day not only arranged, but done, when others were beginning to deliberate on the expediency of leaving their beds." In his business dealings, he was punctual, diligent, and fair; he expected the same from other men. A deeply religious man, his strict moral code and great capacity for work made him intolerant of others less endowed with these qualities, both in business and in politics.[8]

The next move for the rising young merchant was marriage. According to tradition, Laurens met his future wife, Eleanor Ball, at her brother's wedding, and fell in love with her immediately. On 25 June 1750 they married. The union proved both propitious and happy: as the Balls were an established and prestigious low-country family, Henry secured his position among the colony's elite; and his business acumen and industriousness were matched by Eleanor's abilities in the domestic sphere. The available evidence suggests that theirs was a "companionate marriage," one that juxtaposed Henry's patriarchal control with genuine love and friendship. Henry's occasional mention of Eleanor in letters reveals a loving and attentive spouse and mother who enjoyed gardening and excelled in the duties expected of a wife, such as cooking and sewing. These references aside, she remains a veiled figure; a full picture of her never emerges.[9]

The couple had twelve children, of whom only four reached adulthood. Their first son, Henry, was born in 1753. On 28 October 1754 Eleanor gave birth to a second son, named John in honor of his grandfather. Known as Jack, the boy displayed early evidence of talent. At the age of three "he began of his own Accord to draw," and proceeded to copy everything he saw. Jack found the world around him fascinating, both the dust and dash of mercantile Charleston and the flora and fauna of the Carolina coastal plain.[10]

In 1755 the first daughter to survive infancy, Eleanor, whom the family called Nelly, was born. Near in age, the three siblings formed a close-knit team of playmates. It was a happy childhood, supervised by loving and attentive parents, marred only by the specter of death. In August 1758 the younger Henry died. His death was Jack's first encounter with the transitory nature of life, where a loved one's existence seemingly vanished like a mist. Yet life continued and the family grew in size, though death would remain an ever-present reality. A year later Eleanor gave birth to another daughter, Martha, whom the family called Patsy.[11]

Following the steps of other prosperous merchants, Henry Laurens diversified his economic investments. In 1756 he purchased a half interest in Wambaw, a 1,250–acre rice plantation on the Santee River. His brother-in-law, John Coming Ball, managed the plantation, allowing Henry to devote his primary attention to business in Charleston. Ownership of land qualified him for a position in the Commons House of Assembly, and he took a seat in that body on 6 October 1757.[12]

Unlike socially stratified European countries such as Britain and France, the American colonies lacked a genuine nobility. In the colonies wealth was more widely dispersed and a large percentage of white men owned property, which was the criterion that defined autonomous individuals. The richest men in the provinces did not accumulate property to match that held by the English aristocracy; rather, their resources paralleled the prosperity of the English upper middle class. The colonies did, however, possess a natural aristocracy, the men of ability whose property provided them the leisure to live as gentlemen and function as political and social leaders. In South Carolina these gentlemen served in the Commons House of Assembly. Henry's rise to prominence as a merchant, his marriage to Eleanor and ties to the Ball family, his ownership of land, and his election to the Commons House all confirmed him as a Carolina gentleman, a member of the province's patrician class.[13]

Laurens quickly rose to prominence in the Commons House, where he served at intervals for the next fourteen years. Just as the colony's gentlemen modeled their behavior and lifestyle after the English aristocracy, their assembly took for its model the House of Commons in the British Parliament. In what most British subjects considered a balanced government, the Commons protected the rights of Englishmen of property against encroachments by the crown and the House of Lords, which represented the nobility. The Commons House of Assembly viewed itself in a similar light. Throughout the eighteenth century, the assembly gradually increased its power at the expense of the royal governor and the upper house, the council. A seat in the assembly brought both prestige and training in the art of governing. The recurring struggle for power with various governors and the council provided lower house members with valuable political experience.[14]

Despite some personal differences, the political leaders who sat in the assembly maintained a surprisingly united front on most issues of public import. The colony's prosperity made harmony both possible and necessary.

Shared wealth precluded the clash of economic interests among the low-country elite. Yet they owed that wealth to the labor of an overwhelming slave majority. In Charleston, the center of political authority, the ratio of blacks to whites was about even, but in the surrounding low-country parishes dotted by rice plantations, slaves outnumbered whites as much as 7 to 1. The fear of slave insurrections required that whites remain unified and vigilant. At the same time, slaves served as a constant reminder to whites of the consequences of losing one's freedom. Above all else, whites valued their personal independence, which was based on economic independence, their ownership of land and slaves.[15]

As Henry Laurens gained experience in politics, he continued to expand his landholdings. On 5 June 1762 he purchased Mepkin plantation on the Cooper River, about thirty miles from Charleston. Three months later, on 7 September, he bought land in Ansonborough, a neighborhood just outside Charleston. At both places, Henry constructed houses and laid out gardens that he intended to use as his town and country residences. At Ansonborough, he built a wharf that enabled schooners to travel from there to his country plantations. Next to him lived Christopher Gadsden, formerly his close friend but now a political adversary. Gadsden laid out streets in Ansonborough, connecting the neighborhood with Charleston proper.[16]

Young John Laurens spent his formative years at Ansonborough and Mepkin. His father spared no expense in creating an idyllic setting at both locations. Located on a high bluff overlooking Cooper River, Mepkin provided an escape from Charleston, particularly during the warm months, when tropical diseases threatened. Mepkin's tranquil beauty was accentuated by a long avenue of tall live oaks that led to the plantation house. Henry and Eleanor worked together to construct a beautiful house and garden at their town residence. After giving birth on 25 August 1763 to a son, Henry, who was always called Harry by the family, Eleanor devoted personal attention to the four-acre garden, which contained exotic plants and fruit trees. In March 1764 the Laurenses finally occupied their new home. Henry described his dwelling as "a large elegant brick House of 60 feet by 38." The garden was "pleasantly situated upon the River," he wrote. "All this land about Ansonburgh is covered with fine Houses."[17]

As members of the provincial elite, the Laurenses wanted their home to reflect a genteel lifestyle. Their house and garden served as a performance piece, a public exhibit of their refinement. On entering the mansion, a guest beheld several examples of gentility: fine china for display and for formal dinners; a harpsichord on which the girls practiced and performed; a bookcase with volumes that illustrated Henry's breadth of knowledge. Most distinctive of all was the garden. Surrounded by a brick wall, the garden measured 200 yards in length, 150 yards in width. Henry and Eleanor planted an assortment of exotic flora, including a grape vine and banana, fig, olive, and orange trees. The diversity of plants and trees served a dual function: as supplements to the family diet and as conversation pieces when the Laurenses took guests on garden tours.[18]

For John Laurens, the home at Ansonborough served as a quiet haven that contrasted with the commotion of his bustling hometown. The Charleston of John's youth contained over eleven thousand inhabitants. Situated on a peninsula bounded by the Ashley and Cooper Rivers, the city had been planned well. Its wide, unpaved streets, which intersected at right angles, allowed breezes to circulate, thus making life more bearable during the sultry summer months. As the provincial capital and principal port, the city served as the hub of political and economic life. The wealthiest, most influential members of Carolina society resided there for at least part of each year. Their lifestyle befitted their affluence. "No other American city can compare with Charleston in the beauty of its houses and the splendor and taste displayed therein," commented one visitor.[19]

With wealth gleaned from the labor of slaves, the low-country elite lived in comfortable leisure. It seemed, at least to puritanical observers, that the affluent residents of Charleston had sunk to new depths of slothfulness. They spent much time playing cards, gambling, and attending horse races. Doctor Alexander Garden, a prominent physician and naturalist who became a mentor to John Laurens, described these self-styled aristocrats as "absolutely above every occupation but eating, drinking, lolling, smoking, and sleeping, which five modes of action constitute the essence of their life and existence." While growing up, John thus encountered the tension between the luxury and dissipation displayed by many prominent Carolinians and the inflexible standards of a father who viewed wasting time as tantamount to a grievous sin.[20]

Life in Charleston was not without its dangers. High rates of disease and mortality—caused mainly by malaria, yellow fever, and the dreaded smallpox—threatened all South Carolina low-country residents. "Our little spot is a paradise," Henry said, "but we the inhabitants are Mortals."[21] In April 1764 the eldest daughter, Nelly, died. For several days Henry could not conduct any business because of his own grief and his efforts to console Eleanor. He coped with the death of a loved one by submission to the will of God and adherence to his philosophy of life: *Optimum quod evenit,* "Whatever happens, happens for the best," a motto that paraphrased Alexander Pope's line from *An Essay on Man,* "Whatever is, is right." Eleanor took bereavement even harder. When the Laurenses lost an infant, as happened on four occasions, she endured the dual trial of physical suffering and mental anguish.[22]

Henry and Eleanor could not grieve long because there remained three children to mold into useful citizens. Whereas some Carolinians placed great value on personal autonomy and were overly permissive parents who raised unruly children, the Laurenses occupied a middle ground between the extremes of indulgence and authoritarianism. They doted on their offspring, but they also took a keen interest in their children's mental and physical development. Like other parents, as their children grew older, Henry assumed more responsibility for instructing the boys while Eleanor taught the girls domestic duties. Nor was the spiritual realm neglected. Henry read the Bible to the entire family and enjoined his children to study it regularly. Sexual temptation, in particular, concerned him. With some relief, he observed when John was twelve years old that "Master Jack is too closely wedded to his studies to think about any of the Miss Nanny's I would not have such a sound in his Ear, for a Crown; why drive the poor Dog, to what Nature will irresistably prompt him to be plagued within all probability much too soon." Yielding to carnal desires, in Henry's mind, signaled that an individual lacked the moral virtue essential to merit and maintain public respect. Indeed, his ultimate goal was for each child to "become an useful Member of Community. This is the Summit of my desire when I meditate upon the future well being of my own Children in this Life."[23]

An additional concern was Eleanor's health, which grew increasingly fragile. She was sick for several months in the latter part of 1764. Henry described 1764 as "a Year of affliction—a Dead eldest daughter, a sick Summer, a Sick & dying Wife." Eleanor's condition eventually improved, but her health remained precarious. Repeated pregnancies proved physically and emotionally draining. It is unclear from Henry's comments whether he fully made the connection between Eleanor's declining health and her annual ordeal. After one unsuccessful delivery, he wrote, "Poor Mrs. Laurens has been unlucky again this Year. She is confined to her Chamber (as usual once in the round of twelve Months) under the mortifying reflections which arise upon the loss of a very fine Girl." Another time the father observed, with rueful humor, that Eleanor "was safely deliver'd of a fine Boy on the 10th September, but the little fellow finding what a World of vanity & vexation he had come into, went back again the 24th." As for the mother, she "through grief & weakness has been brought very low & barely begins to walk about the House again."[24]

The death of siblings close to his age and the annual, difficult pregnancies of his mother could not have failed to make an impression on young John. In addition to losing his closest playmates, his eldest brother and sister, John also witnessed Patsy's brush with death during a smallpox epidemic in 1759. The Laurenses believed Patsy had died, but shortly before she was to be buried, a doctor examined her and determined that she was still alive. And next door there was additional evidence of the uncertainty of life. In August 1766, "an exceeding hot month," Christopher Gadsden Jr. died. Born in 1750, the younger Gadsden had been John's close friend. Considering the age difference between the boys, John probably looked up to him.[25]

Amid family afflictions, Henry Laurens's business affairs also underwent change. In 1762 Austin, Laurens, & Appleby dissolved their partnership. In poor health, Austin returned to England in July 1763, and Appleby joined him the following spring. Laurens reduced his mercantile activities, in large part because he needed to free himself to take a greater role in John's education. Like his father before him, Henry wanted his oldest son to have advantages he had lacked. Henry had apprenticed as a merchant in England, but with the exception of that training he was essentially an autodidact who never attained the polish a gentleman received from a liberal education. He wanted John to have access to such an education. A liberal arts education at a college would make John an accomplished, fully cultivated gentleman, prepared to make a positive contribution to society. Because South Carolina lacked a college, most of Henry's wealthy contemporaries sent their sons abroad to complete their schooling. Laurens contemplated taking John to England, a prospect he did not relish. He had often urged his countrymen to improve their public schools, and now he lamented their lack of foresight.[26]

In October 1764 Laurens's brother-in-law John Coming Ball died. Ball's death forced Henry to spend more time managing the Mepkin and Wambaw plantations. He continued to increase his property, purchasing rice plantations in Georgia along the Altamaha and Savannah Rivers and obtaining land grants in the South Carolina backcountry. When his friend James Grant became royal governor of East Florida in 1764 and began developing the province, Laurens supplied him with slaves, overseers, and tools. He hoped, in return, that Grant would help him obtain choice Florida land.[27] Henry admitted that his extensive landholdings "denominate me a greater planter than ever I had an idea of becoming. I have been insensibly drawn into such an extent by means & circumstances quite adventitious. However the reflection is comfortable that my Servants are as happy as Slavery will admit of, none run away, the greatest punishment to a defaulter is to sell him."[28]

Laurens's lifelong attitude toward slavery was, at best, ambivalent. Privately, he detested the institution. Yet the ultimate foundation of his wealth, which derived from activities as both a merchant and planter, was the labor of African slaves. As an enlightened patriarch, Laurens exerted firm control over his slaves but also tried to mitigate the cruelty of an inhumane institution with respect for their humanity. In discussing his expectations of an overseer, Henry conveyed his belief that the patriarchal master was responsible for the well-being of his bondspeople: "If he makes less Rice with more hands but treats my Negroes with Humanity I would rather have him to be at their Head, than submit to the Charge of one who should make twice as much Rice & excercise any degree of Cruelty towards those poor Creatures who look up to their Master as their Father, their Guardian, & Protector."[29] When one overseer experienced difficulty managing a bondsman, Laurens wrote, "Take care of him. . . . You say you don't like him but remember he is a human Creature whether you like him or not." In principle Laurens opposed the practice of selling and separating slave families, a procedure he "would never do or cause to be done but in case of irresistable necessity." Yet, as a businessman, he knew that property, in situations of "irresistable necessity," had to be liquidated. Slaves, though "human Creatures," were property first.[30]

Slaves, though "human Creatures," were also potential enemies. Laurens realized that the relationship between master and slaves ultimately rested on coercion, and a hint of violence was always close to the surface. After instructing the captain of one of his vessels to procure a cargo of slaves from Jamaica, he issued an admonition: "Be very careful to guard against insurrection. Never put your Life in their power for a moment. For a moment is sufficient to deprive you of it & make way for the destruction of all your Men & yet you may treat such Negroes with great humanity." Laurens's statement reveals an institution fraught with ambiguity: slaves were antagonists who could never be fully trusted yet also humans who merited humane treatment. Humane treatment, as practiced by Laurens, was based on reciprocity. As enlightened patriarch he provided his bondspeople shelter, clothing, and food; in return he expected their obedience and their labor. When neither response was forthcoming, he did not hesitate to order that a recalcitrant slave be flogged or that an indolent slave be sold.[31]

This ambivalence—acknowledgment that Africans were humans yet insistence on treating them as property to be bought and sold—can be traced through Laurens's involvement in the slave trade after 1762. Though no longer a partner in a merchant firm, he still arranged on several occasions to sell cargoes of slaves for merchant friends in England, and he procured slaves for enterprising young men who were venturing into planting. In late 1769 he supervised the sale of nine recent arrivals, all of whom had suffered from mistreatment during the middle passage across the Atlantic. Laurens told the owners of the slave ship that one woman, a "poor pining creature hanged herself with a piece of small Vine which shews that her carcase was not very weighty." Understandably shaken by his own narrative, he penned a telling postscript: "Who that views the above Picture can love the Affrican trade." Yet he could be equally insensitive, almost anesthetized to the horrors around him. In 1764, when the market for slaves was almost flooded, Laurens, using common nomenclature that dehumanized the human cargo, referred to several shipments of aged and infirm Africans as "refuse."[32]

In private correspondence Laurens counterpoised handwringing over slavery's ill effects on both whites and blacks with an insistence that the weight of public opinion tied his hands and forced compliance with the continued existence of the institution. On such occasions he often shifted blame elsewhere, either on the mother country or on northern merchants. In 1763 John Ettwein, a Moravian missionary with whom Laurens corresponded, argued that reliance on slave labor made whites lazy. Even worse, from Ettwein's perspective, no effort was made to bring Christianity to the enslaved. Laurens agreed, but insisted that laws and customs sanctioned slavery and made it impossible for individuals to effect change. In addition, he contended, "we see the Negro Trade much promoted of late by our Northern Neighbors who formerly Censur'd & condemn'd it, the difficulties, which a few who would wish to deal with those servants as with brethren in a state of subordination meet with, are almost insurmountable." The last phrase reveals the extent to which Laurens was in accordance with his contemporaries. Influenced by ideas propounded by European social theorists like Baron de Montesquieu and Adam Smith, white Carolinians increasingly acknowledged the humanity of their bondspeople, but this admission did not include concessions on the morality of slavery. Slaves, though "human Creatures," were "in a state of subordination," and thus they would remain. Shared humanity did not confer equality.[33]

While Henry Laurens attempted to simplify his business life, he found his political life increasingly complicated by forces beyond his control. During the 1760s, the relationship between the North American colonies and their mother country, Great Britain, underwent a transformation that would forever alter the Laurenses' lives. At the end of the Great War for the Empire in 1763, France ceded to Great Britain its North American lands east of the Mississippi River. As proud British subjects, the colonists rejoiced over this decisive victory. Their mood soon darkened. The British ministry decided to station a peacetime army in America to protect the colonies and the newly acquired lands. Believing the colonists should pay part of the expense of maintaining this force, the British Parliament enacted the Stamp Act in March 1765. Under the provisions of this act, Americans, beginning in November, would have to pay a tax on various official and unofficial papers, such as playing cards, newspaper advertisements, and legal documents. Arguing that the act was unconstitutional, that they could be taxed only by representatives in their own assemblies, the colonists opposed it strongly and in some instances violently.[34]

In late October Henry Laurens, who consistently advocated moderation throughout the crisis, found himself under suspicion and threatened by violence. Late one evening a mob forcibly entered the Laurenses' home at Ansonborough in a vain search for stamps. Though Henry managed to convince the crowd that he harbored no stamps, the disturbance terrified Eleanor, who was then pregnant. A month later she gave birth to James, described by his father as "a very fine Boy, who seems as if he had not been half so much frighted by smutty faces, turned Coats, Cutlasses, & Bludgeons as his Mother was."[35]

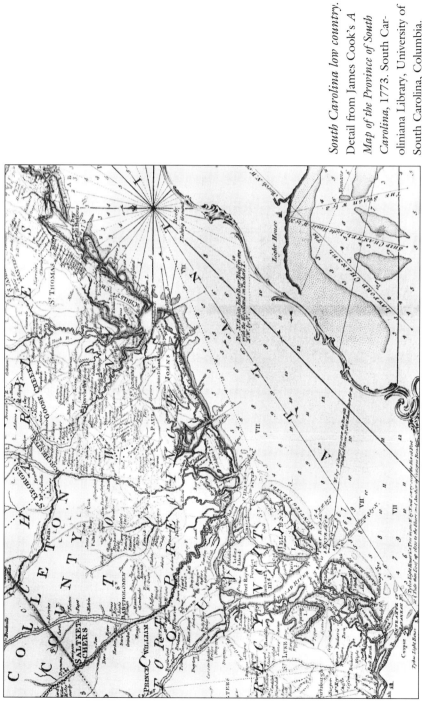

South Carolina low country. Detail from James Cook's *A Map of the Province of South Carolina,* 1773. South Caroliniana Library, University of South Carolina, Columbia.

Faced with growing colonial opposition, including the nonimportation of British goods, Parliament voted to repeal the Stamp Act in March 1766. Parliament did not relinquish the prerogative to tax the colonists, however, and in 1767 it placed duties on all tea, lead, glass, paper, and paint imported into the colonies. Named for Charles Townshend, chancellor of the exchequer in the British ministry, the duties raised American ire and resulted in the eventual renewal of nonimportation.[36]

In the meantime, John continued his education under several tutors, studying French, classical literature, mathematics, surveying, mechanics, and drawing.[37] His learning proved useful when Henry again became personally involved in the growing dispute between Great Britain and the American colonies. In the spring of 1767 Daniel Moore, the new customs collector, arrived in Charleston and began vigorously enforcing trade regulations, probably in hopes of pocketing the profits. When Moore seized two of Laurens's ships, the case went to the court of vice-admiralty, where Egerton Leigh presided. A prominent jurist, Leigh was related to Laurens by marriage. His wife was Martha Bremar, the daughter of Francis Bremar and Henry's sister Martha. Leigh attempted to arbitrate the matter and returned one vessel to Laurens, but condemned the other. In an oversight that was probably intentional, Leigh failed to declare that George Roupell, the customs searcher who made the seizure, had "a probable cause of seizure," thereby paving the way for Laurens to sue for damages, which he promptly did. The jury awarded him a settlement that Roupell could not pay. Roupell responded by seizing *Ann,* another of Henry's vessels. He offered a deal: he would release *Ann* if Laurens dropped the claim for damages. Laurens refused, and the matter again went before the vice-admiralty court. This time Leigh released the vessel, but had Roupell take the oath of calumny, a declaration that he had only performed his duties, and not acted maliciously. This oath prevented Laurens from filing suit again. Caught between his family ties to Laurens and his duty as a royal officer, Leigh tried to reach a compromise that protected both sides.[38]

Henry, however, did not view the matter that way. The litigation consumed time and money, forcing him to postpone his plans to take John to England. Angered by Leigh's handling of the cases, he attacked the jurist in a pamphlet entitled *Extracts from the Proceedings of the High Court of Vice-Admiralty.* Henry acknowledged that portions of the *Extracts* involved collaboration with John, to whom he had turned when he was "puzzled about a Grammatical term or so." John's knowledge of Latin proved especially critical. He translated from Latin into English Samuel Pufendorf's comments on the seldom-used oath of calumny.[39]

Leigh responded with his own pamphlet, a personal attack on Laurens entitled *The Man Unmasked.* He mocked Laurens for using the passages from

Pufendorf "in order that his son (by giving it an English dress) may return the obligation which he lies under to his father, who made use of him to retail out, or rather drop, his dirty poison through the town, like the printer's mercury, who circulates the weekly paper of occurrences." Henry countered with an *Appendix to the Extracts.* He contrasted Leigh's translation of Cardinal Melchior de Polignac's work with John's rendering and concluded that the jurist was "deficient in several Branches of a polite Education."[40] In the end Laurens's position as a merchant victimized by abusive royal officials redeemed him in the eyes of Carolinians who had disapproved of his moderate stance during the Stamp Act crisis. More important, the dispute marked a turning point in his politicization. Though his feelings of loyalty and affection for the mother country remained intact, he never forgot how an arm of the British government had threatened his livelihood and his reputation.

During the pamphlet war, Leigh issued a particularly serious threat to Henry's reputation. In *The Man Unmasked,* Leigh argued that Laurens had resigned from the slave trade as a matter of conscience, but only after amassing riches that he retained, despite their origin from trafficking in human flesh. According to Leigh, Henry's pangs of conscience stemmed partly from his interpretation of Revelation 18. In one of that book's prophetic passages, merchants, whose varied activities include involvement in the slave trade, mourn the fall of Babylon. Leigh's attack carried potentially devastating ramifications for Laurens: if Henry withdrew from the slave trade because he considered it sinful, he implied that his fellow merchants were under condemnation for their continued participation. Henry strongly resented the publicity given to what he considered strictly a private matter. His reply in the *Appendix to the Extracts* was telling: "What Benefit is it to the Public to know the Motives and Principles from which I quitted the *African* Branch of Commerce?" After posing that question, he went to great lengths to provide solely economic reasons for his semiretirement from the trade: he had reduced his involvement because his partners had retired; he found the business too taxing; rather than share continued profits with younger merchants, he referred cargoes to them, but received no commission. A gentleman of strict honor, Laurens could not abide Leigh's imputation that he was a hypocrite who privately questioned the morality of other Carolinians. One's honor, or reputation, rested largely on the esteem and respect extended by fellow gentlemen. In South Carolina those gentlemen, with very few exceptions, accepted slavery without moral qualms. While the economic feasibility of slavery was open to public debate and some slaveholders pondered ways to ameliorate the institution's inherent brutality, white Carolinians drew the line at any suggestion that slavery was unconscionable and indefensible. However much Laurens entertained private misgivings, he could not ignore the prevailing public consensus on the slavery issue.[41]

As the controversy died down after August 1769, Henry resumed his plan to send John abroad and scheduled the trip for the following spring. Eleanor, along with several friends of the family, wanted Henry to accompany John. Alexander Garden believed the youth demonstrated great promise. Unfortunately, Garden concluded, the area did not have "one Man from whom Jack can receive advantages as a Tutor." Henry considered John too "big a Boy to be left Idle." To keep the youth occupied, he occasionally had him copy business letters.[42]

John continued to study Latin, Greek, English, and mathematics. He had not chosen a profession, but the study of medicine appealed to him, partly because of Garden's influence and partly because the youth had been fascinated by the natural world since he was three years old. Colonial physicians earned greater reputations for their contributions to natural history than for their medical practices. Garden, the leading physician in Charleston, possessed an international reputation as a botanist. He regularly corresponded and collaborated with the premier naturalist of the era, Carl Linnaeus. In devoting considerable time to natural history, Garden paralleled other physicians in the colonies. Their focus on science stemmed from training, since medical schools and hospitals in Europe stressed the study of botany and anatomy; from application, as herbs were commonly used in treating patients; and from inclination, since association with European scientists provided the intellectual stimulation and opportunity for renown that the practice of medicine alone did not offer. This aspect of medicine, the pursuit of scientific knowledge, appealed most to young Laurens. John, observed Garden, "appears to me to have some inclination to the study of Natural History." The doctor readily obliged the budding scientist. On one occasion John's artistic talent proved especially useful. For three months Garden kept for observation a freshwater soft-shelled turtle, a creature that had not been previously classified. John copied drawings of the turtle, which Garden sent to London. John's drawings and Garden's description of the turtle were published in the Royal Society's *Philosophical Transactions.*[43]

Henry and Eleanor's other children also developed as distinct individuals. "Patsy is forward in her learning," Henry noted with pride, "she reads well & begins to write prettily, is not dull in the french Grammar, & plays a little on the Harpsichord, but better than all, she handles her needles in all the useful branches & some of the most refined parts of Womens work & promises me to learn to make minced Pies & to dress a Beef Steak." Harry, on the other hand, appeared "a little thick Headed, loves Marbles, Tops, and Tumbling much more than his Books," an observation that reveals as much about the father as it does the son. Much to Henry's relief, James, whom the family called Jamie or Jemmy, was "healthy and clever & seems to be a duplicate of his Elder Brother."[44]

Before Henry could take John to England, he had to wait for Eleanor to deliver another child. On 26 April 1770, she gave birth to a healthy daughter, whom they named Mary Eleanor. The mother, however, did not fare so well. The rigors of twelve pregnancies in less than twenty years finally broke Eleanor's already fragile health. For over three weeks she lingered near death. "This Gloomy prospect distresses me beyond description & in such a manner as you cannot feel," Henry told a friend. "I was waiting a happy Issue of her late circumstance in order to go to England with Jack or at least as far in his way as Philadelphia. . . . In an instant the scene is shifted."[45]

On 22 May, after showing some signs of recovery, Eleanor died. Henry mourned his own and his children's loss. "I have lost a faithful bosom Friend, a Wife whose constant Study was to make me happy," he wrote. "My Children have lost a tender watchful Mother; and I who was well acquainted with her Merits cannot help believing the public Voice upon this Occasion, that Virtue has lost a Friend."[46] John found himself torn by opposing emotions—grief for his mother and disappointment at having, once again, to postpone his education abroad. "Poor Jack is much to be pitied," Henry observed. "He has been almost inconsolable for the Loss of his Mother; and now he sees that another Loss must be sustained in Consequence of the first, the Loss of a year at College in Great Britain." Under the circumstances, John's feelings were understandable. Yet his conflicting emotions undoubtedly troubled and distracted him, perhaps inhibiting his mourning and preventing him from coming to terms with his grief. How selfish he must have felt. Rather than focusing on his family, who had suffered an irreparable loss that could never be fully remedied, he could not help thinking about how his mother's death thwarted his own personal aspirations. It is unclear whether or not he resolved this emotional dichotomy.[47]

Throughout the summer of 1770, the grief-stricken widower found it difficult to devote time to his business activities. He never forgot Eleanor's dying words: "I know you Love me, I know you will take care of your Children." Perhaps her deathbed statement explains his decision not to remarry; perhaps, too, he thought of his own father's hasty remarriage. "I have remained Single," he would say later, "& have no desire to hazard an alienation of my affections from our Children by a second marriage."[48]

Performing the duties of both mother and father consumed much of Henry's time. After Eleanor's death, he could no longer leave Charleston on extended trips to visit his plantations. "My children . . . have large Demands upon me," he observed. Now they depended on him "for that tender Care in domestic Life, which they have always experienced in the Conduct of their dear Mother."[49] He considered John's assistance indispensable. Eleanor's death brought father and son closer together. "His company & conversation,"

Henry admitted, "have been great supports to me in my late affliction." John also assumed the role of tutor to his elder sister and brothers: "I feel an irrestible pleasure result from seeing him act the part of a kind & able friend & Brother to a Sister of 11 Years Old who is now advancing fast in French & is as much a Mistress of English Grammar as any Girl of her age through his assistance. Besides this he brings on a little Harry & Jamie in their learning too."[50]

When Henry became incapacitated for several days in October because of illness, John wrote a letter, in his father's stead, to James Grant regarding a shipping cargo. The East Florida governor, who took great interest in John's progress, was favorably impressed. Having received permission to return to England in 1772, he invited John to accompany him. He offered to "procure Recommendations" for the youth to enter any school that Henry approved. John appreciated Grant's generous offer, but could not put off school any longer. He wanted to make the voyage in 1771. "My dear Papa hopes to conduct me to England the next Spring," he wrote, "and has determined, if he cannot go himself to send me thither before the Month of June. My Wish is that he may go with me."[51]

Despite upheaval in his personal life, Henry remained active in political affairs. In May 1770 he presided over a public meeting that focused on the repeal of the Townshend duties by the new British administration under Lord North. Because the British retained the duty on tea, Carolinians resolved to continue nonimportation. By the end of the year sentiment had changed in Charleston. In December Henry chaired another meeting that reversed the previous decision and agreed to import all articles except tea.[52]

In early 1771 Henry decided to send Harry to London to be taught by Richard Clarke, the former pastor of St. Philip's Church in Charleston, who now headed a school for Carolina boys. He asked his old partner, George Appleby, to meet the boy and look after him until he was placed under Clarke's direction. Harry went ahead, Henry explained, because "his Constitution is not strong enough to bear the extreme Heats and Changes of this Climate." John would follow later in the summer. "I detain him," Henry wrote, "at his own particular desire for a month or two longer, in hopes of going with him. He says, if Harry goes first, he is sure that I will go after him."[53]

Several friends, including Alexander Garden, encouraged Henry to provide "a liberal and extensive Education" for John, including study at a university. Henry agreed with this advice because John expressed "his Desire to study Physick, Anatomy, &ca., and that he has not any Inclination to Merchandize." He preferred, however, that his son choose another profession. "I don't altogether like his turn to Physic, but I will do nothing to obstruct it," he said. "I would rather he should study Divinity, the Law, or apply himself to Trade & Commerce." Henry did not state explicitly why he preferred that John not pursue medicine, but concerns over the social and economic status of physicians probably loomed in his mind. Doctors, along with lawyers and ministers, constituted the three learned professions, but colonial practitioners trailed the other two, both in social prestige and in financial remuneration. South Carolina, with an unhealthy climate and constant threat of illnesses, was at least partially an exception to this rule, for there the best doctors were among the colony's elite. To Henry, however, a medical career still appeared more unpredictable and potentially less rewarding than the other options before John. Henry did not keep his opinions to himself, but he remained determined that John have the final say. It was, after all, his life and his career.[54]

Henry asked Clarke for opinions on schools and universities in Great Britain and the Continent, particularly any in Geneva, Switzerland. If possible, Henry preferred a school far from London, for he did not relish the idea of John being exposed to the temptations of that large city: "Jacky hitherto knows of no other Use for Vacation Time but Study. . . . My grand Aim is to hold him in that Track for a few more Years and then he may be pretty safely trusted with the Reins." Like other parents of his time, Laurens struggled with a basic dilemma: how to shield one's children from a corrupt world. Since complete isolation was out of the question, a sound education and knowledge of the world's snares became essential.[55]

After Harry's departure in April, Henry worked to get his affairs in order. At the same time, John said goodbye to his closest friends. Before leaving, he received a delightful farewell letter from Alicia Hopton, the sister of John Hopton, one of Henry's former clerks. She was stirred by John's promise to send her a sketch he had made of Alexander Pope's "Sweet Retreat," the poet's country estate at Twickenham, England. Employing the language of sensibility then in vogue among women and men, she divulged her idea to create her own "Rural retreat" at her family's plantation on the Wando River. Because John had "such a fine taste" and artistic talent, she requested that he sketch a plan for her sanctuary. There she would retire to pursue intellectual pleasures; there she expected John eventually to visit and lecture her family and friends, stirring them with his scientific knowledge; there, she wrote, you will "find me grown quite a Philosopher, depend on it, it will in part be oweing to you." That all lay in a distant and uncertain future. In the more immediate future lay John's arrival in the mother country, where one's finery made a lasting first impression. Hopton and another friend, Mary Esther Kinloch, "intended each of us to have work'd you a pair of Ruffles, but as time wont permit, we shall both work at one pair, which will be sent down next week. You will wear them I hope for our Sakes." She concluded on an affectionate and whimsical note: "I am Sir, your admirer. (as much as it is possible you can be mine)."[56]

In addition to a new pair of ruffles, John also would arrive in England with an introduction to a respected scientist. Describing John as "a favourite of mine," Alexander Garden recommended the youth to the attention of fellow naturalist John Ellis. "I think he has genius," Garden observed, "and I know he has application sufficient, under good masters, to enable him to become an accomplished man, and to make him a joy and delight to his father, as well as an ornament to his country."[57]

Henry finally decided to take his youngest son Jemmy, "a wild, lively, sensible, good natur'd fellow," along on the voyage. He left his business affairs under the guidance of his closest friend, John Lewis Gervais, an up-and-coming young merchant, and his brother James Laurens. James and his wife Mary occupied the house at Ansonborough and agreed to take care of the two girls, Martha and little Mary Eleanor, who was called Polly. Destined, like other women, for "Domestic Employments," Martha, despite her obvious talents and potential, would remain behind.[58]

On 21 July Henry, John, and Jemmy departed from Charleston. After first sailing to Philadelphia, where they remained until late August, they continued to New York. By 9 September they were ready to journey to England on *Earl of Halifax Packet*. While the pilot boat led their vessel out of the harbor, John reminded Henry that he had "promised to give Patsy an Opportunity of Learning to Draw." Henry quickly wrote his brother to arrange lessons for Martha, if possible. "We are in a fine Vessel just in good Ballast," he observed, "and the Captain except swearing a little too much, seems to be just what we would wish him."[59] Having endured frustrating delays that prevented him from completing his education abroad, John Laurens now watched America recede in the distance. Before him lay new lands, new adventures, and far greater responsibilities and temptations than he had ever known.

Chapter 2

The Voltaire of Carolina
Sojourn in Geneva
October 1771–November 1774

During the Atlantic passage, John Laurens had plenty of time for reflection. Ahead lay not only England but also momentous decisions that would determine his future. The most important choice, which career to pursue, promised to shape his personal and public identity. That decision, like John's future, remained indeterminate. John could not foresee that he would remain abroad more than five years. He departed South Carolina a promising youth with only a vague sense of purpose but returned a man with an overriding mission that would consume his life.

On 9 October 1771, a month after their departure from New York, the Laurenses reached Falmouth, England. They arrived in London on 21 October and reunited with Harry. Henry found his middle son "in very good health, grown tall & improved in his Book." John promptly began his studies under Reverend Clarke's direction. Henry's plans called for John to remain with Clarke for half a year and then enter a university. Observing his eldest son, Henry wrote that "Hitherto I can venture to pronounce him a good Boy, God forbid the tainted air of this Kingdom should infect his Morals & divert his attention from that pursuit in which he at present most delights."[1]

Among the other Carolina boys studying at Clarke's house was Jacky Petrie, son of the late Alexander Petrie, a Charleston merchant who had been James Laurens's brother-in-law. James now acted as young Petrie's guardian, and he asked his older brother to look after the boy. "Your Nephew John is Jacky Petrie's elder Brother in England," Henry assured James. "He loves him, and we both treat him as of our Family."[2]

To remain near Clarke's school, Henry and Jemmy moved in with Robert Dean, who lived on Fludyer Street in Westminster. While the boys worked at their studies, Henry had considerable free time and, true to form, he did not remain idle. He investigated Oxford and Cambridge to determine if they were suitable universities for John. What he found did not please him. "The two Universities are generally, I might say universally censured," he wrote. "Oxford in particular is spoken of as a School for Licentiousness and Debauchery in the most agravated heights." Nor was he happy with Clarke. "I don't like Mr. Clarke's Situation at all," he told James Laurens, "and must prevail upon him to take a more capacious and Airy House." Blame ultimately rested, he argued, on his countrymen and the misplaced priorities that forced him and other parents to send their sons abroad for education and refinement.[3]

Henry Laurens was hardly a naive provincial; he had, after all, spent considerable time in London as a young man training to be a merchant. Yet he was genuinely appalled by the immorality he perceived. "The Height to which Fraud, Perjury, Gaming, Murder, Forgery, and every black and execrable Crime has gain'd in the City," he said, "is equally astonishing and shocking."[4] One could dismiss Laurens's descriptions of English society as mere hyperbole, the product of an inflexible moral code that occasionally lapsed into self-righteousness. His opinions, however, were shared by other leading provincials. Influenced by a Puritan ethic of industry and frugality, some American observers believed England had fallen into a degenerate state. They contrasted an idealized portrait of colonial enterprise and thrift, its simple society and good life, with the extravagance of the English gentry who lived off the high rents paid by tenants and the sale of luxury items and cheap goods produced by the sweat of the working class. Previously the model for the colonies, the metropolitan political system now appeared hopelessly corrupt. Offers of money and patronage bought votes in Parliament; and a bloated bureaucracy contained worthless officeholders motivated by private gain rather than service to the public good.[5]

Despite concerns over social changes in commercial England and anger over Parliament's attempts to tax the colonies, provincials like the Laurenses were still proud to be part of the British empire and continued to express affection for their monarch, King George III. One morning, as Henry prepared to write letters, a friend came by and invited him "to the House of Lords to see the King of England on his Throne." Henry laid aside his work. "There was no denying a Request so very agreeable to my Inclination," he admitted. "I went and was highly entertained." His enjoyment, however, was tempered: "I wish'd heartily for Jack, but he was at Chelsea." Shortly thereafter, John received his own chance to see George III and, as befitted his youth, he reacted more effusively. He informed his uncle with pride that, "I had the Honour . . . of seeing the King in all his Glory on the Throne in the House of Peers, and just afterwards in his State Coach, attended by his Guards."[6]

One day Henry visited the naturalist John Ellis, to whom Alexander Garden had written a letter introducing John. Ellis showed Henry a drawing of a softshelled turtle and asked him "if that was not the Performance of" his son. John did sketch the turtle, replied Henry. Ellis observed that the drawing was "exceedingly well done indeed, and has been much admired at the Royal Society . . . you must send that Son to see me." He recommended that John meet Daniel Charles Solander, a naturalist who had returned earlier that year with Captain James Cook from a round-the-world voyage that won them both wide acclaim. Solander planned another voyage to the South Seas and Ellis believed John should go along. At the very least, Ellis wanted to meet John. "Send him early," the naturalist insisted, "that I may have some time to talk with him, without Interruption. He must come and breakfast with me." John readily accepted Ellis's invitation. The prospect of a venture to the South Seas was definitely tempting to both the youth and his father. "If he had two Years more School Learning," Henry mused, "I should cultivate the hint of his attending Doctor Solander." As it turned out, Solander did not join Cook on his second voyage.[7]

Meanwhile, matters grew worse at Richard Clarke's school. Despite Henry's initial displeasure, his regard for Clarke restrained him from removing his sons. His feelings for the reverend soon received a sterner test. Clarke allowed his "Vagabond Brother" to live in the house. One day Clarke's brother "wantonly and maliciously thrust" a candle in Harry's face. Fortunately, the candle only burned Harry's cheek, but if "an Eye had been struck, it must have perished," Henry fumed. Compounding the incident, Clarke did not offer an apology.

When Henry talked to John, he learned that the problems were rooted deeper. "Mr. Clarke," John reluctantly admitted, "does not keep a proper Discipline." Owing to lack of attention, the boys of "duller Genius must remain Slack or go backward." John's testimony was confirmed when Henry examined Harry's writing books and found that the boy had written nothing for five weeks. Yet the elder Laurens remained reluctant to make a move. Clarke had only seven Carolina boys enrolled, and three of them—John, Harry, and Jacky Petrie—were under Henry's supervision. Removing all three, he feared, would reduce Clarke and his family to poverty.[8]

For the time being, they postponed a separation. In April Clarke planned to move his school to Chinkford in Essex County, a "pleasant and healthy" location about eleven miles from London. With that problem seemingly solved, Henry located a school for little Jemmy. During a visit to Shropshire to see his old partners, George Austin and George Appleby, he placed the boy at

Winson Green, a boarding school near Birmingham. Administered by the Reverend William Howell with the help of his family and three assistants, the school appeared ideal to Henry, especially since Appleby lived nearby and promised to check on Jemmy's progress.[9]

After their return to London, Henry made plans to take his eldest sons to the Continent, as he wanted to inspect foreign universities before deciding where to place John. They would travel, Henry noted, "loaded with Letters of Introduction. For Jack has acquired some very valuable Friends." Those friends recommended that Henry take John to Geneva, a small republic with excellent educational facilities and teachers. If, upon inspection, Geneva matched these appraisals, Henry planned to leave both boys there. He dreaded the idea of separating from his sons, but his desire to make them useful members of society took precedence "in Spite of the strong affections and Inclinations of Nature."[10]

On 30 May 1772 Henry and his two eldest sons began their journey. They traveled through France at a leisurely pace. Even if John chose not to remain in Geneva, Henry was determined that the trip be an educational experience for both boys. He pronounced the French tour a success: "The Young Folks have been highly entertained. . . . John has feasted on several Pieces of fine Painting, some of Carving, and a few in Sculpture. Harry has learn'd to string a few Sentences cleverly together in French and serves me sometimes for an Interpreter."[11]

They reached Geneva in mid-June and found that the area exceeded all expectations. The "delightful City" possessed all the virtues that London lacked, and the letters of introduction produced valuable contacts in the Geneva community. Henry decided to leave his sons there. "They will have as many kind Friends in Geneve as they had in Charles Town," he said, "and more friendly Attention paid to them in all Respects than we could hope for in a Kingdom overwhelm'd by Luxury and Vice. . . . The Anxiety therefore which Distance of Place might have occasioned, must be greatly alleviated, if not wholly remov'd."[12]

An independent Protestant republic located on Lake Leman, Geneva, in effect, was ruled by a small, self-perpetuating oligarchy. Only a small portion of the population of 25,000 actually possessed political rights. Citizens held the reins of power. As male inhabitants whose parents and grandparents had been born in Geneva, they were eligible for public office. The burghers occupied a second tier in Geneva politics. A diverse group of men that included artisans, merchants, and storeowners, they could vote but not hold any office. Together the citizens and burghers, who held the franchise, comprised about 1,500 inhabitants.[13]

Geneva's superior education system attracted students from many countries, particularly England. The republic's leaders supported and supervised an academy, founded by John Calvin two centuries earlier, that trained the able teachers who filled Geneva's schools. Geneva's system balanced flexibility— enterprising young scholars could engage academy professors for private lessons—with government regulation—the state determined the amount these independent teaching masters could charge for their services.[14]

The city of John Calvin and Jean Jacques Rousseau was known for its industry and virtue. Large numbers of hardworking Huguenots migrated to the tiny republic and helped make it the world center of watchmaking. A visitor to Geneva witnessed "a People happy and free . . . who make Temperance the Guardian of their Healths, and who bar up every Avenue to the Blandishments of Luxury." Laws promoted frugality and selfless public service; sumptuary laws attempted to prevent people from becoming addicted to luxury goods; and high officials received little remuneration for performing their duties. George Keate, an English visitor, wrote approvingly of these republican edicts: "This is agreeable to the Spirit of a Republic; which should infuse into its Subjects a Love of Frugality; and teach them to do that from Zeal for their Country, which in other Governments is done out of a View to private Interest."[15] Geneva, in other words, seemed the perfect place for a inflexible moralist like Henry Laurens to have his sons educated.

Henry placed John and Harry at the home of Jean-Antoine Chais, a descendant of French Huguenots. Since 1770 Chais had served on the Small Council of Twenty-Five, the principal governing body in Geneva. The plan mapped out for John required him to study French, Latin, and Greek and to take instruction in drawing until the end of October. During that time, he would decide whether to remain in Geneva or return to England to enroll at either Oxford or the Middle Temple in the Inns of Court.[16]

Satisfied that the boys were finally settled, Henry began the return journey to London. He urged his eldest son to follow his own example of prodigious industry; the proper use of time, he believed, was critical if one were to become a useful member of society. "An Industrious Man," he wrote John, "may gain near 12 Months in a Year over the bulk of his contemporaries. How much Time is lost in what is commonly stiled Pleasure, but deserves no better epithet than barbarous dissipation. Sleep & Indulgence unites in stealing another large Portion of Time from the Sons & Votaries of Pleasure." Recognizing that there were many English students in Geneva, Henry expected John to follow the middle path "between abstaining wholly from an acquaintance with your Country Men in the Place where you reside & an intimacy with them. Of the two extremes the former is prefered."[17]

For the first time in his life, John found himself completely on his own. In addition to following the precepts Henry had laid out, he now acted as surrogate father for his younger brother. Geneva friends were available to offer advice, but no longer could he immediately turn to Henry for direction. Henry could have prepared him for the crowds and commotion of London. Nothing in John's experience, however, could have prepared him for this new environment, so different from the bustling port city and low-country rice plantations with which he was so familiar. He now awoke each day to an awe-inspiring vista of craggy, snowcapped peaks whose reflection shone in the clear blue waters of Lake Leman.

It was also an exciting intellectual climate for John, who found no shortage of people whose interests reflected his own. Though far from home, he had not completely departed the Anglo-American world he had always known. One native described Geneva as "an English city on the continent . . . where one thinks, where one feels in English; where one speaks, however, and writes in French." Visitors thought Geneva differed from other cities on the Continent, where a wealthy elite tended to possess a monopoly on refinement; in Geneva literacy was widespread, and the bourgeoisie, artisans, and laborers balanced their work with intellectual pursuits. John Moore, an English doctor who visited Geneva in the early 1770s, observed "simple workers who, in moments of leisure that their work permits them, relax by reading the works of Locke, Newton, and Montesquieu." To John the cultured bourgeoisie who dominated Geneva politics were kindred spirits, for they patronized the physical and natural sciences more than they did the fine arts.[18]

John's sojourn in Geneva, unfortunately, must be traced largely through Henry's letters, written in response to John's own. For the most part, John's thoughts and emotions have not survived. Clearly he found the adjustment difficult at first. He wrote six letters to Henry during his first month alone in Geneva. In his spare time he agonized over his choice of a career. He was "as cautious," his father commented, "against determining upon a particular branch or Science for his Studies, as a prudent Maid is against the Suits of surrounding Lovers."[19]

While John pondered his future, he found his living arrangements with Monsieur Chais more than acceptable. "My Apartment fronts upon a pleasant Square on the River Rhone," he wrote his uncle, "and I have a delightful prospect of the adjacent Country. The Climate agrees extremely well with Harry and me, nothing is wanting to us here, but our Friends. Thursday is so great a Holiday always among the Genevois, that it is call'd petit-Dimanche. I have devoted it to writing Letters to my Carolina Friends." Two of those friends were his mentor, Alexander Garden, and a former teacher, the Reverend Henry Bartholomew Himeli. John sent them the most recent publications of Voltaire.[20]

Geneva's religious climate had changed greatly since the sixteenth century, when John Calvin made the city a theocracy. During the eighteenth century,

Geneva society as a whole grew more secularized and less spiritual. Most clergymen and professors now received greater attention for liberal religious views than for piety, and many embraced deism and unitarianism.[21] John assured his worried uncle that his teachers's "Lessons have not the least Tincture of their Religious Opinions." He recognized that "under the specious pretext of satisfying the mind with Knowledge," many men had been led away "from the only true Wisdom" and "into Unbelief." Though John admired Voltaire—the aged and eminent writer lived five miles from Geneva at Ferny—he did not accept the Frenchman's strictures against churches. He told James that "with respect to the Christian Religion, I believe Voltaire has done more Injury to it, than any modern Author; for I believe it is greatly owing to him that Deism has crept in even among the younger Branches of the Clergy here . . . but happily Instances of this are rare." When such beliefs prevailed, he observed, "each Man supposes the existence of such a God as best suits his Purpose."[22]

With the exception of a few letters John wrote as a teenager, his surviving correspondence contains few allusions to religion. In that sense John differed from his father, whose heartfelt religious faith manifested itself in public and in private. In that sense Henry differed from most colonial gentlemen, who increasingly devoted their attention to the secularized political and business worlds and focused less on the spiritual realm.[23] Still a teenager, John remained under the sway of his father and thus spiritual concerns loomed large, even to the point that he contemplated entering the ministry. Despite his earlier preference for the study of medicine, John now found it difficult to commit himself to one profession. He approached this decision as he confronted other issues throughout his life: as a romantic idealist.

His idealism was a product of youthful exuberance; his romantic temperament was in keeping with the age. For the latter half of the eighteenth century, in England and in the American colonies, was an era of sensibility, when people of property placed emphasis on cultivating their "moral sense," on developing a bearing that prompted emotional responses to beautiful vistas, to sentimental literature, to family and friends, and to the general sufferings of humanity. Sensibility's roots extended back to the previous century, when some Anglican ministers, reacting against the Puritan view of man's innate depravity and Thomas Hobbes's argument that man was a self-interested creature devoid of virtue, extolled the "natural goodness" of humans. In the eighteenth century, moral philosophers like Lord Shaftesbury, Francis Hutcheson, and Adam Smith extensively analyzed and promoted an ideal of disinterested benevolence. By the 1770s sensibility was embedded in English culture; as an ideal it consumed England's growing middle class. The beneficiaries of a booming economy, the self-conscious bourgeois eagerly copied the genteel lifestyle of the aristocracy but disdained upper-class exclusiveness. Sensibility

proved so appealing because in theory the ethic celebrated a common humanity that bridged class and racial divides. An individual imbued with moral sentiments displayed disinterested benevolence through actions, not mere words
and gestures. The man of feeling, popularized in Henry Mackenzie's 1770
book of the same title, demonstrated his virtue through acts of charity to the
unfortunate and took decisive steps to alleviate societal injustice. Evidence of
sensibility's impact could be seen everywhere: in reform movements that
attempted to secure poor relief, penal reform, more equitable representation in
Parliament, and the abolition of slavery and the slave trade; in popular sentimental novels by authors like Mackenzie and Samuel Richardson, stories that
literally evoked tears from readers; and in the English middle class's intense
interest in exotic locales and native cultures, evidenced by the public acclaim
won by Captain Cook's voyages.[24]

The Laurenses could not help imbibing this culture. On more than one
occasion, they attended church services at John Fielding's orphan asylum for
young girls, which was a famous symbol of sensibility's focus on social reform.
Henry and John also witnessed how different themes in the culture of sensibility—desire for reform, emphasis on a common humanity, curiosity about
the exotic—could merge in a single event. While in London during the holidays, they attended the theater and saw *Oronooko,* a play in which the title character, a noble African king, leads a slave revolt in Surinam. The play depicts
slaves in a heroic light; their white masters, by contrast, appear as villains.[25]

Both Henry and John were men of feeling, but in quite different ways.
Henry, who often employed the language of sensibility in his correspondence,
revealed a sentimental bent in treating his slaves as "human Creatures," and in
his intense spiritual life. Influenced by friends like Richard Clarke and the
Moravian John Ettwein, Henry embraced Pietism, a Continental Protestant
religious persuasion that focused more on an experiential faith and inner spiri-
tuality and less on external questions of doctrine. Thus the elder Laurens,
though he remained an active member of the established Anglican Church, was
open to the beliefs and practices of other Christian denominations and was a
model of religious toleration. Similar to other Pietists, he also demonstrated an
impassioned faith, which made him unusual among the Carolina gentry.
Egerton Leigh derisively commented on Henry's emotional response to the
recitation of the Litany, how he appeared "transcendently moved," "swallowed
up in sublime and heavenly contemplation!"[26]

John styled himself as a man of feeling, but with a definite secular cast. In
his own mind he had clearly constructed a public identity—how he wanted to
live and be perceived by his fellow man. He desired, more than anything, to be
viewed as a man whose life was defined by acts of disinterested benevolence. In
emphasizing benevolence as his credo John drew on a dominant strain in the

culture of sensibility. He also drew on his own heritage. His native Charleston prided itself on its ethic of benevolence; as churchwarden in St. Philip's Parish, his grandfather had duties that included distributing alms to the indigent; and his father had always stressed the importance of service to the community.[27]

Now John's dilemma involved identifying the profession that best suited his perception of self. Despite his father's wishes, he unequivocally rejected a career as a merchant. Indeed, that profession's only positive features corresponded directly with values of sensibility, namely the middle class's increasing interest in the wider world and the emphasis on deeds of disinterested benevolence. The merchant, John conceded, maintained a "Universal Correspondence" that "gives one a Knowledge of Mankind." Moreover, "the continual Flow of Money peculiar to this Employment enables a Man to do extensive Good to Individuals of distress'd Fortunes, without injuring himself as well as to promote Works of publick Utility upon the most beneficial Terms." Those attributes, however, were not sufficient to induce him to follow in his father's footsteps: "I never lov'd Merchandise, nor can I now."[28]

As John weighed the remaining options—divinity, law, and medicine—two desires had the greatest weight: to perform acts of benevolence and to win fame or renown in posterity. Unwilling or unable to reveal his deepest feelings and frustrations to his father, whose opinion on the matter was quite clear, John instead wrote a lengthy letter to Uncle James, in which he expressed his opinions on the three learned professions:

> For my own part, I find it exceedingly difficult, even at this time, to determine, in which of the Learned Professions I shall list myself. When I hear a Man of improv'd Education, speak from the Goodness of his Heart, Divine Truths with a persuasive Eloquence which commands the most solemn Silence and serious Attention from all his Audience, my Soul burns to be in his Place. When I hear of One who shines at the Bar, and overcomes Chicanery and Oppression, who pleads the Cause of helpless Widows and injur'd Orphans, who at the same time that he gains lasting Fame to himself, disperses Benefits to Multitudes, the same emulous Ardor rises in my Breast. When I hear of another, who has done eminent Service to Mankind, by discovering Remedies, for the numerous Train of Disorders, to which our frail Bodies are continually subject, and has given Relief to Numbers whose Lives without his Assistance would have been insupportable Burthens, I can't refrain from wishing to be an equal Dispenser of Good.
>
> Thus I am agitated. 'Tis beyond far beyond the Power of one Man to shine conspicuous in all these Characters. One must be determined upon, and I am almost persuaded that it would be that of the Divine, if this did not preclude me from bearing Arms in Defence of my Country (for I can't read with Indifference the valiant Acts of those, whose prudent Conduct and admirable Bravery have res-

cued the Liberties of their Countrymen, and deprived their Enemies of power to
do them Hurt.)

No particular Profession is in itself disagreeable to me; each promises some
Share of Fame.[29]

The learned professions, as presented by John, were not mere ornaments completing a gentleman's refinement; rather, each profession became a potential
moral crusade with a utilitarian purpose. No longer did John view a medical
career as an opportunity to pursue scientific knowledge for the sake of learning
alone. Now scientific inquiry must be applied, its purpose to find cures for
dreaded diseases. Though some proponents of sensibility's model of benevolence asserted that a man should perform acts of kindness for others not in
hopes of winning public acclaim but because of a natural affinity for the good,
John found alluring the possibility that he would win applause for his achievements. For him the distinction between the act and the public response seemed
blurred, as if he placed more importance on the latter: the "Divine Truths"
spoken by the minister were overshadowed by "the most solemn Silence and
serious Attention" his sermon received "from all his Audience." For the
remainder of his life, John's sense of self-worth was tied to direct participation
in transcendent causes that served humanity, to performing actions that won
the acclaim of others. He saw himself as a dispenser of good, a man whose life
of disinterested benevolence benefitted others: the end result for him, the
benefactor, was both immediate (the approval of his contemporaries) and
removed (the approval of posterity, eternal fame).[30]

Like benevolence born of sensibility, fame required acts of service to the
community. A man who sought fame acted virtuously, not always in hopes of
winning popular acclaim, but in order to merit a reputation in posterity, the
verdict that really counted. To an impressionable youth like John, who grew
up in a disease-ridden environment where life could be cut short in an instant,
the idea of achieving symbolic immortality appeared particularly attractive.
Fame, in essence, was victory over death. The surest path to winning fame was
to serve one's country in time of war. Classical authors such as Plutarch provided numerous examples of heroic self-sacrifice, of valiant soldiers preserving
the liberties of their countrymen. Knowledge of the past century, in which
Great Britain and France fought four major wars, indicated that in the future
additional military conflicts, not peace, could be expected. In its brief history,
South Carolina had constantly faced invasion threats from neighboring Indians and foreign powers. With that in mind, John eliminated the ministry, leaving him to choose between law or medicine.[31]

John's final choice revealed the anxiety of a youth struggling to find his
place as an autonomous individual while mindful of the expectations of others.

In mid-August he announced that he would study law. John's explanation for this decision, a complete turnabout from his preference for medicine and the natural sciences, displayed a stronger desire to please Henry than himself:

> I have weighed the matter very seriously & considering that my Dear Papa & the majority of our judicious friends give a preference to my studying the Law, being conscious too that the World will not loose any considerable discoveries in Physick, because I turn my attention another way & reflecting that I ought not to abandon myself wholly to my own inclinations, but persue & make that agreable to me, by custom, which it is generally thought will render me most useful. I leave my favorite Physick, grieved to the Heart, that it is not to embrace that which I know would give my Dear Papa the most pleasure, but hope that he will accept of me as a student in the Law. My industry & application shall not be wanting & happy shall I be if their fruits shall be found in any degree answerable to the great & uncommon pains which have been taken on my account by the best of Parents.[32]

Was it unfair for John to lay his decision at Henry's feet, to state, in effect, that he gave up medicine, his first choice, because his father preferred that he study law? It is possible that John, despite his love for the natural sciences, chose law because it appeared to provide a surer path to acceptance in the present and to fame in posterity. Among the South Carolina gentry the bar was the third most prominent profession. As the Carolina economy grew more complex during the eighteenth century, the need for lawyers increased. Few men, however, practiced law as their only occupation; most were also planters or merchants. John, for example, told Henry that in addition to studying law, he would "pay particular attention to my Dear Papa's advice with regard to agriculture & Farming, they are very essential studies to one in my station." Many Carolinians considered an understanding of law a useful corollary to public service. Owing to their legal knowledge, lawyers assumed an importance in the assembly that was out of proportion to their numbers. And many followed the path John now chose—prior to 1780, over fifty Carolinians attended the Inns of Court in London. A law career not only proved more pleasing to his father, it also accorded with the values of his Carolina contemporaries.[33]

While John probably weighed these factors, the most important consideration remained his strong desire to win his father's acceptance. To Henry's credit, though he always wanted John to be a merchant, he gave the youth free rein to make up his own mind. On the other hand, Henry clearly favored law over medicine. John, adamantly against becoming a merchant, finally picked law because at least it was Henry's second choice. The decision proved doubly difficult: John said farewell to his "favorite Physick," which was wrenching enough, but he also felt "grieved to the Heart" because he could not fully conform to Henry's hopes. Raised to be a dutiful son, to strive to please his father, John found it difficult to separate his aspirations from Henry's wishes, even though he possessed latitude to make the final decision. His expression that "I ought not to abandon myself wholly to my own inclinations" was indeed telling. John based the first important choice of his life, not on his "own inclinations," but on what he considered his duty: to be the man Henry wanted him to be.

After learning of John's decision, Henry immediately took steps to enter him in the Middle Temple at the Inns of Court.[34] He approved John's plan of study, but doubts lingered. The tone his son had employed worried him. If John felt "grief at Heart" because he had decided to study law instead of medicine, Henry promised to withdraw his name from the Middle Temple. Henry reiterated that the final decision rested with John, that, above all, he wanted him to be happy with his choice. "If I did not act upon such principles," he concluded, "I should risk a defeat of my own purposes, which are to give you such an Education as will best enable you to support a Family with credit & honour, & to be most useful as a member of Society." Five days later Henry wrote John that his godfather George Appleby "had Decyphered" the section of the letter that indicated doubts about the choice of a legal career and "relieved me from my difficulties & distress."[35] Henry's anxiety was eased; thereafter the matter disappeared from their letters.

The Laurenses had lived in Europe for over a year, and Henry considered the time well spent. After receiving a letter from Jemmy that demonstrated marked improvement, the proud father told John that "there does not appear to be a want of Talents in any of you."[36] What surprised Henry and John most was the promise shown by Harry. John told his father that Harry "discovers more Talents than some folks were aware of." Henry had once described his namesake as "a little thick Headed." Jemmy, on the other hand, appeared "to be a duplicate of" John. In many respects, Harry assumed the role of the typical middle child, overshadowed by both of his brothers. Timid and lacking John's charisma, Harry never seemed to win his father's full affection.[37]

Henry's bliss was rudely interrupted when he received news from Charleston of a family scandal that involved his old nemesis, Egerton Leigh. After the death of Henry's sister Martha Bremar, Leigh, her son-in-law, became the guardian of her daughter Mary. While staying in Leigh's house, young Mary became pregnant with his child. Leigh placed the girl on *Carolina Packet* bound for England. Two days after boarding, she gave birth to a boy, but the baby lacked proper medical care and died a few days later. When the ship reached England, Captain William White promptly told the sordid tale to Henry. An outraged Laurens wrote to "The Perjured, Adulterous, Incestuous, Murderer—Egerton Leigh" and threatened to bring him to justice. Only sympathy for Leigh's family restrained him. Still, the scandal fulfilled a didactic purpose. "Read, Read, my Dear Son, my last & other Letters attentively" he instructed John. "Who can tell to what lengths of Vice he may be driven if once he leaves the Path of Virtue."[38]

At various points during his stay in Europe, Henry was stricken with gout, a disorder that plagued him intermittently for the rest of his life. Believing a warmer climate would aid his recovery, he planned a journey to Geneva. Mary Bremar, who seemed truly penitent for her past actions, wanted to accompany him. He decided to take her to France and search for a suitable retreat, a location unlike London, with its multitude of temptations. As evidence of his ecumenical spirit, he placed the girl at the Ursuline convent in Boulogne, France.[39]

Upon arriving in Geneva in May 1773, Henry found that his sons continued to do well. John studied civil law, mathematics, philosophy, and had "just begun a Course of political Eloquence, in which I promise myself great pleasure and Satisfaction." The course, he explained to his uncle, was designed for "Young English Nobleman, and is particularly adapted to the English Constitution." Riding and fencing balanced out his mental exertions with physical labor. Still, John could not fully surrender his real intellectual passion. In Geneva he met Jean-André de Luc the elder, a noted naturalist who numbered among his accomplishments the invention of a hygrometer to measure humidity levels and an accurate barometer that he used to measure Alpine peaks, including the highest mountain in Europe, Mount Blanc. John sent de Luc's *Recherces sur les modifications de l'atmosphere* to a fellow scientist, his former mentor Alexander Garden.[40]

John did not reveal these mixed emotions to his father. Assuming that the matter was closed, Henry now focused on determining the course that the young legal scholar should follow. After returning to London in late July, he conferred with Thomas Corbett, a London barrister who had formerly practiced law in Charleston. Corbett recommended that John continue studying civil law while in Geneva, but added that London was where he must finish his education. In the meantime, Corbett advised, the youth should further his legal knowledge by reading William Blackstone's volumes on English law. Henry promptly sent John a copy of Blackstone's *Law Tracts* and *Commentaries on the Law of England*.[41]

A visit from John's old teacher, the Reverend Himeli, provided Henry with another opportunity to lecture his son on the dangers of succumbing to sexual temptation. After the death of his wife in November 1771, Himeli grew tired of Charleston and departed in May 1773 to return to his native Switzerland. On his journey he formed "an attachment to a Trumpery Woman who Travels with him & whose quality is doubtful." Himeli's scandalous relationship prompted Henry to issue a didactic warning: "There, is a Bar to Fame, to

Honest Fame & peace of Mind, the Work & Hopes of Parents, the Labour & Laudable Ambition of all the Years in Youth, tumbled down, by a Baggage of no Value. The Love & friendship of Good Men, of a whole Community, the prospect of Glory & future good Days, All, All, sacrificed upon the Knees of a little Freckled Faced ordinary Wench. Let other Men Commiserate his Wretchedness & take Heed." Presented with this stark admonition, John could not fail to "take Heed."[42]

Henry frequently used the moral shortcomings of others, whether it be an Egerton Leigh or a Himeli, to reiterate to his eldest son the necessity of a virtuous life. Henry tried to direct his son down "the path of Virtue," meaning virtue in both its private and public contexts. He thus emphasized that John practice industry as opposed to idleness, chastity as opposed to debauchery, temperance as opposed to licentiousness. These virtues governed one's private and public conduct and resulted in a complete, accomplished man. As "useful" and virtuous citizens, his children would prove "the Cement of Society."[43]

Similar to other fathers of his time—indeed, like parents throughout history—Henry attempted to mold his offspring in his own image. He encouraged his children to adopt his lifestyle, which stressed moderation in all things. During the political crises of the 1760s, for example, he consistently urged his fellow Carolinians to pursue a moderate course. As an enlightened patriarch, Laurens emphasized that his overseers strive for the "Medium" between extreme severity and excessive leniency. As a patriarchal father, he preached a similar message to his children. He instilled in them a sense of their duty, the obligations they owed to him and to society. They could best fulfill their duty by practicing moderation. A moderate life required self-control, which could be achieved only through industriousness. "A life of Indolence," Henry believed, was "the Source of all Evil."[44]

As a father, Laurens revealed in practice at least a trace of John Locke's educational theories, which profoundly influenced many Americans. There is no evidence that Henry read Locke's *Some Thoughts Concerning Education,* but he could not have been unaware of that volume's reasoning. His emphasis on self-mastery, on prevailing over one's passions, accorded both with accepted Lockean wisdom and with the prevailing idea that the man of feeling must temper his sympathy with reason lest his emotions prove a destructive rather than a constructive force. Yet if Henry tried to apply Locke's principles to his own children, he did so inconsistently. Whereas Locke emphasized "example over precept," Laurens tended to blur the contrast. He set an example of industry and self-control for his children, yet his insistence on implicit obedience often bordered on imperiousness.[45]

To ensure his children's continued good conduct, Henry employed a device commonly utilized by other parents, instilling in the child the belief that parental approval depended on the child's accomplishments. Once, when particularly gratified at John's actions, Henry wrote "you know how to please your Papa & at the same time . . . you love to please him." Imitation was the sincerest form of flattery. "I shall receive vast Pleasure," he told John, "if you continue to live in Temperance & Regularity, an example worthy the Imitation of your Father." In another letter, he assured young Jemmy that through obedience "You will be more & more beloved by your affectionate Father." There were dangers implicit in such an approach: it indicated that the parent's love was conditional; and if the child did not fulfill the conditions, if he failed to meet parental standards, that love could be withdrawn.[46]

Henry's ties to his children, like his relationship with his bondspeople, were based on reciprocity. So long as he provided the children with a moral and material foundation on which they could secure their future, he expected in return their duty and obedience. For he would always fulfill his duty to them. Henry clearly demonstrated his idea of parental love and obligations when he attempted to effect a reconciliation between George Austin and his son and heir, George Jr. After the elder Austin emotionally and physically disinherited his son, who struggled with a drinking problem, Henry urged his former partner to reconsider. "If he was my Son," he said, "I would not altogether Cast him off." The dispute between the Austins ended tragically, as George Sr. died suddenly before acting on Henry's advice. Revealing both his Christian principles and his sensibility, Henry urged George Jr. "never to Speak Evil of your Father . . . humanity & your own honour Should restrain you from abusing the Memory of a deceased Parent."[47] While Henry implied that his continued love depended on his children's achievements, in reality his love for them was unconditional. His children, whose self-esteem largely depended on parental support and approval, perceived matters in a different light. Image proved more important than reality.

Parental approval was not John's only concern: he faced the additional pressure of fulfilling the high expectations of family friends in South Carolina and England. As usual Henry supplied the reminders: "Your friends on both Sides of the Water will expect to See in Jack Laurens the Man of Honour, Modesty, & prudence, the Scholar, the Christian, the Gentleman. Surely no endeavours on your part will be wanting to answer their utmost wishes & expectations." Proving the truth of this statement, Himeli wrote John and praised his improvement in the French language. "You are going to be the Voltaire of your Province," he predicted. Alexander Garden remained interested in his former protégé. "I have not the least doubt of his daily improvement in knowledge & Science," the doctor told Henry, "yet I own the Interest, which from long acquaintance with his growing Genius I take in his success & progress makes me often anxious to know how he proceeds & in what walks of Science his Genius chiefly delights." After quoting Garden's words, Henry encouraged his son to labor assiduously: "Your Character & Happiness are at Stake."[48]

In Geneva John worked hard, but he did not let his studies prevent him from forming close ties with fellow students and teachers. It marked the beginning of a pattern: he continually centered his life around homosocial attachments to other men. A handsome young man, properly genteel in his comportment, intellectually stimulating in his conversation, John never had difficulty attracting women and men. Women played important roles in his life, but he reserved his primary emotional commitments for other men. L. de Vegobre, who served as John's mathematics teacher, grew especially fond of his American student. John reciprocated by tutoring de Vegobre in English. De Vegobre honed his skills on current English literature, including Samuel Richardson's *Clarissa,* one of the century's best-selling sentimental novels. The young men shared much in common: de Vegobre, like John, was preparing himself to be a lawyer, though he preferred the study of science; moreover, they both spoke the language of sensibility. "I can think of nothing more sadly insipid," de Vegobre told John, "than to live without any affections of the heart."[49] With that sentiment, John heartily agreed.

John's active social life caused him to exhaust his finances by early 1774. Henry, who had set up a fund of £260 sterling for John during his visit to Geneva, considered that amount sufficient to last the young man "to the Month of May in the State of a Gentleman."[50] John feared that his "profligacy," as he termed it, would anger Henry. He promised his father that in the future he would be more frugal and keep regular accounts of expenditures. Henry promptly supplied additional funds and assured his son that he was not angry, for he believed the young man had learned his lesson. And it turned out that John had blown the problem out of proportion. Even though he had spent more than the average young gentleman, his father did not entirely disapprove. As Henry explained to a friend, John "was early taken notice of in Several polite families, & in return for their Civilities & Invitations he has gone into Similar expences for entertaining his friends." Conversations with Genevan visitors to London convinced Henry that these activities did not impinge on the young man's studies. In fact, he had spent less on entertainment than his father feared at first. John, Henry observed, "has been frugal beyond my expectation. . . . However it is not necessary [to] tell him all that." Instead, he instructed John to follow the middle ground between excessive liberality and stinginess unbecoming a gentleman.[51]

John's overreaction can be traced to two imperatives that molded his generation. Like most sons, he dreaded losing his father's acceptance, and Henry, like most fathers among the colonial gentry, encouraged his offspring to practice frugality and strongly opposed any wastefulness. More important, John's extravagance undermined the foundation on which masculinity was constructed. As a young colonial gentleman, he would assume a leadership role in society only if he remained a fully autonomous individual. His independence or freedom rested on his ownership of property. A man protected his property by managing his resources properly, which required that he exercise authority over himself. Male autonomy also rested on maintenance of authority over others, women and children in the domestic sphere and slaves in the rice fields. From Henry's perspective, manhood was demonstrated in a disciplined life of moderation. A man stayed in control; a boy, on the other hand, lacked self-control. Put in this context, John's expenditures take on added significance. When he described his handling of money as "profligacy" and "prodigality," he not only called himself recklessly extravagant. A profligate was also dissolute, debauched, given over to self-indulgence. In short, he identified himself as a boy incapable of self-control. Afraid of failing to meet his father's standards, John debased himself as an act of penitence.[52]

By the time that matter was settled, John had undertaken new responsibilities. Henry sent to Geneva two young Carolinians, Jacky Petrie and Billy Smith, son of the late Benjamin Smith, who had been a leading Charleston merchant. The elder Laurens asked his son to look after the boys and find them suitable lodgings. Because Petrie possessed limited financial resources, John drafted a plan for the boy's education that met a budget of 140 guineas. An additional charge came from London—John Manning, the son of William Manning, a West Indies merchant with extensive business ties to South Carolina. A wild youth, John Manning sorely needed discipline. Henry considered William Manning "a worthy Man" and was "Interested in the happiness of the whole family." Another newcomer to Geneva, Francis Kinloch, arrived from Eton College, where he had been placed by his guardian Thomas Boone, the former royal governor of South Carolina. Kinloch became one of John Laurens's closest friends.[53]

Because he now had even less free time, John's letters to his father became hurried. Henry never failed to point out these faults: haste signified procrastination and time ill spent; a gentleman displayed his refinement with good penmanship.[54] John's haste perhaps explains an ambiguous passage that slipped into one of his letters. He referred to "two people the most addicted of any in the World to Suicide." Alarmed by these words, Henry sent an emotional reply:

What can be meant by, *addicted*, to an Act, which can be perpetrated but once & no Man's devotion to it can possibly be determined from any thing Short of the Commission? But, my Dear Son, I trust that your opinion on that Question is So firm, that you are armed with Such irrefragable proofs of the Impiety as well as

Cowardice of Self Murther, as puts you out of danger of being made a Convert to Error, by any Man be his "Rank & distinction" ever So great, or by the finest thread of declamation tickling the Ears & fatally Captivating the Hearts of Giddy & inexperienced youth.[55]

Not surprisingly, Henry adhered to a conservative, Christian view of suicide as sinful and immoral, rather than to secular Enlightenment arguments that were less hostile and more sympathetic toward suicide. John's reply satisfied his father that the remark was innocuous. To ensure that such a misunderstanding did not recur, Henry urged John to use "forethought & reflexion" before writing. "A hurried Letter," he believed, "ever indicates a confused head."[56] Because John's original letter has not survived, it is impossible to determine the context of his cryptic suicide reference.

On the surface John's remark resembled the romanticism of suicide then popular among young Europeans, which found its ultimate expression in the suicide of the young English poet Thomas Chatterton in 1770, and the publication of Johann Wolfgang von Goethe's *The Sufferings of Young Werther* in 1774. Despite his evident literary promise, Chatterton swallowed arsenic after failing to make a living from his writings. Goethe's work concerned a highly emotional and unstable young man who shot himself because of his unrequited love for a married woman. In response to the book, young men wore Werther's costume, a blue-tailed coat and yellow waist-coat, and some killed themselves in imitation. Chatterton and Werther served as precursors and models for the Romantic movement that swept Europe in the nineteenth century and celebrated the misunderstood and unappreciated young genius who died prematurely, often by self-destruction. Essentially a romantic idealist, Laurens perhaps found these sentiments attractive. At the very least, he could not have been unaware of the ennui and despair that gripped his European contemporaries.[57] On the other hand, John's statement perhaps did not romanticize suicide at all. In writing about "two people the most addicted of any in the World to Suicide" he could have been referring to the citizens of Geneva and England. During the eighteenth century, both areas earned dubious reputations for having high suicide rates. Voltaire observed that Genevans seemed more prone to melancholy than the English; in proportion to population he believed Geneva had a higher suicide rate.[58]

Henry Laurens soon found himself consumed by greater worries than any allusions surfacing in John's letters. The relationship between Great Britain and the American colonies, which had been relatively calm since the repeal of the Townshend duties in 1770, suddenly exploded into turmoil. The colonists had quietly accepted the retention of the duty on tea. But when Parliament passed the Tea Act of 1773, an effort to help the financially crippled East India Company by giving it a monopoly in the colonial tea trade, colonists viewed the move as another attempt by the British government to impose unlawful taxes designed to deprive them of their property. The most extreme reaction occurred in December, when Bostonians disguised as Indians dumped the company's tea in the harbor.

Faced with this blatant destruction of private property, Parliament decided to discipline and isolate Boston, the perceived center of rebelliousness, and teach all Americans a stern lesson. Between March and June 1774, Parliament passed acts that closed the port of Boston to commerce and altered the charter of Massachusetts, replacing local autonomy with royal control. The legislation, rather than isolating Massachusetts, united the colonists as never before. In September the First Continental Congress, a body of delegates from twelve colonies—Georgia was unrepresented—met in Philadelphia and framed a response. Americans again resorted to economic coercion, except this time, in addition to nonimportation, Congress forbade the consumption of British products and banned most exports to the mother country.[59]

As a respecter of the rights of private property, Henry personally believed the Bostonians went too far. He hoped that with the assistance of the other colonies they would pay for the destroyed tea. The response in Charleston, where the tea was landed and stored in the customs house but the duty left unpaid, met his approval. Still, he viewed Parliament's punitive legislation as an arbitrary abuse of power. "People will tell you," he wrote a friend, "the Chastisement is intended only for Boston, but common Sense informs me that in Boston all the Colonies are to Stand or fall." If the British attempted coercion with force, he told John, they had better return home to face the guns.[60]

The uncertain imperial crisis made it imperative that Henry return to Carolina to guard his property and assist his countrymen in their time of need. He wanted John to begin law studies that November, but if the young man thought it wise to remain in Geneva, he would consider the change in plans, though he did "not promise an absolute submission" to his son's opinion. John replied that he wished to stay in Geneva another year, thereby postponing his return to America until 1778, a prospect Henry did not relish. Having recently learned that James Laurens's health had deteriorated, Henry told John, "My presence in Carolina both on his Account & our own is the more necessary." Since John had recently passed a civil law examination, it was time for him to begin studying English law. Though Henry had not made a final decision, he advised his son to get ready to leave Geneva.[61]

Preparations for the voyage home and the resulting excessive activity brought on an attack of gout, forcing Henry to postpone a final journey to Geneva, where he had planned to confer with John before determining whether to leave his sons there or bring them to London. Preferring a private meeting to correspondence, he decided instead to meet John and Harry at Paris. John, however, did not believe his father's health would allow the trip. He and Harry thus traveled the shortest route to London, arriving there on 7 August, only to learn that their father was on his way to Paris. John left Harry with William Manning and "rode Night & Day like a Young Man . . . at all hazards to himSelf" to meet Henry and ease his anxiety. The misunderstanding made John's desire to remain in Geneva a moot point; with Harry already in London, it was impractical to return to Geneva. After removing Mary Bremar from the convent at Boulogne, the Laurenses sailed to England. Mary went to live with the family of her cousin, Martha Parsons.[62]

Henry refused to leave for America until he placed his sons in suitable locations. Acting on John's advice, Henry enrolled Harry at Westminster School, where he could be watched over by his elder brother. Henry decided to leave Jemmy at Winson Green. He had considered taking his youngest son to Carolina, but feared that the boy's health would be impaired by the hot climate.[63]

After spending over two years in Geneva, John found the return to London jarring, and he longed for his former abode. To his friend Francis Kinloch, he confessed: "I am quite like a Creature in [a] new World. . . . The Noise, the Cries the Smoak and Dust of this vast City, makes me sometimes wish myself back at Paquis, I have another Reason too, for wishing myself there, I dont know when I shall get into such a valuable Set of Acquaintance as I left, but perhaps for the present, the fewer Acquaintance I have, the better it will be for me." He concluded the letter on a whimsical note: "Adieu, kiss all the pretty Genevoise for me."[64]

Thomas Corbett, the barrister who had promised to assist the Laurenses, looked for a lawyer who would take John in as a boarder.[65] "My present Prospect," John told Uncle James, "is either to be lodged in the Temple, or in some reputable Family, under the Eye of an honest Lawyer if such a one can be found, and to study the Laws of my Country very digilently for three years." Yet he possessed strong misgivings about his chosen profession that he revealed frankly:

> And a horrible prospect it is, that I am to get my Bread by the Quarrels and Disputes of others, so that I cant pray for success in my occupation without praying at the same time that a great Part of Mankind may be in Error either thro' Ignorance or Design, the only noble Part of my Profession is utterly unprofitable in this world, I mean the Defence of the weak and oppress'd; it is a part however that I am determined never to neglect, for altho' it enriches not, it must make a Man happy, what can be equal to the Heart felt Satisfaction which abounds in him who pleads the Cause of the Fatherless and the Widow, and sees right done to him that suffers wrong. Thus after long wavering I am now fix'd, no more Talk to me either of Physick, or Commerce, Law is the knotty Study which I must endeavour to render pleasant.[66]

The reference to "Physick" was tinged with regret. John chose "the knotty Study" of Law, after all, only because he strongly desired to please his father. Obviously he found little attraction in law. Although provincial society had grown more complex in the eighteenth century, increasing the demand for legal services, many Americans still adhered to negative perceptions from an earlier period—they shared John's belief that lawyers fed on the misfortunes of their fellow man. James Laurens, for example, agreed with his nephew that lawyers "have the greatest incitements to Chicanery & more encouragement from Example, to do Evil, than almost any other sett of men in our nation."[67] To John, the lawyer, like the merchant, gained "Heart felt Satisfaction" from the aspects of his profession that accorded with the values of sensibility. Only the opportunity to perform acts of benevolence and assist the downtrodden made the profession palatable. Though John made a verbal commitment to law, his heart obviously remained uncommitted. He was emotionally unprepared to spend three years studying a field he found so offensive.

In mid-October John moved in with Charles Bicknell, an attorney at Chancery Lane. More than just a landlord, Bicknell would advise John on attendance at the Inns of Court. And the young man could learn much from observing Bicknell's law practice. At the same time, Thomas Corbett remained available to provide continued advice and introductions to other highly regarded lawyers.[68]

Before his departure, Henry had a long-awaited meeting with Egerton Leigh, who had left Carolina during the summer. Leigh admitted his wrongs and tearfully asked for Laurens's forgiveness. Henry forgave Leigh and "dismissed him with a Serious admonition to amend his Course of Life." In addition, Henry received from Mary Bremar assurances that she released Leigh from further obligation in the matter. Thus ended, wrote John, "the late unfortunate Affair of My Cousin Molsy, which seem'd likely to prevent my Father's leaving this for some time."[69]

In late October Henry left London for Falmouth, where he would set sail for Charleston. On the way he visited Thomas Ledyard, an expert on indigo culture. Henry encouraged John to meet Ledyard. "You will find it worth your attention," he wrote, "for you must make Indigo by & by as well as practice Law." On 7 November, after a sojourn in England of three years and one month, Henry began the voyage home.[70]

With his father a continent away, John now assumed weightier responsibilities than he had previously known. In addition to his law studies, he acted as surrogate father for his brothers—surely an awesome task for a twenty-year-old. These new obligations required that he be a model for Harry and Jemmy, that he demonstrate the discipline of a man rather than the flightiness of a boy. Time would tell whether he truly merited his father's trust.

Chapter 3

"I hate the Name of King"
Biding Time in England
November 1774–December 1776

Entangled in the "knotty Study" of law because of his own choice, John Laurens soon found diversions in social interaction with new friends and in the political disputes that increasingly alienated the colonies from their mother country. John's preoccupation with the imperial crisis worried Henry, who insisted that his son focus on his studies and on his duty to his brothers. Unwilling to directly contest Henry's authority, John instead joined in the larger rebellion against another parent, King George III. In the process he constructed a new identity, a role that would define the remainder of his life.

Henry Laurens, after a voyage of thirty-four days, finally reached Charleston on 11 December 1774 and reunited with his daughters, his brother, his sister-in-law, and his friends. Laurens's thoughts, however, often centered on the three sons left behind in England. Shortly after his return, he reminded John that in the Laurens family he was "second in command." During moments of reflection, John should contemplate the responsibilities he would assume upon Henry's death. "In a word you are the Man," Henry concluded, "the proper Man to be my friend while I Live, & the friend of my younger family after my Death, you therefore on whom, next to God, I rely, will meditate on the subject & endeavour to qualify your self for the discharging the Duty which may be required from you."[1]

Daunting words for a twenty-year-old. Yet John performed his duty as the guardian of two younger brothers without hesitation. At the same time, he began the studies that were to prepare him for a legal career. He paid a bond, certifying that he could meet his financial obligations to the Middle Temple. He jokingly told Henry about his introduction to "the Mystery of Mutton Eating, by which alone I can gain the Title of Barrister." His first visits to the Court of King's Bench proved uninspiring, but being "a perfect Novice," he could not "fail of picking up some Instruction."[2]

The Inns of Court—the Middle Temple, Inner Temple, Gray's Inn, and Lincoln's Inn—had long served as the training ground for English lawyers. Of the four, the Middle Temple was the most popular to both English and American students, albeit Lincoln's Inn possessed the best reputation. Since the latter half of the seventeenth century, the inns had discontinued formal education practices such as lectures conducted by senior barristers and moots that gave students the opportunity to discuss legal cases and develop their argumentative faculties. By the time John entered the Middle Temple students were required to attend four terms: Hilary, Easter, Trinity, and Michaelmas. Each term lasted about three weeks, except the latter, which extended an extra week. During a term, the student was expected to dine in the Middle Temple Hall with the benchers, barristers, and fellow pupils. For the most part, however, a student worked on his own; the study of law entailed extensive time alone reading textbooks and legal tomes, supplemented by attendance at court. On occasion, law students gathered at coffee houses to debate current cases or discuss common readings. To be called to the bar, a student had to keep twelve terms. Usually the call came five years after admission to the inns, though exceptions were made. Yet not all students expected to be lawyers; for many gentry youths, a legal education served only as an embellishment to their standing in society. Obviously this informal system allowed them considerable leisure.[3]

Thus John had free time for outside activities, including forming new acquaintances. Although he found his lodgings with the Bicknells at Chancery Lane agreeable, he considered the attorney Charles Bicknell "the merest machine in the world, the most barren in Conversation and least calculated to improve, of any Man I ever was connected with." Conversely, Bicknell's elder brother John proved a stimulating companion; whenever possible, Laurens spent time with him.[4]

He also paid frequent visits to the home of William Manning at St. Mary Axe. In Henry's absence Manning served as an unofficial guardian and advisor to John. The young man enjoyed the congenial atmosphere at the Manning household—particularly, it seems, the companionship offered by the merchant's three daughters, Sarah, Elizabeth, and Martha. In one letter, John issued a mild rebuke in French to his sister Martha: "I am annoyed that you have for so long neglected to write to Mademoiselle Manning, you should have done so right away. She's a very nice young lady; I have the opportunity to see her often at her Father's, and the entire Family is very kind to me." Presumably the "Mademoiselle Manning" in question was Martha Laurens's namesake. During a dinner at the Manning home, John Baker, a prestigious barrister and family friend, noticed a mutual attraction between John and Martha. Having chosen a career, John neared the time when he would, with his father's blessing, choose a bride. In the same letter to his sister Martha, he commented on her reports of marriages in low-country Carolina. "I wish them all . . . much happiness in their Sacred Union," he wrote. "Do you think about it sometimes, my Sister"? John's question implied that he did think about it.[5]

As a young man alone in London for the first time, John inevitably encountered distractions that interfered with his studies. "I am reading Law as closely as I can," he told his father, "but have great Reason to regret every Moment lost at Geneve, as the unavoidable Interruptions to Study here are great and numerous." He promised to "do all in my power to merit, as nothing will make me happier than, to receive your Well-Done." In a more candid letter to Francis Kinloch, he admitted "being strenuously employed sometimes in Study, sometimes in the pursuit of Pleasure." Having been tied to his books for so long, John was now making up for lost time.[6]

The worsening imperial crisis proved the greatest distraction. Whenever possible, John attended Parliament to hear debates on relations between the metropolis and the provinces. He heard George III announce to the House of Lords his determination to uphold the supremacy of Parliament. On occasions when John could not observe the proceedings, he received news from friends he had met in Geneva, such as Lord Stanhope. When the House of Lords made an address of thanks to George III, nine lords, including Stanhope, dissented because they believed the king's speech tacitly approved the measures taken by the previous Parliament. John sent copies of the address of thanks and the nine lords' protest to Henry, who delivered these documents to the *South-Carolina Gazette* for publication. John's letters thus helped his countrymen stay informed of the political climate in Great Britain.[7]

It seemed that John could never get enough information about political events. The growing threat of war absorbed his thoughts and dictated his actions. He no longer identified himself as a British subject; he now spoke with deep emotion as an American, one whose interests diverged sharply from those of the mother country. Taxation imposed by Parliament, rather than the elected colonial assemblies, threatened the property that was the foundation of every man's independence. British imperial policy treated the colonists as inferiors, dependents rather than free people. Born and raised in a slave society, John clearly recognized the implications. "If a British Parliament may prescribe to us the Mode and Quantity of our Taxes," he observed, "we are but Slaves."[8]

John was now but a vicarious participant in the crusade, "the sacred Cause of Liberty." If the British ministry resorted to force, he hoped to join his fellow Americans and was willing to make the ultimate sacrifice. "There is no Man I hope would more gladly expose himself," he said, "or hold his Life more cheap."[9] While John knew that Henry initially would oppose a premature return, he rationalized that his father's sense of patriotism would eventually override any misgivings. It seemed silly to study law for three years when revolution loomed so near. "Why should we spend years in theory," he asked, "when so noble an opportunity offers for Practice?" To Francis Kinloch, who did not share these idealistic sentiments, John wrote, "we can die but once, and when more gloriously than in defence of our Liberties."[10]

Amid thoughts of war, John found time for more pleasant diversions. When two young Carolinians who had studied in England, Thomas Pinckney and James Ladson, returned home in December, a group of their countrymen accompanied them on the trip to Gravesend. John joined this party, which included Jacob Read, a law student at Gray's Inn. After a late night with his friends, John rose early in the morning to write letters. He had considered attending an "agreeable Party" at Cambridge during the Christmas holidays, he informed Henry, but now it seemed wiser to remain in London and devote time to his studies.[11]

These letters, containing extensive details of British political maneuvering, expressions of a desire to return home to fight and perhaps die in defense of American liberties, and accounts of excursions like the trip to Gravesend, did not please Henry, who perceived that John's obsession with the imperial crisis consumed his time and diverted him from his studies. He encouraged John to continue sending the latest news, but emphasized that his education came first. It was easy, Henry believed, to declare one's willingness to die for his country during a coffee house debate. He reminded John that "Life is the Gift of God & we are accountable to him not only for, but for the improvement of, it. Reserve your Life for your Country's call, but wait the Call. Mind your chosen business."[12] In other words, the call to service would not come until John had completed his education.

What bothered Henry most was the company John kept. Jacob Read, in particular, was known for drinking and carousing—activities involving loss of time and reputation that rankled the elder Laurens. Henry rebuked John for associating with men like Read, especially when their moral shortcomings were so obvious. He assumed, despite John's word to the contrary, that his son did attend the party at Cambridge, an event Read probably planned. "Are you so poor in valuable acquaintance," Henry asked, "in Books, in Ideas, as to seek Company which inwardly you disapprove of. It cannot be. Were you under any restraint while your Father was in England? No! you were his Companion his bosom friend. Whence then these retrograde motions immediately after his departure, like a Bird after long confinement fled from her Cage?" After a lecture on proper time and money management, Henry reminded John that "the Eyes of your friends & of your Country are upon you, they are in expectation

& think themselves in view of a valuable Casket, for your own sake, for theirs & for the sake of posterity disappoint them not by coming up a bundle of Carolina Rushes."[13]

These stern words of reproach produced the desired effect—a properly dutiful and penitent response from John. He regretted his involvement with "the Carolina Set, against which I had been forewarned; but the Relation as Countrymen, by degrees stole me into their Society. Notwithstanding all that I knew to deter me from such a Connexion with them. Thank heaven there are none of them now in my Neighborhood." Adding to his remorse, John continued to have difficulty living within his expenses, and he promised to spend the entire summer of 1775 in London, where he would need no additional funds. Despite these efforts to reform, he longed for words of reassurance from his father, the one whose opinion mattered most. Henry's rebuke inflicted a deep wound to John's self-esteem. His pain was obvious in a statement of repentance that became the harshest of self-appraisals:

> I feel my Mind a little eased, tho' it will not be free from Pain and Anxiety, 'till it receive some words of Comfort from you. And I am persuaded that however greatly I have offended, you would pity me, could you conceive the Tort[ur]e of Mind that I have undergone this day. I have experienced the same distressful Sensation in putting Pen to Paper to address you, that an offender does in lifting his Eyes, which Shame had cast down; to meet those of his injured Friend. Oh such a Letter from you my Father, and I, distracting Thought, to have given occasion for it. But your Words are a Seasonable, tho' most severe, and trying Medicine. Yes you have shewn me myself. I was very well satisfied, before your terrible Letter gave the Alarm and call'd me home to Self-examination. You have shewn me such a Man as I almost hate. The more I look into my past Conduct, the more I despise what I was, the more I wish that a long Series of such Deportment, as I now, dares such an irresolute man, say, resolve upon, were already past, and had regained your Confidence. The Remorse I have felt is known to none, but myself, and can only be conceived by one, who has been so unhappy, as to sink in his own, and the Esteem of his best Friend. I supplicate Your Pardon, and Pity, how dare I ask to restore to your Esteem, Your Unworthy, tho much afflicted
>
> > and penitent Son
> > John Laurens.[14]

Viewing this father-son exchange through twentieth-century lenses, John's youthful frolics seem understandable, especially considering his earlier total devotion to his studies. Henry, however, did not view matters that way. Despite his emphasis on moderation, Henry invariably leaned toward a life of Spartan self-denial. A puritanical individual who considered it a grievous sin to waste time or resources, he viewed John's attempt to sow wild oats as an almost unforgivable lapse into debauchery. One's personal deeds were as important as one's actions in the public sphere; a virtuous man was to be a model of rectitude in his private life. A year earlier Henry had itemized for John the principal components of moral virtue, "that system of sound Philosophy the precepts of Jesus Christ. Moderate desires of Riches & Dignity, Temperance & Sobriety, Self denial of irregular Pleasures, Benevolence & Loving our Neighbours as ourselves." To that list he could have appended industry, frugality, chastity—these virtues marked the principal attributes of an upright man. He hoped John's departure from these "precepts" was an aberration that would not be repeated; future good behavior would again merit a father's "Well-Done." When Henry used the metaphor of the "Bird" and the "Cage," he came closer to the truth than he realized.[15]

Henry had mapped out the part John was to play on the world's stage: a virtuous man, both in public and in private, a "useful Member of Society." If his children could not fulfill that role, he once told John, "I would rather wish you all taken from this Life before you could experience more of those Pains & Sorrows which are the Inheritance of the Sons of Men." Doubtless those words now came back to haunt John. He tried to follow Henry's lead. To an extent, he succeeded in fashioning an identity like the ideal set by his father. He acquired the polish expected of a gentleman; he constructed a public role, the man of feeling performing acts of benevolence. In his private life, however, he failed to imitate his father's example. To be sure, some of John's transgressions—his failure to utilize wisely every minute of the day, his difficulties handling money—diverged from the industriousness and self-control expected of most gentlemen. John's social activities with his friends, however, challenged Henry's personal standards, which were stricter than was the norm in South Carolina. For example, one of their contemporaries, John Mackenzie, successfully combined the private pursuit of pleasure with a public career that won him the esteem of his fellow Carolinians. What worked for Mackenzie, however, did not work for Henry or his children. It was John's misfortune to inherit an ideal that he aspired to yet never fully achieved.[16]

On another occasion, John's judgment won his father's approval. During a visit to Parliament, he encountered Egerton Leigh. The following day, when Leigh invited John to dinner, he replied that Henry would not approve. Leigh understood, but hoped for an eventual rapprochement between the two families. Undeterred by this rebuff, the Leighs attempted to renew relations with Mary Bremar. Upon receiving word of these developments, Henry instructed John to tell Mary to have no further dealings with the Leighs.[17]

In the meantime, Henry Laurens became a key figure in South Carolina's gradual move toward independence. Shortly after his return, he was elected to the First Provincial Congress. Upon convening in January 1775, the Provincial Congress reviewed the measures adopted by the Continental Congress the previous October and established committees to enforce the economic sanctions against Britain. When the Congress reconvened in June, the delegates elected Laurens president. Before adjourning on 22 June, the Congress created an executive body, the Council of Safety, to oversee the province's defense efforts, including three newly established regiments. Named president of this thirteen-member board, Laurens now headed South Carolina's executive and legislative bodies. His indefatigable industry proved valuable in the tumultuous days ahead.[18]

Political events took an ominous turn. News reached Charleston that British regulars and Massachusetts militiamen had fought at Lexington and Concord on 19 April. The possibility of harsh British reprisals threatened the vast estate Henry Laurens had accumulated and hoped to bequeath to his children. James Laurens's precarious finances posed an additional concern. James was the surety for his old mercantile firm, Hawkins, Petrie & Co., which owed extensive debts in Britain. Hoping to protect his brother from bill collectors, Henry pledged his credit with William Manning. The Laurenses's financial standing was indeed delicate. "From the complexion of the present times," he told John, "there is more than a bare possibility of your being obliged to depend *wholly* upon practice in your profession for a Livelihood. To qualify your self therefore for encountering the utmost difficulty is your duty, a duty to your self & to Society."[19]

At about the same time that Henry issued this warning, John apologized for almost exhausting his expense account. Coming on the heels of the earlier statement of repentance and self-loathing, John again humbled himself before his father, to the point that he questioned his own moral virtue, his ability to keep his passions in check: "I again confess, and upraid myself for, my Imprudence, and tho' few possess so little of that Virtue, which prevents foolish Actions, yet noone can feel more poignant Regret, when sensible of the Commission of them." In John's defense, membership in an inn of court involved considerable expense. In addition to having to purchase costly legal tomes, students, regardless of their social standing, felt constrained to maintain the lifestyle of an English gentleman. Still, Henry wanted to hear less remorse—he called John's penitent confession "very pretty!"—and more evidence that his son could live within his means. As usual, he emphasized the importance of self-control, a quality John could acquire through practice, until it became habitual, an integral part of his character: "Can't a Man of your sensibility & penetration discovery a way for accomplishing that by Skill, which nature has denied, if it be true that she has denied it; but I deny the fact; Nature has been abundantly kind in *all* respects to the Young Man, but at different stages he has in *many* respects given himself Airs. I say, be it so, let us help Nature, by depriving our selves of the means of doing foolish Acts."[20]

Along with these worries, James Laurens's health continued to decline. Following Henry's advice, James decided to journey to England with his wife Mary and with Henry's daughters, Martha and Polly. They hoped the change in climate would strengthen his constitution. Before their departure in late May, Henry wrote John and instructed him to suggest ways for Martha to improve her education. Polly, though only five years old, already displayed considerable intellectual promise. Henry worried that Mary was too permissive with Polly, and he asked John to communicate those sentiments to his aunt.[21]

On 12 July the Laurenses arrived in England. John, upon meeting his eldest sister for the first time in four years, tested her courage to determine if "her mind" was "superior to the common accidents of life, and the groundless fears of some of her sex." He arranged for the postillion to drive the carriage at high speed through the rolling English countryside, while he scrutinized Martha's reaction for any display of "womanish fears." Satisfied that Martha had passed this trial with flying colors, he announced that "he had found her the same Spartan girl he had left her." It was an eccentric test, to be sure, but one in keeping with the paradoxes of the culture of sensibility. While John cultivated his emotions and formed sentimental attachments with other men, as a counterbalance he desired that his sister shy away from feminine weakness and adopt habits of masculine fortitude.[22]

After a brief stay in London, James, Mary, and the young girls moved to Bristol in order to take advantage of the city's hot wells and sea air. Though John still longed for America and military action, he was delighted to be reunited with his sisters, especially Martha, who was now fifteen years old. Like her eldest brother, Martha consistently demonstrated intellectual curiosity; unlike John, she invariably encountered external barriers to her achievements. Henry supported Martha, but he never failed to remind her of the constraints their culture placed on women. Once when she requested a pair of globes he sent them along with an admonition: "When you are measuring the surface of this world, remember you are to act a part on it, and think of a plumb pudding and other domestic duties." Unable to display her abilities in a civic realm dominated by men, Martha constructed her identity through a personal covenant with God: she pledged to make her contribution to society as a model of virtue and piety. In doing so she reflected her father's intense religious faith. John could not resist teasing Martha about her fervor, and requested from her a letter "in the first vacancy from the important Duties, of commanding, putting on, and Displaying the *Sublime* Inventions of the Millenenil Tribe; I think I may promise myself You will not remain Silent, now. My rashness in hinting at the Distribution of your Time will draw a spirited Harangue, I'll engage for it."[23]

Separated from his entire family, Henry Laurens dealt with feelings of isolation in part by performing the multiple political roles assigned to him. His duty as president of the Council of Safety was most important because that body supervised the daily functioning of the revolutionary movement. He frequently transmitted copies of documents and letters to John, with instructions to print the material in English newspapers. When representatives of the revolutionary government negotiated a treaty with backcountry loyalists, the Council of Safety ordered it published in England; Henry asked John to "see that work done." In another letter, Laurens accused John Stuart, superintendent of Indian affairs, of plotting to unleash Indians and slaves on the Carolinians. Following his father's instructions, John submitted this charge to the *London Chronicle* and it was printed on 3–5 October 1775.[24]

With good reason, Henry continued to worry that his eldest son focused on the war and political events and neglected his education. These fears did ease a little when John wrote that law became more interesting as he progressed to advanced levels of study. If John's letters to his uncle are any indication, Henry's concerns were indeed well founded. John kept Uncle James informed on political maneuvering in London and military developments in America. He also copied for James extensive passages from Henry's letters. Known for his political apathy—he left America in part to escape the rebellion—James probably could have done without these frequent updates. In correspondence, John rarely mentioned his studies, and when he did, it was often as an afterthought. One excursion from London almost proved costly: "My arrival here . . . I have found to day, was just in time to enable me to keep Term."[25]

John mostly wanted to return home. "What have I to do here in the present Circumstances of my Country? what have I not to do at home?," he asked Henry. He longed for permission to leave England, especially now that the likelihood of a peaceful settlement between Great Britain and the colonies seemed remote. His departure, he assured Henry, would have little negative effect on the family. James, with the assistance of William Manning, could oversee the "weaker part" of the Laurens family. "You will be, honorably distinguished by your Services in the foremost Rank of your Fellow Citizens," John predicted, "and I shall act, with no less Ardour in some inferior Station."[26]

Henry reacted decisively. He pleaded with John not to abandon the dual roles of student and surrogate father. He intimated that the young man was attempting to exercise autonomy too soon, prior to his twenty-first birthday, a rite of passage that signified adult independence. Referring to John's plans as "Romantic schemes," he instructed James to convince the young man to remain in England where his duty lay. If John persisted in his determination to leave, Henry resolved, "I Shall give him up for lost & he will very Soon reproach himSelf for his want of Duty & affection towards me, for abandoning his Brothers & Sisters, for disregarding the Council of his Uncle, & for his deficiency of common understanding, in making Such a choice. If these reflections prevail not over him, nothing will. He must have his own way & I must be content with the remembrance, that I had a Son."[27]

Henry employed this threat to manipulate John into submission; he had no intention of actually renouncing his son. But to a son dependent on his father's acceptance, the severest of reprimands—a threat to withdraw affection—was practically tantamount to a death sentence.[28] John thus had little choice but to acquiesce in his father's wishes, at least for the time being. He never intended to give the impression of disobedience; only worry for Henry's safety and America's future influenced him. "If in my zeal I have inadvertently gone too far or have said any Thing which implied a Design or Desire of Independence on you or your Counsels," he wrote, "I sincerely ask pardon." In requesting forgiveness he recited a familiar formula of submissiveness, except that now resentment reached the surface. He began to feel constrained by Henry's patriarchal demands: "No My Dearest Friend and Father, I feel the same Obligation to you, the same unbounded Love at this period of my Life that I have ever hitherto acknowledged. . . . Yes My Dear Father I will obey you fully in all that you require . . . tho Baseness seems to lurk under Duty, and I feel like a Man avoiding the Service of his Country because his Father tenderly commands him to be out of Danger."[29]

John expressed his dilemma more clearly to James: "My Father repeats to me his Commands relative to my Studies, and adds some such Expressions as make my Heart bleed. My good and Dear Uncle what shall I do. Is it not dishonour to stay; and how can I disobey so good a Father[?]" Time did not abate his desire to serve his country; his restlessness only increased. "I am ashamed to own that I am an American," he told James two months later. "Young and free from bodily Infirmities, in England, as a dear Father's Command[s] oblige me to remain in the humiliating Situation being pointed at by others, and almost think[ing m]eanly of myself."[30] Whether or not his contemporaries actually noticed his absence from the scene of action, he clearly thought they did. This admission marked a turning point, for previously John's self-image had depended mostly on Henry's approval. Now he openly sought recognition and respect from his peers.

John's Geneva friends sympathized with his dilemma even as they chastised him for failing to write them more often. It was to be a recurring pattern. Wherever John went, he easily formed close attachments to other men, but then neglected them once he moved. He seemed to reserve all his focus and energy for the matters at hand. Both Francis Kinloch and L. de Vegobre complained when John did not promptly answer their letters. Still, it was difficult for any friend to remain annoyed with John for long, and de Vegobre tempered his reproofs with encouragement. Even if John could not volunteer for military service, de Vegobre believed, he could still prove himself a man: "My dear Laurens! It's the circumstances where you find yourself that a man shows himself; you are exhibiting, doubtless, a male firmness in the midst of misfortune."[31]

De Vegobre had a point, for reasons he could not have suspected. John's claims to the contrary, his presence in England was needed. He served as an important influence on Harry and Jemmy, who benefitted from his attention and needed the guidance that only he could provide. After William Howell, the headmaster at the Winson Green boarding school, suffered a stroke, John concluded that Jemmy was not receiving proper attention. He removed his youngest brother and began investigating private schools in the London area. While he made a thorough search to find an ideal location, he tried to ensure that Jemmy's absence from school did not prove harmful.[32]

In the end he narrowed the inquiry to two schools, one at Greenwich, another at Brompton near Gillingham in Kent. He tended to favor the Greenwich school because William Manning had leverage with the master. On Monday, 4 September, he made a final visit to both schools and decided to place Jemmy at Greenwich.[33]

John rushed back to London. He wanted to notify Henry, and there was still time to dash off a letter at the Carolina Coffee House before the packet boats departed. John also wanted to tell William Manning. When he reached the Manning residence at St. Mary Axe, he encountered Manning's clerk. Unable to restrain his own emotions, the clerk gave John the biggest shock of his young life. During his absence, Jemmy had suffered a critical injury. Always an active and adventurous child, the boy attempted to jump "across from a Footing within the Iron Rails," to John's window, whereupon he fell and fractured his skull. Grief-stricken, John rushed home to his brother's side. The attending doctors concluded that the injuries were too severe; John could do nothing but "pour out fruitless Tears" and await the inevitable. Along with a nurse furnished by William Manning, he maintained a constant vigil until the following night, when Jemmy died. John described the ordeal to his uncle: "At some Intervals he had his Senses, so far as to be able to answer single Questions, to beckon to me, and to form his Lips to kiss me, but for the most part he was delirious, and frequently unable to articulate. Puking, Convulsions never very violent, and latterly so gentle as scarcely to be perceived, or deserve the Name, ensued, and Nature yielded."[34]

After this devastating blow, John with good reason wondered aloud, "what unexpected Cruel Misfortunes await us, of what can we promise ourselves any lasting possession[?]" Jemmy's death, like the earlier loss of his mother and siblings, provided ample evidence of the uncertainty of life, of how a person's loved ones could be snatched away in an instant. In a similar vein John asked, "What is there most dear to us in this world, that we are not liable at every moment to lose by some unforeseen Accident?"[35]

Four days later John wrote what was probably the most difficult letter of his life. Normally he composed letters hurriedly, but this occasion called for careful planning. John realized that the news would wound Henry deeply; his goal was to ensure that the wound did not prove incapacitating. While John's immediate family remained dear to him, he believed that the cause of liberty took precedence over any private concerns. He arranged the letter with those priorities in mind, placing his account of Jemmy's death in the middle and employing the introduction and conclusion to remind Henry that he had public obligations to fulfill. Grief, while inevitable, was to be "indulged as little as possible." He encouraged Henry to "Suffer not one moment to be spent in useless moans for the Dead, which might be employed to the Service of the Living. You have great and important Duties to perform upon the Earth. Your Family your Country looks to you with Confidence." Though John realized that "The Feelings of Humanity must in some degree be yielded to," he remained confident that the combination of "Reason and Religion" would prevail and help Henry overcome his grief.[36]

Hoping to lessen the shock, John described Jemmy's death to Henry less graphically than he had to Uncle James. He also sent the letter through Gabriel Manigault, the prominent Huguenot merchant. Noted for his honesty and integrity, the seventy-one year old Manigault served as a patriarch for Charleston's Huguenot community; it would be left to him, along with Alexander Garden, to break the news to Henry.[37]

Owing to the slowness of communications, Henry did not receive word of Jemmy's death until 4 January 1776. The grief-stricken father was unable to attend the Council of Safety meeting that day. At the first shock, Henry himself contemplated and welcomed death as a release from the intense pain. Upon reflection, he decided that God willed him to remain on earth, where his duty lay: "The Stroke was sudden & unexepected . . . I feel it, feel it, but I will bear it." He still had "two Sons & two Daughters who by God's grace may remain long after me & to whom 'tis my duty to pay attention." Henry realized that John, as Jemmy's guardian, felt some responsibility for the accident. "Console your self my Dear Son I blame you not," he reassured John, "if in aught you have been remiss, your own reflections will be too severe. Henceforward take heed."[38]

Rather than alleviating any guilt John felt, Henry's ambiguous and clumsy attempt to offer condolence more likely compounded his remorse. Obviously

John bore no responsibility for Jemmy's death. Yet it was consistent with his sensitive temperament for him to feel accountable, to believe that somehow he could have, or should have, prevented the accident, especially after his father implied that he had been "remiss." When his mother died, he had reacted with mixed emotions, a response that perhaps repressed his mourning; now another sudden and unexpected loss engendered ambivalence. As surrogate parent, "second in command," the man "on whom, next to God," Henry relied, John reproached himself "and made a case of conscience out of the event, which embittered the natural sorrow, and humbled greatly the spirit beyond the usual exactions of grief." Francis Kinloch attempted to console his friend. "Cast a strict eye upon Your past conduct with regard to Your late Brother," he advised, "& Your conscience will wisper consolation."[39]

Jemmy's tragic death made Henry even more pessimistic about the future. The war, he believed with renewed fervor, could cost him his life and deprive his children of their inheritance. He urged William Manning to exhort John to practice frugality; if necessary, the young man could make his annual allowance last three years. Both John and Martha, he contended, were capable of earning their own bread. If they achieved self-sufficiency, he could allocate the remainder of the family's funds to support James and Mary Laurens and the younger children, Harry and Polly.[40]

Henry's pessimism about the future of the American rebellion led him to reiterate the charge that John persist in his studies. "Be not ambitious of being half a Soldier half a Lawyer & good for nothing," he wrote. He appealed to John's sense of manhood: "'Tis your Interest, tis your duty to yourself, your Duty to your Country, to proceed with manly Resolution to the end of the Course which you have entered upon." The implication was clear: if John deserted his studies he would display the indecisiveness of a boy rather than the resolution of a man. John heeded the admonition but intimated some bitterness when he reminded Henry that law had not been his original choice: "I labour to qualify myself for the Profession to which you have destined me."[41]

The growing political gap between Henry, the reluctant revolutionary, and John, the ardent enthusiast, was best illustrated in their differing reactions to the publication of Thomas Paine's *Common Sense*. A recent immigrant to America, Paine published the pamphlet in January 1776. It became an immediate success. Americans from all social classes eagerly imbibed Paine's vicious attack on the hereditary English monarchy and his call for the colonies to declare their independence. Deliberate and moderate leaders like Henry Laurens remained unimpressed. Henry still held faint hope that a reconciliation could be achieved. Nevertheless, he sent the pamphlet to John, but added the stricture that "nothing less than repeated & continued persecution by Great Britain can make the People in this Country subscribe" to Paine's arguments.[42]

John, on the other hand, applauded the pamphlet and hoped that its popularity among Americans would lead to a declaration of independence. Upon learning that Henry was sending *Common Sense,* John replied that the pamphlet had been printed in England and he had read it "more than once." He believed that once Henry recognized that the British intended to prosecute the war with vigor, he would change his opinion of Paine's work.[43]

Between April and September 1776, while Americans were debating the merits of Paine's arguments and moving to declare independence, John and his school-friend Francis Kinloch held their own political discourse. Influenced by his guardian Thomas Boone, the former royal governor of South Carolina, young Kinloch was a monarchist. For his part, Laurens argued the cause of republicanism with eloquence and vigor.

Though John was far removed from his Calvinist heritage and showed no hint of it in his religious beliefs, he espoused a Puritan ethic of thrift and sacrifice. He apparently saw no contradiction between that position and his own difficulties in handling money. John connected the policy of economic coercion—the ban on importing or consuming British products—with the rejuvenation of American industry and frugality. The longer Americans lived without "Luxuries" and practiced frugality, he argued, "the more will they despise Affluence and it's Incidents, the more will they prize Liberty and the better able will they be to repulse their Enemies."[44]

Kinloch hoped that the mother country and colonies would not separate. He contrasted the differences between a monarchy and a democracy and found the latter form of government wanting. Though he preferred death to slavery under the rule of a tyrant, his ultimate desire was "to live the subject of a monarch. In a democracy you are condemned to a hateful mediocrity." The democratic society, Kinloch believed, viewed with disdain the ambition of educated and talented men to achieve fame. The result was social leveling of the worse kind, with the best men "confounded in a heap of butchers, bakers, blacksmiths, etc." He compared that deplorable scenario with a monarchy, where "every generous principle of the mind is developed . . . [and] ambition becomes a virtue."[45]

In reply John's opening salvo clearly stated his position: "My Ambition Kinloch is to live under a Republican Government. I hate the Name of King." From there John refuted Kinloch's arguments, point by point. A monarchy, Laurens believed, usually resulted in "a foolish or Knavish King" occupying the throne, totally dependent on "designing, servile Flatterers, the Business of whom, it is, to make the foolish Monarch believe and act as will best suit their purposes." These court favorites, whom John likened to seductive women, displaced "Men of Merit." Under a republican government, however, "Men of Education and feeling" utilized their talents in works of public service. Laurens did not accept Kinloch's contention that a democracy condemned talented individuals to "hateful mediocrity." In a democracy able men were not lost in the crowd of "Tradesmen" and "mean Mechanics." Rather, these men won acclaim through service to their country. Only their own indolence caused them to be absorbed in the great mass of humanity. "Under a Republican Government," John argued, "there is the fullest Scope for Ambition directed in it's proper Channel, in the only Channel in which it ought to be allowed, I mean for the Advancement of the Public Good." He contrasted this laudable ambition with the selfishness of individuals intent on accumulating more wealth and power than their "fellow Citizens." Such "pernicious Ambition" established "that odious Inequality of Fortunes, Sources of Luxury and Wretchedness in Society." In writing these words, John perhaps thought of republican Geneva's sumptuary laws that curbed man's natural tendency to become addicted to luxuries. For he concluded that lust for wealth and political power "must fall under the wholesome Rigour of the Law."[46]

Like two fencers, Laurens and Kinloch parried each other's thrusts. To demonstrate that a republican government channeled ambition into civic duty, Laurens cited the example of the classical republics described in the works of Plutarch, where men competed "with each other in the glorious Service of their Country." Kinloch countered that in a democracy the masses were subject to the wiles of the demagogue. In Athens, for example, an ungrateful populace banished several of their greatest heroes. Laurens, on the other hand, considered laborers and artisans the political equals of the natural aristocracy that would preside over a republican government. The "useful industrious part of the Community," he asserted, should be trusted to "choose Men whom they judge worthy of the important Trust of Governing." Kinloch, ignoring the limited franchise in Britain, where only a small percentage of men of property voted, contended disingenuously that Laurens really referred to an existing polity—the revered English constitution, with its balanced government. Laurens urged Kinloch to read "the Maxims respecting Government" in the works of Sidney, Locke, and Rousseau. Upon examining the arguments of those political theorists, which "strike Unison with the Sentiments of every manly Breast," he believed Kinloch would "then be a Convert to the Cause of Humanity, and no longer an Advocate for Kings." Kinloch, in turn, suggested that his friend take a break from newspapers and coffee house debates and reacquaint himself with Cicero, Machiavelli, and Montesquieu. They proved that a mixed government—one that united the finest characteristics of monarchy, aristocracy, and democracy—worked best. The English constitution, Kinloch contended, served as the foremost model of mixed government in practice.[47]

While the debate produced no clear winner, it demonstrated that these young men were far apart in their political assumptions. Kinloch considered republican government, without a monarch to check democratic excesses, as tantamount to anarchy. Laurens, on the other hand, now believed that republics, where men of property elected their representatives, were corrupted by monarchs. He had moved considerably beyond his father and many other colonists who defined republicanism as a system that promoted an active citizenry, a concept that was compatible with a monarchy.[48]

The debate told much about John Laurens. He did more than just express his political views to counter Kinloch's arguments. In essence, he outlined his own moral code, his philosophy of a life spent performing one's civic duty. This time, however, he blended the language of sensibility with ideas drawn from other, equally important sources. Having imbibed the political culture of his native Carolina and Geneva, having read ancient classics and political works of the seventeenth and eighteenth centuries, John wholeheartedly embraced the ideals of republicanism, an ideology composed of disparate sources—the historical examples of ancient Greece and Rome, the discourses of Machiavelli during the Italian Renaissance, and the writings of English commonwealthmen in the mid-seventeenth century. Republicanism, as John interpreted it, emphasized active citizenship and virtuous self-sacrifice for the common good. Whatever his shortcomings in conforming to his father's standards in the realm of moral virtue, John would be second to none in performing selfless acts of public service. He believed "the continual Sacrifice of private Interest to public Good" bestowed "a Happiness which Riches cannot give."[49]

Only in America, only in service to his country, could he fulfill his dreams and demonstrate his virtue. He longed to be among the soldiers fighting for liberty. "I should glory to be one of their Number," he told Kinloch. "In Men there must be always powerful Motives to produce great Actions."[50] The prospect of eternal fame was definitely a motive powerful enough to induce him to perform "great Actions." And selfless service in the cause of liberty promised a solution to a growing crisis of confidence: John's struggle to live a life of moral virtue and merit his father's full approval—in short, the tension between his aspirations and his achievements.

John faced the second major decision of his life. Three years earlier he had chosen law over medicine out of deference to Henry's wishes. Now he faced a similar dilemma: he could either follow his own desires and return to America or he could submit to his father's dictates and remain in England. On the surface, the first choice appeared individualistic, an abandonment of his duty to his family. On a deeper level John saw military service as an endorsement of the principal imperative instilled in him by Henry—to be a "useful Member of Society." In the end John's decision involved elements of self-assertion and self-abnegation.

Volunteering as a soldier promised a solution to his crisis of identity. The man of feeling had failed to fashion himself into a lawyer. As a teenager, he had announced his intention to identify himself with higher causes that would win him fame. In the American Revolution he found that cause, one of sufficient consequence to allow him to break free from the "knotty Study" of law. With his countrymen, he would engage in a cause that transcended America, a struggle to preserve and protect natural rights, "the Liberties of Mankind."[51] Enlisting in the rebellion against the mother country was also an act of rebellion against Henry's patriarchal rule. Far removed from the boy who revered George III, John was now a young man who resented the restraints placed on him by a loving yet exacting father. Therein lay the transition from "I had the Honour . . . of seeing the King in all his Glory" to "I hate the Name of King."

Now the man of feeling pledged to become a gentleman officer. Warfare constantly tested a man. He endured exposure to the elements, inured himself to the privations of encampments, and encountered the danger of battle. These tests of strength and will demanded self-mastery, the essential quality John seemingly lacked. The man who combined the sensibility of the man of feeling with "the highest degree of self-command," wrote Adam Smith, "must surely be the natural and proper object of our highest love and admiration." To this ideal John aspired. In fashioning himself as an officer he would conquer the self he had come to hate, the man who lacked self-control, and become, in Smith's words, "The man of the most perfect virtue."[52]

While Laurens eagerly championed the revolutionary cause, inconsistencies within the struggle for liberty bothered him. In the debate with Kinloch he had cited another important ideological source—John Locke. Lockean liberalism extolled man's inherent right to his life, liberty, and property. On the surface, slavery appeared blatantly incompatible with a revolution based on the rights of humanity. Most whites in Laurens's native Carolina easily reconciled their ownership of slaves with their belief in natural rights: slaves, after all, were their property; and blacks were of an inferior nature and thus did not possess the rights of white men. Laurens, even had he desired to do so, could never accomplish this intellectual reconciliation. His closest English friends would not allow it.

Earlier, Laurens had cultivated a relationship with John Bicknell, the brother of his landlord. Friendship with Bicknell led him to Thomas Day, an eccentric would-be lawyer who maintained lodgings at the Middle Temple. Though called to the bar in 1775, Day never practiced law seriously. Bicknell, despite his legal talents, "had some of the too usual faults of a man of genius; he detested the drudgery of business." Like Laurens, he divided his time between pleasure and law. Finding law unfulfilling, Bicknell and Day fashioned themselves as men of feeling and collaborated on literary works, most notably the antislavery poem, *The Dying Negro*, published in 1773. The melodramatic poem depicts a noble African enslaved by treacherous Europeans. Unable to obtain his freedom, the slave, prior to committing suicide, delivers an impassioned account of his sufferings at the hands of a cruel master. Bicknell and Day formed part of the link between the culture of sensibility and the growing English antislavery movement.[53]

Of Laurens's two friends, Day in particular found the American cause attractive, but Americans' ownership of slaves disturbed him. The hypocrisy of American slaveowners was starkly illustrated in Day's *Fragment of an original Letter on the Slavery of the Negroes.* John was indirectly responsible for this piece. He introduced Day to an unnamed American slaveowner who asked the Englishman to give his opinion on the slavery issue. In 1776 Day wrote the letter, hoping his arguments would convince the slaveowner to free his slaves. Because of his sympathy for the Revolution, he did not publish the pamphlet until 1784. Day attacked slavery as a violation of natural rights and God's will for the happiness of mankind. He ridiculed the American argument that placed the onus for the institution on greedy African kings and rapacious slave traders. Isolation from the slave trade did not excuse the slaveowner from responsibility; the man who purchased slaves was equally accountable for an outrage that violated the laws of nature. "If there be an object truly ridiculous in nature," Day wrote, "it is an American patriot, signing resolutions of independency with the one hand, and with the other brandishing a whip over his affrighted slaves." The pamphlet provides an example of the arguments Day used in debates with Laurens, and its reasoning is reflected in the Carolinian's later statements.[54]

Laurens's first open articulation of these views occurred in the debate with Francis Kinloch. Despite their disagreement on political matters, Laurens believed Kinloch's "Humanity and Love of Justice" would cause him to concede one important point—it was hypocritical for Americans to demand their liberty while they held blacks in bondage:

> I think we Americans at least in the Southern Colonies, cannot contend with *a good Grace,* for Liberty, until we shall have enfranchised our Slaves. How can we whose Jealousy has been alarm'd more at the Name of Oppression sometimes than at the Reality, reconcile to our spirited Assertions of the Rights of Mankind, the galling abject Slavery of our negroes. . . . If as some pretend, but I am persuaded more thro' interest, than from Conviction, the Culture of the Ground with us cannot be carried on without African Slaves, Let us fly it as a hateful Country, and say ubi Libertas i[bi] Patria [where Liberty is there is my Country].[55]

Kinloch's reaction held ominous implications for the future. "I admire your ideas on slavery," he replied. "I heartily agree with you, but at the same time can not flatter myself that our country men will ever adopt such generous principles."[56]

In addition to debates on revolution and slavery, John devoted time to family matters. He worked with his younger siblings, attempting to ensure their continued refinement. When James and Mary Laurens moved from the urban setting of Bristol to the outskirts of Bath in hopes of finding improved health, John worried that his eldest sister's "retired Disposition" prevented her from acquiring "that Grace of Deportment which gives Splendour to every Action." Observing that Martha used "an undecided Tone" when talking, he advised her to develop a positive speaking voice, one that enhanced any polite conversation.[57]

He urged the entire family to refrain from a sedentary life and exercise regularly. During a visit to Bath, he went on horseback rides with James and convinced Martha to take long walks. After his departure, however, they reverted to their old ways. Vivacious little Polly, "skipping and galloping about the Room in spite of all their Efforts to restrain her," remained the exception to that rule. John agreed with Henry that Mary was too indulgent with her youngest niece; but he believed the excessive leniency stemmed from her natural desire, as the girl's guardian rather than natural mother, not to appear too severe. Yet the precocious girl desired even greater freedom. Though only six years old, she recognized the inequities between men and women. "Polly thinks the Restraint incident to her Sex, very mortifying, and asked one day with as much Gravity as Innocence, if they would not let her wear Breeches & become a Boy," John told his father. "She envied Harry his freedom very much and would wish to be upon the same footing with him. When she was told that this Change would not be effectual, she proposed what she thought would infallibly answer the purpose, to be re-christen'd, and have a male Name." While doubtless amused, Henry suggested a way to curtail his youngest daughter's incipient rebelliousness: "a narrative of the history of Joan of Arc may cure the little Maid's ambition for Breeches."[58]

John still watched over Harry in London. He instructed his brother to avoid arguments about the war. Because of the difficulty in communications, he suggested that Harry send duplicates of his letters to their father to ensure that at least one arrived. While pleased with John's wise counsel, Henry could not resist a jab at the inconsistency between his son's words and deeds. "Your Brother probably meant to mark you down for a Merchant by encouraging you to Send duplicates of your late Letters," he told Harry, "a precaution which I could never persuade the Lawyer to take." Despite serving as John's principal role model, Henry could never mold his son completely in his own image.[59]

The summer of 1776, meanwhile, was a turbulent period for Americans in general and South Carolinians in particular. On 28 June a British expeditionary force under the command of General Henry Clinton and Commodore Sir Peter Parker assaulted Charleston. The attack proved a fiasco owing to a combination of incompetent planning by the British and a spirited defense by the

Americans, led by General Charles Lee of the Continental Army and Carolina militia Colonel William Moultrie. For his part, Henry Laurens, in addition to exercising his political authority, volunteered his services for whatever was needed, including carrying messages.[60]

On 4 July the Continental Congress declared the colonies "Free & Independent States," the United States of America. Henry reacted to the news with tears and "the lively sensations of a dutiful Son, thrust by the hand of violence out of a Father's House into the wide World." John, on the other hand, responded with optimism. He had expected, even welcomed, the declaration. The previous October he had sensed that there was no turning back and tried to prepare Henry for the inevitable. "Let us not look with fond regret upon what we were," he wrote, "or what we expected to have been, but act with Courage the most laudable part that can be taken in present Circumstances." Unlike others who worried about the future of America, John now believed that "we have no Reason to be so dreadfully apprehensive as some people would make us believe."[61]

Aware that Americans had crossed their Rubicon, Henry mused aloud, "I am now by the Will of God brought into a new World & God only knows what sort of a World it will be." Then, as an afterthought, he told John, "what may be your particular opinion of this change I know not," surprising words, in view of the young man's unequivocal support of American independence. "Remember you are of full Age entitled to judge for your self," Henry added, "Pin not your faith upon my sleeve, but act the part which an honest Heart after mature deliberation shall dictate & your services on the side you may take, because you think it the right side, will be the more valuable[.]" Considering John's explicit pleas for permission to return home, these words are puzzling. It is possible that Henry, deeply disturbed by the separation from the mother country, projected his own misgivings on his son. Pessimistic about his own and his country's future, perhaps he meant these words as a hint to John, for the family's sake, to ride the political fence, a prudent choice for one residing in England. Yet two days later, on 16 August, Henry informed Jacob Read, who was preparing to return to Charleston, that America was "engaged in a contest which will prove too mighty for her without the help of all her Sons." If he had realized that the declaration of independence was imminent, Henry told Read, "a Young acquaintance of yours now too far from me should have been gratified in requests which twelve Months ago appeared to be altogether improper." The following day he reversed his stance again and instructed John to "neither write nor Speak any thing offensive to the Kingdom in which you reside & in which possibly you may choose to abide."[62]

Henry's agitation, revealed in his contradictory statements, stemmed not only from the political break between colonies and metropolis but also from the

British practice of luring slaves to desert to His Majesty's vessels. Rather than freeing the slaves, Laurens contended, the British would "sell them into ten fold worse Slavery in the West Indies." As a leader of South Carolina's revolutionary government, he had confronted the connection between British policy and slave rebelliousness on two earlier occasions. First, in August 1775 Thomas Jeremiah, a black man who was a harbor pilot, was hanged and then burned for plotting to guide Royal Navy vessels into Charleston harbor. Henry defended the death sentence and sent supporting documentation to John so he could counteract British reports that portrayed Jeremiah as an innocent man falsely accused and barbarously executed by Carolina rebels. The following March, Henry, writing on behalf of the Carolina Council of Safety, condoned an attack on fugitive slaves camped at Tybee Island, Georgia, where they could escape to British ships. He was extremely agitated by "the awful business"—a draft of his letter was replete with canceled sentences. These incidents signified that slaves, as "human Creatures," not only would risk danger and death to win their freedom but they also would capitalize on the disorder of war to accomplish that goal. Though faced with evidence of slaves' fierce determination to be free, Henry remained in denial. His own bondspeople, he asserted, were loyal and compliant and would not attempt to escape. The blame for this turn of events rested not on the slaves but on Britain, a degenerate, once-proud country: "what meanness! what complicated wickedness appears in this scene! O England, how changed! how fallen!"[63]

It is in this context of acute anxiety that Henry's attack on the institution of slavery must be assessed. His 14 August 1776 letter to John is famous for its open avowal of antislavery sentiments. Laurens began his attack on slavery by predictably shifting responsibility elsewhere—this time Britain shouldered the blame for enslaving Africans. The English directed the slave trade, Parliament passed laws authorizing slavery—in short the institution had existed prior to his birth. Thus he was not culpable. Indeed, he never liked slavery, he told John, notwithstanding his ownership of slaves and extensive involvement in the slave trade. He personally opposed slavery on Christian principles: the institution clearly violated the Golden Rule. That determination led him to make the boldest declaration of his life—he proposed to free his own slaves, worth an estimated twenty thousand pounds. "I am not the Man who enslaved them," he reiterated, "they are indebted to English Men for that favour, nevertheless I am devising means for manumitting many of them & for cutting off the entail of Slavery." In a moment of keen self-awareness he recognized the hurdles that stood in the way of progress: "great powers oppose me, the Laws & Customs of my Country, my own & the avarice of my Country Men."

Among those obstacles was that emancipation would deprive his children of much of their inheritance. The future of his heirs, including their place in society and their identity, was tied to investment in human property. Still, he pledged to "do as much as I can in my time & leave the rest to a better hand." He realized that his contemporaries saw no contradiction in enslaving "thousands who are as well intitled to freedom as themselves." Thus, he added, "I perceive the work before me is great. I shall appear to many as a promoter not only of strange but of dangerous doctrines, it will therefore be necessary to proceed with caution."[64]

In his reply, John tactfully overlooked Henry's attempt to absolve himself from any responsibility for the enslavement of Africans, a rationalization that Thomas Day had convincingly refuted. Instead, he heartily applauded his father, but noted that "The equitable Conduct which you have resolved upon with respect to your Negroes, will undoubtedly meet with great Opposition from interested Men." He had discussed the issue with some of these men, including William Manning, who supported slavery. Their defense, which John labeled "absurd," in the end was little more than a profession of self-interest— "Without Slaves," they argued, "how is it possible for us to be rich[?]" John agreed that caution was necessary, not for the reasons Henry expressed—the negative response of white slaveowners—but because slavery had debased blacks and left them unprepared to exercise the rights of citizenship. Despite that obstacle, John had reached a conclusion shared by few white men. He believed that blacks shared a common nature with whites, which included a natural right to liberty. "We have sunk the Africans & their descendants below the Standard of Humanity," he wrote, "and almost render'd them incapable of that Blessing which equal Heaven bestow'd upon us all."[65]

Concerned about the consequences of the move toward independence, Henry again wavered on the disposition of his family. He worried that Americans residing in England would be subject to harassment. Therefore he suggested that James consider moving to another country where he could recover his health and be free from the dislocations of war. "I must confess," wrote Henry, "I should now be glad if possible to have with me my eldest son & Daughter." He believed James could care for the younger children and suggested that Harry be returned to Geneva.[66]

Because of the difficulty in communication—at this time letters took from three to eight months to reach their destination—Henry did not know that John already planned to forgo his remaining year at the Middle Temple and return home, with or without parental permission. In late September he wrote his father that "I think the reasons I shall give, for making myself happy in embracing you, before you have expressly given me Leave will be satisfactory." His plans, he told Francis Kinloch, were definite. Only news of a treaty between the two belligerents could compel him to remain in England.[67]

A month later John received his father's letter of 14 August that encouraged him to decide for himself which side to take in the war for American independence. He conveniently interpreted those words as explicit permission to return home. Obviously in that letter Henry had only wanted John to make a political decision that in no way affected his education. But in later letters, which had not yet reached England, he clearly expressed his desire for John's presence.[68]

John promptly wrote Henry to announce his impending arrival. His firm resolve to leave was perhaps explained by another, more shocking announcement. Toward the end of the letter John casually dropped a bombshell. In departing England he abandoned more than his education and obligation to care for Harry. He also left behind a wife and an unborn child: "Will you forgive me Sir for adding a Daughter in Law to your Family without first asking your Consent. I must reserve particulars 'till I have the pleasure of seeing you. My Wife Mr Manning's youngest Daughter promises soon to give you a Grand Child." Again, in an attempt to soften the impact of shocking news, John sent the letter through Gabriel Manigault.[69]

As usual, the account John addressed to Uncle James was more blunt and revealing:

> Pity has obliged me to marry. But a Consideration of the Duty which I owe to my Country made me choose a Clandestine Celebration lest the Father should insist upon my Stay in this Country as a Condition of the Marriage. The Matter has proceeded too far to be longer concealed and I have this morning disclosed the Affair to Mr Manning in plain terms, reserv[ing] to myself a Right of fulfilling the more important Engagements to my Country.[70]

While John expressed pity, noticeably absent from this passage were any feelings of love for the young woman in question, Martha Manning. John had spent considerable time at the Manning residence and, as John Baker observed, found Martha charming. It is likely that William Manning, attracted by the prospect of an alliance between his family and the Laurenses, encouraged the relationship. What the tempestuous young man probably considered an enjoyable flirtation had, he now admitted, resulted in "an important Change in my Circumstances." His expression of pity most likely alluded to concern for Martha's honor. Honor decreed that he marry the young woman, who was at least five months pregnant. As he interpreted it, honor also decreed that he place service to his country over familial obligations. It was indeed telling that he wrote of "the more important Engagements to my Country."

William Manning rented a house in Chelsea for the newlyweds, where they made their temporary home. John spent time preparing for his departure and locating a suitable school for Harry. He decided to leave his brother at a school supervised by John Bullman, formerly an Anglican clergyman at St. Michael's

Church in Charleston. Harry, for his part, wanted to return to South Carolina with John, but friends persuaded him to remain in England.[71]

Grim news from America only made John more anxious to depart. During the last campaign, the British under General William Howe captured the city of New York and forced the evacuation of General George Washington's Continental Army. At a dinner party attended by John's sister-in-law Sally, a veteran officer of that campaign noted that the American army displayed "more resemblance to a Mob than a regular Army." Despite the published accounts of British victories, John remained optimistic. "I must barely say," he told his uncle, "that Washington's Policy is to avoid a general Engagement, and that there is [no]thing desperate in our Case."[72]

By late December John finished his preparations. At six o'clock on the morning of 27 December he boarded a carriage for Dover. From there he planned to cross the English Channel to France, where he would seek passage on a vessel bound for America.[73] After an absence of five years, John returned to his homeland to become a soldier, leaving behind a wife and an unborn child he would never see.

Chapter 4

"Standing on the verge of Eternity"
The War in America
January–December 1777

In January 1777 John found himself at the beginning of an odyssey that would take him from Britain to France, across the ocean to the French West Indies, back to his native Carolina, and overland to Pennsylvania. By year's end he shivered in winter quarters with the American army at Valley Forge. These twelve months marked a crucial transition in the construction of John's public and private identity. When he joined the struggle against British rule he not only became a gentleman officer but also legitimized his rebellion against Henry's patriarchal authority. In doing so John submitted himself to a higher cause, the struggle for liberty, and to George Washington's Continental Army, the symbol of the American Revolution.[1]

John first traveled to Paris, where he arrived on 7 January. He spent several days seeking a vessel to convey him to America, and finally decided to depart from Bordeaux. While in Paris, he paid three visits to Benjamin Franklin, the internationally renowned Philadelphia writer, inventor, and scientist. The Continental Congress had sent Franklin to France, along with the Connecticut merchant Silas Deane and Arthur Lee, a member of the prominent Lee family of Virginia. The three commissioners sought French military and financial assistance and diplomatic recognition of the United States. From Franklin, John learned that the Americans were more prepared for the upcoming military campaign than they had been the previous year. Whether the French would choose to acknowledge American independence remained an unanswered question, since formal recognition meant war with Great Britain. John thought the French would pursue the prudent course of sending covert aid and avoid risking a war.[2]

At Bordeaux John secured passage on a vessel bound for Saint Domingue, the prize jewel of the French West Indies; from that island, he was certain, "there are good opportunities every day for the Continent." Before leaving, he purchased clothing and shoes for James Laurens's slaves and arranged for those goods to be transported separately. On 28 January he sailed from France, accompanied by John White, a Pennsylvanian who was also returning home to offer his services in the war.[3]

A British frigate, HMS *Thetis,* stopped their vessel two days after it departed Bordeaux. Two British officers boarded and examined the vessel's papers. They recognized the two young men as Americans, Laurens reported, "but they contented themselves with survey[in]g us frequently with their Eyes." After that incident, the voyage encountered no further problems. In late March Laurens and White arrived at Cape François.[4]

At Cape François John learned of Washington's surprise winter victories in New Jersey at Trenton and Princeton. These "brilliant Successes in the cause of Liberty," he believed, "have given a new Face to our American Affairs." Even more anxious to reach America, Laurens and White ignored warnings that British vessels patrolled the area and decided to sail to Charleston on *Rattle Snake,* a schooner belonging to South Carolina's navy. During the thirteen-day voyage, two British brigantines gave chase, but *Rattle Snake* eluded capture. On 15 April, after an absence of almost six years, John Laurens reached his home.[5]

While John was sailing across the Atlantic, Martha Manning Laurens gave birth to a daughter. Frances Eleanor Laurens apparently was born in late January, less than a month after her father's departure from England. The delivery proved difficult for both mother and daughter. Fanny, as the infant was called, suffered "much pain & misery by a swelling in her Hip, & Thigh." The exact nature of the Fanny's ailment remains unclear, but a surgeon considered it necessary to "cut out a great piece of flesh" from her hip. At first William Manning doubted his grandchild would survive, but she eventually grew stronger. He sent Martha and Fanny to the family home at Chelsea "for the change of air."[6]

When John arrived, he reunited with his Charleston friends, but he found that his father was absent. Having been selected to represent South Carolina in the Continental Congress, Henry had traveled to his Georgia plantations along the Altamaha and Savannah rivers to arrange for their supervision during his absence. On 17 April John rode to Wright's Savannah plantation to see his father.[7]

For Henry, the reunion brought mixed emotions. In late March he had received John's letter announcing his marriage and impending return to America. Both pieces of news worried Henry, who termed the marriage "an extraordinary & unexpected event." In marrying so precipitously and under such embarrassing circumstances, John issued a double challenge to Henry's role as family patriarch. First, Martha's pregnancy and the distance separating the Laurenses prevented John from obtaining his father's blessing prior to the marriage. Second, although Henry liked and respected William Manning, a union linking their families did not conform with his dreams for John's future. As a member of Britain's gentry, Martha Manning came from a respectable family, so there could be no objections on that score. But this marriage conferred no advantages to John's future in South Carolina society and politics. Henry had used his ties to the distinguished Ball family to secure his place as a member of Carolina's patrician class. He undoubtedly envisioned for his eldest son a marriage uniting the Laurenses with another of the state's distinguished families. Such alliances often served more as political and business mergers, linking the Carolina elite in an ever-tightening network, than as marriages born of mutual love. Yet any anger Henry felt quickly faded, replaced by concerns for John's safety. He feared that his son would be captured at sea and imprisoned at New York or at Halifax, Nova Scotia. When John arrived safely, Henry's anxiety only increased at learning details of the young man's plan to "offer his Service to his Country." Though Henry disapproved of the circumstances that led to John's hasty marriage, his love for his eldest son did not dim. He could not censure John's return, especially since he had desired it; instead, he was bothered more by John's abandonment of his wife and daughter.[8]

"Perhaps you know more of his Plan than I do," Henry wrote William Manning, "the Subject is too tender for me, I cannot dwell upon it, I have given every Mark of my Esteem for him since his Arr[ival and] every reason to believe that I regard his Wife as one o[f my] Daughters, I am sorry they are at such a distance fr[om each] other, but I trust the happy time will come when we [shall] all meet again." When hostilities ceased, Laurens assured Manning, he planned to grant John an inheritance that would amply support the couple. At present the exigencies of war made Laurens's estate precarious. Regardless of the outcome of events, Henry promised that Martha "and her dear little Girl shall not be unnoticed in my last Will and Testament."[9]

At age twenty-two, John made two critical decisions—to marry and to return to America—without first securing Henry's approval. His arrival marked a new, deeply ambivalent stage in the father-son relationship. Though John had not yet received the property from Henry that would mark him as an independent man, he nonetheless functioned as an autonomous individual. John maintained proper deference toward his father and never failed to seek his guidance on matters of import. But John's decisions were now his own. Henry treated his son more as a friend; indeed, "best friend" was their preferred label for one another. He might disapprove of John's choices in life, but what previously had been admonitions became recommendations.

In mid-June the Laurenses and John White began the long trek north-ward, accompanied by James Custer, a young Swiss who served as Henry's clerk, and Shrewsberry and George, two slaves who were personal servants to the Laurenses. Henry and John were impressed by the productivity and population growth they witnessed as they traveled leisurely through the backcountry region of the Carolinas. Previously pessimistic, Henry now believed that Great Britain's war effort would prove futile. Continuing their inland route, the party reached Philadelphia on 20 July. Two days later Henry took his seat as a delegate to the Continental Congress.[10]

On 4 August, John applied to join General Washington's staff as an aide-de-camp. At this time Washington had three official aides and was unwilling, for unspecified reasons, to add a fourth one. Nevertheless, he did not refuse the young Carolinian who, in addition to being polished, well-educated, and fluent in French, was the son of a member of Congress. He asked John to "become a Member of my Family" and serve as a volunteer extra aid. That same week Washington's army received another new arrival. The Marquis de Lafayette, a twenty-year-old French aristocrat, joined the army as major general.[11]

John left Philadelphia on 8 August to join Washington at his headquarters near Germantown. The young man's departure left Henry shaken: "My heart was too full at parting & would not allow me to enquire into particulars." He was confident that John could perform well in any capacity, but in choosing a military career his son had "made an indiscreet choice for his outset in Life." Henry realized that the field of battle was a social leveler, for bullets and cannonballs proved indiscriminating, felling gentleman officers and common soldiers alike. John's "Talents & his diligence would have enabled him to have been much more extensively & essentially useful to his Country in a different line" Henry wrote, "at the same time to have been the Cement of mine & the builder of a new family." These words echoed the arguments Henry once used to keep John in England working on his studies; now he employed the phrases in regret at an accomplished fact he could not change. He remembered John's rash words, his willingness to die for his country. The chance to act out those assertions appeared imminent. To counter his darkest fears, Henry sought solace in his philosophy of life—"Whatever happens, happens for the best." "Let us hope, my Dear Sir," he told William Manning, "that the measure which he is pursuing will have happy effects."[12]

When John joined Washington at headquarters, he found a general at a loss to explain the movements of the enemy. To most American observers, British strategy for the 1777 campaign posed a perplexing puzzle. Having taken the city of New York the previous year, the British commanders, Sir William Howe and his older brother Vice-Admiral Richard Lord Howe, now turned their attention to Philadelphia, the most populous city in North America. The Howes decided to invade Philadelphia by sea, though they were unsure where to land the army. At the same time, the secretary of state in charge of American affairs, Lord George Germain, authorized General John Burgoyne to mount an offensive from Canada into New York and seize Albany. Germain and Burgoyne believed possession of Albany, a town strategically located on the Hudson River, would isolate New England, the focal point of American rebelliousness. Because the British made little effort to coordinate planning, two armies operated at cross purposes throughout the campaign.[13]

Washington could not understand why William Howe went to sea, thereby eliminating any chance of cooperation with Burgoyne. He believed Philadelphia was Howe's objective, but when the British fleet turned from the mouth of the Delaware River and headed south, many Americans, including Henry Laurens, were left shaking their heads. Some observers suspected that the British intended to attack Charleston again. John Laurens did not agree with those assessments, but should they prove true, he hoped Washington would march north to destroy Burgoyne's army.[14]

The first month with the army was both exhilarating and frustrating for John. He spent his time searching for a servant and horses, but to no avail. These disadvantages might have hindered another officer, but John always could fall back on Henry's financial resources. John solved the first problem by retaining the services of Shrewsberry, who was on loan from Henry. As for mounts, Henry could take care of that matter in Philadelphia. "I am exceedingly in want of a vigorous Steed, that can gallop, and leap well," John wrote, aware that part of his duties involved joining General Washington on daily rides to exercise and to inspect the army and the areas surrounding the camp. To be an officer one needed more than a horse and servant; instruction in the art of war was also necessary. John requested that Henry send military treatises, among them a work by Marshal Maurice de Saxe, a German military authority. The waiting game annoyed the impatient young man: "We are all anxious to hear something that will give us Employment of a different kind from that which we have at present."[15]

John finally received his wish. On 22 August Washington learned that the British were preparing to land at Head of Elk, the northeast edge of Chesapeake Bay. From there they would march the fifty-five miles to Philadelphia. The American army promptly moved to place itself between the redcoats and their objective.[16]

On 9 September Washington positioned the army at Brandywine Creek, a stream that ran parallel to the Schuylkill River. Realizing the British would have to ford the creek to reach Philadelphia, the Americans waited at Chadd's Ford, a main crossing point. Because there were numerous fords in the vicinity, it was imperative that the Continentals remain watchful lest the British secretly cross at an unguarded point and turn their flank. "The enemy must . . . force their passage here," John believed, "or go higher up the country, which will leave their flanks exposed."[17]

Instead, on the morning of Thursday, 11 September, the British executed a flanking maneuver that exposed the right wing of the American army. Sir William Howe feigned an assault on the position at Chadd's Ford. While Washington met that threat, Howe's subordinate, Charles Earl Cornwallis, led eight thousand troops across an unguarded ford to the northwest. Upon discovering that Cornwallis had attacked and threatened to annihilate Major General John Sullivan's right flank, Washington hurriedly dispatched reinforcements under Major General Nathanael Greene.

Along with his staff, Washington rode ahead to investigate. While Greene's brigades filled the gaps in the American line, Washington, his aides, and the Marquis de Lafayette, heedless of the heavy fire, rode among stragglers, encouraging them to hold their ground. John Laurens, in his first battle, was conspicuous for his boldness. Unperturbed by bloodshed and mangled bodies, Laurens, more than anyone on Washington's staff, went out of his way to defy the British volleys. Lafayette, who received a bullet in the leg, could not help noticing John's heroism. "It was not his fault that he was not killed or wounded," the marquis remarked, "he did every thing that was necessary to procure one or t'other."

Resistance proving hopeless, the Continentals began to retreat. Meanwhile five thousand redcoats at Chadd's Ford pushed the Americans back from their position on the creek. Darkness and a British army exhausted from a seventeen-mile march prevented the defeat from turning into a total rout. Not until midnight did the disordered Continentals manage to reassemble at Chester. The Americans lost over one thousand troops, while the British suffered almost six hundred casualties.[18]

With the British capture of Philadelphia imminent, Congress prepared to depart for Lancaster. On the morning of 19 September Henry proceeded by carriage to Bristol, where he met Lafayette, and from there he conveyed the wounded marquis to Bethlehem. During the journey, the two men became fast friends. Lafayette told Henry of John's rashness at Brandywine, news that did little to allay the father's worries. Congress met at Lancaster on 27 September but decided to move to York, where the delegates reconvened three days later.[19]

Though Howe now occupied Philadelphia, he still faced an intact American army. Not wanting to keep his entire army in the city, he spread his forces throughout the area, leaving a large contingent of nine thousand troops at

Germantown, a village five miles northwest of Philadelphia. Despite the defeat at Brandywine, Washington ached for another chance at Howe. Reinforcements had joined his army, and a council of war favored a surprise attack on the unsuspecting camp at Germantown. Having recently learned that the northern army under the command of Major General Horatio Gates had decisively defeated Burgoyne at Freeman's Farm, Washington appealed to his army's pride, exhorting the men to duplicate the success of "their northern Brethren."[20]

Stretching for two miles along both sides of Shippack Road, Germantown could be approached by four different routes. On 4 October, the American army divided into four columns that each marched on one of the four roads. If the plan went according to schedule, the columns would enter the town at 5:00 a.m. Traveling with the Major General John Sullivan's main column on Shippack Road, John Laurens eagerly anticipated experiencing the thrill of battle for the second time in three weeks. At around 5:00 a.m., the army encountered the British pickets. After an exchange of fire, the pickets retreated, with the Americans in hot pursuit. As the shooting began, Laurens was hit "by a Musket Ball, which went through the fleshy Part of his right Shoulder." Ignoring the slight wound, he pressed on with the other troops. A dense fog, blended with smoke, reduced visibility to less than fifty yards, making it difficult to distinguish friend from foe. About an hour after the initial shots, Sullivan's troops came upon a large stone house owned by Benjamin Chew. Over one hundred redcoats had slipped inside, closed the shutters, and blocked the doors. From the second story, they fired on the approaching Americans with deadly accuracy.

At this point, Washington and his officers discussed their next step. They could either neutralize the house and press on or demand that the British surrender, and launch an assault if they refused. Brigadier General Henry Knox, the chief of artillery, favored the latter course, and Washington deferred to his opinion. When an officer approached the dwelling with a white flag to summon the garrison to surrender, the redcoats responded by shooting and fatally wounding him. The Americans then brought up six-pound cannon to reduce the temporary fortification to rubble, but the balls merely bounced off the sturdy stone walls.

The stalemate called for desperate measures, or so concluded a vigorous and impetuous young Frenchman, the Chevalier de Mauduit Du Plessis. Out of the group of American officers, Du Plessis singled out John Laurens, another man more amenable to action than deliberation. Du Plessis proposed to Laurens a daring plan. Why not gather straw from a nearby stable, pile the straw against the front door, and set it ablaze? If cannon proved ineffectual, the young men reasoned, perhaps the redcoats could be forced out by fire. As John gathered the straw, Du Plessis forced open the shutters of a ground floor window and climbed on the sill. Inside the house, a British officer, armed with a pistol, demanded to know what Du Plessis thought he was doing. "I'm only taking a walk," the Frenchman replied with bravado. As the officer commanded Du Plessis to surrender, another redcoat walked in the room and fired a shot, but hit his comrade by mistake, whereupon Du Plessis quickly made his escape. John, who had approached the door with sword in hand, also withdrew, but received "a Blow in his Side from a spent Ball," a minor injury that only caused swelling.

Having wasted half an hour contending with the redcoats in Chew House, the Americans pressed on. Then disaster struck. A separate American column encountered Sullivan's left wing; their view obscured by the fog and smoke, the two detachments opened fire on each other, and heavy casualties resulted. By the time the Americans discovered this mistake, Howe launched a counterattack that threw them into retreat. After two and a half hours of fierce fighting, the battle of Germantown was over. Though it was a British victory, the American soldiers were heartened by the results. This time they were the aggressor, they fought well, almost executing a complicated plan, and they threw a scare into the enemy. The losses were similar to Brandywine: nearly 1,100 Americans were killed, wounded, or captured; British casualties numbered 550. Among the American dead was John Laurens's former traveling companion John White, who had served as Sullivan's aide-de-camp.[21]

Anxiously waiting in York for news of the battle, Henry heard that White was among the casualties. Unable to discover John's fate, Henry feared the worst and prepared once again to submit humbly "to the Will of the Almighty disposer of all events." When a letter finally arrived from John on 8 October, "the well known inscription instantly dissipated every gloomy Idea." Overcome by emotion, Henry burst into tears. He wished to leave Congress and nurse his son back to health. Instead, he was forced to plead with John from afar, to remind him that others needed him. "No Man can doubt of your bravery," he told John, "your own good sense will point out the distinction between ge[nuin]e Courage & temerity nor need I tell you that [it is as much] your duty to preserve your own health & strength as it is to destroy an Enemy."[22]

To his closest friend, John Lewis Gervais, Henry was more blunt about his feelings, revealing fatherly pride, yet bitterness and a sense of resignation—the realization that he could no longer control John, that the young man's fate was out of his hands:

> he has in him qualities more valuable than Courage, he understands the Science of War, in theory & is getting fast into practicable knowledge, he is modest & cool. I know him well. I speak of him not as my Son, but with pleasure as a friend, a

Countryman. . . . I still feel a resentment against him although I judge it best to express it in the softest terms to himself, for the Robberies he has committed, he has taken a husband & Father from his young family, a Guardian from his Brother & Sister, a Son & friend from a dependent Father, & I still look upon him as standing on the verge of Eternity to morrow I may again hear of his bravery sealed by his fall. So let it be! if it be God's Will. 'Tis mine my duty to bear.[23]

If he was reduced to pleading with John not to risk his life needlessly, Henry could still appeal to his son's conscience and sense of duty. He reminded John that there existed other, more pressing responsibilities than public service. An ocean away, a wife and child were without a husband and father. Martha Manning Laurens had sent Henry a letter that contained an unsealed enclosure for John. "I presume the putting an open Letter for you under my Cover was an innocent stratagem of the Dear Girl," Henry declared, "& a modest mode of requesting me to second her efforts, which I mean to comply with most earnestly." Then, he wondered aloud, "what shall we do in this affecting & important circumstance? 'Tis a circumstance in which also your Honour & reputation are deeply Interested, be your present views & feelings what they may."[24]

Martha wanted Henry to support her desire to come to America. Although the young couple had married without parental approval, she hoped Henry would consider her one of his "own Children." However John felt toward Martha, she obviously loved him. "No woman ever Loved more tenderly & Sincerely than I do," she informed Henry. She longed to be reunited with her husband: "Our Separation is indeed cruel, & has been the occasion of very great unhappiness to me."[25]

John earlier had asked William Manning to secure passage for Martha, but the worried father recognized the hazards of an Atlantic crossing and tried to dissuade his daughter from leaving. Manning admitted that he could send Martha in "very safe hands" to the West Indies, "but shou'd the Ship be taken by an American Privateer, she may be exposed to horrid insults." During the voyage from the Caribbean to Charleston, "as much is to be dreaded from English Ships of War." As it was, he told John, "I would by no means have her venture till peace is restored to us, & even then I should not think it prudent . . . without you come for her."[26]

Manning's final option was out of the question, as John had no intentions of leaving the army and returning to England. John hoped instead that one of the Carolina families residing in England would return home and allow Martha to accompany them. When it appeared that his family could not find companions for the voyage, he decided, a month after the battle of Germantown, to prohibit them from leaving. "However great our unhappiness be, in consequence of our Separation," he wrote Martha, "I can never consent my dearest love, that you should expose yourself to all the dangers which now attend a Sea Voyage in a common Vessel and without the guardianship of a particular Friend." He advised her to "Reflect for a moment into how much misery we might both be plunged by your captivity, and say dear Girl whether it will not be better to endure the pain of absence patiently, 'till some eligible opportunity offer."[27]

Before the end of the year, Martha informed John that she had found that opportunity. She planned to sail to America with the family of William Blake, a Carolina lawyer and planter. Upon receiving the letter, John told Henry that her arrival could be expected soon. Showing more concern for Martha than did her husband, Henry worried about the young woman landing in Carolina without the benefit of family or friends to assist her. He told John, "'Tis highly necessary you & I should bestow one moments thought on a Lady who otherwise may find herself even in Charles Town cast on a forlorn Shore." Blake eventually decided to remain loyal to Great Britain and make his permanent home there, thus removing a final avenue for Martha to travel safely to America.[28]

The wife and child left behind in England seemingly occupied little space in John's thoughts. Henry frequently reminded John of his responsibility to his family. While Henry's concern for Martha and Fanny was sincere, he also wanted to steer John away from danger. Henry's efforts achieved no result, for John could not be dissuaded from his chosen path. The choice between fulfilling his private duty in England and performing a public role at such a momentous time, a role that promised ample opportunities to prove his virtue and win fame, really involved no choice at all. In constructing his new identity as a gentleman officer, John threw himself wholeheartedly into the struggle for liberty. He committed himself to fight to the end. So long as the British army remained a threat in America, he would remain an officer, renouncing his family in order to fulfill what he conceived to be his public duty.[29]

Two days after the battle of Germantown, John's public role became cemented when he was named an official member of Washington's staff. In the general orders of 6 October, Washington announced that Laurens was "now appointed Aid de Camp . . . and is to be respected and obeyed as such."[30] As an official aide, John joined a talented group of young men. The constant companions of Washington, they were at the center of the war effort. Washington's staff was composed of secretaries like Robert Hanson Harrison and Tench Tilghman, whose primary job was assisting with the voluminous correspondence at headquarters, and aides like Alexander Hamilton and Richard Kidder Meade, who, in addition to secretarial functions, also gathered intelligence and went on special military and diplomatic missions as Washington's official representatives. Because Washington lacked time to dictate correspondence, he usually instructed his aides on what to write. As Washington admitted, he needed a staff "that can think for me as well as execute orders." He succinctly described their duties and qualifications: "Aid de Camps are persons in whom entire confidence must be placed. It requires men of Abilities to execute the duties with propriety and dispatch, where there is such a multiplicity of business as must attend the Commander in Chief of such an Army as ours. . . . I give in to no kind of amusement myself, consequently those about me can have none, but are confined from Morn' 'till Eve hearing, and answering the applications and Letters of one and another."[31]

The staff formed a close-knit group of young men who were ardently devoted to their commander and to each other. Harrison, a Maryland native who had been Washington's lawyer, was the eldest of the group; he was known as the "Old Secretary." Tilghman, son of a wealthy Philadelphia merchant, joined Washington as a volunteer. Highly regarded for his astute mind, Tilghman won admiration because he was unpretentious by nature. A superb horseman, Meade was primarily used to carry orders and perform reconnaissance missions. Hamilton, a native of the West Indies, was the youngest member of the official family. Prior to the arrival of Laurens, he had served as Washington's French interpreter, an important responsibility considering the evegrowing number of foreign officers in the Continental ranks. Thus it is somewhat surprising that the young men became best friends, since Laurens also acted as interpreter, a role that heretofore had been Hamilton's private reserve. Rather than viewing Laurens as a competitor, however, Hamilton recognized in the Carolinian a kindred spirit.[32]

Both men had much to prove. Born out of wedlock in 1757, Hamilton lost his parents early—his father deserted the family in 1765, his mother died in 1769. Financial assistance from well-wishers enabled Hamilton to migrate to New York in 1772. There he entered King's College, formed strategic friendships with prominent politicians, and even wrote pamphlets that defended the American political position. A proud and ambitious young man, sensitive about his background, Hamilton was anxious, sometimes to the point of rashness, to prove his legitimacy as a member of American elite society and, by implication, his capacity for leadership.[33] For his part, Laurens desired immortal fame and wanted to prove to himself, to his contemporaries, and to a loving yet demanding father that he was truly virtuous, a model republican citizen.

John felt thoroughly at home with his new family. As he had done previously in Geneva with L. de Vegobre and Francis Kinloch and in London with Thomas Day and John Bicknell, Laurens formed intimate, sentimental associations with other men. He spoke, for example, of his "unbounded and inviolable attachment to" Richard Kidder Meade. Hamilton became John's closest friend. The young men expressed themselves in the language of sensibility. "I wish, my Dear Laurens . . . to convince you that I love you," said Hamilton. Perhaps influenced by the loss of his parents at an early age, Hamilton attempted to maintain an aura of reserve that protected him from growing too close and too dependent in relationships with others. John cracked that veneer. "You know the opinion I entertain of mankind, and how much it is my desire to preserve myself free from particular attachments," Hamilton told Laurens, "and to keep my happiness independent on the caprice of others. You should not have taken advantage of my sensibility to steal into my affections without my consent."[34]

To modern eyes these statements, so full of romantic imagery, appear to contain homosexual overtones. That impression is persuasive only if the words of these young men are taken out of context. In an age of sensibility, men typically expressed themselves with affection and effusiveness. Young gentlemen officers drew their models of behavior from the classical world. In an act of self-fashioning, Hamilton recorded excerpts from Plutarch's *Lives,* which contained lessons on virtue that many young revolutionaries knew by heart. From Plutarch's study of Sparta's lawgiver Lycurgus, Hamilton copied a passage on the bonds formed by Spartan males: "Every lad had a lover or friend who took care of his education and shared in the praise or blame of his virtues and vices."[35] Just as American political leaders looked to classical Greece and Rome as republican paradigms, young officers such as Laurens and Hamilton viewed the heroes of that earlier period as examples to be emulated. It was not uncommon for officers to pattern friendships after heroes of Greek literature like Damon and Pythias, whose devotion to each other in the face of death was legendary. In classical Greece, male friendships, which usually included a pronounced homoerotic component, assumed precedence over other relationships, including the bond of husband and wife. Love between men, entailed, above all, virtuous youths inspiring each other to perform heroic acts.[36] While they emulated the heroes of old, Laurens and Hamilton carried their mimesis only so far. Their relationship was platonic, a bond formed by their devotion to the Revolution and mutual ambition for fame.

The Laurens-Hamilton friendship, similar to other noteworthy male relationships, "resonated in the realms of power." Both men enjoyed sensual pleasures and beautiful women, but females remained an afterthought, appreciated for their tender qualities but omitted from serious discussion. Gentleman officers constructed their masculinity before an audience of other men. It was the relationships with other men that mattered most, particularly in a subculture like Continental Army officers, who shared a common bond and viewed themselves as a distinct group. Detached from both the rank and file and the civilian population, officers constituted, in essence, a separate society, with "a certain number of beliefs and practices common to all . . . traditional and thus obligatory." They valued their honor or reputation above all else. Over two thousand years earlier, Aristotle had observed that honor depended "on those who bestow honor rather than on him who receives it." Honor, in other words, was not entirely inherent in the individual. To be sure, a man's character and behavior determined how others perceived him. Yet his self-worth rested on those perceptions. In a sense, therefore, a young officer like John Laurens was forever on stage, performing before other gentlemen in the intimate theater of eighteenth-century warfare.[37]

Depending on the endorsement of others bred insecurity. Indeed, Continental Army officers as a whole were an insecure lot. They coveted an elite position comparable to their British counterparts. In European thinking only a gentleman—in France a man of noble birth, in Britain a man with sufficient funds to purchase a commission—could exercise and maintain proper control over enlisted men. Americans generally agreed, but unlike monarchical France or Britain, theirs was not a deeply stratified society. They lacked a genuine nobility. Property and the status it conferred largely defined one's claims to gentility. Those were at best fragile props. Under such circumstances, officers were capable of irrational displays of bravery, where the symbolic act itself was more important than the result. Laurens's conduct at Brandywine and Germantown fits this mold. On another occasion, Hamilton paraded troops within range of British weapons; the redcoats, perhaps in a combination of surprise and approval, did not open fire.[38]

Yet it would be a mistake to assume that women belonged entirely to a separate, private sphere. Men primarily constructed their masculinity before other men but women played an important, albeit auxiliary, role. In the male world of honor, women performed a function akin to the Spartan females who inspired their men to heroic acts and shamed those who behaved in a cowardly manner in war. On more than one occasion, John Laurens purposely invited encounters with British troops, in part because women were present as spectators. Men of sensibility like Laurens and Hamilton expected females to emulate the fortitude displayed by the women of Sparta and the Roman Republic. Thus John tested his sister Martha to determine whether she remained "the same Spartan girl he had left her." And Hamilton later wanted his fiancé, Elizabeth Schuyler, to imitate the meritorious wives of republican Rome who encouraged virtue in their husbands. "If you saw me inclined to quit the service of your country," he told her, "you would dissuade me from it."[39]

Within the separate society of Continental Army officers, Washington's official family formed its own distinct subculture. Soaring above them all was the imposing figure of the commander in chief, the patriarch of a military family. Washington was by nature a reserved, aloof man, cultivating a distance that served him well as a leader of other men. On a daily basis the aides saw him most. They observed a man who valued honor above all else, who labored selflessly for the new nation. To John Laurens, Washington projected a model of virtue and self-control, an example to be studied and emulated. "If ever there was a man in the world whose moderation and Patriotism fitted him for the command of a Republican Army," said John, "he is, and he merits an unrestrained confidence." Though the general had faults—a strong temper he occasionally failed to mask, a hypersensitivity to criticism, even when it was justified, and a tendency to blame others for his own mistakes—Laurens never reflected on these shortcomings. John, in short, played the role of the ideal subordinate, dutiful and unquestioning.[40]

In the days following Washington's failure to prevent Howe from taking Philadelphia, welcome news came from New York. At Saratoga, on 17 October, Burgoyne surrendered his army of fifty-eight hundred troops to Gates. To members of Congress, Gates's victory stood in contrast to Washington's recent setbacks. Many delegates considered Washington incompetent, and their criticisms of his performance worried Henry Laurens. He requested observations from John on the condition of the army, provided, of course, that the young man remembered that his first obligation was to his commander. John's frequent letters presented an insider's view of military operations that proved useful to Henry in Congress.[41]

Henry soon had even more need of this privileged intelligence. On 31 October John Hancock, the Massachusetts delegate who had served as president of the Second Continental Congress since May 1775, resigned. The following day the delegates, with only one dissenting vote, elected Henry Laurens as Hancock's successor. The lone dissenter was Laurens himself, a move that perhaps represented a ritualistic expression of his disinterestedness—under the prevailing political culture, leaders were expected not to covet higher office—and perhaps signified his acknowledgment that the presidency was a thankless job.[42]

Considering Laurens's opinion of Congress, this turn of events was ironic. From the beginning of his tenure, he had been disappointed by the quality and behavior of his fellow delegates. He considered many colleagues inept and shortsighted, and found appalling what he perceived as their bickering, pettiness, and refusal to sacrifice self-interest for the public good. Members of Congress, the executive body that made decisions affecting the future of the young republic, seemingly lacked the virtue necessary to secure their country's liberty. Now Laurens found himself president of that body. In addition to presiding over sessions of Congress, he assumed responsibility for managing a voluminous correspondence with military leaders, state officials, diplomats, and assorted petitioners seeking Congress's favor. It was a truly awesome responsibility, one he undertook with some trepidation. When John sent congratulations, Henry expressed thanks, but admitted his misgivings. "I feel warm'd by the good wishes of my friends," he said, "but very frigid as to the honour immediately lighting on my self."[43]

After Henry became president, John continued to act as an unofficial go-between, sending his father the latest news from headquarters. Washington's officers, already somewhat sensitive over the comparisons between their performance and the success won by Horatio Gates at Saratoga, grew irritated at the honors accorded his aide-de-camp, James Wilkinson. The problem stemmed from Congress's ebullient reaction to the announcement of Burgoyne's surrender. Gates dispatched Wilkinson to convey the news to Congress, but the aide tarried along the way, arriving in Philadelphia on 1 November, two weeks after Congress had initially learned of the victory. Nevertheless, in accordance with Gates's recommendation, Congress rewarded Wilkinson with a brevet commission as brigadier general. Upon learning of the promotion, other Continental officers reacted with anger. Had Wilkinson performed "any remarkable Service," observed John Laurens, "we should have applauded Congress for bestowing a well merited Reward, but we think there is a degradation of Rank and an injustice done to senior and more distinguished Officers, when a Man is so extraordinarily advanced for riding Post with good News." What Wilkinson really deserved, John insisted sarcastically, was a new horse. The promotion, he informed his father, "is likely to produce many Resignations in the Line of Colonels."[44]

While these issues absorbed the attention of Continental officers, Congress debated the various provisions of the Articles of Confederation, the document that was to serve as the framework for the new national government. The articles were initially drafted in 1776, but had never been approved. Congress renewed discussion in October and reached agreement on 15 November. Presiding over the culmination of this process filled Henry Laurens with pride. He sent a copy of the articles to John. "I know you will Criticise as a Scholar & a Legislator," he told his son, "& I shall be glad to receive your Ideas."[45]

Under the articles, the states maintained their sovereignty and independence. Congress received considerable authority to manage war and diplomacy and expected compliance with its decisions from the states. Yet the national legislature did not possess the power to tax the states directly. Within Congress, representation and power were not in proportion to the population of the different states. Although each state could send from two to seven delegates to Congress, state delegations only possessed one vote. After briefly perusing a copy of the articles, John commented on its prospects: If the people in the states were convinced that it was "a Duty to themselves as most favouring their private and political Interests, to maintain the Confederation, it will be established upon the most permanent Basis that human Affairs admit of and the opinion propagated by Education will pass to remote Posterity."[46]

With the approach of winter, the 1777 campaign appeared over, for typically armies waited out cold weather before resuming operations. After the near disaster at Germantown, General Howe brought his scattered units into Philadelphia. It was now left to the Americans to choose their winter quarters. Washington's generals leaned toward two alternatives—to establish interior lines, stretching from Reading to Lancaster, or make camp in Wilmington, Delaware, twenty-seven miles from Philadelphia. In a letter to Henry, John advocated a different course, one more amenable to the desires of Pennsylvania state government leaders. Any move to the safety of the interior, John believed, removed the army too far from Philadelphia, allowing the inhabitants near that city, "who will be partly seduced by the expectation of Gold," to supply Howe's army. A more attractive plan was to "take a position more honorable, more military, more Republican, more consonant to the popular Wish, in a proper Situation for covering the Country or at least so much of it as Circumstances will permit, and for distressing and annoying the Enemy." As it was, the rank and file needed "Relaxation from the Duties of a Campaign in order to allow them an opportunity of being disciplined and instructed." Because the soldiers were scantily clothed, which decreased their stamina in the cold weather, rest became even more imperative. John recognized that many delegates in Congress wanted more decisive action from Washington's army. His words, therefore, kept Henry informed and supplied a rebuttal to the arguments of delegates who favored continuing the campaign.[47]

A committee of congressional delegates, appointed to consider the feasibility of a winter campaign, visited the army and found compelling reasons for retiring until spring. They recommended that Washington seek winter quarters at a location that allowed the army to watch British movements but prevented the redcoats from attempting a surprise assault. On 19 December Washington moved the army to Valley Forge, eighteen miles northwest of Philadelphia, where Valley Creek entered the Schuylkill River. Located on high ground, the site possessed the necessary assets. It was defensible, close enough to Philadelphia, yet secluded from populated areas where refugees had gathered to escape the British advance. Here "the shivering, half naked defenders of liberty," as John described the troops, camped for the duration of the icy winter. Congress, in the meantime, remained in cramped quarters at York. As for the British, they prepared to enjoy the relative comfort of the largest North American city.[48]

Chapter 5

"Those dear ragged Continentals"
Winter at Valley Forge
December 1777–June 1778

For John Laurens the long winter at Valley Forge provided time to ponder the revolutionary cause to which he had committed his life. He did not like what he saw. As the Continental troops endured harsh conditions in winter camp, their fellow Americans seemed oblivious to their fate. It appeared that Americans sorely lacked the self-sacrificing virtue they needed to win their independence and establish a republic. Desiring some reward for their sacrifices, Continental officers began to demand that Congress grant them pensions. John responded differently. Rather than focus on his own future, he thought about the future of his country. He wondered how the republic could survive when wealth was distributed so unequally, when a few sacrificed so the many could pursue private gain. His immediate response was to advocate subtle government measures designed to equalize wealth. That idea he broached in private conversations with his father. In public he proposed something far more daring. John conceived a plan to augment the dwindling American forces with slaves who would receive freedom in return for their service. His controversial proposal raised a vital question: what role would blacks play in an American republic?

The first priority for the Continental Army at Valley Forge was to build shelter to protect them from the freezing weather. Following Washington's orders, the soldiers constructed small log cabins, which were largely completed by New Year's Day. Prior to moving to Valley Forge, Washington pledged to endure the winter as a common soldier. Impressed by this display of humility, John called his commander "Our truly Republican General." Once the soldiers moved into their cramped quarters, Washington, ignoring his earlier statement, established his headquarters in a two-story stone farmhouse. There, protected from the elements and joined by his wife Martha in February, he passed the winter.[1]

The common soldiers had shelter and little else. They lacked adequate clothing or food, and many were literally naked. When Washington learned on 22 December that a sizable British detachment had left Philadelphia to obtain provisions, he ordered his troops to prepare to counter the redcoats. To his chagrin, he learned that the army could not advance because of insufficient provisions. A few days earlier, a march to confront a British foraging party had been called off for the same reason. "I could weap tears of blood," a disheartened John Laurens remarked. Indeed, the troops were also at the limits of their patience. They engaged in nonviolent protest, chanting across the camp, "no meat, no meat," and imitating the calls of owls and crows. Though the officers managed to quiet their men, Washington feared that a violent mutiny was inevitable if clothing and supplies did not reach the army.[2]

The root of the problem, everyone believed, was an incompetently administered Commissary Department, the agency responsible for feeding the army. John told his father that he had "inquired whence this defect in the Commissarial Department arises." The deficiency, it turned out, rested with Congress itself. In October Thomas Mifflin resigned as head of the Quartermaster Department, the branch that procured and allocated supplies other than food and clothing and directed troop movements. Congress neglected to replace Mifflin for five months. Jonathan Trumbull served diligently as commissary general, but he resigned earlier in the summer because Congress would not pay him a commission or allow him to appoint his assistants. Congress named William Buchanan to replace Trumbull, but he proved inept. Compounding the administrative woes, boats could not transport supplies down the frozen Schuylkill River, and Congress did not offer teamsters sufficient wages, so many drivers preferred to work for private contractors who paid more. Unless Congress made necessary reforms, Washington warned Henry Laurens, "this Army must inevitably be reduced to one or other of these three things. Starve, dissolve, or disperse, in order to obtain subsistence in the best manner they can."[3]

To the president of Congress, the crux of the country's problems was the lack of virtue among its citizens. He especially lamented his own state's loss of zeal. Because fellow delegates Thomas Heyward Jr. and Arthur Middleton had returned home in October, Laurens was the lone South Carolina representative in Congress and was thus unable to cast a vote in Congress's deliberations. Carolinians, it appeared, mistakenly believed their repulse of the British attack on Charleston in June 1776 had removed all danger. Other states also neglected to send qualified men to Congress, which caused the ineffective response to Washington's requests for assistance. Amid these reflections, Henry worried about John. He realized that John had submitted himself completely to the Revolution. John, Henry observed, had forfeited "all feelings for Interest or pleasures. . . . If I may judge from his conduct he has forsaken Father & Wife & Child Houses & Beds & all for the Sake of his Country & the Cause which possesses his whole Heart."[4]

John endured conditions at Valley Forge in large part because Henry supplied him with needed clothing. The young officer required the best clothes and accessories so, as he put it, "I may not disgrace the relation in which I stand to the President of Congress, and the Commander in chief of the Armies of the United States, by an unworthy appearance." On one occasion, he desired powder and perfume for his hair; to make a new uniform, he wanted blue and buff (a soft, brownish-yellow leather) cloth, yellow buttons, and, if Henry possessed sufficient money, gold epaulets; he also requested dimity for a waistcoat.[5]

Continually exposed to the elements, John's clothing deteriorated rapidly. Thus he made frequent requests for new attire, and Henry responded with alacrity. Usually, however, the young man neglected to announce that he had received new garments. Because the clothing could be lost or stolen en route to Valley Forge, Henry warned John, acknowledgment of their receipt was necessary. When John ignored this admonition, Henry, realizing that he could no longer dictate or mold his son's behavior, resorted to plaintive pleading. He had, he told John, "assigned such good reasons for the necessary Check as I should have thought abstracted from the Idea of humouring an old & good friend, would have made a proper impression upon a Man of so much accuracy as I perceive you are when you transact business for or correspond with any body but poor me." After that appeal, John, reminded of his duty as a respectful son, began to acknowledge the arrival of clothing.[6]

At Valley Forge, John performed his normal duties as aide-de-camp. Washington sometimes allowed his aides discretion to issue orders themselves, utilizing their authority as members of the general's staff. With inadequate supplies a recurring problem, John directed several dispatches to Henry Lutterloh, the deputy quartermaster general who acted as Mifflin's temporary replacement, and Clement Biddle, who supervised collection of forage. Laurens, owing to his knowledge of French, drafted most of Washington's correspondence with Count Casimir Pulaski, a troublesome Polish nobleman who commanded a detachment of dragoons in New Jersey.[7]

On occasion aides found leisure moments away from their taxing duties. Laurens and his close friend Alexander Hamilton devoted that precious time to self-fashioning, studying books that reflected their sense of their own identity. The young men's choice of reading material revealed decidedly disparate aims. Laurens devoured as much military literature as possible.[8] Conversely, Hamilton read and took notes on Malachy Postlethwayt's *Universal Dictionary of Trade and Commerce,* a renowned work on political economy that contained extensive statistics on world trade and manufacturing. He also recorded passages from Plutarch's *Lives* and Demosthenes's *Orations.* While Laurens focused solely on the present and his role as a gentleman officer, Hamilton's self-fashioning involved preparing himself to make a future impact on governmental policy. In this respect, among Continental officers Laurens was most likely the rule, Hamilton the exception.[9]

During part of the winter, both John and Henry found themselves embroiled in a dispute between General Washington and his detractors. Two factors influenced the Laurenses' interpretation of this controversy: their esteem for Washington—"his virtues are the only present props of our Cause," said Henry—and a republican ideology that valued jealousy, an attitude of vigilance and suspicion. Because Americans believed that power invariably threatened liberty, it was imperative that individuals remain watchful and move quickly to crush any conspiracies they uncovered.[10]

The problems began shortly after Horatio Gates's triumph at Saratoga. When Gates dispatched James Wilkinson to carry the news to Congress, the young aide lingered along the way, occasionally stopping at taverns to spread gossip. According to Wilkinson, Gates had received a letter from General Thomas Conway, an Irish-born French officer, that criticized Washington's leadership. A sensitive man not prone to accept critiques, Washington reacted angrily when he heard this news. He quickly dispatched to Conway a letter that quoted the passage the Irishman allegedly wrote. Conway denied having made the remark, but admitted that he had disparaged Washington's military advisors. Congress then exacerbated tensions by appointing Conway, who was considered a military authority, inspector general, a position that promoted him to major general.[11]

When Conway reached headquarters in late December to assume his responsibility as instructor to the troops, he received a decidedly cold reception. Washington's staff did not trust or like the man. Wilkinson's gossiping raised suspicions about Conway's integrity; now John Laurens employed gossip to raise suspicions about Conway's manhood. He passed along to Henry the story that "Genl Conway was charged with cowardice at the battle of German Town." John conveniently omitted significant details: during the retreat, Conway had been discovered sleeping in a barn, but this dereliction of duty was caused by physical exhaustion rather than cowardice. Other officers reacted angrily to Conway's promotion, which seemed unfair and unmerited. "His military knowledge and experience may fit him for the Office of Inspector General," John remarked, "but the right of Seniority violated without any remarkable Services done to justify it, has given a deep wound to the Line of Brigadiers." Like the colonels who had protested Wilkinson's promotion after Saratoga, the brigadier generals complained to Congress, even though as a staff officer, Conway had no authority over the line officers he outranked.[12]

Compounding the issue was the composition of the Board of War, a standing administrative committee chaired by Horatio Gates. John Laurens thoroughly distrusted two of the board's members, Gates and Thomas Mifflin: Gates's success as the conqueror at Saratoga was frequently contrasted with Washington's apparent failures, and Mifflin, the former quartermaster general, had criticized Washington's generalship. John saw too many coincidences. Linking the appointments on the Board of War with Conway's new assignment, he concluded that a plot was brewing that threatened Washington. Conway, John informed Henry, "has weight it seems with a certain party formed against the present Commander in chief, at the head of which is Genl Mifflin." Employing the nomenclature of conspiracy, John labeled this group the "Junto." He believed this faction probably exerted its influence to acquire for Conway "the extraordinary promotion which has convulsed the Army." The American revolutionaries, John concluded, faced graver threats from within their own ranks than from the British; he considered these designing men his country's most "dangerous Enemies." He called Henry to action with an unsubtle hint: "I hope some virtuous and patriotic men will form a Countermine to blow up the pernicious Junto."[13]

Apparently Washington also hoped Congress would intervene in the growing controversy. He sent to the delegates copies of his exchange with Conway. For his own records, Henry Laurens copied the Washington-Conway letters. The president also personally interviewed Conway. Though the Irishman denied that his letter to Gates had denigrated Washington, Laurens remained unconvinced. "There was *something*," he told John, "in the manner of his representation, which raised doubts in my mind."[14]

Lafayette, who revered Washington, communicated to Henry Laurens his worry that Congress was divided into parties, one of which had resolved to make Horatio Gates commander in chief. Laurens, too, lamented the existence of parties, which were not permanent coalitions but factions formed because of disagreements on public questions. For his part, he adhered to the political culture of South Carolina that deplored factions and revered the independent individual who followed his conscience and deferred to the public welfare. Although Congress did not meet his exacting standards, he guaranteed Lafayette that "the friends of our brave & virtuous General, may rest assured that he is out of the reach of his Enemies, if he has an Enemy, a fact of which I am in doubt of." In other words, Washington's position vis-à-vis Congress was secure.[15]

Notwithstanding the worries of John Laurens and others, Henry was essentially correct. While there was dissatisfaction with Washington, both in and out of Congress, few delegates seriously considered replacing the commander in chief. Instead, their malaise resulted from the recognition that Americans were involved in a protracted conflict. Prior to the 1777 campaign, many prominent leaders hoped that a decisive stroke would end the war. Forced to flee Philadelphia to uncomfortable and overpriced quarters at York, some frustrated delegates ignored their inattention to the army's supply problems and reacted by blaming the campaign's failure on a readily available scapegoat—the army's high-ranking officers, beginning with Washington. Conversely, Washington and his adherents, sensitive to criticism and aware of their recent defeats, placed the onus on Congress for not equipping the Continentals for battle.[16]

Despite Henry's assurances, matters only worsened in late January when Congress, acting on the recommendation of the Board of War, authorized an expedition to invade Canada and appointed Lafayette as commander and Conway as second in command. Wanting to detach Canada from Great Britain, Congress hoped that the marquis, as a French Catholic, could inspire the Canadians to embrace the revolutionary cause. As for Conway, the delegates considered it prudent to separate him and Washington. Lafayette, however, refused to serve with Conway and demanded that another general be appointed second in command. To several observers at Valley Forge, the expedition appeared to be part of the overall plot to embarrass Washington. After all, Congress had not consulted him on the issue, and few trusted Conway. As John Laurens commented, "it is feared that the ambition and intriguing Spirit of Conway will be subversive of the public Good." Viewing the proposed campaign from a strategic standpoint and, perhaps, through Washington's eyes, John told his father that military and financial resources spent in Canada were needed more elsewhere. In early March, owing to the obstacles John cited— the lack of sufficient supplies and manpower—Congress canceled the proposed expedition.[17]

From this point, most of Washington's devotees regained their composure. Gates and Mifflin, whom John Laurens and other officers deemed suspect, vacated the Board of War. When Congress later investigated allegations that Mifflin had embezzled funds during his tenure as quartermaster general, young Laurens heartily approved its actions. In mid-April Congress directed Gates to resume his former command of the Northern Department. The Laurenses worked together to secure a truce between Washington and Gates. Henry became convinced, after conversing with Gates, that there was "an inclination in him to be upon friendly terms with our great & good General." When John received this news, he communicated it to Washington, who replied that Gates was "only the instrument of more dangerous and inverterate personages." Though their relationship had been strained, the generals again cooperated professionally.[18]

Conway—the man at the center of the supposed plot to supplant Washington—grew increasingly disillusioned because Congress would not offer him an independent command. After Congress accepted his resignation, Conway returned to France, thus ending the so-called cabal that bears his name. In retrospect, it is obvious that there was no organized plot to oust Washington. What is important, however, is that Washington and his supporters, including the Laurenses, believed a conspiracy existed; and they acted quickly and decisively to defeat their adversaries.[19]

During the controversy, Henry deliberated about his family in Europe. He hoped to effect a plan to bring them to America. In late 1777 James and Mary Laurens had moved with Henry's daughters, Martha and Polly, to France, where they planned to wait out the war. Harry stayed behind in London and attended school under the watchful eye of William Manning. Reflecting on their far-flung family, Henry worried that John continued to neglect his duties as husband and father. If John consented, Henry intended to bring Martha and Fanny to America with the rest of the Laurenses. Consumed by his responsibilities at camp, John expressed little concern for his family and offered no advice to Henry. "I may truly say my mind is exercised by this subject," an exasperated Henry remarked, "it is very often so, & as often do I wish for that aid, at least for that alleviation, which might be derived from your conversation. But you seem to be wholly absorbed by one passion. If you have marked for your self any limit, I am ignorant of it. What shall I say to our friends on this head!" John's reply only aggravated Henry's anxiety. "You ask me, my Dear Father what bounds I have set to my desire of serving my Country in the Military Line," he declared. "I answer glorious Death, or the Triumph of the Cause in which I am engaged."[20]

At Valley Forge John was preoccupied with more than the fight to secure American liberty. While his fellow Continental Army soldiers endured winter in makeshift huts, their British adversaries enjoyed secure and comfortable lodgings in Philadelphia. Some observers feared that the American army would wither away. Such a critical time called for desperate measures. John responded with an idea to extend the revolutionary cause to a higher plane, where he could put into practice the ideals he had expressed to Francis Kinloch and debated with Thomas Day, where he could merge two aspects of his identity, the man of feeling and the gentleman officer fighting for liberty. In short, John conceived a plan that offered freedom to the enslaved. Both Laurenses had openly avowed antislavery sentiments. Yet in the end only the younger man proved willing to translate words into action.

Before they will intervene actively to alleviate the suffering of others, people must first believe that a potentially successful strategy exists. Henry Laurens's only strategy to end slavery was to watch and wait. He was a "Conditional Terminator," willing to act against slavery only when time and circumstances were right. Because slaves were a majority of South Carolina's population and formed the bedrock of the economy, the proper conditions for emancipation did not exist. Thus, once Laurens recovered from the shock of independence and the initial threat of slave insurrections, antislavery sentiments disappeared from his correspondence. That is perhaps to be expected from a man whose bywords were "to proceed with caution."[21]

While economic considerations and circumspection born of age and temperament prevented Henry from acting on his noble sentiments of August 1776, John knew no such constraints. Even as a staff officer, he already had won a reputation for bravery in battle that bordered on recklessness. On the slavery issue, therefore, only a catalyst was necessary to inspire him to public action.

A proposal by Rhode Island officers served as that catalyst. In early January they suggested filling their two undermanned battalions with slaves. Receiving their recommendation on 2 January, Washington gave his tacit endorsement and forwarded the proposal to the governor of Rhode Island. Under the plan, which was approved in February by the Rhode Island legislature, slaves who enlisted would receive their freedom, and the state would compensate slaveowners.[22]

John Laurens observed these proceedings with great interest. The war and the concomitant need for manpower, he realized, provided the means to place slavery on the path to extinction. As a young man full of youthful idealism for the American cause and as an officer desperate for a field command, he could not fail to act once the idea was conceived. Two weeks later he asked Henry to release his "able bodied Slaves, instead of leaving me a fortune." With a complement of slaves, John was convinced that he could train and equip a black regiment before the next campaign began. "I am sure of rendering essential Service to my Country," he said. "I am tired of the Languor with which so sacred a War as this, is carried on." Augmenting the Continental battalions with slaves, John argued, would achieve "a twofold good." First, he believed that his plan "would advance those who are unjustly deprived of the Rights of Mankind to a State which would be a proper Gradation between abject Slavery and perfect Liberty." In other words, slaves would earn their freedom by military service, which obviated John's earlier concern that social chaos might result from bestowing freedom on unprepared blacks who had been debased by generations of servitude. Second, he contended that "Men who have the habit of Subordination almost indelibly impress'd on them, would have one very essential qualification of Soldiers." Characteristic of the man of feeling, John took a class-oriented approach to the problem: he based his entire plan on utilzing his inheritance. A less affluent man could not have entertained such notions.[23]

Henry did not reject the idea unequivocally, but he asked questions that the impetuous John had not considered. If John intended to form a black regiment from his inheritance, Henry predicted, he would encounter only disappointment. Henry owned nearly three hundred slaves, many of whom were women and children; thus John could expect to raise no more than forty able-bodied men from his portion of Henry's estate. And if John hoped to augment that force with free blacks, he was mistaken. "Have you considered," Henry asked, "that your kind intentions towards your Negroes would be deemed by them the highest cruelty, & that to escape from it they would flee into the Woods, that they would interpret your humanity to be an Exchange of Slavery a State & circumstances not only tolerable but comfortable from habit, for an intolerable. Taken from their Wives & Children & their little Plantations to the Field of Battle where Loss of Life & Loss of Limbs must be expected by every one every day." A man who viewed blacks as naturally in a "state of subordination," the elder Laurens could not imagine that bondsmen would risk death in battle to secure their freedom.[24]

Despite this initial harsh assessment, John did not back down; rather, he responded with a stirring defense of his plan. Even before Henry's letter, he had assessed the potential obstacles, but remained undeterred: "I was aware of having that monster popular Prejudice open-mouthed against me . . . but zeal for the public Service and an ardent desire to assert the rights of humanity determined me to engage in this arduous business, with the sanction of your Consent." These words not only reflected the attitude of the English sentimental reformer but also suggested that John, in advocating this controversial plan, was prepared to forego the approval of his contemporaries in favor of some distant arbiter, whether it be God or future generations. "I have long deplored the wretched State of these men," he said, "and considered in their history the bloody wars excited in Africa to furnish America with Slaves, the Groans of despairing multitudes toiling for the Luxuries of Merciless Tyrants." He reminded Henry of their conversations about slavery and their mutual desire to restore natural rights to slaves. "When can it be better done," John wondered, "than when their enfranchisement may be made conducive to the Public Good."

In response to Henry's caveat that few slaves would be willing to leave the relative comfort of the plantation and subject themselves to the dangers of war, John replied, "I am tempted to believe that this trampled people have so much human left in them, as to be capable of aspiring to the rights of men by noble exertions, if some friend to mankind would point the Road, and give them a prospect of Success." John understood what Henry refused to see. He repudiated the idea that slavery had debased blacks so much that they were content with their present condition. Instead, he argued that slaves compared themselves with their masters, and that "Self-Love" aroused "ardent wishes for a change." Rather than run from military service, each man would find hope in the prospect of moving from slavery to freedom; "those who fall in battle will not lose much," John reasoned, "those who survive will obtain their Reward."

Under John's plan, furthermore, any degeneration produced by slavery would be erased. His arguments reveal the influence of John Locke's cognitive theory that all men were born with a clean slate. Young Laurens reasoned that blacks were not innately inferior to whites; rather, their apparent mental deficiencies resulted from generations of enslavement. Given the opportunity to bear arms in the cause of liberty, they would confirm his conviction that blacks were of the same human nature as whites. When John wrote that blacks felt "Self Love," he meant that they were capable of recognizing their long-term self-interest. In short, blacks possessed the same psychological faculties as whites: they were ruled by their passions but they could achieve self-control by cultivating good habits; then they could aspire to the higher moral virtues. Still, John thought that blacks were years away from revealing their full potential. Because the institution of slavery had denied nearly all blacks any opportunity for education or refinement, he believed, it was imperative that they progress toward freedom gradually. His plan provided a step-by-step approach.[25]

In concluding the defense of his proposal, John revealed more of his personal motivation than he perhaps realized. "Upon the whole my dearest friend and father," he said, "I hope that my plan for serving my Country and the oppressed Negro-race will not appear to you the Chimara of a young man deceived by a false appearance of moral beauty, but a laudable sacrifice of private Interest to Justice and the Public good." While John found slavery inimical to the principles of liberty and was sincere in opposing the institution, deeper, more personal reasons drove him. Henry suspected that behind the slave regiment plan lay his son's passion for fame. If John desired a field command so desperately, Henry asked, why not return to Carolina and use his social status to raise a regiment of white men? The question cut John to the quick. The man of feeling, Lord Shaftesbury had argued, was to balance his self-love, or private interests, with his "Natural Affections," his consideration for the public good. While both concerns were necessary and motivated man to be virtuous, he was to maintain them in equilibrium. Now Henry implied that John was motivated more by personal ambition than by public virtue and sympathy for the fate of slaves. John's touchy response indicates that his father hit close to the mark: "I am very sensibly affected by your imputing my Plan in so large a degree to Ambition."[26]

As commander of the slave regiment, John would find ample opportunities to win fame on the battlefield. Perhaps more important, the nucleus of the regiment would come from his inheritance. In essence, he proposed to sacrifice his future prosperity to secure freedom for both his country and the enslaved. Like his contemporaries, Laurens believed that disinterestedness, which entailed restraining desires for private profit while serving the public, was synonymous with civic virtue. In this respect the gesture—foregoing the prospect of future revenue—was as important as the result—sustaining the war effort and paving the way for emancipation. In one sweeping act John could demonstrate his selfless virtue and achieve symbolic immortality as the progenitor of liberty. "As a Soldier, as a Citizen, as a Man," he wrote later, "I am interested to engage in this work." Those words suggest the multiple considerations involved: desire for military fame, ardent patriotism, and humanitarian sentiment.[27]

John Laurens's ulterior and unconscious motives do not lessen the significance of his views. Still, it is important to note that his concerns about slavery and its effects on individuals, albeit sincere, focused on slaves in the abstract. Though not cruel by nature, he nonetheless could be insensitive when dealing with his personal servant, Shrewsberry. John made frequent requests to his father for clothing and accessories that befitted an officer and aide-de-camp. Reflecting conventional thought toward slaves, however, he considered Shrewsberry's needs far more modest. Prior to the winter at Valley Forge, Henry sent a "Hunting shirt and a Check shirt" for Shrewsberry. John expressed gratitude, but added that "if there be any difficulty in getting him Winter Cloths, I believe he can do without."[28]

While awaiting a definitive answer from his father, John prepared for his command. For the proposed regiment, he even envisioned uniforms that would be coordinated with the skin color of the troops. "If you should give me leave to execute my black project," he told Henry, "my uniform will be a white field, (faced with red), a Color which is easiest kept clean and will form a good Contrast with the Complexion of the Soldier."[29] Having heard more than enough of "the Negro scheme," Henry dispatched a strongly worded letter that he hoped would bring the young man to his senses. He reiterated his argument that the average slave would be unwilling to exchange his present condition for service in the army, "which will be esteemed by him infinitely worse than Slavery." Since John made no claims as their master, Henry asked, "upon what ground of justice will you insist upon their inlisting for Soldiers, as the condition of their infranchisement. If they are free, tell them so, set them at full liberty, & then address them in the Language of a recruiting Officer to any other free Men." If four men out of the original group of forty agreed to enlist, Henry would be surprised; of that number, he predicted, at least three would desert before too long. The argument was both ingenious and insincere. While Henry implicitly granted slaves the right to refuse to bear arms, his suggestion that John first offer them freedom effectively undercut the whole emancipation scheme.[30]

More important, Henry focused John's attention on his public image. Because the young man talked only of his plan, Henry caustically remarked, "the conclusion that your whole mind is enveloped in the Cloud of that project, is unavoidable. If any good shall arise from a prosecution of it, the merit will be solely yours. For now, I will undertake to say there is not a Man in America of your opinion[.]" He had cautiously sounded out other delegates in Congress, but none favored the idea. By continuing to promulgate the black regiment plan John would become a laughing stock to his contemporaries; and his descendants would be humiliated. Indeed, it appeared that John's wife and child were out of sight and far from thought. He seemed unconcerned how the disposition of his property would affect their future, whereas Henry, as family patriarch, worried about preserving an inheritance for his other children. Stung by this rebuke, John announced that he would abandon the plan since it was obvious that his father would not approve. Henry applauded John's decision to renounce the idea. Had he persisted alone, Henry explained, "you would not have heard the last jeer till the end of your life." Such a far-reaching plan required "mature deliberation by the Collective Wisdom of States."[31]

For the time being, John shelved his idea. On one point, however, John refused to yield—he desperately wanted an independent command. "Nothing would tempt me to quit my present Station," he wrote, "but a prospect of being more useful in another. The ambition of serving my Country and desire of gaining Fame, leads me to wish for the command of men." He observed with respect the soldiers at Valley Forge who stoically endured adversity; he wanted to share in their hardships and eventual triumphs. "I would cherish those dear ragged Continentals," he told Henry, "whose patience will be the admiration of future ages, and glory in bleeding with them."[32]

Indeed, "those dear ragged Continentals," the rank and file John admired, possessed more republican virtue than their officers. Whereas privates usually endured the privations of inadequate food and clothing in silence, officers demanded that their own sacrifices be acknowledged by Congress. When many officers, disgusted by pay that was too low to support a gentleman, began to leave the army, the remainder, in effect, used these departures as leverage in dealing with Congress. They demanded that the delegates grant officers a half-pay pension, payable after the war. Officers, considering themselves gentlemen, valued their honor above all else. Their reputations, however, depended in part on public recognition of their service and professional skill. Half pay, the officers believed, provided acknowledgment of their value to their country. If Congress voted against pensions, the officers could resign and still claim that they were not selfish because their honor was at stake. John Laurens, however, believed that service to one's country was a sacred trust that could not be broken. As he told a lieutenant who wanted to leave the army, "every officer is bound by the Laws of Honour . . . to retain his Commission as long as he has any prospect of being serviceable to his Country."[33]

Supporters of half pay, such as General Washington, argued that the measure was necessary to keep qualified officers in the army. The issue proved divisive in Congress, where delegates split into opposing camps. Political pragmatists who favored the measure did not believe the call to virtuous self-sacrifice was sufficient inducement for men to serve in the army and forego material gain. Doctrinaire revolutionaries such as Henry Laurens argued that loyal patriots did not need financial incentives to serve their country. To support this position, Henry cited his own example, his willingness to lose his estate and his children's inheritance in order to secure America's liberty. Though he revered Washington, he did not hesitate to express his opinion that half pay was unrepublican. The officers, he told the commander in chief, were practicing a form of extortion. If Congress acquiesced and granted half-pay pensions, the officers would become "a seperate Body to be provided for by the honest Yeomanry & others of their fellow Citizens many thousands of whom have equal claims upon every ground of Loss of Estate health &c."[34]

Henry and John reacted so strongly to the half-pay issue because they were republican purists, firmly opposed to mixing public service and private gain.[35] To some extent, they resembled their fellow revolutionaries. Like other Americans, the Laurenses fused their republicanism with Lockean liberalism, which extolled industrious labor as a virtue and emphasized man's natural right to enjoy the fruits of that labor. Thus they did not disavow the accumulation of wealth, for to have done so meant repudiating the family's fortune. The God who willed that their family experience tragic personal losses also blessed them with material wealth, an estate that owed much to a combination of frugality and toil—both Henry's own labors and those of his slaves. That estate, in accordance with both republicanism and Lockean thought, placed an obligation on the Laurens family—the duty they owed to society. Henry's property allowed him entry into the natural aristocracy of wealth and talent that was destined to rule in a republican society. His financial resources enabled him to pay John's expenses, so the young man drew no pay for his military service. John could play the role he craved—the model republican citizen, an example of public virtue to all observers. "I have drawn no pay," he remarked, "and would wish never to draw any, making to my country a pure offering of disinterested services." That same wealth separated Henry and John from most other Americans. The Laurenses became intolerant purists, disdainful not only of those who saw the war as an opportunity to make private profits but also of war-weary patriots who could not afford the continual financial sacrifices, who needed additional compensation for their service. Regardless of their motives, such individuals placed their personal needs over the cause of liberty at a time when independence seemed literally to hang by a thread. Over a decade earlier, Henry made the point succinctly: "private Interest must not be set in competition with public good." Other men might agree in principle, but few were willing to take this ideal to the extent that Henry and John did.[36]

While the Laurenses practiced their brand of pure republicanism, many Americans took the accumulation of property to an extreme that John Locke had not endorsed or envisioned. These people translated liberalism into an acquisitive individualism and simply wished to be left alone to pursue their own private interests. To a farmer in eastern Pennsylvania, for example, rational self-interest perhaps entailed selling produce to the British, who paid in specie, rather than to a Continental Army that could offer only worthless paper. Other Americans, like John's fellow officers, were willing to serve, but only if they could reconcile their self-interest with their sacrifice for the common good. John had drawn on Locke when he attacked British taxation for threatening liberty and slavery for depriving blacks of their natural rights. In attacking what he perceived to be excessive individualism, however, he drew specifically on republican thought, an ideology tailor-made for a reactive jeremiad. He lamented the lack of virtue among his countrymen in general and his fellow officers in particular. Officers who threatened to resign over the half-pay issue, he believed, "would merit eternal Infamy." Such men were "destitute of virtue and unworthy to be free." "I require such virtue in those of the Army," he wrote, "as to esteem the loss of estate a cheap price to pay for the honor of establishing the Liberties of their Country." One year after his return to America, the idealistic young man was disillusioned: "Upon a nearer view I have a far less respectable Idea of my Countrymen, than when I beheld their Struggle from afar." Yet a tinge of idealism remained: his views of human nature revealed more naivete than realism; his political ideas were still inchoate and inconsistent. The previous fall, in his response to the Articles of Confederation, he recognized that Americans held both private and public interests and implied that the two might come into conflict. Now he denied that Americans, as republican citizens, held separate interests; and he strongly opposed employing self-interest to tie the people to governmental policy. "I was thunderstruck at hearing a System adopted of governing men by their vices," he wrote, "and putting Public virtue and Patriotism out of the Question as non-entities, a System so subversive of Republicanism, that if it prevails, we may bid adieu to our Liberties."

While John expected the army to be virtuous and sacrifice all, he knew that many citizens remained home, tilled their land or engaged in commerce, and contributed nothing to the war effort. He questioned how America's republican experiment could endure when citizens placed their selfish needs over the public good. He wanted "the burthens of Society as equally distributed as possible, that there may not be one part of the Community appropriating to itself the Summit of wealth and grandeur, while another is reduced to extreme indigence." Yet he was unsure how to involve the entire population in the struggle for independence; that question must be left to "wise Legislators" to decide.

Perhaps, John reasoned, the burden could be more equitably distributed "by Taxes on Luxuries, which would be felt only by the rich. In a Republic these ought to be the Penalties of sumptuary Laws and should be so severe as to amount to a Prohibition." When John advocated sumptuary laws, he perhaps drew from his observations in Geneva, where statutes prohibited amassing luxury items, and from Montesquieu, who contended "that the less luxury there is in a republic, the more it is perfect." John adhered to the accepted wisdom that republics were inherently fragile, dependent on the virtue of the populace. Unequal wealth distribution, which split the community into the vain rich and the jealous poor, was the bane of all republics. Thus he believed that "if Mediocrity could be established generally . . . it would ensure us virtue and render our indepency permanent. But there never will be virtue in the poor, when there are rich in the same Community. By imperceptible and indirect methods, we should labor to establish & maintain equality of Fortunes as much as possible, if we would continue to be free." John envisioned a republic of virtue, a homogeneous society whose citizens shared moderate fortunes and similar interests.[37]

These ideas on the surface appear radical, yet John merely reflected prevailing republican thought. When he advocated luxury taxes, however, he went further than his contemporaries were willing to go. Most American political leaders conceded that wealth would be distributed unequally in society. Unlike John, they stressed equal opportunity for all, not equality of condition. They desired a republic that based social and political rank on merit rather than birth. John tended to blur these distinctions.[38]

If John seemed radical in advocating luxury taxes to equalize estates and preserve virtue, he was quite conventional in his views on who should rule. In the debate with Francis Kinloch he had argued that industrious artisans and laborers could be trusted to elect qualified representatives. Those representatives would be men like himself, gentlemen of character who possessed a liberal education and the independence accorded by wealth. The reins of government belonged in their hands, safe from the influence of "our lowest

Mechanics . . . Men who are as contemptible for their Ignorance, as they may be pernicious by their obstinacy." His thoughts on this question were best expressed in his reaction to the temporary constitution established in South Carolina in 1776, which tightened property qualifications for elected officials and prevented eligible voters from electing the upper house and executive. John heartily approved: "It has answer'd a very good End in removing the power and Controul from the hands of the giddy Multitude, to the better Management of Men of Weight & Character."[39]

Just as John championed the rights of blacks yet assured his father that Shrewsberry did not need winter clothing, he also saw no hypocrisy in advocating social leveling in one breath and then in the next requesting clothing and accessories appropriate to his rank. Upon receiving news of a mid-January fire that destroyed over three hundred dwellings in Charleston, he wrote, "I deplore the misfortune in Charles Town if it has fallen upon Individuals of moderate fortune; if it affects only a number of rich men & will contribute to equalizing estates I shall not regret it." In a postscript to the same letter, John, having "but one pair of breeches that are wearable," asked his father to procure white cloth. Henry's sardonic reply put the young man in his place: "Beleive me my Dear Son the present times present us with a variety of modes, which contribute to, & effectuate, the equalizing Estates which though very wicked are still infinitely preferable to burning a whole Town." As for the request for clothing, he explained that none could be found in York. He chided John for not reserving extra clothing for such an emergency. The young radical, Henry mused, would "find the Doctrine of equalizing altogether inconsistent with Military uniformity." These words found their mark; John's next letter commented on the fire's ill effect on commerce.[40]

Congress haggled over the half-pay issue until a compromise was reached on 15 May. The delegates rejected half pay for life, but supported pensions for a seven-year period after the war; to qualify, officers had to serve for the duration of the conflict.[41] To the Laurenses, the half-pay question remained just another indication that Americans lacked the virtue and the will to secure their independence. They considered American-born officers selfish; in some instances, the foreigners appeared even worse.

On several occasions John, utilizing his influence as the president's son, wrote for a foreigner a letter of introduction to Henry. As president, Henry dealt with foreign officers on a regular basis. In general the Laurenses admired these foreign adventurers and supported their pretensions to rank so long as the claim equaled the merit. Too often, however, the Frenchmen demanded too much and expected promotion over veteran American officers. John regretted that Congress did not confer promotions solely on the basis of recommendations from superior officers. Instead, anyone who boasted of their abilities and whined to the delegates rose through the ranks; ultimately, the reputation of Congress suffered.[42]

Distressed at the overall lack of enthusiasm for the war effort, Henry contemplated resigning from office as soon as South Carolina sent new delegates to Congress. He lamented the lost "Spirit of Patriotism which flashed in 1775," the original passion Americans expressed for their glorious cause, and concluded that any chance for victory rested with the starving and freezing army at Valley Forge. Alarmed by his father's pessimism, John encouraged him to remain in Congress. Because Congress as a "body collectively" had "fallen into disrepute," John asserted, "firm disinterested patriots are more than ever wanted. I entreat you in the name of your Country not to lessen their number at this critical epoch of our Affairs." Despite John's plea, Henry remained adamant. From South Carolina, he learned that the assembly had elected four new delegates, including William Henry Drayton, a controversial jurist. The assembly, moreover, consented to Henry's return once his replacements arrived, but, as an endorsement of his service, they reelected him to Congress. Though embarrassed by this turnabout, Henry still resolved to leave; he only wanted to embrace John before departing.[43]

John remained persistent. "I am grieved that you persevere in your resolution of retiring from Congress," he told Henry, "your reelection is a testimony of the good opinion of your Countrymen." Though new delegates were coming from Carolina, John reminded his father that Drayton was a man "whose great Talents from a defect of probity render him the more dangerous." It was imperative, therefore, that the elder Laurens continue as "a guardian of the liberties of these rising States," and not "leave the fate of this Empire, this last Asylum of Liberty" in the hands of self-interested politicians. Having completely submitted himself to the cause of liberty, placing his military service over family concerns, John expected Henry to do likewise. He urged Henry to subordinate his reason for leaving, whether it be poor health or anxiety for his property, to public duty.[44]

At first Henry was noncommittal. "I listen attentively to your reasonings & flatterings for inducing me to continue in the present appointment," he responded. "No Man has so much influence over me as my worthy friend my Virtuous Son John Laurens. If after half an hours conservation he will confirm his present advice. I will be governed by it." After Drayton arrived at Congress in late March, Henry did change his mind. Owing to his reelection and a feeling that his presence was needed in Congress, he decided to remain. John's exhortations had carried some weight, but there were additional factors. As Henry explained in early May, "the public aspect is now somewhat brightned, the approaching season not the most inviting to a Southern Journey, Congress not yet so respectable as it probably will be a Month hence. I have resolved to continue here a little longer."[45]

Several developments contributed to Henry's conclusion that "the public aspect is now somewhat brightned." First, between March and April congressional reforms improved the supply system. Congress recognized earlier errors and allowed the new commissary general, Jeremiah Wadsworth, to appoint his own deputies, who now received commissions that rewarded them for their purchases rather than a fixed salary. Acting on Washington's recommendation, the delegates named Nathanael Greene quartermaster general and also gave him authority over his subordinates. An able administrator, Greene promptly sent foraging parties as far south as Maryland to procure supplies for the army at Valley Forge. Though still not without problems, the supply system functioned more efficiently, and the soldiers began to receive much-needed rations.[46]

Even more important to the army's esprit de corps was the arrival of Baron von Steuben as inspector general. A Prussian adventurer, Steuben embellished his military record, claiming that he had been an important subordinate to Frederick the Great. He won over Congress when he offered his services, asking only that his expenses be paid. The delegates sent the baron in late February to Valley Forge, where he volunteered to train the ragged Continentals. Washington responded by naming Steuben acting inspector general. John Laurens, who served as interpreter during Steuben's interview with Washington, was highly impressed. He believed the baron would provide an indispensable service: "He seems to understand what our Soldiers are capable of, and is not so starch a Systematist as to be averse from adapting established forms to stubborn Circumstances."[47]

Steuben proved Laurens's prediction correct. While the army remained at Valley Forge, he taught the troops close-order drill and the manual of arms. Steuben realized that American soldiers were unique. They were fighting to establish their independence, to create a republic, and a concomitant of that struggle was the desire for individual autonomy. Thus Steuben could not exact obedience through fear; rather, he had to explain the utility of proper training. Once the troops understood that a properly executed close-order drill would save lives and make them better soldiers, they were willing to obey. Before Steuben's arrival, officers had avoided the parade ground, considering it beneath them as gentlemen. The baron, however, argued that officers should not only closely supervise training but also care for their men, ensuring that they were properly fed, clothed, and housed—in short, officers were to develop feelings for their men that paralleled Laurens's "dear ragged Continentals" statement. A relationship based on mutual respect would induce troops to follow their officers into battle.[48]

Possessing limited knowledge of English, Steuben relied on Laurens and Hamilton as interpreters. To disseminate his reforms throughout the army, Steuben wrote his own drill regulations in French. His assistant, Pierre Du Ponceau, provided an English translation. Laurens and Hamilton then edited the drill regulations, making them intelligible to the common soldier. Slowly but surely the Continentals took on a new appearance; their discipline improved and their professional pride increased. John gave Henry an enthusiastic report: "Baron Steuben is making a sensible progress with our Soldiers; the Officers seem to have a high opinion of him and discover a docility from which we may augur the most happy effects. It would enchant you to see the enlivened scene of our Campus Martius." On 5 May, as a reward for these services, Congress officially appointed Steuben inspector general.[49]

Most important of all, France acknowledged the independence of the United States on 6 February 1778, consummating the efforts of the American commissioners. Prior to formal recognition, the French sent covert aid to the Americans, but the British were aware of the flow of arms and relations between the two countries grew strained. Once the French signed the treaty of friendship and commerce and concluded a defensive alliance with the United States, war between the great powers appeared imminent. In early March the French broke off diplomatic relations with the British. The following month, Count de Vergennes, the French foreign minister, made the first move: he dispatched to America a naval squadron commanded by Count d'Estaing.[50]

On 2 May, the treaties reached America, where Congress promptly gave its assent. John Laurens congratulated his father and expressed cautious optimism. "If the general languor can be shaken off," he said, "and that this event instead of increasing our supineness stimulates us to vigorous exertions, we may close the war with great eclat." For his part, Henry again experienced pangs when he thought of the mother country. "I am not without feelings for poor old England," he confessed.[51]

Following the announcement of the alliance, the Laurenses became concerned, albeit for different reasons. John inferred correctly that the war would take a new course, with Great Britain and France conducting a naval war. Perhaps, he surmised, the British would feel compelled "to negotiate a disgraceful peace." He fretted that the war's end would deprive him of one more shot at military fame. More than anything, it seemed, he wanted to consummate his service with conspicuous bravery in a climactic battle that secured American independence. "It gives me concern that there is no immediate prospect of closing the war with brilliancy," he told Henry. "A successful general action, or some happy stroke upon one of the important points of which the enemy are at present in possession would be very desirable as it would clearly establish the military reputation of our Country, render us more independent of our allies, raise the character of our General, and give all young soldiers one more opportunity of distinguishing themselves in the dear cause of their Country." John was careful to employ the plural form "soldiers," but in reality he thought of fame in singular terms. As befitted his age, Henry had quite different concerns. He worried that Americans would be deluded by the recent alliance and consider the war already won.[52]

The British did not remain idle. When Lord North, the prime minister, learned of the Franco-American alliance, he secured passage of a bill in Parliament that offered to repeal the punitive legislation of 1774 and promised to tax Americans only for purposes of regulating trade. Parliament also established a commission to negotiate peace and authorized the commissioners to offer significant concessions to the Americans: for example, the British would recognize the Continental Congress as a permanent body, but it would remain subordinate to Parliament. There was, moreover, turnover in the army's high command: General Howe resigned as commander in chief and was replaced by Sir Henry Clinton, commander of the garrison at New York. Upon his arrival in Philadelphia in late March, Clinton received orders to evacuate the city and move to New York. The British ministry also concluded that the French entry into the conflict necessitated a redefinition of war aims. They considered shifting their strategic focus to the South, a sparsely populated region weakened by economic dependence on slaves, and inhabited, the British believed, by numerous loyalists.[53]

The peace commissioners raced across the Atlantic in a vain attempt to reach America ahead of official confirmation of the alliance with France. Congress greeted the commission coldly. On 22 April the delegates had resolved to open negotiations only after American independence was recognized or British troops were withdrawn. Thus any attempt at conciliation was simply unacceptable. Moreover, Clinton's preparations to evacuate Philadelphia undercut the peace commission's position; Congress, temporarily at least, held the upper hand.[54]

One tactic the commissioners used—John Laurens considered it their main ploy—was to bring from England private letters for prominent Americans that urged acceptance of a peaceful settlement. One of the commissioners, George Johnstone, former governor of West Florida, delivered to John correspondence from his wife and his father-in-law. William Manning informed John that his return to England "would greatly contribute to our felicity, & I flatter myself you will soon, & with propriety have it in your power." Manning hoped Congress would accept the commission's terms and not form an "unnatural Alliance" with France. Henry received a letter from Manning and one from a former Scottish trading partner, Richard Oswald. Despite these letters of introduction, the Laurenses opposed acceptance of peace overtures. John, in fact, knew the commission's secretary, Dr. Adam Ferguson, from Geneva, where Ferguson had served as Lord Chesterfield's tutor. Though John thought highly of Ferguson, he hoped "Congress will not even suffer the Secretary of the Commission to wait upon them, Nor do any thing that looks like listening to their proposals." Henry and his colleagues agreed. Spurned by Congress, their mission a failure, the commissioners sailed to New York.[55]

Throughout this period, John and Martha had employed various maneuvers to transmit correspondence during wartime. Martha, for example, sent letters through Arthur Lee, one of the American commissioners at France. John often dispatched mail to his wife via South Carolina, and even routed one letter through New Orleans. Perhaps stung by Henry's rebukes, the young man began to talk about Martha more frequently. After the Franco-American alliance was announced, John believed that he could bring her to America. Yet he often reverted to his earlier posture of nonchalance, dismissing letters from Martha as "containing nothing new."[56]

While Martha remained in London and Chelsea, she was not an isolated single parent. When she was not busy with Fanny, she mingled with several Carolinians who resided in London. Among the Carolinians in her social circle were Ralph and Anne Izard, the loyalist William Blake, and Gabriel Manigault II. As a student in Europe, Manigault followed in John Laurens's footsteps. After a residence in Geneva, he moved to London in June 1777 to study law. There he boarded with Charles Bicknell, who, along with his wife, was frequently in Martha's company. On one occasion Manigault and Francis Kinloch, who had also left Geneva, walked to Chelsea to have tea with Martha. Another caller was Lady William Campbell, wife of Carolina's last royal governor. Martha's letters to John detailed these visits.[57]

Meanwhile the British secretly prepared to evacuate Philadelphia. The Continentals, who were ready to march at a moment's notice, impatiently waited for the redcoats to make a move. The early days of June illustrated an essential facet of warfare: much of an army's time was spent in camp, where boredom was the rule and the greatest danger lay in the unsanitary conditions that spread disease. On 10 June Washington directed the army to a new location, a mile from the old camp at Valley Forge. John explained the move to his father: "the unwholsome exhalations from the ground which we occupy, has made this measure necessary . . . and while we are condemned to inactivity, we shall not swallow the effluvia arising from a deposit of various carcases and filth accumulated during six months." A few days later he was even more restless and eager for action: "We pass a most tiresome time of inactivity and Suspense in Camp."[58]

On the morning of 18 June, after sending his heaviest supplies and about three thousand loyalists ahead on transport ships, Sir Henry Clinton and his ten thousand troops began the march to New York. Washington, upon receiving confirmation of the evacuation, ordered his army to leave Valley Forge in pursuit.[59] After six months of inactivity, it appeared that the Continentals finally would have a chance to test their newfound cohesiveness in combat. John Laurens had worried earlier that the war would end with a whimper—the result of a negotiated settlement rather than a decisive last battle. His fears allayed, he now rode with the army, in search of that battle and a final opportunity to achieve symbolic immortality.

Chapter 6

"That bravery which becomes freemen"
The 1778 Campaign
June–December 1778

The New Jersey weather in June was hot and humid. Frequent rain made the roads muddy and impeded the progress of the two armies. The British, with a supply train of fifteen hundred wagons that stretched for twelve miles, moved at a snail's pace. Their destination was Sandy Hook, where Clinton hoped to meet his navy and sail to New York. By 24 June, Washington and his army of over ten thousand Continentals reached Hopewell and camped at a site reconnoitered by John Laurens and the French engineer Louis DuPortail. Washington held a council of war and found his officers divided. Some, like Nathanael Greene and the fiery Pennsylvanian Anthony Wayne, strongly urged an attack. Lafayette believed the supply train offered an inviting target. Others, led by Charles Lee, advocated caution.[1]

Major General Lee, who had commanded the defense of Charleston in 1776, was captured by the British later that year. Held by the redcoats until a prisoner exchange was arranged in April 1778, he rejoined the army in May and now served as Washington's second in command. Lee, an eccentric character who preferred the company of his dogs to that of his fellow men, was considered a military authority by virtue of his previous experience in Europe. His opinions, therefore, carried some weight. Washington, however, favored action. The Continentals continued their march and camped five miles from Englishtown on 26 June. The British reached Monmouth Court House that same day. Both armies spent 27 June recuperating from their arduous trek.[2]

At Englishtown, five miles west of the British camp, an advance party of five thousand Continentals prepared to attack Clinton's rear as soon as his army renewed their march. Despite his earlier reservations, Lee asked to command this detachment, a request Washington graciously granted. Early on Sunday morning, 28 June, the British began to break camp. Washington promptly sent Lee discretionary orders to attack. Before the commander in chief moved the main army toward Monmouth Court House, he dispatched John Laurens to examine the ground ahead.[3]

As Laurens rode away to reconnoiter the terrain, he felt pleased at this turn of events. Before Clinton evacuated Philadelphia, John, hoping to spark the decisive battle of his dreams, advocated aggressive tactics. Washington had planned to use the New Jersey militia to obstruct Clinton's line of march and harass his flanks. John wanted to supplement the militia with a detachment of about three thousand handpicked Continentals who would block Clinton's progress, allowing Washington time to bring up his main force to engage the British army. "The Country is favorable to this kind of combat," John believed. "The loss of the Enemy in killed wounded, and deserters in repeated skirmishes would be considerable. And some opening may be given for such a stroke as would ruin Mr Clintons Army." At the same time, John realized that the unhealthy state of Washington's army, coupled with the shortage of wagon teams to transport supplies, necessitated "more prudent conduct." His scenario, he admitted to Henry, came from "a man of more zeal than judgement."[4] Now Washington had adopted tactics in keeping with John's aggressiveness. Two facets of John's character influenced his perception of events on that hot and sultry Sunday: his propensity for reckless action and his instinctive suspicion of any man who challenged Washington.

The land Washington chose for an encounter with Clinton was suited more for irregular warfare than a pitched battle. Between the two armies on the road to Monmouth Court House lay a sandy and swampy wooded area traversed by three large ravines. A mile north of town, Lee's force encountered the British. While Lee believed he could surround and crush the British rear, Clinton had other ideas, and moved four thousand reinforcements to support his rear guard of two thousand troops.[5]

John Laurens, with Baron Steuben and his aides, reconnoitered the ground between the two armies. When they ventured too close to the British lines, Clinton recognized Steuben's Silver Star of the Order of Fidelity, which the baron always wore on his chest. Hoping to nab such a valuable prize, Charles Earl Cornwallis, second in command of the British army, ordered his dragoons to pursue the baron's party. Laurens and Steuben managed to elude capture only because the dragoons feared "an ambuscade of infantry."[6]

Once Lee realized that his force was outnumbered and that a successful British attack could trap the Americans against the ravines, he ordered a general retreat. An exasperated Laurens could not believe his own eyes. Based on his observations, he thought the redcoats were retreating, that their force was small and vulnerable. He presented to Lee a dispatch from Washington that asked how the engagement was going. Lee told John that "he really did not know what to say." In fact, Lee himself was angry because his orders had been disobeyed. Even before he realized that the British possessed superior numbers, his left wing had initiated an unauthorized retreat that caused similar withdrawals across the American line.[7]

Already irritated by Lee's decision to fall back, Laurens became more upset when he looked to the right and noticed that artillery commanded by Lieutenant Colonel Eleazer Oswald lacked infantry support. Without that protection, Oswald's cannons were easy prey for the redcoats. Cognizant of the danger, Oswald asked Laurens to obtain help. As John surveyed the field, he chafed at "all this Disgraceful retreating, passed without the firing of a Musket, over ground which might have been disputed Inch by Inch."[8]

Laurens thought the American withdrawal was chaotic. Considering the extreme temperature, however, the troops retired in as orderly a way as possible. Their commanders ordered brief rests in wooded areas where the shade provided some shelter from the suffocating heat. Lee surveyed the ground and decided to form his line on a hill behind the westernmost ravine. If the British wanted battle, they had to cross the ravine, where the Continentals would wait, possessing the advantage of higher ground.[9]

As Washington continued forward with the main army, he encountered a fifer who brought news of the retreat. Deciding to investigate matters, the general, accompanied by his aides, rode to the scene of action. Nearing the field, they met additional weary stragglers, some of whom complained about the withdrawal. When Washington found Lee, he demanded an explanation. Surprised by Washington's imperious tone, the normally talkative Lee managed only to stammer, "Sir? Sir?" Upon regaining his composure, Lee justified the withdrawal, pointing out that the redcoats had superior numbers. Intelligence indicated, Washington countered, that the Continentals were retreating from a "covering party of the enemy." At that point, he assumed personal command and directed the army to form a line of defense. Ironically, he positioned the troops on the same hill selected earlier by Lee. Laurens, who witnessed the confrontation, considered Washington's arrival fortuitous "for the honor of the Army, and the welfare of America."[10]

After Washington gave his orders, he perhaps had second thoughts about his conduct toward Lee. He returned and asked Lee to assume command of the front line, while the remaining troops formed a column behind the ravine. For almost an hour, Lee's command held off a British attack, giving Washington precious time to form his defensive line. Positioned on the hill, the main

American line withstood further assaults and forced a British withdrawal. The Continentals, with Laurens among them, then crossed the bridge that spanned the ravine and pursued the retreating redcoats, only to encounter a fierce counterattack from an elite battalion of grenadiers. During the savage hand-to-hand combat that ensued, John's horse was shot from under him, and he received a slight contusion from a musket ball. He ignored the wound and stayed in the middle of the fray. Both Laurens and Hamilton "exhibited singular proofs of bravery," reported an eyewitness. "They seemed to court death under our doubtful circumstances, and tryumphed over it as the face of war changed in our favor."[11]

Unlike Brandywine and Germantown, in this battle the redcoats retreated, leaving their dead and wounded behind. The Continentals, nearly spent from the stifling heat and close fighting, awaited further assaults. His troops equally exhausted, Clinton decided to call it a day, believing that his supply train had been secured. "We remained looking at each other with the defile between us till dark," Laurens observed, "& they stole off in silence at midnight." The Continentals had held their ground, and John could not resist an exultation: "Our officers and Men behaved with that bravery which becomes freemen and have convinced the world that they can beat british Grenadiers."[12]

Washington's military family took special pride in their role in the battle. "The Merit of restoring the day is due to the General, and his conduct was such throughout the affair as has greatly increased my Love & esteem for him," John gushed. Without drawing attention to his own conduct, he applauded his fellow aides "who acted as military men on this occasion, and proved themselves as worthy to wield the sword as the pen." While the aides patted themselves on the back, they reflected on what they perceived as a lost opportunity. Rather than taking into account British valor and difficulties of terrain and weather, Laurens and Hamilton placed full blame on Lee. Had Lee pursued the enemy, they believed, a great victory, perhaps the decisive stroke bringing peace and recognition of American independence, would have been within their grasp. The young aides did not hesitate to express these sentiments. Hamilton believed Lee's "conduct was monstrous and unpardonable." "Genl. Lee I think must be tried for misconduct," John confided to his father.[13]

As the Continentals rested by the Raritan River, the British continued their march to Sandy Hook, where they met transports and sailed for New York on 5 July. Charles Lee, meanwhile, seethed in his tent. Expecting an apology from Washington and receiving none, Lee dashed off a letter, complaining that he had been ill-treated. His generalship, after all, had saved the army, "the success of the day was entirely owing" to the "manoeuvres" he supervised. Lee did not blame Washington for their encounter on the battlefield, believing instead that the commander in chief had been "instigated by some of those dirty earwigs who will forever insinuate themselves near persons in high office." Foremost among those "dirty earwigs" were Laurens and Hamilton. Washington responded hotly, accusing Lee of "making an unnecessary, disorderly, and shameful retreat." Stung by these words, Lee demanded a court-martial. Washington readily obliged.[14]

Lee faced three charges. First, he disobeyed orders when he failed to attack the redcoats at Monmouth; second, he made "an unnecessary, disorderly, and shameful retreat," an echo of Washington's words; finally, Lee's post-Monmouth letters had shown "disrespect to the commander in chief." During the trial, which was held between 4 July and 9 August, the principal witnesses for the prosecution included Brigadier Generals Charles Scott and Anthony Wayne, whose unauthorized retreats had resulted in confusion across the American line. Obviously both men could avoid scrutiny of their conduct by directing attention toward Lee's actions on the battlefield. In addition, Washington's entire staff testified against Lee. These young men had a vested interest in expediting Lee's downfall, for anything less than a full conviction would undermine the position of their chief and, by implication, their own status. Most damning to Lee was the testimony of Laurens and Hamilton.[15]

Both men appeared before the court on 13 July. Laurens testified first. He reiterated his opinion that the British force had been small, no more than fifteen hundred to two thousand troops. The unnecessary American retreat, he contended, was executed "in some disorder." He emphasized that Lieutenant Colonel Oswald's cannon had lacked infantry support, which implied that Lee neglected essential details.

"Were the orders that you heard General Lee give the 28th of June, given distinct and clear?" asked the court. "I thought General Lee seemed to be a good deal embarrassed, and that his orders were indistinct," John replied.

To insinuate that he had lost his composure was too much for Lee, who was managing his own defense. He pressed Laurens during cross-examination: "Did you impute my embarrassment to my uneasiness, by having been counteracted by some officers under my command, to the contradictory intelligence I received, or to my want of a personal tranquillity of mind?" John remained adamant: "I imputed it to want of presence of mind." In a sharp counterattack Lee sarcastically pointed out Laurens's youth and inexperience. "Were you ever in an action before?" Again, John held his ground and gave an equally acid reply: "I have been in several actions; I did not call that an action, as there was no action previous to the retreat."[16]

Hamilton did not withstand Lee's acerbic tongue as well as Laurens. Earlier, on 4 July, he had appeared before the court. On that day, under cross-examination, his testimony appeared to acquit Lee of the first charge. Hamilton acknowledged that Lee's orders were discretionary, that Washington did not expect him to attack a vastly superior British force. On 13 July, upon following Laurens, Hamilton met additional embarrassment. When the prosecution asked if Lee's orders were "distinct and clear," Hamilton replied that the general "seemed to be in a hurry of mind." Lee quickly reminded the young aide of a battlefield conversation during which Hamilton had observed that the general appeared calm and collected. Remembering his own rather foolish behavior at Monmouth, how he had brandished his sword and pledged to die on the spot, Hamilton retreated and moderated his appraisal of Lee's demeanor.[17]

Like Washington's staff, Lee's aides, Captains John Francis Mercer and Evan Edwards, strongly supported their chief's case. Lee produced several additional witnesses unconnected to his staff who defended his actions and countered the testimony of Laurens and Hamilton. In particular Lee wanted to refute the accusation that he had lost his composure on the field. Ten officers asserted that Lee, though angry at the unauthorized retreats and concerned about the effect of the heat on his troops, remained poised throughout the battle. Among those officers, ironically, was John Fitzgerald, one of Washington's aides, who admitted that "Lee appeared serious and thoughtful."

Laurens's insinuation that Lee had neglected to protect the artillery received an unequivocal rebuttal. Both Lieutenant Colonel Eleazer Oswald, whose cannon Laurens had seen uncovered, and another artillery officer, Captain John Cumpston, affirmed that Lee made every possible effort to guard their field pieces. When Lee asked Oswald why his cannon had been temporarily exposed, the artillery commander replied that the problem resulted "not from any want of precaution in you, but from the heat and fatigue of the day, both men and horses being exceedingly fatigued." Contrary to Laurens's testimony that the retreat was chaotic, two officers swore that it was orderly, even though the troops were exhausted.[18]

Lee spoke eloquently in his own defense and mocked the testimony of Washington's staff. While Laurens and Hamilton both irritated Lee, it was the latter aide's allegations that bothered him most. Hamilton's imputation that Lee was unsteady, the general admitted, hurt him because it was "an impeachment of my qualifications as an officer." He could not resist a dig at both aides. "If Colonel Hamilton's sentiments were really opposite to what his precise words were," said Lee, "I cannot help thinking it somewhat extraordinary that he and Colonel Laurens should have seen with so very different optics from those of every other gentlemen who had an opportunity of observing me that day."[19]

Although the prosecution's case was flimsy at best, the court found Lee guilty on all charges and suspended him from the Continental Army for one year. They did moderate the second charge. Whereas Washington accused Lee of conducting "an unnecessary, disorderly, and shameful retreat," the altered verdict read that Lee had made "an unnecessary, and in some few instances, a disorderly retreat." Obviously Lee acted with disrespect toward his commander and was thus guilty of the third charge. Anything less than a guilty verdict on the other charges would have been a blow to Washington's authority. Forced to decide between Washington and Lee, the court ignored the weight of evidence and cast its lot with the commander in chief.[20]

During the trial, John's testimony had been seriously called into question. While there is no evidence that he knowingly lied, his perception of the Monmouth battle and his memory of events were obviously colored both by his close ties to Washington and by an impulsive temperament that tolerated no retreat from danger. Yet unlike Hamilton, Laurens withstood Lee's stern cross-examination and proved one of the prosecution's strongest witnesses. His influence on Lee's fate did not end with the trial. Lee promptly appealed his case to Congress, hoping the delegates would reverse the verdict. Prior to the court-martial, Congress, which had now reconvened in Philadelphia, received reports of Monmouth that were strongly biased against Lee. Hamilton and Laurens again played prominent roles in spreading the stories. Hamilton's letter to New Jersey delegate Elias Boudinot, which condemned Lee's conduct at Monmouth, was published in the *Pennsylvania Packet.* John convinced Henry that Lee's conduct had been suspicious. The president of Congress, who regarded Washington with "Love & reverence," was thus hardly disposed to grant Lee's appeal an impartial hearing. Like the officers who presided over the court-martial, many delegates viewed the Washington-Lee dispute as a power struggle in which the latter was destined to lose. Most likely, therefore, the delegates, once they found time to review and debate the case, would uphold the court's verdict.[21]

In addition to influencing Henry's opinion of Lee, John gave his father a detailed account of his own part in the action at Monmouth, including the narrow escape from Cornwallis's dragoons. He omitted, however, any reference to his slight wound. Henry learned that information from Elias Boudinot, the recipient of the letter that described how Laurens and Hamilton courted death. Having heard more than enough, the worried father again pleaded with his son to take care and remember his family. "You have had many escapes," he told John, "but I submit it to your wisdom and Philosophy whether it be necessary to tempt the fates or to brave them, and to your friendship whether a person so dear and so much beloved, is not entitled for the sake of his Connections to ordinary protection. I shall never be surprised until I hear you have in one instance attended to the preservation of your Life by means which the bravest Man on Earth would not blush to adopt."[22]

John did not have much time to reflect on his prominent role in the battle of Monmouth and the Lee court-martial. Word arrived from Congress that

Count d'Estaing and his fleet had arrived off the coast of North America after an eighty-seven-day voyage. For the first time the efficacy of the Franco-American alliance was to receive a military test. Washington promptly dispatched Laurens to meet d'Estaing at Sandy Hook. The general planned to take the Continentals across the Hudson River and move south toward New York, and he hoped the French fleet could cooperate against the British garrison that held the city. Washington assured d'Estaing that Laurens was a trusted and valued aide "to whom you may safely confide any measures or information you may wish me to be acquainted with." The Marquis de Lafayette, a distant relative of d'Estaing's, wrote a letter to introduce John and verify that he was an authentic emissary. The marquis astutely recognized that Laurens, son of the president of Congress and aide to Washington, was well connected and thus merited special treatment. "You will greatly please the general and Congress," he instructed d'Estaing, "by receiving him with distinction and *that will have many good effects.*"[23]

On 16 July Laurens reached d'Estaing's fleet at the Shrewsberry River, an estuary just south of Sandy Hook. Facing shortages of food and fresh water, the admiral wanted to replenish his supplies immediately. When the French explored the coast seeking access to fresh water, several rowboats sank in the dangerous currents, and four sailors and one officer were drowned. John soon experienced these perils firsthand. While being conveyed in a rowboat to d'Estaing's flagship, the young aide narrowly escaped a watery grave. An admiring d'Estaing noted that Laurens's "patriotism and his Courage made him brave the most imposing dangers of the Sea, with the same firmness as the Fire of the English."[24]

Washington realized that the pilots might not locate a channel deep enough for d'Estaing's vessels to pass Sandy Hook. As an alternative, therefore, he proposed that d'Estaing consider sailing to Newport, Rhode Island, which was held by a British garrison commanded by Sir Robert Pigot. In laying siege to Newport, the French fleet would cooperate with a Continental-militia force under Major General John Sullivan. Washington ordered Sullivan to augment his force with five thousand militia from Rhode Island, Connecticut, and Massachusetts. At the same time, the commander in chief sent his other French-speaking aide, Alexander Hamilton, to confer with d'Estaing. Hamilton was accompanied by several captains and pilots familiar with the treacherous approach to New York.[25]

The pilots agreed that it was impossible for the heavy French vessels to pass Sandy Hook. Laurens and Hamilton found additional pilots who proved equally intransigent. The admiral offered an award of 50,000 crowns to anyone who would accept the job, but there were no takers. Frustrated at the sight of the British masts in the bay, so close yet inaccessible, d'Estaing ordered his fleet to proceed to Newport. On Sunday night, 19 July, Laurens returned to headquarters with the disappointing news. Washington immediately ordered two Continental brigades under Lafayette to reinforce Sullivan at Rhode Island. The general then dispatched Laurens to Providence, where he was to meet Sullivan and explain in detail how the Americans were to cooperate with d'Estaing.[26]

Laurens arrived in Providence exhausted by a journey completed "in 48 hours over the worst and in some parts the most obscure road that I ever travel'd." There was no time for rest, for it was important that he convey Washington's directions to Sullivan. An ambitious, vain officer, still smarting from a poor performance at Brandywine, Sullivan desperately craved success. He had worked hard to obtain reinforcements and supplies, but was not ready to begin operations against the British at Newport. The redcoats, it turned out, had not been idle. Sir Henry Clinton sent two thousand reinforcements from New York to bolster Pigot's strength. Newport, Sullivan believed, was now garrisoned by seven thousand troops, so it would be a while before the Americans possessed sufficient numbers to launch the siege. Compounding his worries, Laurens brought news that d'Estaing was on the way.[27]

After conferring with the general, John proceeded to Point Judith, forty miles south of Providence. He took with him several pilots who would guide the French fleet into Newport harbor upon its arrival. Laurens and his party gathered boats, including eight "whale-boat privateers," and called out the local militia. Upon their arrival at Point Judith on 25 July, he posted guards to watch for d'Estaing's approach. Realizing that his position was a cul-de-sac and that the redcoats could approach from the rear and cut off a retreat, Laurens stationed the remainder of his party about four miles inland. "Our situation commands a view of the several entrances . . . so that nothing can pass to or from New port unnoticed," he informed Washington.[28]

Three days after their arrival, Laurens's detachment found their view obscured by a dense fog. On 28 July, D'Estaing finally arrived with twelve ships of the line and four frigates. The mist concealed the fleet until the following morning, when, John observed, "the Fog cleared away and the appearance of [the] French Squadron was as sudden, as if they had been brought to view by raising a curtain." He immediately boarded d'Estaing's ship, *Langue-doc,* and delivered a letter from Sullivan that proposed an assault on the British garrison at Newport.[29]

The French, still facing a severe water shortage, were anxious to commence operations, but Sullivan's letter dashed those hopes. They must postpone an attack, he said, until Lafayette arrived with the Continental brigades; his current force was too small, despite his efforts to procure reinforcements. Moreover, most of the troops at hand were militia whose tenacity under fire was suspect. There was one untested regular unit, a battalion formed after passage of the bill to enlist slave units—Colonel Christopher Greene's First Rhode Island Regiment of slaves, free blacks, and Narragansett Indians.[30]

What concerned d'Estaing most was the weakened condition of his force. After four months at sea, numerous Frenchmen suffered from scurvy. In addition to a replenished water supply, they desperately needed fresh fruit and vegetables. With his supplies nearly depleted, the admiral decided to remove his sick from the fleet. Laurens helped establish a hospital for the sick in houses on the western shore of Conanicut Island, located in Narragansett Bay across from Newport. D'Estaing deeply appreciated the young man's "zeal & infinite useful care." Laurens, he informed Washington, "runs twenty four hours at a stretch to procure us assistance, and afterwards remains on board many long & tedious days with the patience of an Ancient Seaman."[31]

On 4 August Lafayette's two thousand Continentals reached Providence. Sullivan now had over six thousand troops at his disposal, and additional militia were arriving. Washington also sent his quartermaster general, Nathanael Greene, a native of Rhode Island. The allied commanders could finally implement their plan of action. Located on the southern tip of an island, Newport was surrounded by two channels. Covered by d'Estaing's frigates, the Americans were to land on the eastern side of the island, while French troops subsequently disembarked on the western shore, adjoining Narragansett Bay. The two armies would then quickly form a line of attack. Sullivan placed Laurens in command of an advanced detachment of the American army's light corps. The allies scheduled the combined assault on Monday, 10 August. Realizing that an attack was imminent, Pigot ordered troops posted at redoubts on the northern end of the island to evacuate their positions and withdraw to the main defenses at Newport.[32]

On 9 August, after redcoat deserters verified that the northern posts had been abandoned, Sullivan ordered his force to cross over to the island, a move designed to prevent the British from reoccupying the batteries. When Sullivan informed d'Estaing that the Americans were landing a day early, the admiral reacted with disapproval—the French national pride had been wounded. From John Laurens's gendered perspective, the French displayed the pettiness of women succumbing to private desires rather than the resolution of men participating in a great cause. "This measure gave much umbrage to the french officers," he informed Henry. "They conceived their troops injured by our landing first, and talked like women disputing precedence in a country dance, instead of men engaged in pursuing the common interest of two great Nations."[33]

D'Estaing overcame his initial irritation and directed four thousand troops to land on the island and join the Americans. As the admiral proceeded ashore to meet Sullivan, he received the shock of his life. The morning fog dissipated, revealing a large fleet holding course in Rhode Island Sound. D'Estaing counted thirty-six sail: a British fleet under the command of Vice Admiral Richard Lord Howe had arrived from New York.[34]

Howe could not have made a more dramatic entrance. With the British waiting off shore, d'Estaing believed his only alternative was to meet the threat. On the morning of 10 August d'Estaing sailed away, leaving behind three frigates and a brigantine to protect the Americans, and his assurances that the French fleet would return after defeating Howe. Lacking sufficient French naval and land support, the disappointed Sullivan concluded that the siege had stalled. He feared, he admitted to Henry Laurens, that the delay would allow the British to send additional reinforcements to relieve Pigot. In fact, while Sullivan put his concerns on paper, Sir Henry Clinton busily prepared to send a relief expedition from New York.[35]

Despite Sullivan's problems, numerous militia continued to arrive. As his force now contained over ten thousand troops, Sullivan decided to continue the siege without French assistance. Then forces out of his control again intervened. On the evening of 11 August, a violent gale struck Rhode Island. For two days the storm raged, pelting the unprotected troops with rain and wind. Despite their own misery, John Laurens remarked, they felt "anxiety for the french Squadron" out at sea. By 14 August the gale subsided, but the army's ammunition was soaked and useless. Sullivan's former optimism turned to gloom. "Your Brave and worthy Son is a fellow Sufferer with me in This Fatal Island," he wrote Henry Laurens.[36]

Nevertheless, Sullivan resolved to continue. Early on the morning of 15 August, the army moved toward Newport. John Laurens, as usual, served in the forefront and marched with his detachment about a mile ahead of the main force. The army halted less than a mile and a half from the redcoat defensive line before Newport and began to construct fortifications. Having regained his confidence, Sullivan assured the president of Congress that the American army would take Newport. "I promise your Excellency," he wrote on 17 August, "that by tomorrow (noon) I shall be able to keep up so warm a Fire upon them, as to render the Properties of a Salamander essentially necessary to their existence." Henry Laurens was unimpressed, and thought of John Burgoyne's arrogance prior to his humiliation at Saratoga in the fall of 1777. "If General Sullivan falls short of his views of the 17th," he wrote John, "his Letter will be christened a Burgoynade."[37]

On the afternoon of 20 August the French fleet returned. American spirits soared, only to be dashed. The gale struck and severely damaged d'Estaing's ships while they were in the open sea maneuvering against the British fleet. Under orders from the French government to sail to Boston if a superior

British fleet appeared or if an accident occurred, d'Estaing believed he had no choice but to depart, taking with him the entire French fleet.[38] Sullivan and his officers strongly objected, claiming that the ships could be repaired at Newport. "The honor of the french Nation, the honor of the Admiral, the safety of his fleet, and a regard for the new alliance required a different conduct," said John Laurens. He believed that d'Estaing, who began his career in the army, was influenced less by the orders and more by pressure from subordinate naval officers who resented his leadership. As the navy sailed away on 22 August, Sullivan and his general officers met and drafted a protest against the French departure. They contended that d'Estaing, by "abandoning" the American army at Newport, dishonored his nation and damaged the Franco-American alliance. Sullivan directed Laurens, who at that moment was writing to his father, to board a brigantine, sail after the French fleet, and deliver the "solemn protest" to d'Estaing. John hurriedly concluded his letter to Henry: "I was going on but am called away upon the most important business."[39]

John returned the following day, having failed to catch the French squadron. He quickly informed Washington of the recent turn of events and chastised the French for "abandoning the American Troops in the midst of a very important expedition, and reducing them to the necessity of making a desperate attack, or a precipitate Retreat." Concluding with an apology for his "confusion of ideas for want of Sleep," John presumably then retired for a well-deserved nap. While Sullivan pondered his next move, matters were taken from his hands. On the evening of 24 August he received word from Washington that the Newport garrison might receive reinforcements. Sullivan now had no choice but to withdraw to the island's northern fortifications, where he would await d'Estaing's return. The army broke camp on Friday evening, 28 August.[40]

Sullivan's force stopped at Butts Hill, about seven miles north of Newport, and constructed a defensive line that traversed the island. The rear guard under John Laurens and Colonel Henry Livingston, commander of the light corps, assumed posts three miles south of the main army to watch the two approaches from Newport. Laurens's detachment of Continentals and militia guarded the West Road. After the early morning fog disappeared, the British saw that the Americans had withdrawn, and Pigot immediately ordered a pursuit.[41]

By 7:00 a.m. a detachment of Hessians under General Friedrich Wilhelm von Lossberg encountered Laurens's party. Though Laurens posted his troops behind stone walls, the outnumbered Americans were unable to turn back the Hessians. After brief skirmishing, he ordered his troops to retreat. "The weakness of the party, both in numbers and composition," he noted, "rendered it unfit for any very obstinate opposition; the militia executed the order to retreat

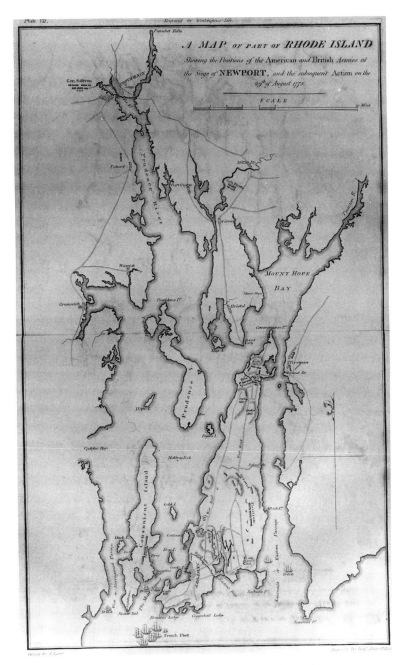

A map of the siege of Newport, Rhode Island that shows the positions taken by the two armies at the battle of Rhode Island.
Drawn by S. Lewis and engraved by Benjamin Jones, from John Marshall, *The Life of George Washington; maps and subscribers' names.* Philadelphia: C. P. Wayne, 1807.

too rapidly, the continentals behaved better; we kept up a retreating fire for the distance of 4 miles."

Along the East Road, Livingston's troops provided stiff resistance before falling back. Seeing his advance parties in danger, Sullivan sent two regiments to reinforce Laurens and Livingston, along with orders to make an orderly withdrawal to the main army. The reinforcements proved useless, Laurens thought, because they "were too much employed in seeking advantageous ground to be of any service." Waving his sword, John rode among his own troops and urged them to take cover from the enemy. As they retreated, the troops under Laurens and Livingston continued their "Fire upon the Enemy," Sullivan remarked, "and retir'd in Excellent order."

The British and Hessians did not initially hazard a frontal attack on the main American line, choosing instead to form positions on Turkey Hill and Quaker Hill. On the other side of a wide valley the Americans at Butts Hill awaited further assaults. They found themselves in a precarious position, surrounded on all sides by water. To the west, in Narragansett Bay, four British ships maintained constant fire on Sullivan's force. On land the two armies exchanged artillery fire for several hours. Early in the afternoon von Lossburg launched a major attack on the right wing under Greene. Along this line a fierce struggle continued for about an hour, before the combined British-German force retreated "in worse disorder than they did at the battle of Monmouth."[42]

With the exception of some brief skirmishing and artillery exchanges, the battle of Rhode Island was over. It was a hotly contested fight—one-fifth of the combatants were casualties. The Americans suffered 30 killed, 137 wounded, and 44 missing; British casualties were slightly greater—38 dead, 210 wounded, and 12 missing. Stationed along the right line, the First Rhode Island Regiment fought well. John Laurens, who fell back with his light troops to this area, could not have failed to observe that the slaves and free blacks displayed coolness under fire. Though the Americans drove back their attackers, John remained unsatisfied; as always, he desired a complete triumph. "If I have anything to regret," he told Henry, "it is that we did not make a general attack upon the enemy. Their numbers, at least those that appeared, could not exceed three thousand; our men were full of confidence, and I am persuaded victory would have declared for us; but however this is a matter which must be delicately touched." Still, John admitted that "there were some good reasons against such an attempt," and he praised Sullivan's leadership. John's own performance received public notice from both Sullivan and Greene, the latter providing the most glowing accolade. After recognizing the accomplishments of the junior officers, Greene told Washington that "it is not in my power to do justice to Col Laurens who acted both the General and the Partizan. His command of regular Troops was small but he did every thing possible to be done by their numbers."[43]

The following morning Sullivan received a letter from Washington containing intelligence that the British fleet had again departed from New York, apparently with reinforcements for Pigot. From Boston came word that d'Estaing's return was delayed indefinitely. Their position no longer tenable, the Americans decided to abandon the island. By the early morning hours of 31 August, the entire army had been ferried to Tiverton on the mainland.[44]

The evacuation occurred in the nick of time. On 1 September, Sir Henry Clinton reached Newport with four thousand reinforcements. Clinton, rather than just relieving Pigot, had planned to block Sullivan's line of retreat. Had the British fleet arrived two days earlier, Sullivan's entire force could have been trapped.[45]

After the American army reached the mainland, Laurens went to Boston, having decided that his mission entailed a visit to d'Estaing. Ten days had passed since the French fleet departed Newport. During that time, the Americans had conducted a successful retreat and won some semblance of honor in battle. John realized that it was now time to heal any hurt feelings caused by the failed siege. He also had reason to regret his own harsh words. "It will be my greatest happiness," he wrote Washington, "if I can be useful in explaining the causes of mutual Jealousy and Uneasiness which have subsisted between the Officers of the allied powers . . . and be any ways instrumental in restoring that harmony which the common interest requires." Prior to the British victory in the Great War for the Empire, the English colonists viewed the French as their mortal enemies. Laurens knew that old prejudices died hard, and he feared that d'Estaing's departure from Newport would revive anti-French sentiment. He summarized for Washington a letter d'Estaing had written in response to the intemperate American protest, which Sullivan had forwarded to Boston. Though his pride was offended, the admiral maintained his cool. John believed the groundwork had been laid "for restoring harmony and a good understanding." He hoped Sullivan would work toward that end.[46]

While in Boston, Laurens stayed at the home of John Hancock, who strived to ensure that the French felt welcome. Despite these efforts, the tension between the French and the Bostonians was palpable. Laurens "saw very plainly . . . that our antient hereditary prejudices were very far from being eradicated." Before leaving for headquarters at White Plains, New York, John met with d'Estaing and received letters for Washington. After an extended absence, the young aide was in a hurry to return to the main army's camp. He left behind heavy clothing (which he later needed for winter) and took a shortcut along the way that prevented him from delivering a letter entrusted to him by Hancock.[47]

Congress attempted to minimize the damage caused by Sullivan's tactless reaction to d'Estaing's departure. The delegates resolved not to publish copies of the protest Sullivan sent to Boston. According to the official version promulgated by Washington, the gale that damaged d'Estaing's ships caused the expedition to fail. John Laurens spoke for many, including himself, when he commented that whereas Americans first reacted by heeding "their chagrin rather than good policy," deliberation produced "more cautious behavior."[48]

The Rhode Island campaign added more laurels to Laurens's reputation. There was also renewed talk of his excessive recklessness, especially in the wake of false rumors that he had been wounded in battle. Afterward he received another stricture to take care, but the warning came not from his father but from the other South Carolina delegate to Congress, William Henry Drayton. Though consistently at political and personal odds with Henry Laurens, Drayton showed genuine concern for John's safety. "A Man who is ever vigilant to discharge his duty to his country, is pleased to have objects pointed out," said Drayton. "Give me leave to point one. The public is fully convinced tha[t] in you they possess a most valuable Officer, & upon this point great hopes are established. It is your duty then in action to take some care of such an Officer, & not unnecessarily expose those hopes to a blasting shower of balls."[49]

Shortly after his arrival at headquarters in early September, John met his old friend Francis Kinloch, who had recently returned from England. Laurens could not forget how he and Kinloch had debated the merits of republicanism and constitutional monarchy. Remembering Kinloch's earlier opposition to the revolutionary cause, he viewed with skepticism his friend's change of heart. "I am sorry that Kinloch did not return to America sooner," he told Henry, "his former sentiments on the present contest, give reason to suspect, if he is a convert, that success on our side, has alone Operated the change." In fairness to his friend, John did acknowledge that as a youth Kinloch had been strongly influenced by his guardian, former Carolina royal governor Thomas Boone.[50]

Now that John had returned safely, Henry could think about the future. As 1 November—the expiration date of Henry's one-year term as president of Congress—approached, he again contemplated retirement from public life and a return to Carolina. His private affairs suffered from his absence. Unlike John, who had given himself completely to the Revolution, Henry's public service did not cause him to forget his family. As he told John, "I have a duty to you, to your Brother, to your sisters, and some to myself which call on me." He longed for a reunion with his eldest son: "If I retire without seeing you, what a lump will be dragged from hence to Charlestown, and what a heavy hearted Creature shall I exhibit to our friends there." Before departing, he wanted to discuss plans for Harry's future, as the boy was now fifteen years old. "Do you never think of your Brother?" he reproached John. "You know I postponed determinations respecting him upon an opinion of your own. I want much to see you on that important account."[51]

John ignored Henry's reproach and instead focused on his father's plans to leave Philadelphia. "The Public interest and my own lead me to wish that you may continue in the august Assembly of the States," he wrote. "I dread your being so remote from where my duty places me." He wanted to visit Henry, but he had to remain at headquarters, where there was considerable anxiety over British activities in New York. Obviously the British were preparing an expedition, but the question was, where? With the French in the war, the valuable sugar islands in the West Indies, not the rebellious American colonies, became the point of contention between the two great powers. Thus in November Clinton dispatched five thousand troops to St. Lucia. He also sent an expedition of thirty-five hundred redcoats to Georgia. The focus of the war had shifted to the South.[52]

By late October John finally received leave to journey to Philadelphia. After an extended separation, father and son were finally reunited. The initial days together proved professionally rewarding for both men. When Henry reminded Congress that his one-year term as president had expired, the delegates expressed appreciation for his service and asked him to remain as president a while longer.[53] Three days later, on 5 November, the delegates resolved that John Laurens "be presented with a continental commission of lieutenant colonel in testimony of the sense which Congress entertain of his patriotic and spirited services as a volunteer in the American army." In particular, Congress cited his performance during the battle of Rhode Island. The delegates directed Washington to give Laurens a line command "whenever opportunity shall offer." John had long desired "the command of men," a prerequisite for winning lasting fame. Finally, he had achieved his goal.[54]

As John pondered a response, concern over how others would perceive his actions delineated his range of options. More than anything, he wanted to employ a mode of self-presentation that won the approval of other men of honor. Rather than simply accept Congress's offer of a commission, he used the tactic advocated by Adam Smith in his *Theory of Moral Sentiments.* John adopted the role of an "impartial spectator," which involved stepping outside himself and viewing his conduct as would another man.[55] How would his fellow Continental officers and his colleagues in Washington's family react if he accepted the commission? During this period, the problem of rank continued to divide officers. Foreign adventurers still complained to Congress, which readily granted commissions to the loudest whiners. In mid-October John had told his father that the delegates had "brought rank into disgrace." He now realized that his connection to the president probably influenced Congress's decision to offer the commission. Having recently made rank an issue, arguing that Congress should distinguish between politically motivated promotions and those based on merit, he did not desire to become part of the controversy himself. Nor did he want to offend his closest friends, his fellow aides on Washington's staff. He realized, as a man of sensibility, that he could not in good conscience accept the commission "without injuring the rights of the Officers in the line of the Army; and doing an evident injustice to my Colleagues in the family of the Commander in chief. Among the former a regular mode of rising is established which I have no desire to infringe, the latter are my seniors and from length of service as well as merit I humbly conceive have prior claims." He decided to say no, but then couched his words carefully, concerned also about how Congress would view him. He assured the delegates that "the approbation of the august Representatives of the united States is the first object of my ambition." Congress, it turned out, viewed John in exactly the light that he desired: as a paragon of selfless republican virtue. On 6 November the delegates passed a resolution that "highly" approved "the disinterested and patriotic principles" he expressed in his refusal letter.[56]

In early December Congress found itself embroiled in two controversies. The delegates had recalled Silas Deane, one of the commissioners to France, because of his indiscriminate issuing of commissions to foreign adventurers. Deane returned home in June, but Congress procrastinated and took no definite action regarding his case. The delegates were divided between Deane's supporters and others, such as Henry Laurens, who suspected that the Connecticut merchant, while procuring supplies for the American war effort, had padded his own pocket. Ever the republican purist, Laurens tolerated no mingling of public duty with private gain. Impatient with the holdup, Deane vilified Congress in a piece published in the *Pennsylvania Packet* on 5 December. Laurens, though himself often critical of Congress, nevertheless believed Deane had impugned that body's honor and that the delegates could not allow this public affront to pass by unchallenged. When his fellow delegates appeared unwilling to condemn Deane, Henry resigned as president on 9 December. Though the resignation did little to alleviate tensions within Congress over the Deane affair, it did place Laurens on the floor, where he could more actively participate in debates.[57]

On the day Deane's attack appeared, Congress, after a long delay, approved the military court's ruling in the Charles Lee case. Lee anticipated the adverse decision and published a defense of his actions at Monmouth in the *Pennsylvania Packet* on 3 December. For the first time, he also openly questioned Washington's military ability and judgment. The essay never mentioned John Laurens. Yet the young aide reacted angrily to the aspersions cast on his chief. He wanted to frame a rebuttal, but doubted that his facility with the pen was equal to the task. "An affair of this kind ought to be passed over in total silence," he reasoned, "or answered in a masterly matter." So he asked Alexander Hamilton, who was already an accomplished essayist, to draft a response. Apparently Hamilton accepted the assignment, but his rejoinder never appeared in print.[58]

Aware of his limitations—he was more a man of action than words—Laurens challenged Lee to a duel. "I am informed," he told Lee "that in contempt of decency and truth you have publickly abused General Washington in the grossest terms. The relation in which I stand to him forbids me to pass such conduct unnoticed. I therefore demand that satisfaction which I am entitled to." John issued the challenge, not because of Lee's publication, but on the basis of rumors that Lee, in conversations with his friends, had attacked Washington's character.[59]

At the time, Lee was in the process of warding off a duel with Baron Steuben, who believed Lee had insulted him during the court-martial. Lee successfully assuaged the baron's injured honor, but he decided to confront Laurens head on. The aide, after all, was one of the "dirty earwigs" whose testimony had led to his dismissal from the army. Yet, the acerbic Lee mused, if Washington's honor had been denigrated, it was up to him, not Laurens, to issue the challenge. It appeared that young Laurens sought to renew the medieval custom of *pro viduâ*, an element of trial by combat whereby knights championed the honor of widows, elderly women, and priests. Under the eighteenth-century code duello, men fought their own duels. There was one exception, which occurred infrequently, when a son replaced his father, so long as the elder man "was not the aggressor." Laurens violated that convention, since Lee had never challenged Washington. Nor was Washington his father, albeit the young aide venerated his commander, the patriarch of a military family.[60]

Though Laurens issued his challenge on 3 December, the day Lee's publication appeared, they postponed the duel, allowing the aide to return briefly to headquarters and giving Lee time to recuperate from injuries sustained from a fall from his horse and to recover from an attack of gout. On 22 December Lee wrote Laurens and scheduled their engagement for the following afternoon at half past three o'clock. Barring rain, the two men, accompanied by their seconds, would meet and duel with pistols. "I would willingly bring a small sword at the same time," Lee apologized, "but from the effects of my fall and the quantity of Physick I have taken to baffle a fit of the Gout . . . I do not think myself sufficiently strong on my legs."[61]

On Wednesday afternoon, the twenty-third, Lee and his second, Evan Edwards, arrived early at the meeting place, the edge of a wooded area outside Philadelphia. When three o'clock passed without any sign of Laurens and his second, Alexander Hamilton, Edwards suggested that they might not show up. In dueling the antagonists forged an ironic bond: a duel defined a man, for only gentlemen fought duels and staked their lives on their honor. Lee thus defended his opponent, responding that "Laurens was a man of unquestionable bravery" and would definitely make his appearance. Proving him right, Laurens and Hamilton arrived shortly thereafter.[62]

Lee suggested that each man approach the other and fire whenever ready. Laurens agreed. The two men took their positions and walked toward each other, opening fire at a distance of about five or six paces. Laurens, who was unhurt, had just started reloading his pistol when Lee announced that he was wounded. Believing the wound was serious, Laurens and the seconds rushed forward to assist the general. Lee assured them that the injury was slight, that the bullet only grazed the skin. He requested a second fire, and Laurens consented. The seconds, however, strongly objected, arguing that honor had been satisfied. When Lee persisted, Hamilton asked him if he "was influenced by motives of personal enmity." Conscious that Laurens's honor was at stake, Hamilton did not press his point too far. When both principals prepared for another exchange, Edwards repeated his opposition. Lee then replied that he would accept whatever decision Edwards and Hamilton made.

While the seconds conferred, Laurens and Lee discussed the events that had prompted the duel in the first place. He came only to defend his honor, Lee said, and bore no hostility toward Laurens. For his part, John reiterated that he felt obligated, as a member of Washington's family, to contest aspersions against the commander in chief. Lee admitted that he had expressed to friends his opinion of Washington's military ability, and most likely would do so again. That, after all, was his right, and he did not have to answer to Laurens for such statements. As a gentleman, however, he assured John that he had never slandered Washington's character. The seconds then appeared and announced that the duel was ended. Both principals being satisfied that the affair had been conducted honorably, the four men returned to Philadelphia.[63]

Hamilton and Edwards promptly published an account of the duel that served to dispel rumors. Following a nonfatal duel, a participant normally departed the field of honor with deep admiration for his foe. While Lee admired John's courage, the statement attributed to him—"I could have hugged the noble boy, he pleased me so"—is probably apocryphal. Instead, he accorded Laurens an "odd sort of respect."[64]

Laurens's motives in initiating the duel are somewhat suspect. Lee drew parallels between himself and Thomas Conway, and the similarities in the downfalls of both men are striking. In each case John played a prominent role. When Washington considered himself threatened by Conway and Lee, Laurens, as well as Hamilton, strongly defended their chief and spread stories about his adversaries that were only partly true. Yet different imperatives seemed to govern the friends: Laurens acted on impulse, inspired by love for

Washington and influenced by the attitude of jealousy that was an essential component of republican ideology; Hamilton, though affected by jealousy, also acted from ulterior motives. While Laurens viewed Washington with adoration that bordered on blind idolatry, Hamilton saw how an alliance with the commander in chief could advance one's career. Hamilton, who encouraged Steuben to pursue a duel with Lee, probably also urged Laurens to tender a challenge. Once the affair was arranged, however, he acted in a subsidiary position, and probably envied the prominent role his friend played. Whatever their motives, the young men helped to eliminate from the scene Conway and Lee and, to a lesser extent, also succeeded in shoving aside Horatio Gates. Washington faced no further serious challenges to his authority and prestige.[65]

As John Laurens summarized the events of 1778, forming a self-narrative of his role in the campaign, he could reflect proudly on the progress he made in his quest for virtue and fame.[66] He served bravely at Monmouth and Newport; proved, for the most part, an effective liaison between Sullivan and d'Estaing; and successfully defended the honor of Washington. Most important, Philadelphia was again in American hands. William Henry Drayton in private and Congress in public confirmed that John had achieved the public recognition he craved: they identified him as "a most valuable Officer," a gentleman of "disinterested and patriotic principles." While their acclaim was gratifying, it remained insufficient. John wanted more—a decisive battle, a defining moment that allowed the grandest possible display of selfless virtue. Earlier in the year he told Henry that he desired either a "Glorious Death, or the Triumph of the Cause in which I am engaged." His public achievements meant little if his ultimate aspiration, the "Triumph of the Cause" to which he had completely submitted himself, remained unfulfilled. Now there appeared ominous signs from the South. While Henry and John spent the holidays together, a British expedition captured Savannah, Georgia.[67] After the redcoats consolidated their hold on the southernmost state, they most likely would turn their attention to a more important prize. Once again, the havoc of war threatened the security of Charleston.

Chapter 7

"White Pride & Avarice"

The Limits of Independence in
the South Carolina Low Country
January–December 1779

In 1779 the British focused their full attention on conquering the South. This turn of events prompted John Laurens to return to South Carolina, and over the next three years he struggled to drive the enemy from his home state. John placed no limits on service to his country, no limits on self-denial in behalf of a higher cause. In four major battles he had willingly risked his life; to secure American independence, he was willing to relinquish his inheritance in slaves, the very property that marked him as an autonomous individual. He discovered, however, that his fellow low-country Carolinians placed definite limits on the sacrifices they were willing to make to win independence from British rule. In a real sense the question of limits defined the remainder of Laurens's life.

During the first month of 1779, John remained in Philadelphia, where General Washington conferred with Congress about the upcoming campaign. Washington and his wife Martha stayed at Henry Laurens's quarters. Life in the largest American city was more comfortable for an aide than it was at the main army's winter camp at Middlebrook, New Jersey. Yet Philadelphia presented different hazards. The staff, accustomed to constant activity and occasional danger, found that inaction quickly led to ennui. Such an existence, commented Tench Tilghman, was fine for a man of wealth "whose pursuit is idleness and dissipation." For young aides in search of military fame, however, it was an unbearable existence.[1]

John found some distraction in the political controversies involving his father. Henry believed that the wealthy Philadelphia merchant Robert Morris collected private profits while he managed Congress's mercantile affairs as chairman of the Commercial Committee. When Laurens made allegations of financial misconduct before Congress, Morris defended his actions in the press. After an investigation, the delegates exonerated Morris of any wrongdoing, much to Laurens's chagrin. As an outgrowth of that feud, he fought a blood-less duel with his political enemy, John Penn of North Carolina. Within one month, both father and son had engaged in affairs of honor. At least eight duels occurred in Philadelphia during this period, prompting some caustic observers to label the "barbarous and unjustifiable practice" of dueling the cur-rent craze.[2]

The elder Laurens also remained involved in Silas Deane's continuing trou-bles with Congress. Thomas Paine, the contentious author of *Common Sense,* attacked Deane in a series of articles published in the *Pennsylvania Packet.* In one piece Paine, apparently using information provided by Laurens, mentioned that the Carolinian had been unanimously reelected as president on 2 Novem-ber 1778. Using the pseudonym "Philalethes," an anonymous author coun-tered Paine's charges against Deane. On 23 January, Philalethes scrutinized Laurens's reelection and argued that Congress, lacking both adequate candi-dates for president and a sufficient number of delegates for a vote, merely asked him to remain in office a while longer.[3]

Sensitive about his honor and aware that his thirteen-month-tenure exceeded the normal limits of presidential terms, Henry drafted a rebuttal. Writing as "Philopatros," he explained that Congress unanimously requested that he remain as president. He never insisted that details of the proceedings appear in the journals of Congress because he wanted only to "serve his coun-try," not elevate his reputation.[4]

A written rejoinder was one means of defending one's honor; a duel was another. Not one to remain on the sidelines as an observer, John decided to intervene on his father's behalf, just as he had earlier sought redress for his mil-itary father, George Washington. Alexander Hamilton informed him that Colonel John Parke wrote the articles signed by Philalethes. When John visited Parke, he readily admitted that he was the author. John presented Parke with another account of Henry's reelection, presumably the rebuttal written under the pseudonym "Philopatros." He asked Parke to print that version "with a proper preface, signifying that . . . the account he had given of the late presi-dents Resignation in his last paper was inaccurate." Parke agreed to publish the new account.[5]

Despite Parke's promise, the article was not printed, even though Laurens, on three separate occasions, insisted that the piece appear promptly. After a fur-ther delay, Laurens wrote Parke and instructed him to revise the preface and explain why the retraction had not been published sooner. Parke had already submitted the article to John Dunlap, the publisher of the *Pennsylvania Packet*. He agreed to change the preface, but insisted that the matter was out of his hands, that it was up to Dunlap to print the piece. "I am determin'd to affront no Man, designedly," said Parke, "but if Col. Laurens is resolved to break the Peace, he will be so good as to inform me."[6]

This time John managed to avoid a duel. When the two men met again in Philadelphia, John acknowledged that Parke had done everything possible to ensure publication. He decided to try a different tactic. Since the original piece by Philalethes contained information known only to members of Congress, he asked Parke who had been his source. Parke replied that it was Silas Deane.

Deane, of course, was not a member of Congress, so obviously Parke had been mistaken. Hoping to discover the true identity of Parke's collaborator, Laurens visited Deane. The former diplomat admitted that he supplied Parke with documents "to serve as detections of Common Senses falsehoods." The actual article, however, had been written by Parke and William Duer, a delegate from New York who frequently opposed Henry Laurens in Congress. Because so much time had elapsed, John wondered aloud, perhaps it was pointless to publish the retraction. Speaking from his own experience, Deane agreed. "As many people shewed such a captious disposition," he told John, "and there was such an inundation of controversial papers, the less any Gentleman appeared in print the better."[7] The Laurenses chose to follow Deane's advice: Henry never printed his rebuttal; the original allegations by Philalethes went unchallenged.

John correctly perceived that this dispute was largely inconsequential. Of much greater importance was the British threat to South Carolina. In late January the Laurenses learned that the British had taken Savannah. Concerned for the fate of Carolina, both men longed to go home. "I am exceedingly anxious to return to my own Country at this critical juncture," said Henry, "my Son if possible is more desirous." Washington granted John leave of absence to journey southward, but told him that he was welcome to rejoin the official family once his duty there had been completed.[8] The young man hoped to offer more than himself to South Carolina; he revived his proposal to raise a regiment of slaves, an idea that had lain dormant for almost a year.

Either outside assistance "or the adoption of my black project alone can save" South Carolina, John told Henry. He wondered if "the force of example, Argument, and above all that of impending Calamity will determine our Countrymen to embrace the salutary measure which I propose." If there was a chance of success, it was important that the Laurenses work together. "You will have the glory of triumphing over deep rooted national prejudices," John assured Henry, "in favor of your Country and humanity at large, the former may perhaps have reason to call you her deliverer. The sacrifice you make, will be effaced by the most delicious and enviable feelings." Henry, in other words, would experience the sublime sensation of the man of feeling who gave objective form to his virtue by extending assistance to the oppressed. "For my part," concluded John, "it will be my duty and my pride, to transform the timid Slave into a firm defender of Liberty and render him worthy to enjoy it himself."[9]

John spent the month of March preparing for his departure. Time was running out for Carolina, he believed. "Dont you think it would be saving time," he asked Henry, "to obtain a Recommendation from Congress to the State of So Carolina to raise black Troops for her defence." His enthusiasm proved contagious: Hamilton wanted to accompany his friend to the new scene of action, but Washington could not afford to lose two valuable aides simultaneously. Hamilton could only participate vicariously by writing a letter to John Jay, president of the Continental Congress, endorsing the black regiment plan and extolling Laurens's qualifications.[10]

On 10 March John reiterated to Henry that Congress needed to act. He desperately wanted to be on his way. Late winter in Carolina, noted for its mildness, "affords very good fighting weather," he observed. He realized that the journey southward would consume much time, followed by another delay—South Carolina's assembly, "from the opposition of private interest" could not be expected to embrace his plan. "I must confess I am anxious," he admitted, "for if I am engaged in a plan of this kind my reputation is at stake." With that in mind, he wished to spend considerable time "disciplining and instructing my Soldiers before I introduce them to the enemy." It was imperative that the black regiment be ready for use in the upcoming campaign. "As a Soldier, as a Citizen, as a Man," John declared, "I am interested to engage in this work, and I would chearfully sacrifice the largest portion of my future expectations to its success."[11]

In an about-face, Henry Laurens now supported his son's idea. At least two factors influenced this transformation. First, unlike the previous year, in 1779 South Carolina faced a direct British threat. Because the majority of South Carolina's population was black and the state lacked sufficient white manpower, the plan could be justified strictly on military grounds. Second, Henry realized that he could not dissuade John this time. As a protective father, he did not want his son to go it alone. He recognized, more clearly than John, the inflexible opposition that lay ahead. Perhaps the sanction of Congress would win John a warmer reception in Carolina. Though no longer president of Congress, Henry's opinions still carried political weight.

Faced with an imminent British invasion, South Carolinians anxiously awaited assistance from Congress. Governor John Rutledge dispatched Daniel Huger to Philadelphia to make a personal plea for military aid. The form of aid that Rutledge wanted most was Continental army and naval reinforcements. Thomas Bee, the lieutenant governor, wondered why Carolina was isolated in her hour of need. In a letter to William Henry Drayton, Bee revealed low-country South Carolina's growing disillusionment with the government in Philadelphia: "If Congress mean we should make the best Terms for ourselves we can, I wish they would be Explicit."[12]

Daniel Huger's arrival in Philadelphia coincided with the formation of a congressional committee, proposed by Henry Laurens, that deliberated on ways to defend the threatened southern states. Though Carolina delegates Laurens and Drayton were normally political enemies, on this pressing occasion the two men fully cooperated. The five-member committee, which included Laurens, met with Huger, who informed them that it was impossible for South Carolina to raise large numbers of militia because most men remained "at home to prevent Insurrections among the Negroes, and to prevent the desertion of them to the Enemy." Based on this discussion, the committee concluded that the state should turn a weakness into a strength and enlist slaves as soldiers. When asked his opinion, George Washington contended that if Americans recruited slaves, the British would follow suit and initiate a race to determine which side could "arm fastest." He therefore considered the issue "a moot point, unless the enemy set the example." Laurens, Drayton, and Huger turned this argument on its head and asserted that a force composed of blacks not only offered military advantages but also prevented the British from inciting "revolts, and desertions by detaching the most Enterprising and vigorous Men from amongst the Negroes."[13]

On 25 March the committee presented its report to Congress. Up to this point, Congress officially forbade the enlistment of blacks, whether slave or free, but winked when individual states used blacks to fill gaps in their Continental battalions. An endorsement by Laurens and Drayton, coupled with Huger's account of Carolina's predicament, convinced Congress to depart from previous practice and endorse the plan. Four days later, on 29 March, the delegates resolved that South Carolina and Georgia raise "three thousand able bodied negroes," who would be commanded by white officers. Congress agreed to pay one thousand dollars to the owner of each slave who passed muster; all blacks who served loyally for the duration of the war would, after returning their arms, receive their freedom and fifty dollars. There was, however, a loophole. Because the committee cautioned that the "measure may involve inconveniences peculiarly affecting" the two states, Congress only recommended that blacks be armed. The state governments would have the final say.[14]

After passing the resolution, Congress commissioned John Laurens lieutenant colonel. Furnished with the commission and Congress's endorsement of the slave regiment plan, and authorized by Henry to employ the family slaves as circumstances dictated, John began his journey southward. Few delegates in Congress failed to recognize the revolutionary implications of the resolution. William Whipple of New Hampshire wondered how the southernmost states would react. If the plan were "carried into effect," said Whipple, "it will produce the Emancipation of a number of those wretches and lay a foundation for the Abolition of Slavery in America."[15]

Having rejected a commission from Congress only four months earlier, John soon had second thoughts about accepting this offer. He worried that he had placed his private interests over the rights of others, and wondered how his fellow officers viewed him: did they consider him selfish? Hamilton assured his friend that he acted correctly. It was proper that he receive a line commission since he was to command the black regiment. Had the commission been dated retroactively to Laurens's admission into Washington's military family in October 1777, however, Hamilton would not have approved. On two separate occasions Congress had attempted to grant Laurens "a privilege, an honor, a mark of distinction . . . which they withold from other Gentlemen in the family. This carries with it an air of preference, which, though we can all truly say, we love your character, and admire your military merit, cannot fail to give some of us uneasy sensations." Having hinted that Laurens's position as the son of the former president brought special rewards, Hamilton reassured his friend that any fault for this favoritism rested with Congress alone. John's own conduct had been unimpeachable. Yet Hamilton could not resist a playful dig at Laurens's penchant for handwringing, his excessive concern about his reputation, demonstrated by his reluctance to accept the commission: "You rejected the offer when you ought to have rejected it; and you accepted it when you ought to have accepted it; and let me add with a degree of overscrupulous delicacy. It was necessary for your project; your project was the public good. . . . In hesitating, you have refined upon the refinements of generosity."

Hamilton enclosed to Laurens letters from the Manning family in England. Despite their close friendship, he seemed not to have known that John had a daughter, which again suggests that Martha and Fanny remained far away, not only physically but also emotionally and mentally. After mentioning Laurens's immediate family, Hamilton concluded the letter on a playful note and asked his friend to procure him a wife from South Carolina. His specifications included youth, beauty—"I lay most stress upon a good shape"—moderate intelligence, and, proving there is truth in jest, wealth. Hamilton insisted that his own characteristics be accurately described to the potential lover, and was careful to underline for emphasis "*size*" and "*body*." "In drawing my picture," he instructed Laurens, "you will no doubt be civil to your friend; mind you do justice to the length of my nose and don't forget that I. . . ." At this point, unfortunately, someone, presumably a Hamilton descendant, thoroughly marked through the remainder of the sentence and made it completely illegible. Yet the implication was clear then and now: a common double entendre of the period involved comparisons between the length of a man's nose and the size of his penis; it was a running joke throughout Laurence Sterne's *Tristram Shandy,* a work popular among devotees of sensibility. Obviously, and not surprisingly, the young officers shared a propensity for bawdy humor. Ultimately, however, the passage is similar to much of Laurens's surviving correspondence: it raises more questions than it answers.[16]

John had little time for such jocularity. He hoped to convince his fellow Carolinians, who were ill-prepared to resist an enemy invasion, to save themselves by arming slaves. Little did he know that low-country South Carolina was already in the middle of a major crisis. Since taking charge of the Southern Department, Major General Benjamin Lincoln had encountered problems that plagued previous commanders in that region—civil officials jealous of their position and unwilling to share authority with Continental general officers, a local populace more concerned with private advantage than the public good. Daniel Huger's testimony to Congress had been accurate. There were few Continentals in the state. Compounding the military weakness, members of the militia, who were not under Lincoln's control, feared potential slave insurrections and preferred to remain home. Indeed, the South Carolina militia, during the thirty-five-year period prior to the rebellion, functioned more like a slave patrol than a military body.[17]

In response to these problems the assembly enacted a stringent militia law that authorized fines on able-bodied men who refused to turn out. In addition, the legislature delegated authority to Governor Rutledge and the Privy Council "to do every thing that appeared to him and them necessary for the publick good." Rutledge, in other words, possessed virtually unlimited political power. He stationed about three thousand militia at Orangeburgh under his direct command; from that strategic location in the center of the state, they could be dispatched to points of emergency.[18]

At Savannah, General Augustine Prevost commanded a force of five thousand troops. Lincoln, a cautious man who rarely acted without calling a council of his officers, suddenly made a reckless move. On 19 April he and his officers decided to invade the Georgia backcountry and establish a post at Augusta, where they hoped to stop the passage of supplies to Prevost from an area heavily populated with loyalists. Before leaving, he stationed Brigadier General William Moultrie with one thousand troops, primarily composed of militia, in Black Swamp, across the Savannah River from Georgia. Lincoln realized that Prevost might attempt a diversionary incursion into South Carolina. If he did, Moultrie was to delay the British at the various river crossings leading to Charleston, thus allowing Lincoln time to return. Instructed by Congress to secure Charleston against an enemy assault, Lincoln now left the city exposed.[19]

Prevost readily seized the opportunity. On 29 April he crossed the Savannah River with two thousand troops. He planned to utilize Lincoln's absence to obtain much-needed provisions for his army. In response Moultrie ordered his force to the Coosawhatchie River, where they prepared to make a stand. If Lincoln did not return quickly, Moultrie believed, the redcoats would make it all the way to Charleston.[20]

John Laurens encountered this perilous situation when he reached South Carolina. He hurried to the scene of action, arriving on 1 May at Moultrie's new camp at Tullifiny Hill, which the general believed was a more secure position to defend. Concluding that Prevost was indeed heading for Charleston, he placed sentries at each ford along the river and left behind a rear guard of 100 men at the main crossing point. Two days later on 3 May, with Prevost's force approaching, Moultrie decided to remove the rear guard. Laurens volunteered to perform that duty, and Moultrie consented, considering the young man "to be a brave and experienced officer." Laurens took with him 250 troops, including 150 hand-picked riflemen to protect his flanks.[21]

The mission was simple—Laurens and his detachment were to escort the rear guard back to the army at Tullifiny Hill. Laurens, however, had other ideas; he wanted to engage the enemy and win military fame in an action defending his native soil. He took his entire force, along with the rear guard, across the Coosawhatchie River. The decision revealed imprudence rather than foresight, for he failed to secure some vacant houses on a hill overlooking his position. The British, meanwhile, were not so obtuse and promptly occupied the houses, giving them an unobstructed view of the hapless militia. From this vantage point, the redcoats opened fire with their muskets and artillery, killing two Americans, and wounding seven others, including Laurens. His horse shot from under him and his right arm wounded, John retired from the field, but not before he instructed his subordinate, Captain Thomas Shubrick, to maintain the position a while longer before withdrawing. After Laurens departed, Shubrick wisely ignored these instructions and ordered a hasty retreat across the causeway that spanned the river. Had Shubrick remained, the entire detachment, comprising one-third of Moultrie's army, would have been captured.[22]

At Tullifiny Hill, Moultrie heard the volleys and assumed that Laurens and the British were exchanging potshots while the rear guard evacuated. To his surprise and dismay, Laurens appeared with news of the unauthorized engagement. Moultrie repressed his anger and merely asked a question: "Well Colonel what do you think of it?" "Why sir," replied Laurens, "your men won't stand." Moultrie ordered the army to withdraw from Tullifiny Hill. Laurens's insubordination had foiled his plans. "Had not Col. Laurens discouraged the men by exposing them so much and unnecessarily," Moultrie wrote, "I would have engaged Gen. Provost at Tullifiny, and perhaps have stopped his march to Charlestown." It was risky to place troops under Laurens's command, he concluded: "Col. Laurens was a young man of great merit, and a brave soldier, but an imprudent officer; he was too rash and impetuous."[23]

Moultrie's assessment proved correct: Laurens's ill-advised move had indeed "discouraged" the militia. They began deserting in droves, "every one running to look after his Wife Children & property." The Americans could do little but retire before the British advance. As they retreated, Moultrie's force destroyed bridges and felled trees, hoping to hinder Prevost's progress. Along their line of march, the redcoats looted, collected slaves, and burned and destroyed all property they could not carry. Prevost changed his original plan and now made for Charleston, finding the defenseless city too tempting to ignore. Moultrie urged Lincoln to return. "Pray follow them & let us Burgoine them," he implored.[24]

Prompted by Moultrie's pressing messages, Governor Rutledge departed from Orangeburgh with five hundred militia on 4 May. By 6 May Lincoln, who earlier considered Prevost's invasion a feint, finally sensed that a crisis was at hand. His council of officers agreed that the army should return to South Carolina. After crossing the Savannah River, however, Lincoln moved slowly, seemingly unaware that time was running out. Moultrie, meanwhile, reached Charleston on 7 May, and Rutledge arrived a day later. "There is a strange consternation in Town," Moultrie informed Lincoln, "people frightened out of their wits, they long that you should . . . soon be among the Enemy with your Army."[25]

Though Charleston was prepared for an attack by sea, its land fortifications remained unfinished. The Carolinians hastily constructed lines of defense across Charleston Neck between the Ashley and Cooper Rivers. On 11 May Prevost's force crossed Ashley Ferry, where perhaps Moultrie should have made a stand. After brief skirmishing, the antagonists settled down for the night. The two sides possessed nearly equal manpower—approximately twenty-five hundred troops apiece—although some reports exaggerated Prevost's strength, leading Rutledge and his council to believe that they faced a force of almost eight thousand. The British lacked the equipment to commence siege operations, so the city's defenders, expecting Prevost to attempt a sudden assault, set tar barrels on fire to prevent a surprise.[26]

Rutledge knew that Charleston's fortifications were unfinished and weak and he was convinced that the enemy possessed overwhelming numerical superiority. He also thought of Laurens's recent arrival, not with news that Continental Army reinforcements were on the way but with Congress's suggestion that South Carolinians arm their slaves. As the leaders of a state with an economy dependent on slave labor yet under constant fear of slave insurrections, Rutledge and his council could not envision arming blacks, much less paving the way for their eventual emancipation. Whether in panic or in a fit of pique or in an attempt to stall the redcoat advance, Rutledge asked Moultrie to send a white flag to find out what surrender terms Prevost would offer should the city capitulate. Lieutenant Colonel James Mark Prevost, the brother of the British commander, replied that all inhabitants who rejected royal authority would be made prisoners of war. Moultrie refused to accept those terms but suggested that each side appoint representatives to negotiate further.[27]

Rutledge and the Privy Council, joined by Moultrie, the Polish officer Count Pulaski, and John Laurens, met to consider their options. The three military men insisted that the city could be held. Laurens argued that the fieldworks, while not as secure as "a permanent fortification," would, along with the artillery, hold off the redcoats. John did not expect Prevost to storm the city because he could not risk the high casualties. A siege, on the other hand, allowed Lincoln time to arrive and trap the British, or "Burgoine" them, as Moultrie had suggested. Laurens regretted that the initial overture to Prevost had been made. For his part, he said with typical bravado, he would gladly defend "the weakest point of the lines, with the worst troops," though he had only one hand. Influenced in part by Laurens's impassioned appeal, several council members opposed further negotiations. Rutledge, implying dissatisfaction, commented "that it was extraordinary after Gentlemen had been so unanimous for a measure that they sh[oul]d change their minds." Laurens returned to his family's home at Ansonborough, believing the matter was settled.[28]

After Laurens's departure, the civil authorities again hesitated, fearing "the calamities and cruelties which the Inhabitants would be exposed to" if the British stormed the defenses. At another meeting, Rutledge and the council, by a vote of five to three, drafted surrender terms:

> That he [General Prevost] should be permitted to take possession of it [Charleston], provided the State and Harbour should be considered as neutral during the War, the question whether it [South Carolina] belonged to Great Britain or the United States to be waived until the conclusion of it, and that whenever that should happen whatever was granted to the other States, *that* [South Carolina] should enjoy.[29]

Another meeting was called at the lines. Moultrie and some members of the council asked Laurens to take a flag to Prevost. He would not go, he replied, until they told him what the mission entailed. When they revealed their intentions, John flatly said no, "that he would do any thing to serve his country; but he could not think of carrying such a message as that." He could not believe his ears, and likened the shock to "a thunderstroke."[30]

Moultrie finally found two officers willing to carry the message to Prevost. As they awaited a reply, Rutledge asked Moultrie what he thought of the proposed surrender. He opposed it personally, the general answered, "yet he thought the other States had no reason to complain, as they had not fulfilled their engagements to it in giving it aid and assistance, from which promise that State came into the Union."[31]

The officers returned with Prevost's answer. Because he came as a military commander, not in a civil capacity, he refused to deal with Rutledge and the Privy Council and repeated his demand that the entire city surrender as prisoners of war. As Rutledge and his council looked on, Moultrie framed his response. He informed Prevost that the conference was over. If the British wanted Charleston, they would have to take it. John Laurens jumped to his feet and exclaimed, "thank God! we are upon our legs again."[32]

The following morning the defenders discovered, to their delight, that Prevost had withdrawn across the Ashley River. Proving the accuracy of Laurens's military analysis, Prevost determined that the breastworks, "mounted with a great quantity of Artillery," could be stormed only at great cost. Aware also that Lincoln's arrival was imminent, Prevost could not afford to remain and expose his entire force to capture.[33]

Lincoln belatedly arrived on 14 March. Had he moved with any alacrity, he could have pinned down Prevost and won a decisive victory. Instead, a stalemate ensued as Lincoln camped at Ashley Ferry to watch Prevost's movements. Despite Lincoln's requests, Rutledge and the Privy Council declined to send reinforcements from the garrison in Charleston. To no avail, Laurens urged the council to reconsider; he argued that a large detachment of "good Men" could be dispatched to Lincoln without endangering the city. Though Rutledge refused to assist Lincoln, he still expected the general to defeat Prevost's army, which he branded as "Thieves, Robbers, & Plunderers." The governor said that Carolinians, "many of whom have been pillaged & ruin'd," expected Lincoln to avenge those crimes. These were markedly different words from the man who sought neutrality only a week earlier.[34]

Was the surrender proposal only a ploy to buy time until Lincoln arrived, as some contemporaries claimed? After all, the two sides spent an entire day in negotiations. Or did Rutledge and a few leaders, angry at what they perceived as an indifferent Congress, seriously intend to submit and remove South Carolina from the war?

Prominent Carolinians like Henry Laurens attempted to portray this affair in a positive light. In letters to northern political colleagues he used the same tactics he employed to excuse the presence of slavery: first rationalizing and then projecting the blame elsewhere. Because South Carolina's dire needs had been ignored by her sister states—particularly North Carolina and Virginia—Rutledge and his council deserved understanding rather than censure. Some Carolinians tried to deny reality altogether. Peter Timothy, printer of *The Gazette of the State of South Carolina,* insisted that the neutrality proposal never occurred because "THE PEOPLE were entirely strangers to it."[35]

Other observers took a less charitable view. Mercy Otis Warren, in her history of the American Revolution, considered the surrender proposal "the only instance in America of an offer made so derogatory to the honor of the union." After mocking the "much boasted Virtue & honour of the inhabitants of South Carolina," who broke their commitments "on the approach of real danger or whenever they think it will suit their private views," an anonymous writer in the *Georgia Royal Gazette* posed an intriguing explanation for the offer of neutrality: "Sometime ago the State of South Carolina made requisition to the Continental Congress for a supply of Troops. . . . Congress sent young Jno Laurens to recommend it to them to Arm their domesticks & at the same time recommending Jn. Laurens as a proper person to Lead them, This is said to be the Cause of the Carolinians Willingness to remain in a state of Neutrality."[36] Even when allowances are made for British-loyalist sarcasm, that account is most likely accurate.

In offering to surrender, Rutledge and a majority of the council demonstrated that their allegiance to the United States was volitional. Whereas John Laurens dedicated himself completely to winning independence and was willing to adopt any means necessary to achieve that end, other low-country Carolinians maintained a limited commitment to the cause of liberty. Reciprocal obligations, which governed relations with their slaves, also governed relations with Congress. William Moultrie made the point clearly: the other states in the Confederation "had no reason to complain" because they had failed to fulfill their obligations to South Carolina "in giving it aid and assistance." To Carolina's leaders, slavery was strictly an internal matter, not to be tampered with by outsiders. They unhesitatingly bid farewell to a revolution that required them to place arms in the hands of slaves.

Laurens's performance during the emergency showed him at his best—and worst. His unauthorized excursion across the Coosawhatchie River nearly produced disaster. As it was, the setback lowered the militia's fragile morale, caused many desertions, and forced Moultrie to retreat toward Charleston. On the other hand, he rightly opposed surrender upon any grounds and correctly assessed Prevost's military options. As the brief crisis demonstrated, the young man's desire to prove his virtue and win fame proved potentially dangerous, as at Coosawhatchie; yet his high ideals also produced sound judgment and exemplary behavior, as evidenced in his refusal to countenance the surrender proposal.

After Prevost's withdrawal, Laurens again presented the slave regiment proposal, this time in writing. He used the argument of military expediency while downplaying the social ramifications of the plan. "Those very blacks which have hitherto been regarded as our greatest weakness may be converted into our greatest strength," he contended. He argued further that, accustomed to discipline, their physiques hardened by regular labor and exposure to the elements, slaves would make excellent soldiers.[37] There were, in fact, historical precedents for arming slaves in South Carolina. During the Yamasee War in 1715, blacks played an important role in the fighting. Since the Stono Uprising of 1739, however, whites, fearing additional insurrections, had moved to restrict slave autonomy. Still, John had some reason for hope. Carolina slaveholders allowed free blacks—always a small minority of the population—to serve in the militia. At the Coosawhatchie River a free black man had been killed fighting under Laurens's command. Carolinians seemed unconcerned when a few blacks bore arms.[38] The real issue standing in John's way was numbers: the image of large numbers of armed blacks was a nightmare few whites wanted to contemplate. Rutledge and the Privy Council thus reacted predictably. On 26 May the governor delivered a terse response: "I laid your Letter respecting the black Levies before the Council yesterday but they adhere to their former sentiments on that subject." One councilor, Christopher Gadsden, was more blunt. "We are much disgusted here at Congress recommending us to arm our Slaves," he told Samuel Adams, "it was received with great resentment, as a very dangerous and impolitic Step."[39]

While John convalesced in Charleston, unable to serve in the field because of his wound, Lincoln cautiously watched Prevost's force, which constructed fortifications at Stono Ferry on the mainland across the Stono River from Johns Island. On 16 June Prevost loaded most of his troops on boats and sailed to Savannah. His excursion into South Carolina, based on the booty his troops seized, was a success, though the unrestricted plunder embittered many low-country Carolinians, some of whom had previously been well disposed toward a renewal of British rule. Prevost left behind nine hundred Hessians, Scottish Highlanders, and loyalists under the command of Lieutenant Colonel John Maitland. The time seemed ripe for an attack. On 20 June, after receiving the long awaited reinforcements from Charleston, Lincoln struck the British position. The battle of Stono Ferry proved a devastating defeat for the Americans: their losses totaled over three hundred, while the redcoats suffered less than half that many casualties. After the battle, Maitland did evacuate his post and retreated south to Port Royal Island. Lincoln returned to Charleston. The American setback at Stono Ferry was followed by a period of inactivity, largely necessitated by the sultry summer weather.[40]

Lincoln, who was probably prompted by Laurens, urged Rutledge to reconsider Congress's recommendation to raise slave battalions. It was imperative that the state government fill the Continental line and thus maintain a standing army, ready to respond to the next British attempt on South Carolina. The previous campaign demonstrated the folly of relying on "frequent calls of the Militia," which involved a "great expence of time and money." Notorious for their unreliability, the militia often returned home as soon as their time of service expired, even if a campaign was in progress. Rutledge remained adamantly opposed to the slave regiment plan. He offered a counterproposal—to fill Continental battalions with militia drafts. That idea, Laurens argued, was infeasible: it would prove unpopular with Carolinians, who avoided militia service when possible—in large part because they were afraid to leave their slaves behind unguarded. Laurens believed that the average white male would definitely resist protracted service in the Continental line and that the slave regiment plan was the only means of saving South Carolina from British rule. Having been elected to the South Carolina House of Representatives the previous December, he intended to introduce his plan at the July session. He wished he was a more eloquent advocate, that his words alone could persuade Carolinians to take action. He recalled a similar situation in ancient history, how Demosthenes, the Athenian orator, tried to rally Athens against the Macedonians. "Oh that I were a Demosthenes," John lamented, "the Athenians never deserved more bitter exprobration than my Countrymen."[41]

Unfortunately, the records from the first session of the House of Representatives are not extant. When the legislature reconvened on 31 August, the house renewed debate on "A Bill for the More Effectual Defence of This State," a measure that had been drafted in the previous session. During that initial session, Laurens apparently introduced an amendment to this bill to fill the gaps among the Continentals and militia with able-bodied slaves. What is clear is that his proposal met overwhelming defeat. One of the amendment's supporters, Dr. David Ramsay, a Pennsylvania native who had moved to Charleston in 1774, commented that "The measure for embodying the negroes had about twelve votes: it was received with horror by the planters, who figured to themselves terrible consequences." When one considers that an average of seventy-two members voted on each measure during the second session, the magnitude of Laurens's defeat becomes apparent. At best his proposal received support from about 17 percent of the representatives.[42]

These men, who had rebelled against what they perceived as British tyranny threatening to enslave them, considered the idea of arming their own slaves a worse form of slavery. There were definite limits on how far they would go to win their independence. It seemed far better to risk the renewal of British rule than to resort to a measure that contained such potential for social upheaval. At the beginning of the war, white Carolinians endured a prolonged slave insurrection scare. Then Henry Laurens had protested when two slaves

suspected of plotting rebellion were sentenced to be flogged and then banished from South Carolina. "If they deserve any punishment," he wrote,
"nothing less than Death Should be the Sentence, & at this critical time no
pardon or mitigation Should be granted." Now his son promoted a plan to
arm slaves, whom Christopher Gadsden had once labeled "precarious property," and other whites regarded as "very dangerous domestics." Doubtless
many legislators pondered the likelihood of a British counterstrike with black
regiments of their own. Prevost's invasion force returned to Georgia with three
thousand slaves; perhaps from that group the British would arm "the most
Enterprising and vigorous Men" and employ them against their former masters. In addition to concerns over the social implications of arming slaves, there
was also the question of emancipation. To be sure, South Carolina already contained a small free black population, and three thousand slaves were a low percentage of the total slave population of between eighty and ninety thousand.
Yet most slave owners realized that offering freedom to some slaves would
cause discontent among the rest. The ramifications extended far beyond the
original three thousand.[43]

Certainly economic motives influenced many men to oppose the idea. As
David Ramsay commented, "White Pride & Avarice are great obstacles in the
way of Black Liberty." Yet there was an additional factor rooted in Carolina
political culture. The proposal asked slaveholders engaged in a struggle for liberty to relinquish their property. To Carolinians, and indeed to eighteenth-
century Americans in general, the foundation of liberty was independence,
which, in turn, was based on ownership of property. Liberty rested not only on
the ownership of property but also on the freedom to dispose of that property
as one saw fit. If they freed their slaves, therefore, Carolina planters placed their
own liberty in jeopardy.[44] Finally, although Congress had installed safeguards,
such as disarming the slaves after the war and allowing whites to determine
whether their service merited freedom, the proposal left unanswered a vital
question: where would these ex-slaves settle after the war? Even southerners
who questioned the morality of slavery held the racist supposition that blacks
were of an inferior nature. Unable "to envision a truly biracial republican society," men such as Thomas Jefferson and George Wythe of Virginia agreed that
colonization, that is, resettlement of blacks outside America, must accompany
the end of slavery. Focused more on an immediate objective—enlisting slaves
to win American independence—than on distant ramifications, John Laurens
apparently never pondered this crucial obstacle to emancipation, a problem
that older, more experienced leaders recognized, yet never resolved.[45]

Even the few supporters of the slave regiment plan in South Carolina were
divided on its efficacy and effects. Advocates such as Daniel Huger and William
Henry Drayton probably viewed the idea solely as a military expedient. To a

lesser extent Henry Laurens shared this view, though he hoped for slavery's eventual demise. David Ramsay ardently wished that slavery be eradicated. Yet he supported the proposal only as a step toward emancipation; based on his observations, he was convinced that slavery had debased blacks and rendered them totally unfit for military service.[46] Only John Laurens unequivocally embraced the plan on both grounds.

Those closest to John offered commiseration. "I learn your black Air Castle is blown up, with contemptuous huzzas," Henry wrote. "A Man of your reading & of your Philosophy will require no consolatory reasonings for reconciling him to disappointment."[47] Henry's remarks, combining consolation with sarcasm, strongly hinted that he hoped John would relinquish his idea for good. Hamilton agreed, but for different reasons. He wanted John to return to more earthy concerns, such as corresponding with his closest friend. In early September Hamilton observed that John was so wrapped up in his own affairs, namely the political maneuvering surrounding the slave regiment proposal, that he had written only one letter since leaving headquarters in March. For his part, Hamilton had dispatched at least five letters southward. "I should have written you more had you made proper return," he added. "But like a jealous lover, when I thought you slighted my caresses, my affection was alarmed and my vanity piqued. I had almost resolved to lavish no more of them upon you." The arrival of Laurens's one letter, however, "disarmed my resentment and by a single mark of attention made up the quarrel. You must at least allow me a large stock of good nature."[48] In this relationship of two self-fashioned men of feeling, Hamilton invariably played the role of the ardent pursuer. Laurens, as he had demonstrated earlier when he failed to answer letters from Kinloch and de Vegobre and when he ignored Martha and Fanny, became distant when separated from a friend or family member by time and space.

Hamilton's protests to the contrary, John did think about his friends to the north, but with a trace of self-indulgent envy. He worried that the British in New York would encounter Washington's army in a decisive battle while he fruitlessly pressed South Carolinians to arm slaves. He spoke of the "many violent struggles I have had between duty and inclination," and seemed to wish to be in two places at once. "If any thing important shd. be done in your quarter while I am doing daily penance here, and making successless harangues," he wrote Hamilton, "I shall execrate my Stars—& be out of humour with the world."[49]

Laurens, it turned out, received another opportunity for military fame, while his friends on Washington's staff remained largely inactive. On 1 September word reached Charleston that Count d'Estaing had arrived off the coast of Georgia with twenty-five ships of the line and about five thousand troops. After a naval victory in the West Indies, d'Estaing had received orders to return to France. Considering those commands discretionary and wanting to atone for the failure at Newport the previous year, he yielded to pleas for assistance from Lincoln and Rutledge. Lincoln ordered Laurens to meet d'Estaing and discuss plans for a joint operation against Savannah.[50]

As Laurens prepared to leave, a French frigate arrived off Charleston bar. François, Viscount de Fontanges, adjutant general of the French force, came ashore to confer with Lincoln. Fontanges informed Lincoln that the French had to act quickly, since at most their troops could stay on shore for eight days. Lincoln promised to supply at least one thousand Americans for the expedition. Both men agreed that it was imperative that the British force at Port Royal Island be isolated. Laurens took notes of the meeting and recorded Lincoln's proposal that the French blockade the town of Beaufort and place vessels at Broad River to prevent Lieutenant Colonel Maitland from reinforcing the garrison at Savannah.[51]

On 6 September, while on board *Languedoc,* d'Estaing wrote to Laurens. He was confident of success, but he remembered the controversy and recriminations that erupted at Newport. Once again, he relied on Laurens to act as mediator and prevent misunderstandings. "I need someone who is living proof of our cause," said the admiral, "who demonstrates to your generals the worth of what we are doing. You will be this, it is not possible to have a better spokesman." John expressed similar goodwill, albeit in hyperbolic fashion. He told d'Estaing that his "presence at this particular moment is like that of a guardian angel. You are going to destroy the common enemy and spread joy and gratitude in every heart."[52]

Lincoln departed Charleston on 8 September with fifteen hundred troops, a majority of whom were militia. A mixed lot, some were seasoned veterans with a martial bearing while others scarcely resembled soldiers. Laurens commanded the South Carolina Continental light infantry and dragoons. He left with high hopes. "It will be our fault if we fall short of a great stroke upon the Enemy at Savanna & Beaufort," he wrote Henry. Heavy rains retarded the army's progress, preventing their arrival at the outskirts of Savannah until 16 September.[53]

To his chagrin, Lincoln discovered that d'Estaing, who reached the town with his troops the previous day, had peremptorily summoned Prevost to surrender, behavior reminiscent of John Sullivan's hauteur at Newport. Prevost stalled and requested a twenty-four-hour truce to consider terms. While the Franco-American force awaited Prevost's reply, Maitland arrived from Beaufort with reinforcements. Their spirits bolstered and their fortifications more secure, the British, who now numbered twenty-five hundred, resolved to fight it out.[54]

As soon as the Americans calmed down from their initial resentment at d'Estaing's clumsy attempt to appropriate the spoils of victory for France, a

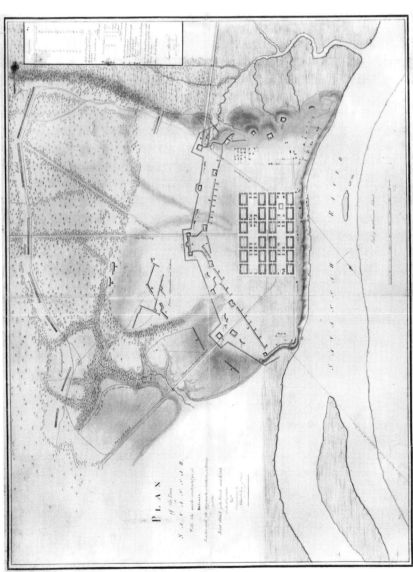

"Plan of the Town of Savannah, with the works constructed for its Defence; Together with the Approaches & Batteries of the Enemy, and the Joint Attack of the French and Rebels on the 9th: of October 1779. From a Survey by John Wilson 71st Regt. Asst. Engineer." William L. Clements Library, University of Michigan, Ann Arbor.

new controversy arose. How had Maitland reached Savannah? Each side
attempted to blame the other. Fontanges denied having agreed that the French
would block the entrance to the Broad River. In fact, while en route to Savannah, d'Estaing, unaware of Fontanges's arrangements with Lincoln, observed
the entrance to the Broad River and ordered ships to block the passage, but
pilots from Charleston refused to guide the vessels into the river. For his part,
d'Estaing believed Lincoln should have pinned Maitland at Beaufort, but
instead the American general came directly to Savannah because of greed for
military glory.[55]

Fontanges harshly criticized the Americans in Laurens's presence. D'Estaing was surprised that Laurens, "a superlatively brave officer . . . took no
offence at what Fontanges said." After all, the admiral reflected, had not Laurens once fought a duel to defend George Washington's honor? He expected
the young man to respond in kind to aspersions against the American army. "It
must be," d'Estaing concluded, "that his conscience reproached him somewhat, imparting a gentleness not natural." By "conscience" the admiral presumably meant that Laurens tacitly conceded that the Americans were to
blame for Maitland's timely arrival. It is more likely that John remembered the
lessons of Newport better than did d'Estaing. Diplomacy, in this instance, prevailed over honor.[56]

With Maitland's arrival, the allies missed their best chance for victory. They
settled down for a siege. After the troops dug trenches and erected batteries,
d'Estaing ordered a bombardment on 3 October. For five days the French batteries rained shells on Savannah. The bombardment terrified civilians, caused
minor casualties and extensive property damage, but left the fortifications largely
intact. D'Estaing had gone far beyond his original eight-day limit for land operations, and the British still held firm. Rather than withdraw and risk the enmity
that followed the Newport siege, the admiral resorted to a tactic that should
have been executed the first day: the allies would storm the garrison.[57]

Located on a bluff along the west bank of the Savannah River, Savannah
was protected on its northern border by a wooded marsh, Yamacraw Swamp.
The defenders had constructed earthworks surrounded by a ditch and abatis—
fallen trees arranged with sharpened edges pointed outward. On the northern
side lay Spring Hill redoubt, considered by both forces as the weak link in the
defenses. D'Estaing decided to direct his main attack there. The marsh allowed
the allies to move unnoticed until they were near the redoubt. Yet there was
enough space between the redoubt and the swamp for additional detachments
to advance toward the river and attack other batteries along the enemy's right
flank. An advance guard of French grenadiers was to storm Spring Hill. The
two main French columns would mount assaults farther down the British right
wing. The French left column was to receive support from two American

columns: the 1st and 5th South Carolina Regiments; and the light infantry, 2nd South Carolina Continentals, and 1st Battalion of Charleston militia commanded by Laurens. Lincoln headed the reserve, composed mostly of Carolina militia and free blacks from the French West Indies.[58]

Because the allies failed to get their troops into position, the assault, scheduled to commence at 4:00 a.m. on 9 October, fell behind schedule. Shortly after daybreak, d'Estaing ordered his French vanguard to attack, even though the main columns were not yet prepared. Unsupported by the rest of the force, these troops, well-defined in their white uniforms, were sitting ducks. Some men reached the enemy lines but immediately fell back. The main columns then launched their assault farther down the British right, but they were also forced to withdraw after a savage struggle.

The Americans fared no better. Count Pulaski, at the head of the cavalry, rode ahead of Laurens's column. While attempting to force a passage through the abatis, he was mortally wounded. Laurens led his troops against Spring Hill redoubt. They cut their way through the abatis and crossed the ditch, eventually reaching the rampart, where they briefly planted the 2nd Regiment flag. At that point their progress ended. They could not climb the high parapet. As the Carolinians crowded on the narrow rampart, unable to take cover, they faced repeated musket volleys from the British at Spring Hill redoubt, while adjacent batteries fired on them from the side. Still the Carolinians did not budge. Lieutenant Colonel Maitland then ordered a bayonet charge, and some of the war's fiercest hand-to-hand combat ensued. Laurens's men fought with desperate bravery, parrying bayonet thrusts, using their muskets as clubs. Soldiers from both sides punched and clawed, kicked and screamed, gripped by a fighting frenzy that stripped away all vestiges of humanity. About an hour later, Laurens sensed that further resistance was futile and withdrew his troops, leaving a heap of bodies behind in the ditch.

Compounding Laurens's problems, he lost contact with much of his force. When Pulaski's cavalry veered left to avoid fire from the garrison, they encountered part of Laurens's column. The momentum of the horses forced the infantry into Yamacraw Swamp. There Laurens met American officers who had just arrived with the second column. Major Thomas Pinckney remarked that "such a scene of confusion as there appeared is not often equalled." Laurens asked if they had seen his men.[59]

Although d'Estaing attempted to rally his disorganized force for another attempt, it was obvious that additional attacks would only waste lives. The battle, the bloodiest for a single side since Bunker Hill, was over. French losses, in particular, were heavy, totaling 151 killed and 370 wounded. The Americans suffered 231 casualties. For their part, the British lost only 18 killed and 39 wounded.[60]

As Laurens's reputation for heroic recklessness grew, stories inevitably abounded about his exploits, some of them wholly apocryphal, some containing elements of truth. One story that initially seems to belong in the former category appeared in Mason Locke Weems's biography of Francis Marion. Weems, hardly known as a careful chronicler of history, described Laurens's reaction to the failed assault. When the retreat was ordered, he looked down on his fallen men and exclaimed, "Poor fellows, I envy you!" He then angrily flung his sword on the ground and left the field. Upon meeting fellow Carolinian Peter Horry, Laurens said, "Horry, my life is a burden to me; I would God I was lying on yonder field at rest with my poor men!" Horry attempted to reason with the disconsolate officer. "No! no! none of that, colonel," he replied, "none of that, I trust we shall live to pay them yet for all this."[61] Before Weems is completely dismissed, one must consider a similar account in John C. Hamilton's biography of his father, Alexander Hamilton. Hamilton described Laurens at the moment of defeat, standing facing the British volleys, "with his arms wide extended," inviting death. When a comrade criticized his display of rashness, Laurens replied, "My honour does not permit me to survive the disgrace of this day."[62] While the stories differ in detail, the point is the same: Laurens recklessly courted death at Savannah, an attitude in keeping with his desire for "Glorious Death, or the Triumph of the Cause in which I am engaged."

Despite Lincoln's protests, d'Estaing decided to terminate the siege. Unable to continue without French assistance, the Americans withdrew on 18 October. After boarding their land forces, the French fleet set sail three days later. D'Estaing returned to France, leaving behind a squadron commanded by Count de Grasse. The admiral had failed again, but unlike the previous year's debacle at Newport, Americans did not vilify him, in part because Lincoln possessed more tact than Sullivan. As he did after the Newport siege, John Laurens praised d'Estaing, "to whom we are as much indebted as if his efforts had been attended with the most complete Success." Ironically, while d'Estaing lost at Savannah, he fulfilled his objective of the previous year. Alarmed by the Franco-American cooperation, Sir Henry Clinton evacuated the garrison at Newport and concentrated his forces in New York. More important, however, the British had maintained their foothold in Georgia, allowing them to plan another attempt on Charleston.[63]

When John returned to Charleston on 21 October, he found that Congress had unanimously elected him secretary to Benjamin Franklin, who now served as sole minister to France. Henry Laurens had mixed emotions about the honor accorded his son. He knew John was qualified for the task. Yet he realized that debates over foreign affairs in general and the Deane affair in particular had caused much dissension in Congress. Service in the diplomatic corps could prove detrimental to "a Man tender of his reputation." While the final decision was up to John, Henry hoped he would refuse the appointment. "If he reads my heart," said Henry, "he will return thanks & decline acceptances."[64]

John's future plans had hinged on the outcome of the operations at Savannah. Prior to leaving for Georgia, he resolved to return to his position as aide-de-camp to Washington if the British garrison capitulated. For the first and only time he displayed some ambivalence about his status as an officer, which heretofore had constituted his public identity and primary avenue to acquire fame. He "might have accepted" the post of secretary to Franklin, he told Henry, "had our Siege been suc[cessful] but in our present circumstances I must decline it."[65] John had returned south with two aspirations—to form a black regiment and help drive out the British invaders—and thus far had accomplished neither goal. His future lay with his native state—while South Carolina faced an impending British invasion, he would not leave.

Although it was obvious that the British would next make a concerted effort to take Charleston, the city remained unprepared. The bitter feelings that surfaced in the spring lingered. Charlestonians felt abandoned. After d'Estaing departed, one man informed Lincoln that "since Congress has exerted itself so little to our Support in Men, we ought to accept the best Terms that can be obtained." The state government remained steadfast in its unwillingness to consider drastic measures to counter the British threat. While Lincoln was too tactful to say it aloud, he saw clearly the limits of revolutionary commitment in the South Carolina low country. He informed Congress "that little may be expected from this State unless they rescind their late resolutions." In the last assembly session the representatives had rejected proposals to fill the Continental battalions with either militia drafts or blacks and refused to place the militia under the Continental articles of war. Lincoln reluctantly provided this information to Congress "because it may seem like a reflection on the State . . . but you ought to know what are our resources, and expectations, or you cannot provide against the worst." Realizing that more help was needed from outside the state, he decided to dispatch Laurens, "whose knowledge in War, and critical observations" would provide "the most perfect intelligence," to Congress to request more aid.[66]

Because d'Estaing had ordered de Grasse to proceed to Chesapeake Bay and obtain provisions, Lincoln believed that this French squadron could escort transport ships loaded with reinforcements for Charleston, thus enabling the troops to avoid the arduous trek by land. John Laurens reiterated this point to his father. If Congress sent an insufficient number of Continentals or directed them to travel overland, he asserted, it would be better to leave them with Washington's main army. He began his journey to Philadelphia on 3 November.[67]

As John prepared to travel north, Henry accepted a new challenge. Congress elected him commissioner to negotiate a loan and a treaty of amity and commerce with the United Provinces of the Netherlands. Despite his belief that diplomatic service brought more retribution than rewards, Laurens doubtless breathed a sigh of relief that he was finally leaving Congress, where he had been the center of controversy since resigning the presidency. Before making the voyage to the Netherlands, he wanted to return to South Carolina, where he would report to the state assembly and attend to his affairs. He departed Philadelphia on 9 November.[68]

John reached Philadelphia eleven days later. During a meeting with congressional delegates, he stressed Charleston's strategic and economic importance to the American cause. If the British subjugated the city, they would obtain a valuable harbor, useful for trade with their islands in the West Indies. Moreover, numerous loyalists in both Carolinas would openly declare themselves and provide the British with an invaluable manpower resource. John's commitment to liberty and independence was unlimited, but he, too, believed in reciprocal obligations. "The terms of the Confederation," he reminded the delegates, "require Congress to exert its force to the utmost" to prevent the fall of Charleston. "Interest & Duty are united."[69]

From Philadelphia he proceeded to Washington's headquarters at Morristown, New Jersey. While there, John learned that the British were preparing to detach a large force from New York. Though their destination was unknown, everyone assumed that Clinton planned to reinforce Georgia. After meeting with his aide, Washington determined that South Carolina and Georgia were "in a more defenceless condition than I had ever apprehended." Prior to Laurens's arrival, the general had dispatched North Carolina's two regiments to Charleston. Now he advised Congress to send the Virginia Continentals southward, a suggestion the delegates readily approved. To Laurens's disappointment, Congress decided that the Continentals would make the trek on foot because de Grasse's squadron had never sailed to the Chesapeake as expected. John worried that the British fleet from New York would reach Charleston ahead of these reinforcements.[70]

Amid these activities, Laurens formally declined the appointment to serve as secretary to Franklin. The appointment was an honor, a sign of Congress's esteem; most young men would have found it impossible to refuse. In fashioning a public identity during the Revolution, a gentleman faced two choices: to be an officer or a statesman. Both roles were honorable, but the former fit Laurens's romantic temperament and youthful energy; military service also provided greater opportunities to win renown. So initially he displayed no ambivalence about his decision. In a letter to Samuel Huntington, the president of Congress, John expressed appreciation for the confidence shown in his abilities. "At the same time," he added, "conscious of my inexperience in politics and diffident of answering their expectations in a commission of such importance, I must request their leave to persevere in a line of duty to which my inclinations as well as profession more naturally attaches me until an honorable termination of the war." He placed his public duty, as he perceived it, over private gain, and concluded with words that accurately reflected his highest personal aspiration—to win fame through selfless acts of virtue. "The motives for declining an appointment, in every private view so flattering to myself," he wrote, "will I hope be a sufficient excuse with Congress. I beg leave to assure them that it is my constant wish to devote myself to the public service, and my greatest ambition to merit their approbation."[71]

Several delegates attempted to change his mind. Huntington told Laurens that he had been the unanimous choice, and it would be difficult to select a compromise candidate because Congress remained divided by factions. One delegate, perhaps James Lovell of Massachusetts, informed John that there was support for the candidacy of Gouverneur Morris, a former delegate from New York, "to whom the world in general allows greater credit for his abilities than his integrity." The delegate vowed to prevent Morris's election. Despite this pressure, Laurens adamantly refused to reconsider.[72]

When John left Philadelphia on 16 December, he immediately had second thoughts: "I fell into a train of serious Reflexion and self examination." He adopted the position of the "impartial spectator" and scrutinized his motives. Had he acted according to the public good, or had he followed his own private desires? Did his decision reveal, to other gentlemen, his disinterestedness or his selfishness? John could not abide the latter possibility:

> I agitated the grand question whether a citizen has a right to decline any office to which his countrymen appoint him, upon what that right is founded, and whether it existed in my case. After undergoing the severest conflict that ever I experienced—sometimes reproaching sometimes justifying myself—pursuing my journey or turning retrograde—I determined that I had been deficient in the duties of a good citizen.

He returned to Philadelphia and met with Huntington and two other delegates. Rather than relent and accept the post as Franklin's secretary, however, John chose a middle course and suggested that Congress consider another option. It was his duty, he said, to "recommend a person equally qualified in point of integrity—and much better in point of ability" than himself. He suggested that Hamilton be nominated for the post. If Hamilton were not an acceptable candidate, concluded Laurens, and it became "absolutely necessary to exclude a dangerous person or to prevent pernicious delays, I shd. think it my duty to obey the orders of Congress." John then informed Hamilton that he would be nominated. "I am sorry you are not better known to Congress," he told Hamilton, "great stress is laid upon the probity and patriotism of the person to be employed in this commission. I have given my testimony of you in this and the other equally essential points."[73]

Congress took new nominations the following day. James Lovell proposed Hamilton. Lovell himself was nominated by William Ellery of Rhode Island. John Mathews of South Carolina put forward Gouverneur Morris. When the vote was held, Samuel Huntington's prediction proved correct: in a two-way race between Morris and Lovell, neither man received the required seven votes. Because the delegates could not resolve the deadlock, the post of secretary remained unfilled.[74]

Hamilton could not have been surprised at the result. He appreciated Laurens's recommendation and coveted the position, but realized his chances were slim because some delegates distrusted him. According to rumors, the young aide had once imprudently wished aloud that Washington and the American people join together to oust a do-nothing Congress. To Laurens, however, Hamilton downplayed this factor, citing instead his lack of property and political connections. His first response to disappointment was to seek a field command so he could join Laurens in the southern campaign, but Washington blocked that alternative. Desperate for military fame, wanting the same opportunities Laurens received yet refused, Hamilton, with his romantic bent, wistfully thought of a martyr's death. He expressed himself in terms that his friend well understood: "In short Laurens I am disgusted with every thing in this world but yourself and *very* few more honest fellows and I have no other wish than as soon as possible to make a brilliant exit. 'Tis a weakness; but I feel I am not fit for this terrestreal Country."[75]

Laurens left Philadelphia on 18 December, before the delegates voted for the second time to choose Franklin's secretary. Thus he conveniently avoided having to fulfill his promise to accept the position if an inordinate delay ensued. While his actions regarding that post clearly indicated his desire to do what was best for the public good, on another occasion prior to his departure he showed that there were limits to his selflessness, that he, too, was subject to private, very human ambition. He asked Congress to rescind his 29 March commission as lieutenant colonel. The delegates had granted the commission under the assumption that Laurens, when he took command of a black battalion, would supersede and thus offend other officers in the South Carolina Continentals. "A mistaken notion that justice to the officers of that line would require my entering as youngest Lt Colonel," said Laurens, "a greater anxiety to avoid infringing the rights of others, than attention to my own, and an eagerness to pursue my journey made me acquiesce." Upon deliberation, however, he realized that the commission made him subordinate to officers who entered the service after he did. He regretted not insisting that the commission be dated retroactively to October 1777, when he officially became aide-de-camp to Washington. With proper deference, he apologized to Congress for any inconvenience. His private ambition and the public good, he believed, were one and the same: "it would argue an indifference to the honor of being in their service, if I did not sollicit a restoration of my rank, when it can be so easily effected." Samuel Holten of Massachusetts moved that Laurens's request be granted; Congress referred the motion and Laurens's letter to the Board of War. There is no evidence, however, that the board ever acted on the matter.[76]

Only eight months had elapsed since John agonized over accepting this same commission. Then the date of the commission was not even an issue; he had worried instead about antagonizing his comrades, especially his brother officers in Washington's official family. Hamilton had gone to great lengths to assure him that his actions had been correct. In fact, the other aides would have found fault with only one thing: a commission dated back to October 1777. Now six months of arduous service in the South had produced a realignment in John's concerns: if others placed limits on their self-sacrifice, why should he relinquish a rank that he considered rightfully his?

His mission fulfilled, Laurens began the journey to South Carolina. Unable to secure passage on a vessel headed south, he traveled on horseback. He was ever the young man in a hurry. "My wish to exclude the possibility of being absent from any Renewal of military operations," John explained to Henry, "and my anxious desire to embrace my dear father before he leaves America, induces me to take what will probably be the surest and most expeditious mode of travelling." The day after Christmas Sir Henry Clinton set sail from New York with almost eight thousand troops. The stage was set for another encounter at Charleston.[77]

Chapter 8

"The greatest and most humiliating misfortune of my life"

The Fall of Charleston

January–December 1780

As John Laurens rode toward South Carolina, he could not foresee the frustrations that lay in wait. His fellow low-country Carolinians would again demonstrate their limited commitment to independence. In the most ignominious American defeat of the war, Charleston would become a British prize. And John would spend six agonizing months as a prisoner of war, a time in which he worried about his honor, fretting over the possibility that he might spend the duration of the conflict on the sidelines as an idle spectator.

Laurens reached Charleston on 11 January and presented to General Lincoln letters from Congress and General Washington. After a separation of over nine months, John was reunited with his father. Henry Laurens spent his time seeking a vessel to carry him to Europe. Though his search proved frustrating, he did not remain idle, but took a seat in the House of Representatives. That body unanimously extended to him their appreciation for his service as a delegate to Congress. John, having assumed command of the marines, accompanied Commodore Abraham Whipple of the Continental Navy on a cruise off the coast of South Carolina. A concerned father could not help reflecting on his son's passion for military service. John, remarked Henry, seemed "determined to pursue the Enemies of his Country in every element."[1]

From his station on board the Continental Navy frigate *Providence*, John wrote his father and asked him to use his "influence to procure the levy of a few black battalions." Congress, during his visit to Philadelphia, restated its recommendation that South Carolina arm slaves. John hoped the renewed

British threat proved "sufficient to awaken our Countrymen from their Lethargy. The measure in question has been so long and absurdly delayed." He reasserted his belief that blacks could tip the balance of power in South Carolina's favor: "They will render much service in the line [as] fatigue and fighting men, as will ensure the safety of our metropolis."[2]

During the brief cruise, Whipple and Laurens searched for signs of the armada from New York. They captured 2 sloops that had been used to transport horses. Laurens examined a logbook and interrogated the prisoners, who told him that the expedition, commanded by Sir Henry Clinton himself, consisted of 140 vessels convoyed by 12 ships of the line. John doubted the validity of these rumors. He knew Charleston was threatened, but he found it difficult to comprehend so vast an enemy force. When Whipple's flotilla spotted a squadron of 14 British vessels anchored off Tybee Island at the mouth of Savannah River, the commodore deemed it prudent to return to Charleston. Having gathered intelligence, it was time to prepare the harbor defenses.[3]

From 30 January until 12 February, John attended the proceedings of the House of Representatives. He apparently urged Lincoln to press the slave regiment issue again, for the general asked Governor Rutledge to either form black battalions or employ one thousand blacks to assist artillery crews and function as laborers. Henry Laurens chaired the committee formed to consider Lincoln's request. If Henry advocated John's plan, he did so in private. On 1 February he read the committee's report, which recommended using one thousand slaves to help man batteries and perform garrison duty but made no mention of black battalions. At some point during the deliberations that first week of February, John brought up the black regiment plan. The House responded that his proposal "was premature . . . and that it ought to be adopted only in the last extremity." An overture to the Privy Council met with even greater disapproval. The councilors refused to leave the door open to the possibility that as a last resort blacks could be armed, and declared "that the plan ought to be removed altogether." Members of the House of Representatives were unwilling even to allow slaves on artillery crews, and amended the committee's report to strike out the word "Artillery." Never one to back down, John refused to concede another component of his proposal—emancipation. As the House of Representatives debated the committee's report, a member—it is hard to imagine anyone but John Laurens—introduced an amendment: "That such of the said Negroes who shall behave themselves during the time they shall be in said service shall be enfranchised at the expiration of their term of service." The House journal merely recorded that the motion received a second, a debate followed, and the issue was voted down. While arming blacks caused them great alarm, Carolina's legislators definitely wanted to avoid freeing nearly a thousand slaves. They had other concerns, namely compensating masters whose slaves were killed, severely injured, or captured while performing public service. An amendment labeled these property owners "sufferers." The House eventually adjourned on Saturday, 12 February, before final action was taken on this report.[4]

Sir Henry Clinton's invasion force, meanwhile, arrived off the coast. On 11 February the British began unloading men and supplies on Simmons (present-day Seabrook) Island at North Edisto Inlet, thirty miles south of Charleston. From there they made a slow trek through the marshes on James and Johns Islands. Despite plenty of advance warning, Charleston had not fully prepared for the British threat. "The Carolinians as usual have been superior to foresight and precaution," John said. "The delay of the enemy produced no other effect than to increase their supineness, and finally to introduce a disbelief of the enemys intentions. But they begin to be roused."[5]

The garrison quickly constructed defenses to protect the northern border of the city. At the center of the line lay an eighteen-gun fortress known as the "old royal work" or "Horn Work," with walls composed of tabby, a mixture of oyster shells, lime, sand, and water. It was flanked by redoubts on both sides. The left works, however, remained detached from the rest of the line, and were thus vulnerable to attack. In front of the fortifications, they dug a canal, six feet deep and twelve feet wide, that stretched across Charleston Neck. "The number of men within the lines [was] uncertain, but by far too few for defending works of near three miles in circumference," observed John, "especially considering many of them to be citizens, and unaccustomed to the fatigues of a besieged garrison, and many of the Continental troops half naked."[6]

Henry Laurens continued preparations for his departure. Lincoln reserved a brigantine to take him to Martinique, an island in the French West Indies; from there he would proceed to the Netherlands. At first inclement weather delayed the departure. Then a more serious obstacle presented itself. The British fleet made its appearance off Charleston in late February, forcing Henry to proceed overland to Georgetown and secure passage on a vessel in that port. With Charleston facing a protracted siege, he felt torn between duty to his country and concern for his property. "In these circumstances," he remarked, "were I to study my own private Interests & desires I should remain here & stand or fall with my Country; whatever her fate may be, exceeding heavy losses to me will be the consequence of my absence at this critical conjuncture." As before, John encouraged his father to place public duty over private concerns. "I hope your success will be equal to your merit," he said, "and that you will establish your own fame while you give stability to the rising empire. Your exertions in the other hemisphere are as essential as ours here."[7]

As the siege prevented the dispatch of letters from Charleston to Europe, John entrusted to Henry a packet for his wife. The father and son said goodbye, not knowing whether they would see each other again. "I strained stoicism to the utmost, before we parted," John confessed a few days later, "but a separation convinces me either that this philosophy is vain, or that I am incapable of it."[8]

The besieged placed much hope on Charleston bar, an immense sandbank that lay outside the harbor. Only small vessels and frigates that lightened themselves could cross the bar. Initially, Lincoln expected Whipple and his fleet to guard the approach to the bar, but the commodore and his officers contended that their vessels could not be anchored close enough to the sandbank to defend its entrance. To trap the garrison at Charleston, therefore, the British navy needed only to pass the bar. On 20 March Vice Admiral Marriot Arbuthnot, the naval commander, sent his frigates and three larger vessels, which had been lightened, over the bar and into the harbor.[9]

Since Whipple's fleet was now vulnerable and useless, Lincoln ordered the sailors and guns ashore to bolster the city's defenses. The Americans scuttled four frigates and "some smaller hulks" at the mouth of the Cooper River. It was imperative that the river stay open. While it remained under American control, John wrote Henry, "the Enemy cannot complete their investiture, we have an opening to receive succours, Refreshments &c and even for Retreat in case of the last necessity."[10]

John knew Charleston could not hold without outside assistance. "As the Enemy is determined to proceed by regular approaches," he wrote Washington, "all his operations are submitted to calculation, and he can determine with mathematical precision that with such & such means in a given time he will accomplish his end. Our Safety then must depend upon the seasonable arrival of such Reinforcements as will oblige him to raise the siege." The North Carolina Continentals, seven hundred strong, arrived on 3 March, but the garrison still awaited the arrival of the Virginia Continentals. To John, the additional Continentals, while important, remained insufficient. He wanted Washington himself to come. "Your Excellency in person might rescue us," he insisted. "All Virginia and NoCarolina would follow you. The Glory of foiling the Enemy in his last great effort, and terminating the war, ought to be reserved for you."[11]

While he probably smiled inwardly at the effusive pleas from his spirited young aide, Washington knew he could not be spared from his position with the main Continental Army at Morristown, New Jersey. "I lament that your prospects are not better than they are," he replied. "The impracticability of defending the bar, I fear, amounts to the loss of the town and the garrison." Thus he believed it best for Lincoln to concede the city and withdraw the army, but he refrained from stating this opinion emphatically. "I suspend a definite judgment," he told John, "and wish you to consider what I say as confidential." Normally a reserved individual, Washington was touched by his aide's letter: "Be assured my dear Laurens that I am extremely sensible to the expressions of your attachment, and that I feel all for you in your present situation which the warmest friendship can dictate. I am confidant you will do your duty and in doing it you must run great hazards. May success attend you, and restore you with fresh laurels to your friends, to your Country, and to me."[12]

On land Clinton continued to move slowly. His force did not cross the Ashley River to Charleston Neck until 29 March. The following morning at 9:00 they marched down King Street Road, the main route to the city. Lincoln placed Laurens in command of a battalion of light infantry and ordered him "to watch the motions of the Enemy and prevent too sudden an approach." After posting his troops in an advanced breastwork, Laurens accompanied by Major Edmund Hyrne, deputy adjutant general of the Southern Department, Laurens decided to reconnoiter the advancing force. They ventured too close, however, and received fire from a flanking party of Hessians, who hid behind trees alongside the road. Wounded in the cheek, Hyrne fell from his horse. Laurens "had barely time to cover his Retreat and drive off his horse."

Upon returning to the safety of his original position, Laurens waited to see what the Hessian vanguard would do next. The Hessians brought up a field piece and sent parties of cavalry and infantry to outflank his battalion. Clinton, however, came up and ordered them to stop. Lincoln, in the meantime, dispatched Jean-Baptiste Ternant, a French officer, with reinforcements and orders that Laurens should avoid a battle. Acknowledging that "the advantages of a serious affair were all on the side of the Enemy," Laurens ordered his troops to fall back, one platoon at a time. As his troops retreated, the two sides continued to exchange fire. A Hessian captain observed that there "were very good marksmen" among the American force. Once Laurens's battalion completed their withdrawal, a small detachment of Hessians occupied the abandoned breastwork.

When Laurens first encountered the enemy, he requested two cannons. That afternoon the field pieces arrived, though he was not sure why, since Lincoln insisted that he avoid a major encounter. John then decided to disobey the letter of his instructions and order a bayonet attack on the position his force had previously held. He did so, he explained, "in order to gratify my young officers," but in reality his behavior followed the pattern set the previous year in the near disaster at the Coosawhatchie River. Overwhelmed by superior numbers, the Hessians fled, leaving behind a dead jaeger who had earlier grabbed Hyrne's hat as a souvenir.

Afterward the two sides exchanged artillery fire while several Charleston women watched from the safety of the fortifications. Despite the loss of Captain Joseph Bowman of the North Carolina Continentals, "a valuable captain of Infantry," Laurens considered the artillery duel a success. "Upon the whole," he said, "it was a frolicking skirmish for our young soldiers." On such occasions eighteenth-century warfare became a stage where gentlemen officers could display their manly virtue before an audience of men and women. At dusk Laurens withdrew his force to the American lines. The opening clash of the siege resulted in minor casualties on both sides. Seven American privates received wounds. One Hessian was killed, two were wounded. Hyrne's facial wound proved minor, but he was out of action for the duration of the siege. Contradicting Laurens's sanguine assessment, one American officer accurately labeled the skirmish "a mere point of honor without advantage."[13]

Laurens's battalion assumed a new position at the "Horn Work." He ordered three of the family slaves—Stepney, Exeter, and Jacob—to work at the lines, where the defenders constructed a lateral redoubt, hoping to secure their right flank. The British commenced siege operations about eight hundred yards from the American lines. They began a parallel, a series of trenches and redoubts. Once the parallel was completed, the redcoats dug saps—trenches that approached the American position—while other troops provided cover from the redoubts. Known as "regular approaches," this process, common to eighteenth-century siege warfare, continued until the assaulting force made the garrison's position untenable, at which point the two sides negotiated surrender terms.[14]

When General William Woodford arrived on 6 April with 750 Virginia Continentals, Lincoln was able to construct batteries on the eastern shore of the Cooper River opposite the city. The British continued their approach. Surveying the American fortifications, Laurens believed that they could withstand an assault, "but must finally yield to a perseverance in regular approaches which appears to be Clintons present plan." Timely reinforcements under Washington, he still hoped, would save the city from surrender.[15]

From headquarters in Morristown, Alexander Hamilton explained that further reinforcements were not forthcoming because "the unanimous sentiment is against it." Lacking supplies and money, the Continentals could not even consolidate their force. "Indeed my friend," continued Hamilton, "our distress is so great that if there were no objection to parting with the men it would be almost impossible to convey them to you." Aware of John's rash temperament, Hamilton concluded with an admonition that in substance resembled Henry's earlier warnings but in tone was tinged with gallantry: "Adieu my Dear; I am sure you will exert yourself to save your country; but do not unnecessarily risk one of its most valuable sons. Take as much care of yourself as you ought to for the public sake and for the sake of Yr. affectionate A. Hamilton[.]"[16]

On Thursday morning, 13 April, the British bombarded Charleston with round shot and combustible bombs known as "carcasses." At that moment, Henry Laurens's secretary, James Custer, was supervising a group of slaves who hurriedly moved family belongings out of the Ansonborough mansion and into the garden. When the house took several direct hits, rendering it "uninhabitable," the work party fled the neighborhood to find a spot beyond range of the British cannons. As houses burned, Governor Rutledge and three members of the Privy Council, among them John Lewis Gervais, left the city. In the event Charleston fell, the council deemed it advisable to send a few civil officials to safety so they could provide at least some semblance of government. In response to the shelling, Lincoln called a council of officers to debate options. Without hope of additional reinforcements, with the supplies dwindling and the fortifications weakened, he considered evacuating Charleston while an escape route was available. In the end, however, he vacillated and deferred a final decision until a later date. The following morning the decision was taken out of his hands: a detachment of British cavalry and infantry seized Monck's Corner, thirty miles north of Charleston at the tip of the Cooper River. Escape was now virtually impossible.[17]

The British artillery did considerable damage to the American fortifications. Noticing that the gunnery crews were now exposed, John Laurens asked how he could help. One officer replied that fascines—bundles of sticks bound together and used to strengthen ramparts—would be helpful, but he doubted there were any "in the beleaguered city." Laurens took his light infantry to his father's famous garden at Ansonborough, where they used the shrubbery to make fascines. They returned to the front line "and repaired the breaches in the fortifications, where most required, and then resumed their post of danger."[18] On 19 April, after the works along the Cooper River had been completed, Lincoln sent Laurens and his battalion to man the battery at Lemprière's Point, at the entrance to the Cooper and Wando Rivers.[19]

By that time Clinton's force was within 250 yards of the American lines. Lincoln sent a proposal to Clinton and Arbuthnot, offering to surrender the city intact if the Continentals and militia were allowed to leave with their arms and supplies. The British commanders found Lincoln's terms unacceptable and practically demanded an unconditional surrender. Laurens remained at Lemprière's Point during the negotiations, but afterward he made it clear that he unequivocally opposed surrender. He retained some hope, even though the garrison's provisions were nearly depleted. "A Country full of resources has by the inactivity of Civil and Staff officers been withheld from the Army which defends it and reserved for the use of the Invaders," he complained to Lincoln. "But it may not be too late to reestablish our affairs, by collect[in]g Negroes & Tools to enable us to keep pace with the Enemy in works, and provision to subsist the Garrison until the arrival of Succours."[20]

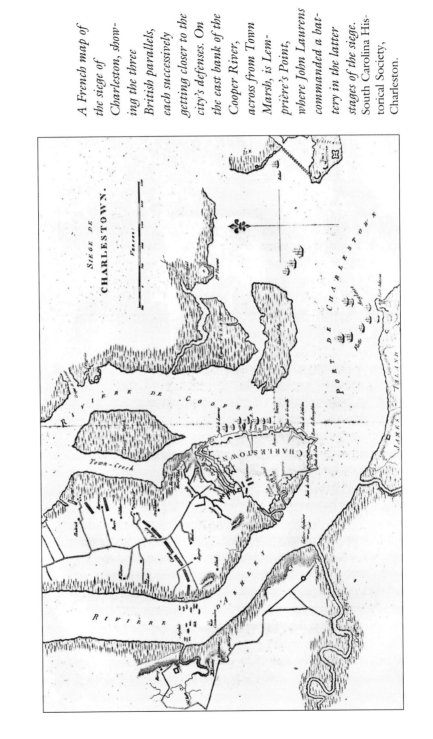

A French map of the siege of Charleston, showing the three British parallels, each successively getting closer to the city's defenses. On the east bank of the Cooper River, across from Town Marsh, is Lemprière's Point, where John Laurens commanded a battery in the latter stages of the siege. South Carolina Historical Society, Charleston.

Laurens's opinion to the contrary, it was only a matter of time before Clinton won his prize. Lincoln ordered Laurens to bring his light infantry into the city on Monday, 24 April. Two days later the garrison received a report that confirmed what many already realized—no relief expedition or additional reinforcements were forthcoming. On 8 May a council of officers voted overwhelmingly to seek surrender terms. Of sixty-three Continental and militia officers present, only eleven advocated continued resistance. Not surprisingly, John was among that group.

When Lincoln attempted to obtain favorable terms for the militia and civilians, Clinton and Arbuthnot refused, and hostilities began anew. Throughout the night of 9 May the British maintained a relentless bombardment. During those terrifying hours, numerous houses went up in flames. Their spirits broken, over three hundred civilians petitioned Lincoln to renew negotiations and accept the terms stipulated by the British commanders.

On 12 May an exhausted and ragged American garrison marched out in humiliation, with their colors cased and their drums beating a Turkish march. Clinton and Arbuthnot refused them the usual honor of marching out with their flags unfurled, while their drums played a march of the victor. It was a standard courtesy of eighteenth-century warfare, in which the victor complemented the vanquished for a brave defense, and the latter, in turn, saluted their conqueror. While losses were light—less than three hundred on each side—almost fifty-five hundred Continentals and militia became prisoners of war, making it the worst setback of the war for the Americans.[21]

Clinton paroled the militia and some Continental officers and allowed them to return to their homes. Laurens waited to depart for Philadelphia with Lincoln. The young man hoped to secure an early exchange. "It is the greatest and most humiliating misfortune of my life," John wrote Washington, "to be reduced to a state of inactivity at so important a juncture as the present." He asked the commander in chief to intervene if possible. As before, he worried that the decisive battle of the war was approaching and he was going to miss it, a prospect he found unbearable. Though Laurens fretted over captivity after only two weeks, he realized that the fall of Charleston, while regrettable, was not disastrous to the cause of independence. "The Loss of this Place," he mused, "does not appear to me of so much general importance to our affairs, as it is usually represented."[22]

Henry Laurens anxiously awaited news of Charleston's fate at Wilmington, North Carolina, where he had sailed, expecting to find a vessel that would convey him to Europe. Once again his plans were thwarted. Compounding his frustration, he found himself temporarily debilitated by an attack of gout. When it became clear that Charleston would fall, he wrote to inform South Carolina's delegation in Congress. Henry could not help reflecting on what might have been had the state assembly adopted John's proposal to raise black battalions. In the process he revealed that his views did not wholly coincide with those of his son. Carolinians, he seemed to imply, should have risked freeing some slaves so that the institution as a whole might be saved. "When we shall have lost our Slaves," he asserted, "we may find it necessary to help ourselves. . . . Had we made a wise disposition of a few of those miserable Creatures to whom we owe some gratitude, we should have saved the whole."[23]

On 12 June John departed Charleston on a truce ship that transported Benjamin Lincoln's staff northward. A few days earlier Sir Henry Clinton had returned to New York, leaving the Earl Cornwallis in command of the southern forces, with instructions to complete the pacification of South Carolina and then to extend British control northward. Their strategy now rested on subjugating the South, a region they believed abounded with latent loyalism. Once the British secured rebellious areas, they would employ the loyalists as a police force, thus allowing the redcoats to invade other regions. Henry, believing Wilmington would soon receive visits from British vessels, decided to proceed to Philadelphia by land, where he would appear before Congress. The Laurenses left South Carolina, one as prisoner of war, the other as reluctant envoy, just as their native state became the dominant battleground of the war.[24]

After Henry made a report to Congress explaining the difficulties he had encountered, the delegates resolved that he leave for the Netherlands as soon as possible. As for John, he had pledged on his word of honor to remain in Pennsylvania until he could be exchanged for a British officer held by the Americans. He could go anywhere within Pennsylvania as long as he did not cross the state's borders. The terms were generous, but John felt trapped, as if he literally were in chains. He longed to be free. It was not possible, Hamilton informed him, for Washington to use his influence to facilitate an exchange. To do so would violate unspoken rules of impartiality. It simply was not fair for Laurens to be exchanged, while officers captured before him remained prisoners on parole. "Don't appear too impatient of your situation nor too solicitous of being freed from it," advised Hamilton. "Though *I* should be satisfied you acted from a laudable desire to be useful; others might give your conduct a construction to your prejudice. You must not have the air of bearing captivity worse than another." Hamilton expected Laurens, as a man of feeling, to feel the pangs of captivity yet project a veneer of resolution before observers. He encouraged his friend to "play the Philosopher if you can and improve your captivity in improving your mind."[25]

While John pondered how to deal with his predicament, Hamilton's correspondence provided some relief from the tedium of captivity. Hamilton announced his engagement to Elizabeth Schuyler, a member of one of the wealthiest and most prominent families in New York. She matched some of the specifications Hamilton listed earlier, namely money. While Schuyler was not beautiful, Hamilton found her "fine black eyes" alluring. Laurens urged Hamilton to marry and get his initial ardor out of his system. "In spite of Schuylers black eyes," replied Hamilton, "I have still a part for the public and another for you; so your impatience to have me married is misplaced." Betsy Schuyler, in other words, would not encroach on the male world of honor, status, and power.[26]

Hamilton also communicated to Laurens his ideas on America's future. The young nation's efforts to finance a war had proved disastrous: Congress borrowed money until its credit was exhausted; excessive emissions of paper money caused rampant inflation; and the Continental Army's old supply problems continued unabated. Believing that the times called for decisive measures, Hamilton proposed convening a constitutional convention to grant Congress greater authority, specifically the power to tax, a prerogative the states refused to relinquish. To improve the nation's credit and to facilitate taxation, he advocated the establishment of a national bank. The bank also presented a partial solution to the army's supply problems, which, he believed, could be further alleviated if Congress instituted a tax in kind and secured a substantial foreign loan. John earlier believed naively that his fellow Americans, as republicans, were bound together by common interests. He had developed no scheme to deal with the country's economic woes beyond a tax on luxuries designed to promote moderate fortunes, which was not surprising since he focused his attention solely on his black regiment plan and the British threat to South Carolina. After three years of frustration, including firsthand experience with the low country's limited commitment to the United States, John was receptive to Hamilton's ideas, including, it seems, a proposal to grant officers half pay for life. That proposal's time had come, Hamilton argued, for half pay had the "advantages of securing the attachment of the army to Congress. . . . We should then have discipline, an army in reality, as well as in name." Neither young man, however, gave much thought to a plan devised to secure the attachment of the common soldiers, who continued to endure privations with a stoicism lacking in their officers. In any event, John expected few concrete changes, at least not immediately. He approved Hamilton's "remedies," but doubted that they "would go down at this time." Hamilton insisted that "necessity must force them down; and that if they are not speedily taken the patient must die."[27]

Laurens's year in South Carolina had been a political education. He saw that appeals to the common good proved unavailing: common interest dictated that the state arm blacks to preserve liberty and prevent the renewal of British tyranny; private interests dictated that masters relinquish no control over their slaves. Because the citizens—and the states—seemed to lack republican virtue, he believed it was imperative that Congress, the symbol of national unity, have greater coercive powers, particularly the prerogative to raise revenue. John's receptiveness to half pay demonstrated that he now understood that the struggle for independence could not subsist on civic virtue alone. Mass mobilization required appeals to rational self-interest. The passion for fame and concern for honor that kept John in service carried less weight with other men, who wanted compensation now, not in a distant, unforeseeable future. John had dreamed of an American republic of virtue whose citizens shared similar interests. Reality forced him to modify his ideas and acknowledge that the republic's citizens held separate interests, quite different from his own. Selfishness, rather than selflessness, spurred others to action. Despite this rude awakening, John remained at heart an ardent republican. If others required an appeal to their self-interest, he would be different, offering his country only himself, pure and disinterested, desiring nothing—both in the present and future—but the approval of his fellow gentlemen, the ones whose opinions really mattered. As a prisoner on parole, however, he could offer his country nothing. He felt helpless and unworthy, and brooded because he could not fulfill his ambition to serve a transcendent cause. Only an exchange would restore him to his rightful place: the officer leading his troops on the battlefield, bringing victory to the cause of liberty.[28]

For a captured officer seeking a speedy exchange, it helped to have friends in high places. On 10 July Thomas Bee, former lieutenant governor of South Carolina and now a delegate to Congress, moved that the Board of War, "[f]or special reasons," work to facilitate Laurens's exchange. To some delegates, this measure smacked of favoritism. Samuel Holten of Massachusetts moved to strike the phrase "for special reasons," but Congress elected to maintain the original wording by a seven to four vote, with two state delegations dividing on the question. The delegates then approved Bee's motion. Resistance to the proposal continued—eight states voted in favor, while five states opposed it.[29]

While John waited for the resolution to produce the desired result, Henry made final preparations for his diplomatic mission to the Netherlands. On 13 August Henry departed Philadelphia on the brigantine *Mercury,* a packet owned by Congress that was considered "an excellent Sea Boat & as fast a sailer as any in America." The father and son postponed their parting as long as possible. John accompanied Henry down the Delaware River until their vessel reached Fort Penn. There they said goodbye, John disembarked, and *Mercury* continued the voyage.[30]

A sixteen-gun sloop of war, *Saratoga,* was to convoy *Mercury* to the Banks of Newfoundland. After six days at sea, however, it was obvious that *Saratoga* could not keep pace with the swift packet. "Considering the Sloop as a very slender defence," Laurens told its captain to return to Philadelphia. On Sunday, 3 September, HMS *Vestal*, a twenty-eight-gun frigate commanded by Captain George Keppel, overtook *Mercury*. When the British fired three warning shots over the packet, the Americans promptly surrendered. Henry noticed that his secretary Moses Young appeared crestfallen. As was his custom, Henry used his philosophy of life—"Whatever happens, happens for the best"—to put a positive face on misfortune. "I feel a satisfaction . . . in being Captured by a British Ship of War," he told Young, "I shall now be sent to England where I shall be of more real service to my own Country than I could possibly be in any other part of Europe."[31]

Keppel proceeded with his prize to St. John's, Newfoundland. When they arrived on 13 September, Henry wrote John and informed him that he had been captured. As the British treated him well, there was no need for John to worry. Henry assured John that he was in good spirits: "through all the changing sc[e]nes of Life, you know my [mi]nd."[32]

Four days later Keppel departed Newfoundland and conveyed his prisoner to England. Upon reaching London, Laurens, contrary to his expectations, received a rude welcome. On 6 October, after being interrogated by prominent officials, he was confined in the Tower of London as a state prisoner on "suspicion of high Treason." The British did allow relatives and close friends to visit Henry—among them was Harry, who had not seen his father for almost five years. On 29 November Martha Manning Laurens brought Fanny to meet her grandfather. In an apparent attempt to avoid the imputation of association with a rebel, Martha used her maiden name during her visit to the tower.[33]

In the meantime, John grew more agitated as he waited to be exchanged. A French army of about five thousand troops under Count de Rochambeau had landed at Newport. If French naval reinforcements arrived and gave the allies superiority at sea, they could commence operations against the British garrison at New York. Laurens worried incessantly that he was about to miss the decisive campaign that appeared in the offing and a last opportunity to win fame. His friends offered encouragement. "For God's Sake, My dear friend," wrote Lafayette, "let's work as hard as we can to get you exchang'd." Believing that Laurens complained too much, Hamilton tendered a gentle reproof. "Tell me not of the difficulty," he said. "I expect you will surmount difficulties which would bear down other men with your sensibility and without your fortitude." In an effort to rationalize his failure to write more frequently, Laurens explained that he could talk only of mundane, personal concerns. Hamilton refused to accept this excuse. "Remember that you write to your friends," he replied, "and that friends have the same interests, pains, pleasures, sympathies; and that all men love egotism."[34]

John followed with great interest Lincoln's negotiations with the British. Lincoln attempted to conclude a prisoner exchange that would liberate his staff and other officers, including Laurens. If this effort proved successful, "the negotiation will make an epoch in our lives, and we shall feel ourselves eternally indebted to you," wrote Laurens with typical hyperbole. "Captivity is such an insupportable evil," he continued, "that I am induced to put in practice every plan for a release, that affords the least glimmering of hope." Lincoln's mediation was his "last resource, and a disappointment would make me capable of rash resolutions."[35]

Though Laurens did not specify what "rash resolutions" he would take, a letter from Hamilton provides a clue. "For your own sake, for my sake, for the public sake, I shall pray for the success of the attempt you mention; that you may have it in your power to act with us," wrote Hamilton. "But if you should be disappointed, bear it like a man; and have recourse, neither to the dagger, nor to the poisoned bowl, nor to the rope."[36] The words are Hamilton's and perhaps were facetious, but most likely he responded to statements contained in Laurens's letter. A reference to suicide was typical of the romantic embellishment the two men often employed. Yet the allusion to self-destruction also suggests that Laurens was capable of contemplating suicide as an alternative when his aspirations were thwarted.[37]

Laurens's identity, indeed his very being, was tied directly to his status as an officer. "An Exchange would restore me to life," he wrote Washington. In this respect he resembled other gentlemen officers. Typical of most was Lieutenant John Kilty, whose reaction to captivity and idleness paralleled Laurens's conduct. "The circumstances I am under," Kilty informed his commanding officer, "must be in the highest degree distressing to an Officer, who prizes the Attributes of that Character above his life." Captivity was, as Laurens termed it, "an insupportable evil," injurious to one's honor.[38]

Like his fellow officers, Laurens valued his honor or reputation above all else. Honor, more than anything, defined a man. Yet for all the similarities with other gentleman officers—the emphasis on status, the importance of honor, the passion for fame—something about John was different, even unsettling. Hamilton noticed that his friend protested confinement too much. On the battlefield he stood apart, too often for the wrong reasons. Laurens's bravery, many contemporaries recognized, verged on recklessness; his conduct violated societal norms. Bravery, to be sure, was expected of any officer, but his exploits displayed a self-destructive bent. He went out of his way to encounter danger and even seemed to court death.[39]

Like his fellow officers, John had his honor to uphold and much to prove. But the imperatives that drove all officers carried even greater weight for John. Military service fulfilled his search for identity, providing him a means to make his mark on the world and win eternal fame. Unable to emulate his father and present to others a life imbued with moral virtue, John compensated with great public achievements. The more he seemingly lacked moral virtue in his private life, the more he labored to prove his worth in the public sphere. Whether on the battlefield, where he repeatedly flirted with danger, or in politics, where his plan to arm slaves invited both financial loss and public scorn, he behaved as the most virtuous and self-sacrificing of all Americans, a man who chose to relinquish everything to a cause more important than life itself, to a duty that transcended love for self and family.[40] The need to be exceptional produced in him a distinctive vulnerability that did not go unnoticed. Laurens's "intrepid spirit was coupled with a self-distrust, a confiding weakness of temper, which awakened in his friends surprise and love," wrote John C. Hamilton in his biography of his father. "While to others his heart was all kindness and benevolence, he was unjust only to himself; and while the world saw him graced with every virtue, he was still aspiring to some higher excellence,—an ideal perfection, which is denied to our nature, and exists only in the warm conceptions of a mind deeply tinged with romance." To a degree his friends understood and admired his aspirations, even as they deplored his methods. "No man possessed more of the amor patria," Washington wrote of his aide, "in a word, he had not a fault that I ever could discover, unless intripidity bordering upon rashness, could come under that denomination; & to this he was excited by the purest motives."[41]

Laurens won renown for his heroism in battle. More successfully than anyone else, he played the role of the disinterested young republican gentleman and received the applause of public men. Yet he never found fulfillment in his accomplishments. In aspiring to do more he initiated a vicious cycle: as his aspirations rose, he found it increasingly difficult to attain success, and his self-image deteriorated. And so it went. There were never enough opportunities for him to prove himself. In South Carolina to introduce the black regiment plan on which he had staked his reputation, he worried about missing major military actions elsewhere. At the Coosawhatchie River he disobeyed orders and turned a routine assignment into a near disaster. In the Charleston siege he initiated an unauthorized artillery duel before an audience of men and women. John desired, it seemed, to perform the final intrepid act in the climactic battle of the war. His continual risk-taking involved more than an outward combat against British tyranny; he also engaged in personal combat against an inner self he had rejected, the irresolute man who lacked self-control.[42]

In defying danger on the battlefield, Laurens literally flirted with death. Death was no stranger to him. In a sense he had struggled with death his entire life. He grew up in a fragile, unhealthy environment that provided constant reminders of the fleetingness of life. As a child, he witnessed the deaths of two siblings—his older brother Henry and his sister Nelly. As an adolescent, he lost his mother, a death that produced ambivalence and emotional confusion. As a young man, he saw Jemmy die after a tragic accident, and again felt ambivalence, his grief mixed with guilt. As an officer, he now pursued fame, which constituted a denial of death. John knew that the hero who sacrificed his life for his country merited renown in posterity. Death did not annihilate that man, removing him from historical memory; rather, he was enshrined in the annals of his country. Small wonder, then, that Laurens chafed as a prisoner on parole. Forced inactivity removed him from the public stage, where each heroic exploit and each brush with death potentially brought him closer to symbolic immortality.[43]

The manner in which a man met death defined his life for posterity. Because honor and fame were bestowed by an audience, the world became literally "a theatre for heroism." Regardless of an individual's personal failings, his willingness to die for a transcendent cause exonerated him in the eyes of posterity. A heroic death, in short, granted a man absolution for his prior sins.[44] During the Revolution, John André provided the ultimate example of a courageous death that produced redemption.

André, the adjutant general of the British army, served as courier during the plotting that led to the treason of Benedict Arnold, the most successful American battlefield general. Only the capture of André foiled Arnold's agreement to surrender West Point, a strategically vital fort that protected access to the Hudson River. Because André was apprehended behind American lines while wearing civilian clothing, his captors had no choice but to sentence him to be hanged as a spy. While the traitorous Arnold managed to escape, André met his death bravely, as befitted a gentleman. His refined manners and gallantry won him the admiration of all American observers, who focused more on his comportment and less on the carelessness that led to his capture.[45]

No American lamented André's death more than Hamilton. He poured out his feelings in a letter to Laurens. Both young Americans doubtless identified with André as their counterpart on the British side, a man suddenly cut down at "the height of his career," a fate they could well envision for themselves. But in large part Hamilton reacted so emotionally because he witnessed another man win lasting fame by confronting death with equanimity. André, in short, had lived and died by the code of honor that Laurens and Hamilton revered. "I am aware that a man of real merit is never seen in so favourable a light, as through the medium of adversity," observed Hamilton. "The clouds that surround him are shades that set off his good qualities." It was essential, therefore, that the man endure misfortune before an audience, his display of virtue becoming a theatrical event. "His spectators who enjoy a happier lot are less prone to detract from it, through envy," Hamilton wrote, "and are more disposed by compassion to give him the credit he deserves and perhaps even to magnify it."[46] In public, heroic death lay the ultimate vindication.

Compelled to remain in Pennsylvania, Laurens could only experience the shock of Arnold's treason and the tragedy of André's execution through letters and newspaper reports. While impatiently awaiting an exchange, he sat before the artist Charles Willson Peale. Peale painted a miniature portrait that reveals a handsome young officer in his prime. His hair powdered, Laurens wore a dark blue uniform with yellow facings, gold buttons, and epaulettes. Laurens's personal charm and vitality are clear: his sharply angled features express determination; adding to the effect are his piercing blue eyes, dark eyebrows raised with an air of inquisitiveness, an aquiline nose, and lips pursed in a slight smile. His self-presentation reveals a combination of confidence and pride bordering on arrogance.[47]

By early November he finally received his wish. Along with Lincoln, he was included in a general prisoner exchange that involved over six hundred officers and privates. Without the intervention of Congress, which made Laurens's exchange a priority, it is doubtful that he would have been liberated so soon. Other officers captured at Charleston remained prisoners on parole for almost two years.[48]

John immediately asked Washington for permission to return south for the next campaign. "I profess myself too much a continentalist to be affected by local interests," he said, "but I indulge a hope that my acquaintance with the country and connexions as a southern man may enable me to be of some utility in the new theatre of the war." Washington freely granted his aide's request. "The motives which led you to the Southward are too laudable," observed the general, "and too important not to meet my approbation." He informed Nathanael Greene, the new commander of the Southern Department, that he could expect Laurens's services.[49]

Before John could begin his journey southward, he once more found himself entangled—against his will—in congressional factional politics and wrangling over foreign policy. As before, the issue was Benjamin Franklin. The septuagenarian minister failed to provide Congress with frequent, detailed accounts of his service in France and news of the European political climate. Within Congress there was renewed interest in appointing a secretary to assist Franklin. In response to Franklin's repeated requests for assistance with mercantile concerns, the delegates elected William Palfrey, former paymaster general, to serve as United States consul in France. They hoped Palfrey would facilitate the dispatch of military supplies from France. Several delegates, either because they distrusted Franklin or believed he was over the hill, wanted to take stronger action. Congress thus considered nominating a special minister to negotiate a loan with France.[50]

While both supporters and opponents of Franklin realized that the appointment of a special minister would embarrass him, there was more than political conniving behind the idea. Pressing economic needs demanded immediate attention. With the public credit exhausted, the army existing on a day-to-day basis, unsure if essential supplies would arrive, and with the British posed for a major offensive in the South, the Americans desperately needed more financial and military assistance from the French. In addition to desiring naval superiority, which would allow the allies to take the war to the redcoats, Congress wanted to obtain a loan of twenty-five million livres. Since France had supplied ten million livres to the American cause the previous two years combined, this new request was at best unrealistic. Still, the delegates hoped that an emissary with up-to-date knowledge on the state of the army and the economy would succeed in prying open the French treasury.[51]

On 9 December four men were nominated for the post of envoy extraordinary to France. Among them were Laurens and Hamilton. When the delegates voted two days later, Laurens was elected unanimously. John carefully weighed his response. He was "sensible that the duties to which a citizen is called by his country ought in general to be considered indispensable." Yet, he believed, "particular circumstances in my case . . . create an exception to the general rule." Again, he chose to refuse an appointment offered by Congress and suggested Hamilton as the attractive alternative. "Congress have it in their power on the present occasion to command the services of a man superiorly qualified in every respect to accomplish the object in view," Laurens explained in a drafted response. "A firm persuasion that the public interest will be promoted by his appointment, and a hope of being useful in the military line to which my studies have been principally directed, dictate my conduct." Having constructed a public identity as an officer, Laurens had no desire to serve as a diplomat, a role that required cautious diligence rather than reckless bravery. From a more immediate standpoint, Congress had interrupted his plans to reintroduce his proposal to form a black regiment. With Charleston in British hands and the state of South Carolina virtually subjugated, he apparently concluded that his distressed countrymen would now agree to arm slaves. He already was making the necessary arrangements. Out of his own funds, he acquired clothing for the regiment and contracted with the commissary of military stores to repair four hundred "Stands of Arms." While there seemed a chance of success, he wanted to pursue the idea that had consumed his thoughts for over two years. Realizing that some delegates would question his motives—after all, his refusal of the secretary's post had resulted in that position remaining unfilled—he concluded his letter with an apology: "My motives being those of the general good to which I profess myself devoted, will not I hope be disapproved by Congress."[52]

Hamilton again desired a post awarded to his closest friend. Lafayette, well aware of Laurens's rash temperament and perhaps concerned about potential clashes with his countrymen, favored Hamilton and lobbied on his behalf, hoping to secure his election. Nevertheless, the Carolinian remained Congress's first choice; it appeared he was the only nominee on whom the delegates concurred. Either they remained unaware of Hamilton's ability, as Laurens concluded, or they still remembered his earlier controversial statement advocating a military coup. Several delegates pressed John to acquiesce, contending that his refusal would lead to "the total failure of the business." It all closely resembled the scenario of the previous year, except this time he gave in to pressure and changed his mind. John never sent the letter refusing the post, and wrote a new one, in which he emphasized that he accepted the commission with great reluctance, because it had "assumed the form of an indispensable Duty."[53]

On 21 December, the day Laurens's letter of acceptance reached Congress, James Duane of New York moved that the new emissary's appellation be changed. It was more than a matter of semantics. The title of envoy extraordinary suggested that Congress intended to supplant Franklin, a connotation his supporters wanted to avoid at all costs. As Thomas McKean of Delaware observed, "the appointment of an Envoy on this occasion seems to imply a want of confidence in our Minister's attention, abilities or something else." With the notable exception of the South Carolina delegation, Congress voted to change Laurens's title to minister.[54]

"Devoted to the public service, my first wish is to be instrumental on all occasions in promoting it," Laurens wrote Washington, "but I feel a diffidence in the present which nothing but Your Excellency['s] particular instructions and couns[el] can counteract." He found reassurance, he admitted, only in the prospect of a forthcoming meeting with his commanding general.[55] With much trepidation Laurens undertook the most important assignment of his public career. He was a neophyte diplomat, and he knew it.

Chapter 9

"His inexperience in public affairs"
Special Minister to France
December 1780–September 1781

While Congress directed John Laurens to secure from the French a loan, supplies, and assurances that they would achieve naval superiority in American waters, astute observers realized that the former objective was most important. As Alexander Hamilton explained, "A loan of money is the *sine qua non.*" The delegates instructed Laurens to obtain from the French favorable terms for repaying the loan; they preferred to defer payment on the principal and interest as long as possible. Furthermore, Congress emphasized that disbursements to the United States be made in specie.[1]

Delegates who supported Benjamin Franklin realized that he would perceive Laurens's appointment as an affront. Slightly apprehensive at the prospect of dispatching a young, untested diplomat on a critical mission, they included in Laurens's instructions a directive to consult Franklin and take advantage of his experience. Congress informed Franklin of Laurens's imminent arrival, assuring him that the young man came because his service in the army qualified him to give up-to-date information on America's faltering military and financial fortunes. If Franklin received this notice before Laurens reached France, he was to initiate negotiations for the loan and supplies immediately.[2]

Laurens did not expect to obtain the entire loan requested by Congress, but he hoped to come as close to that sum as possible. Like previous American diplomats, he began with no practical experience; he would learn from on-the-job training.[3]

To assist him as secretary, Laurens chose Major William Jackson, a native of South Carolina and former aide-de-camp to Benjamin Lincoln. His first choice for that position had been Thomas Paine. The author of *Common Sense,*

Laurens believed, would prove useful when it came time to present to the French in writing a convincing case for additional aid. Aware that he was detested by many delegates in Congress—in large part because of his biting attacks, in league with Henry Laurens, against Silas Deane and Robert Morris—Paine declined the offer, but he agreed to accompany John in an unofficial capacity. Paine had ulterior motives. A controversial figure, embittered because he believed his adopted country did not appreciate his contributions to the war for independence, he longed to retreat to Europe. Laurens's mission provided him that opportunity.[4]

Another factor may have led Laurens to Paine. The pamphleteer was influential in shaping American views of international relations. He had injected an element of idealism in the arena of foreign affairs, where issues were normally decided by power rather than moral considerations. Paine envisioned an independent United States fashioning a new world, where open commerce between nations promoted mutual understanding and peaceful relations. Laurens provided no written evidence that he had thought that far into the future. Up to now John's ideas, including his black regiment plan and his endorsement of constitutional reforms, were connected primarily to winning the war. The amateur diplomat did grasp the fundamental reality of European diplomacy—that questions of power and interest dictated the decisions of nations. With that understanding and with a single-minded focus on gaining money, supplies, and naval support for the American war effort, John departed Philadelphia.[5]

When Laurens began his journey to headquarters to confer with General Washington, he left behind one man who neither supported the appointment of a special minister nor expected the mission to prove successful. That man was the Chevalier de La Luzerne, the French minister to the United States. From the beginning, La Luzerne discouraged Congress from seeking additional loans from France. He believed the groundwork for Laurens's mission was overstated; dispatching a diplomat with a letter of credence addressed to Louis XVI, he warned, could prove potentially damaging to American influence abroad if the mission failed. Most likely La Luzerne prompted the delegates to change Laurens's title from envoy extraordinary to minister. While La Luzerne publicly predicted that little aid would be forthcoming, privately he informed Count de Vergennes, the French foreign minister, that the Continental Army desperately needed relief, as the soldiers continued to endure lack of pay, clothing, and provisions.[6]

A crisis erupted before Laurens reached Washington's headquarters at New Windsor, New York. Some common soldiers had finally reached the limits of their endurance. On 1 January one thousand troops of the Pennsylvania line encamped at Morristown, New Jersey, revolted and marched toward

Philadelphia to seek redress for their grievances. Laurens learned of the mutiny as he traveled through New Jersey with Lafayette. The marquis and Major General Arthur St. Clair, ranking officer of the Pennsylvania line, journeyed ahead to Princeton, where the soldiers had halted temporarily to meet with their commander, Brigadier General Anthony Wayne. When Laurens arrived, the troops grew nervous at the sight of so many officers; suspecting subterfuge, they told their superiors to leave. Laurens and his companions heeded the warning and left for Morristown.[7]

On 7 January Laurens wrote to Washington from Morristown. As usual John had complete faith in Washington and expected him to arrive in person to end the mutiny. Having observed the mutineers, John was "persuaded nothing but a superior investing Force, will induce them to reason." Lafayette and St. Clair, in separate letters, concurred with this assessment. The soldiers appeared confident, Laurens noted, and had appointed their own officers to lead them. "In my opinion the sooner decisive measures are taken," he concluded, "the greater facility there will be in terminating this unhappy affair, and the fewer lives will be sacrificed."[8]

Unable to assist the Pennsylvania officers, Laurens and Lafayette continued toward headquarters and arrived on 11 January. Washington, despite Laurens's expectations, wisely stayed put, allowing the civil authorities of Pennsylvania to negotiate with the mutineers. A settlement reached on 8 January granted the troops immunity, new clothing, eventual back pay, and discharges for those whose terms of enlistment were under dispute.[9]

On 15 January, after Laurens consulted Washington at New Windsor, Alexander Hamilton drafted the commander in chief's impressions of America's capacity to continue the war. Washington admitted that the young nation had made mistakes in its fiscal policy, but he emphasized that abundant natural resources would allow the Americans to repay a loan promptly once independence was secured. His arguments, sharpened by Hamilton's pen, gave Laurens the basis for his appeal to the French ministry and boosted his confidence. Laurens drafted Washington's letter to Governor John Hancock of Massachusetts. Congress had ordered the frigate *Alliance,* moored at Boston, to convey Laurens to France. Washington urged Hancock to use his influence to procure a crew and supplies so the vessel could set sail without delay.[10]

Laurens reached Boston, only to find that the frigate was not ready for departure because of a lack of money and manpower. In an appeal to the state legislature, he expressed surprise that a state "which took the lead in the present glorious Revolution, and has ever been distinguished for its energy, will refuse so trifling a succour, when the most extensive and important consequences are to be derived from it." Despite John's efforts to shame the representatives into action, the General Court, in accordance with the state's constitution, refused to authorize an impressment.[11]

The General Court did, however, provide specie to pay volunteers from the garrison at Castle William, a fortress in Boston harbor. With the addition of those troops and volunteers from the Continental army recruited by Laurens's old commander Benjamin Lincoln, there were enough sailors to man the vessel. The presence of the new recruits made John rest easier, as they served "as a counterbalance" against several British prisoners who had been enlisted earlier.[12]

As Laurens waited to depart, letters arrived with instruction and encouragement. Washington informed him that part of the New Jersey line mutinied on 20 January. This time Washington decided to use force to quell the uprising. A detachment of New Englanders surrounded the mutineers, who promptly surrendered. Two mutinies in one month starkly demonstrated not only that the rank and file's store of fortitude was exhausted but that the objectives of Laurens's mission were of critical importance to the American cause. Washington, with more intensity than usual, reiterated the need for more French support at sea: "How loud are our calls from every quarter for a decisive Naval superiority, and how might the enemy be crushed if we had it!"[13]

Lafayette wrote several letters to his contemporaries in France, recommending Laurens and asking them to render him assistance. The marquis, who had supported Hamilton's candidacy for the position of special minister, advised Laurens to keep his emotions in check. "I am Much affraïd, My dear Sir, You will Not Get the Whole of the Sum," he wrote. Should the French ministry fail to respond favorably to American requests for aid, Lafayette asserted, it would be because they believed their finances were insufficient. "So that don't Get Angry," he concluded, "and Be sure that theyr Intentions Are Good." Despite the marquis's efforts, many, if not all, of these letters did not reach Laurens before he departed for France.[14]

With the possible exception of Henry Laurens, Hamilton understood John's temperament better than any other man. He knew that his friend's recklessness, while sometimes appropriate on the battlefield, occupied no place in diplomacy. A successful diplomat was circumspect rather than direct. After reassuring Laurens that he was confident in his abilities and harbored no ill feelings about his election as special minister, Hamilton offered wise advice on diplomatic protocol: "In the frankness of friendship allow me to suggest to you one apprehension. It is the honest warmth of your temper. A politician My Dear friend must be at all times supple—he must often dissemble. . . . I suspect the French Ministry will try your temper; but you must not suffer them to provoke it." On occasion, Laurens should admit that Congress had made mistakes, yet attribute those errors to the "inexperience" of a young nation.

"When you wish to show the deficiency of the French Administration," Hamilton wrote, "do it indirectly by exposing the advantages of measures not taken rather than by a direct criticism of those taken. When you express your fears of consequences have the tone of lamentation rather than of menace." From the French perspective, the Americans derived the greatest benefits from their alliance. It was best, Hamilton recommended, that John concede this point yet still "take every proper occasion of showing the advantages of the revolution to France without however seeming to insist upon them."[15]

On Sunday evening, 11 February, *Alliance,* commanded by Captain John Barry, set sail from Boston. The voyage proceeded smoothly until Thursday evening. Suddenly, at about 9:00, a loud crash rang out. At first the crew thought the vessel had run aground or hit a rock. When they viewed the area around them, they found that the ship was surrounded by a sea of icebergs. The wind increased to gale strength, tearing one of the sails in half. There was nothing Barry could do but order the ship to lay to, leaving their fate to the wind. Having defied death in several actions on land, Laurens now experienced a close call at sea. About two hours after *Alliance* first encountered the icebergs, a large chunk tore away the ship's larboard quarter gallery, where he had been standing a minute beforehand. "The pleasure occasioned by his escape," Paine said, "made us for a while the less attentive to the general danger." For almost seven hours, the ship was buffeted by wind and ice. Finally, *Alliance* cleared the icebergs and they "began to hear the agreeable noise of the water round the sides of the ship." After daybreak, when the crew and passengers sighted a large mountain of ice, they could not help wondering how many icebergs of similar size they had passed or almost struck the previous night.[16]

On 9 March *Alliance* reached the port of L'Orient. Laurens discovered that William Palfrey, the newly appointed consul who was to assume responsibility for transporting goods secured from France, had not arrived. The fears that Palfrey's vessel had been lost at sea proved true. His death made John's job more difficult: now he had to personally handle mercantile arrangements and ensure that any specie or supplies he obtained were shipped promptly to America.[17]

Laurens originally intended to travel immediately to Passy, the Paris suburb where Benjamin Franklin resided, but he delayed his departure upon learning that the Marquis de Castries, minister of the marine, was expected to pass through L'Orient. Castries was on his way to Brest to supervise logistical arrangements for a naval squadron destined for the West Indies. When two days passed without any sign of the marquis, Laurens left for Passy. On the way he encountered Castries. During a brief meeting, Laurens stressed the importance of French naval supremacy in American waters. Castries hedged, being unable to provide the guarantees John desired. He explained that plans had already been made to station in the Caribbean twenty ships of the line under the Count de Grasse, whose primary concern was to protect France's valuable sugar islands and coordinate operations with her Spanish allies. That fall de Grasse would detach ships to the North American coast; the allied army, therefore, should be prepared to cooperate in combined land-sea operations. Beyond that, Castries refused to give Laurens more specific details, in part because he believed republics like the United States, where power was diffused, were "unsuited to secrecy."[18]

Laurens proceeded to Passy, where he arrived on 15 March. He found that Franklin had not been idle. When the old doctor received the dispatches from Congress explaining the need for a loan and informing him of Laurens's appointment, he promptly applied to Count de Vergennes for additional aid. Because of the depreciation of American currency, Vergennes asserted, the young country's credit in Europe was poor and it would be impossible to grant the large loan requested by Congress. The French instead responded with a gift of six million livres. As an expression of their doubt in Congress's financial judgment, they insisted that only Washington could employ the money to purchase supplies for the army.[19]

In the same dispatch to Congress that announced the gift, Franklin, citing his age and poor health, asked to be replaced. As this move coincided with the news of Laurens's arrival, it is more likely that pique induced him to retire. In Congress reaction depended on how individual delegates viewed Franklin. His opponents attributed the resignation to Laurens's appointment, and there was even speculation that the young man would become the new minister plenipotentiary to France. To Franklin's defenders, the gift of six million livres proved that there had been no need to dispatch Laurens in the first place. "Your having negotiated the business for which he was sent before his arrival," wrote one delegate to Franklin, "proved, that his errand was unnecessary."[20]

John was well aware of two suppositions of European diplomacy—that it was imperative that the balance of power be maintained, so no one nation grew too strong and eclipsed others, and that states invariably acted according to their own interests.[21] Over the next two months, these ideas influenced his tactics in meetings with Charles Gravier, Count de Vergennes. To obtain his objectives Laurens needed to persuade Vergennes that American wants were indispensable and not unreasonable. A career diplomat, Vergennes was prudent, tireless, and totally devoted to preserving and strengthening the dominion of his sovereign, Louis XVI. To achieve that end he sought to restore the balance of power in Europe. Great Britain, by virtue of victory in the Great War for the Empire, had upset that delicate balance. In pledging to support American independence, Vergennes operated under the assumption that the loss of the colonies would weaken Britain and make her equal to France. By 1781, however, he had grown impatient with the Americans, who relied too much on financial support from France. The Continental Congress and its army, he believed, needed to awaken from their lethargy and do more to achieve independence. By the time Laurens arrived, Vergennes even pondered ending the war on the basis of status quo, requiring the British to relinquish New York but allowing them to hold South Carolina and Georgia.[22]

Vergennes could not ignore the mounting costs of financing the war. Notwithstanding the reforms of the director general of finances Jacques Necker, France's obsolete fiscal system was encumbered with mounting debt and the country tottered on the brink of collapse. Either Laurens was unaware of French financial woes or he conveniently chose to ignore them. In any event, his insistence that France could, and should, do more placed him at odds with Vergennes from the start.[23]

In his first conference with Vergennes, Laurens stressed that the gift of six million livres obtained by Franklin was inadequate. His country, he warned, was dangerously close to "being reduced to the british domination." Terrible consequences loomed ahead if France refused to grant the aid requested by Congress. John painted an ominous picture, an image he brought up continually in the weeks ahead. The thirteen colonies, he contended, had long been the source of Britain's strength. If American "commerce and those resources of wealth and power" were "restored to the tyrant of the European Seas, The ancient rival of France," the scales of power would be tipped in Britain's favor indefinitely.

John then presented to Vergennes a memorial that included extensive extracts from the 15 January letter furnished by Washington. Since the credit of Congress was bad, Laurens suggested that the French offer a loan guaranteed by Louis XVI. After all, he argued, French finances were sound, and an additional loan would "be infinitely more advantageous, than suffering the war to languish by affording partial and inadequate assistance." Along with the memorial, Laurens delivered the Board of War's list of supplies needed for the American war effort.[24]

The American "demands are excessive," Vergennes responded. It appeared that they intended to have France carry the entire "burthen of the war" upon her shoulders. France, he explained, had already incurred great expenses from prosecuting a world war and her finances were strained to the limit. Still, he assured Laurens that the French would provide all the assistance within their power.[25]

There remained the additional question of American supply needs. Vergennes asked Laurens to submit a revision of the Board of War's list, including only "the articles of most urgent necessity." After consulting with Franklin, Laurens responded with a list that included artillery, small arms, ammunition, clothing, and medical supplies. He preferred that the clothing be made in France if it could be ready for the upcoming campaign. If not, he asked that the fabric be sent to America. "It may be necessary to remark to Your Excellency that the want of cloathing has been one of the great obstacles to recruiting our Army," he told Vergennes, "and, that altho' the distresses arising from this defect have been hitherto borne with unexampled patience by the Soldier they are now become unsupportable." Time was the most pressing factor. Laurens emphasized that his country needed the supplies and funds without delay, "that the success of the common Cause depends upon it."[26]

Vergennes directed the list to the War Department. For the time being, he postponed a final decision on Laurens's requests until the Marquis de Castries returned to Paris. "My expectations are very moderate," John admitted, but he continued to press his case. In his zeal to obtain as much aid as possible, he went too far and forgot Hamilton's advice to be circumspect and indirect; instead, he allowed himself to be swayed by jealousy, the same attitude of suspicion that had colored his opinions of Thomas Conway and Charles Lee. He wondered aloud if the French had been devious, that "instead of being actuated by a generous and enlightened policy, the Court of France had systematically protracted the war, in order that Britain and America might mutually exhaust themselves, while she had reserved her power to decide only in the last extremity." If France indeed conspired in this way, John announced, the time for intervention had arrived: America had reached "the last extremity."[27]

The French ministry ignored this affront and reminded Laurens that their credit, though sound, was not without limits. Moreover, Vergennes was disturbed by Congress's resolution of 18 March 1780, in which the delegates repudiated the depreciated Continental currency, an act that was a virtual declaration of bankruptcy. "The administration of the American Finances," the French concluded, "was not calculated to inspire confidence." It was impossible, John replied, to sustain "paper credit without a foundation of specie." The loan he sought would go a long way toward establishing that support.[28]

Laurens also emphasized the need for additional French naval support. When Castries returned to Versailles, the young diplomat observed indiscreetly that the marquis's absence had delayed "the most important decisions relative to the common cause of France & America." He reminded Castries of an obvious point—the foundation of British military might was their navy. British naval supremacy proved essential to their success during the siege of Charleston. It was imperative, John said, that French "naval superiority be permanently maintained on the American Coast." Assurances that the French navy might achieve momentary supremacy were woefully inadequate. The "success of all military operations and the event of the war," Laurens contended, "depend directly and even exclusively on the State of the maritime force in

America." As before, the stubborn Castries was noncommittal, though he assured Laurens that there was a strong possibility of at least temporary French naval superiority in the upcoming campaign.[29] Laurens's insistence on permanent mastery at sea probably annoyed the French ministry. They did not need a youthful American to tell them that naval dominance was crucial to winning the war, but they simply lacked an armada capable of matching the stronger British navy in a global conflict.[30]

On 1 April Laurens received an invitation to come to Versailles from Dominique-Louis Ethis de Corny, the commissary of war. The Marquis de Ségur, the minister of war, had appointed Corny and the Chevalier de Veimerange, an intendant general of the army, to confer with Laurens. For several days, the three men discussed how to procure the requested supplies. Laurens initially hoped that clothing could be obtained from military surpluses, but he discovered that French regiments made individual contracts, so there was no stock of clothing available. Corny and Veimerange did agree to release to him clothing stored at Brest, which originally had been intended for Rochambeau's army. While this quantity fell far short of his request, he had no choice but to accept their offer.[31]

Thus far Laurens's efforts had produced little. While at Versailles he continued to pester Vergennes for a definite and favorable answer to his supplications. "Mr. Laurens is worrying the minister for more money," Franklin commented wryly, "and we shall I believe obtain a farther sum." His prediction proved accurate. On 8 April Vergennes notified Laurens that the king had agreed to guarantee the principal and interest of a loan of ten million livres that would be opened in the Netherlands. And the French had decided that the costs of the clothing and military supplies were to be subtracted from the gift of six million livres obtained by Franklin.[32]

Laurens expressed gratitude, but then observed that the loan fell far short of American needs. He requested that the arms and ammunition, which came from French arsenals, be granted to the United States on credit. The clothing alone, he observed, consumed much of the six million livres. In addition, he reminded Vergennes that it would take at least three months for the loan in Holland to be approved and opened. "A single instant is precious," Laurens said, "the least delay becomes of the most dangerous consequence." To expedite matters, he asked that Louis XVI grant the ten million livres out of the royal treasury, which would be reimbursed when the loan was opened: "This arrangement it appears to me can be attended with no possible inconvenience to the finances of France."[33]

John stressed that shipments of specie be sent to America promptly. Though he urged Vergennes and Necker to provide immediate remittances, two obstacles blocked his requests. Fearful of a capture at sea, the French court had no intention of forwarding a large sum of money. And out of the gift of six million livres, Laurens could carry with him only two million because the French retained money to pay for bills of exchange drawn by Washington. Laurens was undeterred. To the first obstacle, he responded that the French navy could provide a stronger convoy; as for the second, he believed no bills would be drafted on the gift granted to Franklin. An exasperated Vergennes observed that Laurens "was not sufficiently impressed" with the assistance France had already rendered.[34]

Vergennes said more in a letter to Lafayette. Including four million livres appropriated to pay for the bills of exchange drawn by Congress on Franklin, France had supplied twenty million livres to the Americans in 1781 alone. Vergennes trusted that General Washington would appreciate France's considerable financial and military sacrifices on America's behalf: "He is too enlightened to be unmoved by it or to allow himself any feeling other than gratitude. I have done what I could to inspire his aide-de-camp with this attitude, but I have not succeeded at all." Vergennes provided a pointed assessment of a callow and tactless diplomat:

> Mr. Laurens shows zeal, but I tell you in confidence that he did not express it in a manner suited to the nature of his mission. We did not take offense, because we attributed his behavior only to his inexperience in public affairs. I think I should speak to you about this officer because it is possible that, because he was annoyed at not obtaining everything he asked for, or rather insisted upon—that is, weapons, clothing, munitions, and 25 million besides—he may give a biased account to his chief.

Vergennes asked Lafayette to warn Washington to expect from Laurens a prejudiced, not wholly accurate report.[35] A wide gulf existed between Vergennes and Laurens. Vergennes constantly endeavored to persuade the Americans that feelings of generosity influenced French policy. He expected his allies to reciprocate with appreciation and "gratitude." To a great extent he was staging a charade, since both sides acted out of interest, but undeniably the French had been generous with their financial support. Laurens, however, resolutely refused to perform Vergennes's script. The young diplomat's actions reflected his belief that the French were motivated solely by their self-interest, and an appeal along those lines was the tactic most likely to win their aid. Franklin, who practiced a "diplomacy of gratefulness," acted as Vergennes expected and was thus highly successful and respected at Versailles. Laurens, on the other hand, "insisted" rather than "asked" for additional funds and permanent naval superiority. When he expressed gratitude, as he did upon learning of the loan, it appeared as an afterthought, and barely moderated the intemperate language of his petitions.[36]

Laurens viewed the United States as a sovereign state in every respect equal to France. He realized that his country desperately needed French aid, but that fact did not make Americans a charge of the Bourbon monarchy, subject to ministerial whims. The mutual benefits gained from the alliance outweighed any advantage the French thought they possessed. Their relationship was based on reciprocity: the French supported American independence, and together the allies weakened Britain. Laurens's haughtiness both amused and irritated Vergennes, who knew from La Luzerne's dispatches that the Americans were on the verge of collapse. According to William Jackson, at one meeting John lost his composure when Vergennes implied that the United States was dependent on French benevolence. "You have so lately left headquarters," said Vergennes in response to Laurens's peremptory manner, "that you forget you are not now delivering General Washington's orders." When the count referred to "the favors which America has received from the King," John responded with characteristic fervor: "Favors! Mons Le Comte, the respect I owe to my country will not admit the application of such a term."[37] This approach, emphasizing French self-interest and American autonomy, rankled the urbane and polite Vergennes.

Most of the difficulties stemmed from Laurens's rush to wrap up the mission. "It is impossible to express the impatience which I feel to return to my military functions," he said.[38] He had never coveted the diplomatic post, and only accepted Congress's appointment under duress. For all John knew, a decisive campaign was in progress in the South, where he had wanted to be at the head of a black regiment, while he wrangled with Vergennes over money and supplies. Small wonder, then, that he acted as a "militia diplomat" and ignored the rules of European diplomacy. Whereas other American diplomats, such as Benjamin Franklin and John Adams, normally followed protocol and displayed discretion, Laurens had little time for such niceties.[39] He repeatedly showed either ignorance or disdain for diplomatic protocol. Rather than address Vergennes with tact, he employed bluster. Rather than follow proper channels, he maneuvered behind Vergennes's back. He both violated conventions and made a strategic error as he attempted to maneuver his way through the labyrinthine world of politics at the French court. "I used every argument of national interest," he commented later, "and added such personal motives as I thought applicable to the different Ministers." In attempting to play ministers against one another, he inflamed tensions even more, for Necker and Castries were rivals of Vergennes.[40] From Laurens's perspective, each day spent in deliberation increased the likelihood that he would miss a last chance to win military fame.

Before Laurens could leave, he still faced two vexing problems that required resolution. First, he refused to accept Vergennes's decision to send smaller shipments of specie at intervals. The two million livres destined for

John's frigate seemed "so inconsiderable compared with our necessities." Second, the clothing stored at Brest fell short of the quantity needed, and most French woolen manufacturers were located far from the coast. "The providing this article," he mused, "I fear will be attended with great difficulties and delays."[41]

As Laurens pondered these concerns, an unexpected savior arrived from Holland. Alexander Gillon, commodore of South Carolina's puny navy, himself needed a deliverer. In 1778 the state legislature commissioned Gillon to purchase three frigates in Europe. As of 1781, his efforts had produced little. The previous year the Chevalier de Luxembourg had leased to the state a ship originally owned by France—*L'Indien,* an imposing forty-four gun frigate capable of carrying thirty additional guns and a crew of 550 men. Gillon renamed the vessel *South Carolina.* Partially loaded with clothing, the ship now lingered in port because he was unable to pay debts totaling ten thousand pounds. Gillon made an offer Laurens found too tempting to refuse. If Laurens paid Gillon's debts, the commodore agreed to relinquish the clothing and convey the cargo to America.[42]

Laurens found the proposal attractive for three reasons. First, he gained the additional clothing he wanted. Second, the large ship, in his opinion, eliminated "a powerful objection on the part of the Ministry against augmenting the first remittance of specie." Finally, the arrangement made the ship, potentially a decisive force at sea, available to South Carolina.[43]

On 28 April the two men signed an agreement that transferred to Laurens clothing and naval supplies worth approximately fifteen thousand pounds in return for his assumption of Gillon's debts. Gillon agreed to proceed directly to Philadelphia with his cargo and deliver it to Congress. He was to vary course only if he encountered storms, "a succession of contrary winds," or stronger enemy vessels, and under no circumstance was he to cause inordinate delays by pursuing potential prizes.[44]

As Gillon's purchases had not filled the ship's cargo space, Laurens contracted with Jean de Neufville, an Amsterdam merchant, to procure additional supplies. An ambitious man, anxious to profit from the war, de Neufville was also dimwitted and prone to irrational schemes. He had meddled in American affairs earlier. Among the documents the British found when they captured Henry Laurens was a 1778 unofficial draft treaty between the United Provinces of the Netherlands and the United States, negotiated by de Neufville and William Lee, "two dilettante diplomatists." In December 1780 Britain had used the document as a pretext to declare war against the Dutch.[45] "The confidence placed in him by Your Excellency," Laurens wrote John Adams, "was my only inducement for accepting the offer of his services on this occasion." It is unclear if de Neufville produced a written endorsement or if he merely claimed to have Adams's trust. In any event, Adams, who had replaced Henry Laurens as American minister to the Netherlands, did not disavow the merchant; and he commended Gillon as a man "whose Industry, Skill and Perseverance, have merited every assistance that can be legally given him."[46]

Laurens dispatched William Jackson to Amsterdam to oversee the arrangements made with Gillon and de Neufville. Necker agreed to send one million livres to be shipped on *South Carolina*. Laurens urged Jackson to safeguard that valuable cargo. He ordered his secretary, moreover, to inspect Gillon's freight and select the items that best conformed to American needs. His instructions regarding dc Neufville's purchases, though couched in a decisive tone, ultimately were subject to Jackson's interpretation: "I request your inspection as far as circumstances will allow of the purchases to be made in Holland. You will be best able to judge upon the spot whether the frigate is capable of receiving the whole quantity of supplies specified in the List delivered to Mr de Neufville, but my intention is that the purchases sh[oul]d not extend beyond the capacity of the Frigate."[47]

Franklin possessed strong reservations about the entire enterprise. He had dealt with Gillon before and thoroughly distrusted the shifty adventurer. His suspicions were partially allayed by Laurens, who claimed that he had broached the matter to Vergennes, who intimated approval. Franklin thus reluctantly consented to pay ten thousand pounds to relieve Gillon of his debts. When Laurens did not provide a precise estimate of how much money was needed to fill the ship's remaining space, Franklin pledged an additional five thousand pounds to cover the expense.[48]

After Jackson's departure, Laurens discovered that an adequate supply of blue cloth had been shipped on *Marquis de Lafayette,* a vessel escorted to America by John Barry and *Alliance.* He promptly "wrote to stop the purchases of that Article in holland, that we might not make unnecessary provision."[49] It is unclear whether this letter reached Jackson in time to affect de Neufville's expenditures.

Not satisfied with the concession made by Necker, Laurens asked the finance director to remit additional specie. He assured Necker that "the strictest Laws of prudence would not be violated in shipping the amount of Six millions on board of two frigates, well armed and good Sailers dispatched from ports distant from each other." Laurens preferred that a higher allotment of specie be sent via *South Carolina,* which was by far the strongest vessel.[50]

While awaiting an answer, Laurens, with assistance from Corny and Veimerange, arranged to ship armaments (howitzers, mortars, muskets, and shells), tents, and medical stores from Brest and Nantes.[51] He also concluded a contract with Sabatier Sons & Despres, a merchant firm "nominally under the authority of the War Department," that was to deliver supplies, consisting of

clothing, pig lead, tin, and German steel, to Brest in time for Laurens's departure, which was scheduled for the end of May. He specified that both the quality and prices of the goods be comparable to those furnished to the French
military; Corny and Veimerange agreed to verify that his directions were followed.[52]

The ministry's final decision proved disappointing. In response to Laurens's
requests for more specie remittances, the French agreed to divide one million
livres between *South Carolina* and *La Résolue,* the frigate that was to convey
him from Brest to America. That amount fell far short of his expectations.
Moreover, the Dutch, distrusting American credit, delayed approval of the loan.
There was, however, encouraging news. The French crown pledged to supply
ten million livres if the loan failed to go through. On the question of naval superiority, Vergennes told Laurens that de Grasse's West Indies squadron would
spend about three months off the North American coast. While the exact timing of the fleet's arrival was indeterminate, Vergennes stressed that the American army should prepare to commence joint operations as soon as Laurens
arrived.[53]

With negotiations completed, Laurens took leave of the French court. In
what was more a formality than a sign of royal favor, Louis XVI presented him
a parting gift, the king's portrait, centered on a gold snuffbox embroidered
with diamonds.[54]

While John had definitely been a nuisance, William Jackson's negative
story, related in fanciful old age, should be laid to rest. According to Jackson,
Laurens, tired of being snubbed, told Vergennes that without aid America
would lose the war and he would be compelled to draw his sword against France
as a British subject; then he violated etiquette by presenting his case directly to
the king at a levee. Vergennes did inform La Luzerne that Laurens "made several requests not solely with some importune insistence, but even resorting to
threats." Before concluding that this statement corroborates Jackson's tale,
however, one should note that the major had already left for Holland before the
supposed encounter occurred. His story merely exaggerates and distorts a point
Laurens hammered repeatedly: a forced reconciliation between Britain and the
colonies portended disastrous consequences for France. Vergennes, in his assessment of Laurens, probably employed hyperbole to describe the young diplomat's unrelenting pressure and overbearing manner.[55]

Even after the conclusion of formal business, John remained an irritant.
"Despite the enormous efforts we are making for the United States, we have
not been able to satisfy Mr. Laurens," Vergennes wrote Lafayette. "That officer has much neglected me since I announced to him His Majesty's decision.
I know he is complaining rather indiscreetly. . . . [M]ake him realize the necessity of giving Congress the most temperate account of the mission he carried

out in France." He sent a similar report to the Chevalier de La Luzerne and instructed him to minimize any damage the Carolinian might cause with a biased report to Congress. Obviously relieved that Laurens had taken leave of the court, Vergennes told La Luzerne, "I hope that no one will be sent back here."[56]

Before leaving Paris, John finally turned his attention to another pressing concern: his father, imprisoned in the Tower of London. From a correspondent in London—probably William Manning—he learned that the British made life miserable for their prisoner. John asked ministers at the French court to intervene on his father's behalf. They replied that they had no influence over British policy and suggested that the Continental Congress threaten to retaliate against a prominent British prisoner if Henry continued to receive ill treatment. John Jay, the American minister to Spain, even advocated raids on the English coast for the purpose of kidnaping British ministers. In the end John could do little but send twenty-four hundred pounds to Babut & Labouchere, a merchant firm in Nantes, to be applied to his father's account. Observing that Manning supplied Henry with money—"but private resources, in time of war . . . are very precarious"—he asked Franklin to grant additional relief from public funds.[57]

Henry Laurens, already stricken with gout, endured frequent insults during his imprisonment. His captors restricted visitation, initially refused to grant him pen and paper, and confined him to his quarters for extended periods. Compounding the indignities, they forced him to pay his own expenses. After the British ministry learned that John was in France, rumors abounded that treatment of the state prisoner would be even more uncompromising "now that Mr L's son had in his present Employment professedly declared himself an Enemy to his King and Country." Henry scoffed at such talk. After all, he observed, John had served the revolutionary cause for almost four years. For him the last straw occurred when his captors suggested that he censure John's activities in writing. Henry's response revealed that the surface differences between the temperate father and the reckless son were more of degree than of kind. They shared the same core values. Dominant among the tenets by which they lived was the belief that a man's honor was more important than his life. "My Son . . . is of Age, & has a Will of his own," wrote Henry, "he engaged in the present defensive War, without consulting me, nay he knew it was contrary to my Wish. I know he is so full of love and Duty to me, he would sacrifice his Life to serve me rightly; but he would not sacrifice his honor to save my life; his Maxim is my Country first and then my father. & I applaud him."[58]

On 17 May John Laurens began his journey to Brest. At first Thomas Paine resolved to remain in France, claiming that he could not return to America, where he "had experienced much thankless treatment." Laurens urged Paine to reconsider. He did not want to be alone on the voyage home with "nobody to confide in," especially if he were to suffer an accident. Paine gave in, as Laurens's "importunities for my returning with him were pressing and excessive, and he carried them to such a height."[59]

Laurens reached Brest on 21 May. Despite his impatience to leave, he encountered delays, but again the French proved cooperative. Upon discovering that essential supplies of clothing, cannons, and small arms had not arrived from Paris and Nantes, he received permission from local military commanders to procure replacements from the magazine at Brest. The specie was stored aboard *La Résolue,* which would convoy two transports loaded with military supplies. Two additional vessels, *La Duque Frouin* and *Le Rusé,* were scheduled to depart from Brest later. At port in Nantes, J. D. Schweighauser, a merchant and commercial agent for the Continental Congress, loaded medical provisions and tin on the ship *Active.*[60]

Because Louis XVI agreed to advance ten million livres if the loan were not approved in the Netherlands, Laurens expected France to deliver additional shipments of specie. Up to the moment of his departure, he issued last-minute requests and instructions. He urged Franklin "not to suffer . . . the farther transmission of specie to America, to be procrastinated. What is now sent from hence and from Holland will produce its effect if properly and immediately seconded, but unsupported it will degenerate into the merest palliative, and we shall find ourselves reduced to a more desperate situation than when Congress first applied for succour." In a similarly worded letter, he told Vergennes that a second remittance of specie should be shipped by July.[61]

Though Franklin realized that Laurens preferred military service, he suggested, either out of courtesy or conviction, that the young man would make an ideal replacement as minister to France. Congress "could not put their Affairs in better hands," he wrote. John made it clear that his ambitions lay elsewhere. "I repeat to Your Excellency that it was only a principle of obedience that brought me to Europe on the present occasion," he responded, "that I have not the most remote inclination to engage in the diplomatic line, and if I had the greatest, I sh[oul]d feel too strongly the disadvantage of succeeding your Excellency ever to form a desire on the subject, unless you would cast your mantle upon me and give me at the same time abilities to succeed to your reputation."[62]

Once the ships were loaded, calm winds delayed the departure for two days. John hurriedly wrote a letter to his sister Martha, who, along with Polly, Uncle James, and Aunt Mary, had settled at Vigan, a small town in southern France. Believing they could help Henry, Martha had applied to Franklin, on her uncle's behalf, for passports to travel to England. John considered the petition well-intentioned, but a visit to an enemy country was a potential political embarrassment. He encouraged Martha to "reconsider the matter. . . . It will have a very ill effect both in france and America, in a public point of view, and I do not conceive any good that can arise from it to our dear and respectable father." His pressing duties allowed him no time to see his family, despite a separation of four and a half years. He told Martha that he regretted "quitting France without having the happiness of passing a moment with you, except in imagination. Devoted to the service of my Country I submit to this sacrifice."[63]

On 1 June the small convoy finally set sail from Brest. John spent the long hours at sea pondering ways to procure additional shipments of specie. Eight days later, when *Engageante,* a ship of war that provided a brief escort, returned to France, he used the opportunity to convey a plan to Franklin. Rather than have Franklin retire, John believed, the solution was to provide a secretary to shoulder the paper work. He recommended William Temple Franklin, the elder statesman's grandson, for the job. To counter any charge of nepotism, he suggested that the young man present himself personally to Congress. Then Laurens revealed his ulterior motive: Franklin's grandson could also bring to Philadelphia a second remittance of specie and additional clothing for the army. Franklin appreciated Laurens's gesture, but he could not part with his grandson even briefly, as the young man already acted as his unofficial secretary.[64] By the end of the summer, Franklin rescinded his resignation. When Congress appointed him to serve with John Adams, John Jay, and Henry Laurens (even though he was a prisoner) on a commission to negotiate peace with Great Britain, he accepted gratefully.[65]

After John Laurens's departure, Franklin graciously praised the young diplomat in his public dispatches. "The most perfect Harmony subsisted between us during his Residence here," he told John Adams. "His indefatigable Endeavours," he informed Congress, "have brought the good Dispositions of this Court to a more speedy Determination of making an Addition, than could well have been expected, so soon after the former Grant." Though still fond of Laurens, he moderated his appraisal after conferring with Vergennes. "He was indefatigable while he stayed and took true pains," Franklin said privately, "but he *brusqued* the ministers too much, and I found after He was gone that he had thereby given more offense than I could have imagined. . . . The offense he gave will I hope have no durable effects, though it produced me some mortifications. Good humor and a kind disposition towards us seem again to prevail."[66] Franklin believed that appealing to French self-interest and emphasizing reciprocal obligations produced the opposite effect from what John had intended. A year later Franklin doubtless thought of Laurens when he wrote that telling the French "that it is their *interest* to help us, seems to say, help us, and we shall not be obliged to you. Such indiscreet and improper language has been sometimes used here by some of our people, and produced no good effects."[67]

Whatever one thought of Laurens as a diplomat—and he had defenders, namely his colleagues Paine and Jackson, and American leaders who despised Franklin—there was no denying that he had been "indefatigable." John Adams, who believed Franklin treated the French too softly, told Jackson that Laurens had "done more for the United States in the short Time of his being in Europe than all the rest of their Diplomatic Corps put together." Adams jeered at reports that Laurens had offended the French. "I have long since learned that a man may give offence and yet succeed," he commented. "The very measures necessary for success may be pretended to give offence." Laurens's diplomatic style, in fact, greatly resembled Adams's most recent dealings with Vergennes, whom he did not trust. While charitable in praising the young diplomat, Adams attempted to appropriate some of the mission's success for himself. He claimed that his memorial of 4 May to the Dutch government, which proposed that the Dutch negotiate a treaty of amity and commerce with him, had pressured the French to back the loan of ten million livres, even though the memorial was presented a month after Laurens obtained the loan.[68]

In the meantime, *La Résolue* and the transports proceeded slowly across the Atlantic. *La Duque Frouin,* escorted by *Magicienne,* reached Boston in mid-August. Dismasted in a gale, *Le Rusé* had returned to France. Because these ships departed from Brest eight days after Laurens, anxiety for his safety increased in Philadelphia. On 25 August he finally arrived in Boston after "a passage in which we experienced every contrariety." He originally intended to land at Philadelphia, but decided that a northern route to Boston would elude British raiders.[69]

After over eighty days at sea, he was anxious to get to Philadelphia, make his report to Congress, and rejoin the army. He borrowed on his own credit forty guineas to cover travel expenses. Laurens and Paine journeyed together past Providence, when the sulky carrying Paine broke down. They split the money, which left Paine with six guineas, and then parted. Paine, who later borrowed a dollar to cross a ferry, could not resist sarcasm: "Perhaps two such travellers as Col. Laurens and myself on such a national business is a novelty."[70]

Laurens continued his journey, arriving in Philadelphia on Sunday night, 2 September. Before retiring, he wrote for Congress a detailed account of his diplomatic mission. With the report completed, he desired a quick release from his assignment. "I entreat the farther orders of Congress," he wrote, "being exceedingly sollicitous to lose no time in rejoining the army." After reviewing the report and related papers, Congress resolved that all the supplies, which were valued at 2,289,109 livres, be delivered to the Board of War. Robert Morris, the recently appointed superintendent of finance, assumed control of the specie.[71]

After advancing Laurens $720 to cover his expenses, Morris made arrangements to transport the money from Boston to Philadelphia. Fourteen wagons hauled by fifty-six oxen and lead horses conveyed the specie to Philadelphia. The convoy arrived on 6 November and delivered the money to the United States treasury. Morris used $254,000, which amounted to more than half the total, to establish the Bank of North America, the first commercial bank in the United States. The bank made short-term loans to the government and facilitated credit.[72]

The Chevalier de La Luzerne, in accordance with his instructions from Vergennes, admonished Laurens for his conduct in France. "He appeared," La Luzerne reported, "to be sensible of his errors, and said he was a soldier, little acquainted with the customs of Courts, but warmly attached to his country; and that this sentiment may have made him pass the boundaries in which he ought to have kept himself." In discussions with Congress, Laurens, much to La Luzerne's satisfaction, emphasized French generosity and good will. When asked questions about Franklin, he responded with appropriate discretion and reserve. In short, he performed quite unlike the impulsive diplomat at Versailles. La Luzerne concluded with words that made Vergennes breath easier: "I do not believe that he has let escape here any of the complaints that he wrongly indulged in at Paris."[73]

On 5 September Congress unanimously expressed appreciation to Laurens for services that deserved "public Approbation." Thomas McKean, the president of Congress, sent him the resolution. "This is the greatest reward which Congress can bestow," wrote McKean, "or the most virtuous Citizen receive. . . . May you long continue to merit and receive the esteem & thanks of your country. You, Sir, at least exhibit one proof to the World, that in the United States the road to honor is thro' the temple of virtue."[74]

If Laurens ever needed confirmation, the thanks of Congress and McKean's laudatory statements proved that his had fulfilled his highest aspirations: his contemporaries considered him a paragon of public virtue, the model republican gentleman. A letter was a form of self-presentation. In writing a reply to McKean, John proclaimed the central tenet by which he lived and wanted others to regard him: virtuous self-sacrifice for the public good. He was, he told the president, "invariably devoted to the general interest. . . . I shall ever esteem the approbation of Congress delivered in the name of the people as the most exalted recompence that a citizen can receive on any occasion." McKean's cover letter made the thanks of Congress even more cherished. "I shall religiously preserve it as a monument of your desire to encourage the servants of the people in their duty," he concluded, "and inspire them with principles of public virtue."[75]

His business in Philadelphia concluded, John hurried to rejoin the army. So great was his haste that he completely forgot a promise to Tom Paine that he would ask Congress to compensate the pamphleteer. Instead, John left a request for Paine to pick up a pair of boots that he left behind with a shoemaker, but he enclosed no money to pay for the repairs. "I wish you had thought of me a little before you went away," Paine chided.[76]

While Laurens left behind a disgruntled Paine, Congress could not have been more pleased with the results of his mission or with his conduct. He played the role of the virtuous republican citizen to perfection, even surrendering the snuffbox given to him by Louis XVI. "Republican strictness, & the utility of the precedent," he explained, "lead me to refer it to the supreme Representative of the Majesty of the American people, the Organ of that sovereign will to which I am devoted." When Congress declined the offering, Laurens presented the snuffbox to Sarah Smith Bee, the wife of South Carolina delegate Thomas Bee.[77]

None was more impressed than James Duane, who headed a special committee that examined Laurens's report and papers. "Col. Laurens is returnd having executed his Mission with great Reputation to himself and Advantage to his Country," said Duane. "His Expences were within 300 Guineas: he refused any other Compensation and applied immediately for Leave to take the field." What was "more remarkable" to Duane was that "this patriot is deprived of his whole fortune by the Course of the War." Duane's picture of selfless virtue directly mirrored how Laurens wanted to be perceived by an approving audience of fellow gentlemen. Laurens, he told George Washington, displayed "A disinterestedness which forms a striking Contrast between him and some other Characters!"[78]

The mission won particular applause from leaders who were unhappy with Franklin. Laurens's accomplishments, Governor John Rutledge told the South Carolina delegation, "will convince many of what I have often said to you, that our not having recd. more powerful Support & effectual Aid, from France, is to be attributed solely, to the want of proper application for it."[79] As Laurens departed to rejoin the army, his brief stint as a diplomat appeared, to all observers, to have been a splendid success.

Or so it seemed. While Laurens crossed the Atlantic Ocean with specie, arms, ammunition, and clothing, the haste with which he had executed his assignment spawned controversy, headaches, and near disaster for American financial interests in Europe. The problems stemmed from his instructions to William Jackson and from the young major's inexperience and incompetence. Ordered by Laurens to supervise the purchase of supplies "as far as circumstances allow," Jackson provided scant oversight. Given considerable leeway, Jean de Neufville purchased fifty thousand pounds sterling in supplies. Once *South Carolina* was loaded, enough freight remained to fill two additional ships, which Jean de Neufville & Son leased in partnership with other merchants. Shocked by the excessive expenditures, Franklin at first refused to honor Jackson's bills. Only when Jackson returned to Paris and lied, claiming that Laurens had authorized the purchases, did Franklin relent.[80]

In the meantime, the French ministry, upset because the goods acquired in the Netherlands were manufactured in Britain, initially declined to provide further financial aid, which in effect terminated their promise to advance the loan of ten million livres. Vergennes contradicted Laurens's earlier story and denied any knowledge of the arrangements with Gillon and de Neufville; the count expressed annoyance at the entire undertaking. Franklin thus lacked the funds to pay for Congress's drafts on its other foreign ministers. Faced with potential damage to American credit abroad, he desperately needed money. When he learned that the specie on board *South Carolina* was part of the gift of six million livres from France rather than an advance on the loan negotiated by Laurens, he promptly ordered that the 1.5 million livres be removed so he could pay American debts. Jackson protested indignantly, but to no avail.[81]

Additional difficulties arose in the Netherlands. Jackson and de Neufville believed that Gillon, since he was responsible for transporting the supplies, should pay for leasing the two additional vessels. Because Jackson also questioned Gillon's loyalty to the American cause, they initially withheld from the commodore the ten-thousand-pound payment that Laurens had promised. To escape his creditors, Gillon sailed outside the territorial waters of the Netherlands, leaving behind the two transport ships. After putting the irate Jackson off at Corunna, Spain, Gillon continued an odyssey that eventually took him to the West Indies, where *South Carolina* seized five prizes and took part in the capture of the Bahamas. He finally reached Philadelphia in May 1782. Depending on one's point of view—and opinions varied widely—he was either a hero or a scoundrel.[82]

Robert Morris wanted to prosecute Gillon for not honoring his contract with Laurens, but the South Carolina delegates opposed any proceedings against the commodore. Having sanctioned Gillon's mission to Europe, the state's leaders hoped to forestall any investigation that might call into question their own actions. Moreover, Carolinians were still embittered at what they perceived as Congress's feeble response to their pleas for military assistance. Because anti-Franklin sentiment prevailed among several delegates, Congress never censured Gillon. Instead, a committee formed to investigate Franklin's suspension of the specie shipment strongly condemned the aged diplomat. Rather than provoking further controversy, the "unfair hostility" of the committee's report received no endorsement from the other delegates. On 1 November 1782 Congress approved a motion by the South Carolina delegation that any questions regarding Gillon's contract with Laurens be settled by arbitration. Thus the matter was closed quietly.[83]

In the Netherlands the de Neufvilles and their syndicate refused to release the remaining goods to either Adams or Franklin and demanded payment for damages. "This piece of business has been managed as ill as any that has ever been done for Congress in Europe," commented the exasperated Adams, who claimed that he had never been involved in the affair. So matters rested until Thomas Barclay, the new American consul in France, assumed control of the supplies. Because Congress had banned the import of British merchandise into the United States, Barclay exchanged those goods for clothing. When the first of the costly shipments reached Philadelphia in September 1782, Robert Morris found there was not enough clothing to distribute to the army; he ordered that the clothing be sold to help pay the country's mounting debts. Morris's opinion regarding the goods from the Netherlands—"would to God that they had never been purchased"—stands as the last word on a venture that was mismanaged from the start.[84]

The contract to guarantee the loan of ten million livres was approved jointly by the Netherlands and France on 5 November 1781. By that time the loan had been absorbed by Laurens's purchases and the previous drafts made by Congress.[85] Its impact on unstable American finances, therefore, was negligible. After subtracting the costs of the supplies and drafts from the ten million, the French treasury had to pay 134,065 livres to Sabatier Sons & Despres for the goods they furnished in accordance with their agreement with Laurens. In August 1785 the Board of Treasury, in response to a report submitted by the French chargé d'affaires, recommended that Congress reimburse the French government for the expense. Beyond that, the delegates took no further action for the remainder of the Confederation period. As late as 1792, the French and American governments still haggled over the debt.[86]

Laurens's mission, in the final analysis, was only a middling success. Congress should not have been surprised at the repercussions of their decision to send to France "a young Beggar instead of an old one." Temperamentally unsuited for the often tedious work of diplomacy, Laurens conducted himself in a manner more befitting an officer leading a frontal attack on an enemy post.[87] His lack of patience, tact, and reserve, essential qualities for a diplomat, might have fractured Franco-American relations had not Vergennes and the other ministers recognized a young man's inexperience and excused his indiscretions.

Chapter 10

"The single voice of reason"
Military Triumph and Political Defeat
September 1781–February 1782

John Laurens had good reason to be in a hurry to rejoin the main Continental Army. A major campaign, perhaps the decisive moment of the long war, was in the offing. He could not afford to miss a final chance to win military fame. After all, he was a soldier, a gentleman officer. It was an integral part of his identity, and he had bent his mind and will in preparation for such a moment. His service as diplomat, he had asserted repeatedly, was transitory, a simple matter of obedience to the commands of Congress. As Laurens rode southward on a small wagon, he knew he was returning to his element.

While John had been away to France, Earl Cornwallis and Nathanael Greene conducted a campaign in the Carolinas that left the British exhausted and weakened by costly engagements, particularly the battle of Guilford Court House on 15 March, where Cornwallis lost one-fourth of his army—troops he could not replace. Convinced that the Carolinas, contrary to projections, contained few loyalists, Cornwallis decided to try his luck in Virginia. He moved there in early May and joined an expeditionary force that Sir Henry Clinton had dispatched to operate in the Chesapeake Bay. Greene promptly moved into South Carolina and assaulted the vulnerable British outposts in the backcountry. Though Clinton was angered at Cornwallis's unauthorized move, he directed his subordinate to select a base and construct fortifications. The earl chose Yorktown, a congenial, peaceful town located on the York River.

True to their word, the French established temporary naval superiority in American waters. Count de Grasse, commander of the fleet in the West Indies, informed Washington that he would sail to the Chesapeake and remain until mid-October. Washington dropped plans to lay siege to New York and focused attention on Cornwallis. Leaving a small force on the Hudson River to watch Clinton's garrison, he moved south with two thousand Continentals and the French army under Count de Rochambeau. The French squadron stationed at Newport, commanded by Count de Barras, slipped past the British navy and joined de Grasse. Shortly after his arrival in Williamsburg on 14 September, Washington learned that a French fleet of thirty-six ships of the line blocked Cornwallis's escape by sea.[1]

When he realized that Washington and his staff had journeyed ahead of the main army, Laurens, full of "anxiety to arrive in time for reconnoitring the theatre of our operations," considered boarding one of the transports at Head of Elk, Maryland, that were conducting troops down the Chesapeake. Apparently, however, he continued overland. As he explained to Benjamin Lincoln, supervisor of the embarkation, he did not want to lose his two horses, "which are essential to me in the Campaign." By 18 September he reached Williamsburg.[2]

At Williamsburg the largest allied army of the war gathered. Washington's Continentals united with a detachment under Lafayette that had been dispatched to Virginia earlier in the summer. With the addition of 3,000 Virginia militia, the Americans amassed a force of 8,845. Rochambeau brought 7,800 men to Yorktown and Admiral de Grasse had 3,000 troops with his fleet. Cornwallis commanded a force of 6,000, composed of British redcoats, Hessians, and loyalists.[3]

For Laurens it was a time of reunion with close friends and old comrades. He learned that Hamilton was no longer a member of Washington's staff. In mid-February, a brief quarrel between the two men led to Hamilton's resignation, but the rift gave him what he had always wanted—a line command. Washington, in a display of magnanimity and in acknowledgment of Hamilton's services, made the young man commander of a battalion of light infantry.[4]

Though Hamilton had worked closely with Washington for over three years, he did not like his commander. "I have felt no friendship for him and have professed none," he declared. As head of a military family, Washington stood in the way of Hamilton's path to renown, similar to the manner in which patriarchs often prevented their sons from controlling their inheritance and gaining independence. Hamilton grew to resent the constraints placed on him as an aide-de-camp. Holding a staff rather than a line appointment, he had no chance to lead troops and win military fame. Despite his frequent requests for a command, Washington always found excuses to say no; he simply valued the young man's assistance too much to let him go. While Laurens was aware of these frustrations, it is unclear if he knew the extent of Hamilton's resentment. If Hamilton conveyed these sentiments, it did nothing to lessen John's esteem for either man; he continued to venerate Washington and love Hamilton.[5]

To be sure, Washington could be a difficult superior. As a young man he had possessed a violent temper and was prone to emotional outbursts. Though he labored to master his passions, there still were occasional eruptions, prompted by a stressful job and painful toothaches. Whether or not Laurens ever experienced his wrath, he always spoke of the commander in chief in a tone that combined respect with an adoration born of youthful enthusiasm. It was perhaps easy for Laurens to revere Washington, since the general granted him ample opportunities to win fame in military campaigns. He experienced none of the frustrations that vexed Hamilton. Because John was properly deferential, and thus gratified Washington's vanity, relations between them were invariably amicable. Among cultured gentlemen, the salutation and complimentary close of a letter indicated the extent of the relationship between correspondents. On more than one occasion, Washington, displaying warmth he reserved for only a few intimates, prefaced a letter—"My dear Laurens"—and concluded with expressions of "every sentiment of esteem and Affection" or "cordiality and true affection." When Hamilton referred derisively to "a man to whom all the world is offering incense," he perhaps forgot that among those worshipers was his closest friend.[6]

Laurens promptly resumed his position as aide-de-camp. His arrival, from Washington's viewpoint, could not have been better timed. He needed Laurens's fluency in French for communications with de Grasse. To Washington's dismay, the admiral decided to leave two vessels at the mouth of the York River and take the remainder of his fleet out to sea where they could maneuver. John drafted for Washington a strongly worded yet respectful letter that urged de Grasse to reconsider. Without his fleet, the campaign was certain to fail, Cornwallis would escape, and the allies would lose an opportunity they could never expect to have again. If the admiral remained, success was assured, and "the surrender of the british Garrison will be so important in itself and its consequences, that it must necessarily go a great way towards terminating the war, and securing the invaluable objects of it to the Allies." At this point, in words reminiscent of his petitions to the French ministry, Laurens appealed to de Grasse's honor, his personal stake in the campaign: "The dearest interests then of the common cause, and Your Excellencys personal Glory being thus deeply concerned, nothing I am persuaded can determine Your Excellency to withdraw your cooperation." Upon perusal, Washington deleted this sentence, apparently concluding that the language exceeded the bounds of propriety.[7]

Two days later Washington received favorable word from de Grasse. He had decided, in council with his officers, to remain and block the entrance to the James and York Rivers. With this welcome news, the allied army began the march from Williamsburg to Yorktown. On 28 September, when they reached the outskirts of Yorktown, Cornwallis surprisingly offered no opposition and evacuated his outer line of defense. The allies spent over a week transporting and installing artillery. Once there was sufficient covering fire, they would open their first trench (or parallel) and begin "regular approaches," a series of parallels and redoubts, each one constructed closer to enemy fortifications until their position became indefensible, whereupon surrender negotiations commenced.[8]

At the beginning of the siege, one man's misfortune paved the way for Laurens to receive a line command. On 30 September, Colonel Alexander Scammell, a popular officer, was captured and mortally wounded while reconnoitering the enemy lines. In response Washington divided Scammell's regiment into two battalions, one to be under Laurens.[9]

On 6 October the allies began the first parallel. By the ninth, batteries were in place, and both French and American cannons opened fire, although the latter had less effect, as the French were the best artillerists in the world. An incessant bombardment continued through the night, inflicting considerable damage on the fortifications and agitating soldiers and civilians alike.[10]

Work began on the second parallel, three hundred yards from the British lines, on the evening of 11 October. So far the siege had proceeded without interference, but now two advanced redoubts opposite the American right prevented them from extending the parallel to the river. Washington ordered a night attack. The French were to assault the stronger of the two redoubts, called No. 9. The commander in chief conferred to Lafayette the honor of supervising the attack on the other redoubt, No. 10, which was two hundred yards from the river. Hamilton, who heretofore had missed the opportunities for military and political fame that Laurens regularly received, realized that this daring mission presented a last chance to win renown on the battlefield. Accordingly, when the marquis chose his aide-de-camp as commander, Hamilton protested directly to Washington, who relented and awarded his former aide the honor of leading the assault. The plan called for Hamilton to lead a frontal attack on the redoubt, while a separate column of eighty men under Laurens came in from the rear and blocked the enemy's escape.[11]

Commanded by Major James Campbell, redoubt No. 10 had a small force of forty-five British and Hessians. To thwart an attack, they had placed abatis and palisades around the redoubt and had dug a moat. Shortly after nightfall on 14 October, the assault force of four hundred men moved into position. Laurens's men went first, sneaking between the two redoubts until they were positioned behind No. 10. The main force then advanced swiftly across the sandy plain with muskets unloaded, for it was to be a bayonet assault, with surprise the key to success. Alert British sentries, however, spotted the approaching attackers and sounded the alarm; the garrison immediately opened fire and hurled hand grenades at the Americans massed in the moat below. Heedless of the obstructions—waiting for their removal subjected the troops to murderous volleys—Hamilton's troops mounted the parapet and swarmed into the redoubt. At the head of his detachment, Laurens entered simultaneously from the rear and personally captured Major Campbell. It was over quickly. Despite earlier talk of retaliation against the redcoats for past atrocities—there were rumors that Scammell had been wounded after he surrendered—the "soldiery spared every man, who ceased to resist." American losses were light: nine killed and thirty-one wounded. Eight defenders were killed or wounded and twenty were taken prisoner. The French had equal success at redoubt No. 9 but suffered greater casualties, partly because they assaulted a stronger redoubt and partly because they halted to remove obstructions.[12]

The successful attacks sealed the enemy's fate. On the night of 16 October, Cornwallis, desperate to escape, ferried troops across the river to the town of Gloucester. During their crossing, a violent storm erupted and halted the attempt. The next morning the earl requested a twenty-four-hour cease-fire to discuss surrender terms. He proposed that each side select two officers to meet at the house of Augustine Moore, located near the river, half a mile behind the first parallel.[13]

Washington selected Laurens to represent the Americans; Rochambeau designated Lafayette's brother-in-law, Viscount de Noailles, to act for the French. They met the British commissioners, Lieutenant Colonel Thomas Dundas and Major Alexander Ross, the following day. The negotiations stretched into the night. While the two commanders had already resolved some issues—Washington refused Cornwallis's appeal that British and German prisoners be paroled and allowed passage to Europe—other questions waited settlement. As gentlemen merited special treatment, Laurens and Noailles permitted officers to travel on parole to Europe or to American ports occupied by Britain. The allied commissioners also consented to the British demand that the loyalists in the area around Yorktown not be punished for openly declaring their allegiance to the crown.[14]

The British objected to Washington's insistence that they receive the same honors granted to the garrison at Charleston. Sir Henry Clinton had insulted Benjamin Lincoln, compelling his force to march out of the city with colors cased, while their drums played a Turkish march. Washington probably employed intentional irony when he selected as his representative Laurens, who had endured the humiliation at Charleston.

According to one account, this dispute sparked a heated exchange between Laurens and Cornwallis's aide-de-camp, Ross. This narrative, in its particulars, is probably apocryphal, but the rival commissioners did haggle over the surrender conditions far longer than anyone had expected. Most likely this condition produced a great deal of testiness, for it involved a question of honor between gentlemen officers from contending armies.

"This is a harsh article," Ross observed. "Which article?" inquired Laurens. "The Troops shall march out with colours cased, and drums beating a British or a German march." "Yes, Sir," acknowledged Laurens, "it is a harsh article." "Then, Col. Laurens," Ross pressed, "if that is your opinion, why is it here?"

"Your question, Col Ross, compels an observation, which I would have gladly suppressed," said Laurens. "You seem to forget, Sir, that I was a capitulant at Charles Town—where Gen. Lincoln, after a brave defence . . . was refused any other terms for his gallant garrison, than marching out with colours cased, and drums *not* beating a British or German march." Ross's reply was immediate: "But my Lord Cornwallis did not command at Charles Town." "There, Sir," said Laurens, "you extort another declaration. It is not the individual that is here considered—it is the Nation. This remains an article or I cease to be a Commissioner."[15]

Ultimately, this dispute was subject to a compromise that allowed the British to preserve a sense of their honor. Because their garrison at Gloucester had not been assaulted, it was allowed to march out with swords drawn and trumpets playing. Toward midnight Laurens and Noailles returned to headquarters. British temporizing had so delayed the negotiations that Laurens could only furnish Washington a rough draft of the surrender terms. Washington reviewed the articles and largely gave his assent. The treatment of loyalists being a matter for civil authorities, he rejected the article that guaranteed their safety. He then had a better copy made and forwarded the document to Cornwallis.[16]

On Friday morning, 19 October, Cornwallis affixed his signature and sent the articles of capitulation to the allied commanders. That afternoon the surrender ceremony took place. The allies formed separate lines, and many observers noted the contrast between the resplendent French and the tattered Americans. Differences in clothing aside, one American remarked proudly, the Continentals "exhibited an erect, soldierly air, and every countenance beamed with satisfaction and joy."[17]

None could have been prouder than John Laurens. To his former fellow aide, Richard Kidder Meade, he wrote, "This is an illustrious day my dear friend for our national honor and interests."[18] Laurens, along with "those dear ragged Continentals," had contributed so much to the glorious victory. It is possible, however, to exaggerate his contribution. To be sure, French naval superiority proved the indispensable element in the allied success at Yorktown. Less clear is the role Laurens's diplomatic mission played in French naval planning. When he met the Marquis de Castries in mid-March, the French minister was headed to Brest to supervise the departure of de Grasse's squadron. Laurens alarmed Castries with reports that the American war effort was on the brink of collapse, but the French ministry had already decided that de Grasse, though his principal objective was to cooperate with the Spanish in the Caribbean, would detach part of his fleet to American waters. De Grasse's presence at Yorktown with a large fleet was owing to two factors wholly unconnected to Laurens. First, the Spanish allies never got ready for combined operations; second, Castries gave de Grasse considerable latitude in making decisions, so the admiral arrived early at the Chesapeake Bay and stayed later than was originally expected. Ultimately, Laurens's arguments reinforced convictions already held by Castries and other French ministers.[19]

"My eyes are sore, my body and mind fatigued by an uninterrupted flow of business," John remarked after the siege. Despite his exhaustion, he certainly felt ironic pleasure. He had negotiated the surrender of Charles Earl Cornwallis, constable of the Tower of London. In effect, he captured his father's jailer. It was too tempting an opportunity to let pass. He asked Lafayette to sound out Cornwallis and discover if he favored an exchange involving himself and Henry Laurens. The earl approved the idea but doubted that the British ministry would release their state prisoner.[20]

Using Major Ross as intermediary, Laurens and Cornwallis discussed the matter further. Since Congress had recently offered to exchange John Burgoyne for Henry Laurens, John believed that the delegates would sanction his idea. John broached the proposal to Washington, who agreed with that assessment but maintained that he had no authorization to act, as prisoner exchanges were the province of Congress. In his zeal to bring about his father's release, John misconstrued Washington's response. He informed Carolina delegate Thomas Bee that the commander in chief agreed to "second the matter on his arrival in Philadelphia." What Washington actually said was garbled even more during John's discussions with Cornwallis. The earl concluded that Washington had authority to approve the exchange, thereby expediting what was normally an involved process. Three months later, when Sir Henry Clinton inquired about the promise that the Cornwallis-Laurens exchange would proceed, a slightly embarrassed Washington replied that "I could never have given an assurance that His Lordship should be exchanged for Mr. Laurens, the Father of the Colonel, as I had no authority to make any such stipulation."[21]

Laurens's official duties as aide-de-camp kept him at Yorktown until 5 November. At that point Washington traveled to Philadelphia to meet with Congress. Hamilton had departed for New York shortly after the surrender, anxious to see his bride, who was expecting the couple's first child. As for Laurens, he received leave to make the journey he had postponed a year earlier. He returned to South Carolina with a dual purpose—to serve under Greene and to make a final attempt to convince his native state to embody black regiments.[22]

Since the fall of Charleston in May 1780, South Carolina had been the scene of the bitterest fighting of the war. Much of the conflict did not involve Continentals and redcoats, but rather pitted Carolinians against each other, rebel against loyalist. Devoid of law and order, portions of the state, particularly the backcountry, degenerated into virtual anarchy as both sides conducted raids, pillaged, and destroyed property with impunity. Nor were the Continentals or British regulars above involvement in the melee. In need of supplies, Continentals impressed private property, at times without authorization, and alienated many Carolinians. Those redcoats who favored a harsh policy to extinguish the rebellion often failed to distinguish between friend and foe and thus drove both potential supporters and neutrals into the ranks of the revolutionaries. By late 1781, Greene's army confined the British to the area around Charleston. South Carolina was an exhausted state where widespread skirmishing persisted; its inhabitants desperately needed a respite from the fighting.[23]

Upon his arrival in South Carolina in early December, Laurens wasted no time in reintroducing his black battalion proposal. He consulted Governor Rutledge, who had been steady in his opposition to the plan. The British, Laurens contended, "may be forced to evacuate Charles Town in the course of the present Campaign, provided the Council of this State will enter vigorously into the measure of reinforcing General Greene with a well chosen Corps of black levies." Rutledge apparently gave Laurens reason for some hope; most likely he merely wanted to get rid of the persistent young man.[24]

Laurens found an influential ally to second his efforts. Despite the victory at Yorktown, Nathanael Greene did not regard the war as over. He sent an eloquent appeal to Rutledge, urging him to utilize the state's untapped resource of black manpower. It was hardly a coincidence that Greene penned the letter on 9 December, shortly after Laurens's arrival, for he probably pressed the issue at the young man's insistence.

"The natural strength of this country in point of numbers," Greene observed, "appears to me to consist more in the blacks, than the whites. . . . The number of whites in this State are too small, and the State of your finance too low, to attempt to raise a force in any other way." He connected the havoc of the previous two years to the state's refusal to sanction Laurens's proposal in 1779. "I believe it is generally agreed," wrote Greene, "that if the natural strength of this country, could have been employed in it's defence, the Enemy would have found it little less than impracticable to have got footing here, much more have overrun the country." Because the legislature rejected Laurens's plan, "the Inhabitants have suffered infinitely greater loss, than would have been sufficient to have given you perfect security."[25]

Not surprisingly, Greene found no more success than Laurens. When Rutledge presented Greene's letter to the Privy Council, they refused "to adopt the Measure recommended . . . as a Proposition of that Kind had been, almost unanimously, rejected, by the last Assembly." In addition, Rutledge told Greene, the councilors believed any decision to deviate from that course should be left to the next legislature, which was to convene soon. Since Laurens had been elected to the House of Representatives in elections held in mid-December, he would have a final opportunity to espouse his idea.[26]

Whatever disappointment Laurens felt was temporarily allayed by the prospect of winning more military fame. Along with Lieutenant Colonel Henry Lee, he planned a surprise assault on a British post on Johns Island. Lee commanded an independent corps of cavalry and infantry, known as "Lee's Legion." The Legion had won acclaim for its exploits, such as the capture of the British post at Paulus Hook, New Jersey, in 1779, and valuable service in Greene's Southern campaign in 1781. A daring yet prudent commander, proud and temperamental, "Light-Horse Harry" Lee viewed the attempt on Johns Island as the consummation of a brilliant military career. Upon completing the coup, he expected to receive leave to return to his native Virginia.[27]

Located between the estuaries of the North Edisto and Stono Rivers, Johns Island was occupied by about four hundred redcoats under Major James Craig. The Americans discovered that the inlet separating the island from the mainland was passable at low tide at a site known as New Cut. Timing was of the essence; at best the inlet could be crossed two times each month shortly after midnight, when "the depth of water was not more than *waist high*." A galley and two gunboats, stationed about four hundred yards apart, guarded this passage, but Lee believed the crews relaxed their vigilance at night. If performed according to design, the scheme would rank among the boldest of the war. Laurens could barely contain his excitement. "I need not add how anxious I am to engage in an enterprise that promises such important consequences," he told Greene.[28]

Despite such enthusiasm, Greene was skeptical. There was little margin for error, he contended, particularly as the operation involved an island assault. Another concern was relations between the two young officers. Laurens, whose commission predated Lee's, was to command the operation. "I have told him of my willingness to serve under him," Lee assured Greene, "so that no difficulty has arisen on this point." Greene, however, read between the lines and wondered if Lee and Laurens were indeed collaborators. The proposals and plans to attack the island, for the most part, came from Lee alone. "I expected you and Col Laurens would have cooperated with each other," responded Greene, "and reported together the issue of the business." Still, he valued his subordinates' judgment. If Lee and Laurens considered the attempt practical, he agreed to provide support.[29]

With much anticipation, Laurens looked forward to the assault. "No Lover was ever so anxious to hear from his Mistress when he expected an assignation," he wrote Lee, "as I am to receive a letter from you."[30] Lee and Laurens decided to assault Johns Island on Saturday, 29 December, when the tide was most conducive to a safe crossing. Upon learning that the redcoats had stationed troops on James Island, across the inlet from Johns Island, they "most reluctantly" canceled the operation. They refused, however, to give up their plan, and continued to watch the enemy's movements.[31]

Two weeks later they agreed to make the attempt. The assaulting force planned to cross at New Cut on Sunday evening, 13 January, while Greene simultaneously marched there with the main army, so he could provide support in case the operation went awry and the redcoats dispatched additional troops to assist Craig. "The consequence of reinforcements on both sides can only terminate in a general Action," concluded Laurens, "in which it appears to me that we shall have great advantages on ours." Greene's presence would "exclude the possibility of any serious misfortune to us."[32]

On the cold and rainy night of the thirteenth, Laurens and Lee rendezvoused at a prearranged spot less than a mile from New Cut. Greene and the main army had broken camp the previous day and marched toward Johns Island.[33] Like his counterparts in the British army, Laurens felt compelled to inspire his troops with bravery.[34] As they waited to ford the inlet, he delivered a stirring address he had prepared for the occasion and appealed to their honor and patriotism.

"Col. Laurens congratulates the gallant troops which he has the honor to command," he said, "on their being selected by the General for the execution of a brilliant and important Enterprise. Their past glorious Successes, the mutual confidence subsisting between the Men and Officers, their patriot zeal and soldierly Sense of honor, are pledges of Victory." After issuing instructions on how the men were to cross the inlet without dampening their arms and ammunition, he assured them that "sure and intelligent Guides" would direct the march. Because their commanding officers had procured detailed intelligence of the enemy's numbers and position, the troops could "advance with the greatest confidence."

He ordered his men to maintain "the most inviolable silence and absolute attention to the commands of their officers." None of them was "to fire or advance without orders, confusion only can arise from unconnected individual efforts." He emphasized that looting was strictly prohibited: "Sh[oul]d there unfortunately be any man so blinded by dishonorable motives as to commit this crime, he will be punished with instant death. The Col. orders the Officers to be inexorable on this subject."

A call to arms required a rousing finale, and Laurens was up to the challenge. His peroration reflected the common bond that tied officers to their men: the belief that they all fought for a transcendent cause:

The Col[onel] entreats the troops to place their principal Reliance on the bayonet, which is the Weapon of the brave, and when they are ordered to charge, to rush forward with that decisive ardour which characterises the Defenders of Liberty & the Rights of Mankind. In all circumstances, he depends upon their inflexible maintenance of order, and bids them remember that bravery alone extinguishes Danger. . . . The Cause in which we are engaged, our Countrys honor & our own must inspire us with Sentiments which are the presage of Victory.[35]

When he finished the oration, "A burst of applause ensued from the ranks, evincing the delight which all felt in knowing that victory was certain, unless lost by misbehavior."[36]

Laurens divided the detachment into two columns, one commanded by Lee, the other under Major James Hamilton. The march commenced shortly after 1:00 a.m., when the tide ebbed. As overall commander, Laurens accompanied Lee's advance column to the fording location. Lee sent one of his most enterprising officers, Major John Rudulph, across first with part of the Legion infantry. While they waded through the shallow water between the British vessels, redcoat lookouts on both sides called out, "all's safe." The Americans were elated; victory seemed assured.[37]

Their euphoria soon subsided. The rear column failed to appear. Accompanied by guides and a small number of soldiers, Laurens immediately set out to discover Hamilton's whereabouts. After a search that lasted more than an hour, but must have seemed to him an eternity, they found Hamilton. His detachment was hopelessly lost. When the two columns failed to begin their advance simultaneously, he lost contact with Laurens and Lee. Compounding Hamilton's problems, his guide deserted, leaving his troops unable to find their way through the darkness. With the tide steadily rising, Laurens had no choice but to recall Lee's column, which had already crossed to the island, and cancel the operation. On their return Lee's troops found themselves "middle deep with mud, weeds and water," and several soldiers became "stuck fast and were obliged to be pulled out." A potentially glorious success ended in bitter disappointment. Laurens's frustration was palpable. When he returned after finding Hamilton's column, he appeared "most unhappy of the unhappy."[38]

Greene, upon hearing the bad news, resolved to bring in a boat to convey troops across the inlet. "Having lost our chance of surprising the enemy," he observed, "we determined to force our way upon the Island." On Monday, 14 January, the Americans fired on the galley and the two gunboats, but the British vessels maintained their position. That night the ships slipped away and Craig evacuated the island.

The following day Laurens, with a small party of infantry and cavalry, crossed in the boat. With the exception of some stragglers, whom the Americans promptly captured, they found the island deserted. Discovering that the redcoats had loaded their supplies on a schooner, and considering "the Schooner with all their baggage and a great deal of valuable Stores . . . an object worth attempting," Laurens ordered an attack. At first the American volleys "threw her Crew into great confusion," and the schooner almost ran aground. The redcoats quickly regained their composure and, using their baggage as protection, opened fire on Laurens's detachment. The schooner then moved away slowly, hindered by a calm breeze. "If I had a three pounder . . . perhaps She might still be taken," Laurens informed Greene. The general dispatched a cannon, but it arrived too late to be of service, a fitting end for an operation marred by bad luck and poor timing.[39]

"The failure of the enterprise," said Greene, "was not a little mortifying to me but much more to Laurens and Lee. Had it succeeded it would have been both important and splendid." Lee lapsed into depression, his hopes of finishing his career with one more brilliant stroke blasted. As commanding officer, Laurens knew he had missed a golden opportunity to cement his military reputation and doubtless felt responsible, even though he could not have foreseen or prevented the misfortunes that plagued the assault.[40]

John had little time to reflect on what might have been. Less than a week later, he journeyed to Jacksonborough, a sleepy village on the west bank of the Edisto River where the state legislature had convened. While it contained only "four or five tolerable good frame houses and a number of smaller houses," Jacksonborough was about thirty-five miles from Charleston, removed from the British yet close to the protection offered by Greene's army. Laurens took his seat in the House of Representatives on Monday, 21 January.[41]

That same day Greene wrote Governor Rutledge, reiterating his appeal that Carolinians form slave regiments. Greene's timing, once again, apparently owed much to Laurens's influence. "It appears to me that the Governor & Council should not lose a moment in carrying the black levy plan into execution," John had written Greene in late December, "but I know that unless they are goaded upon the subject, their deliberations and delays will lose the opportunity which now offers." In this letter Greene pressed his points harder and drew lessons from the recent past. Had Carolinians armed blacks earlier, they might have prevented the fall of Charleston, discouraged the British ministry, and attained the peace everyone longed for. Now an alarming scenario loomed: Greene warned Rutledge that the British ministry might negotiate peace with the Americans on the basis of *uti possidetis,* allowing them to retain all territory held by their army. Under this arrangement, Charleston would remain a British possession.[42]

At Jacksonborough were gathered some of the most distinguished leaders of the Revolution in South Carolina. Few men had emerged from the conflict unscathed; many of the legislators had served in the military and lost property or suffered physical hardship during the war. After almost two years of British occupation and rebel-loyalist discord, bitterness ran high. In his address to both houses, Governor Rutledge enumerated the tribulations Carolinians had endured. Almost four months earlier the governor had offered pardons to loyalists who surrendered within thirty days and enlisted in the state militia for six months. Now he placed before the legislators a potentially divisive issue— whether or not they should confiscate the property of loyalists. The general mood was not conciliatory.[43]

Laurens served on nine committees. His most consequential assignments included work on the committee that drafted a bill to fill the state's Continental battalions and another that considered ways to furnish laborers for the army. More important, he served as chairman of a seven-member committee to determine which loyalists' estates should be confiscated or sequestered "and to what purposes the Profits arising from them may be best applied."[44] Laurens's appointment to this crucial position indicates that his colleagues respected his probity, despite his antislavery views. These committees shared a common characteristic—each dealt with the role of human chattel in time of war.

Ordered by the Continental Congress to raise two battalions, the legislature decreed that every man who enlisted for the duration of the war or for a three-year-term would receive one slave for each year of duty. Offering such inducements was a widespread practice. For example, partisan leader Thomas Sumter used slaves seized from plantations as bonuses for troops under his command. Among soldiers from the Carolina backcountry in particular there was an insatiable demand for slaves. Gone forever was the possibility of fulfilling Christopher Gadsden's 1769 prophecy of a backcountry populated by non-slaveholding small farmers who would serve as a counterweight against slave insurrections in the low country. In 1782 enterprising backcountry farmers recognized that ownership of slaves fulfilled their dreams of accumulating more wealth. Few legislators seemed to comprehend the incongruity of promising slave ownership to men in return for their service in a struggle for political freedom. The ready acceptance of an expedient that increased the number of slaveholders did not bode well for Laurens's black regiment plan.[45]

As chairman of the committee on loyalist estates, Laurens conceived a novel idea. Why not, he proposed, take twenty-five hundred slaves from the confiscated estates and form them into regiments under white officers? It was an adroit move, quite unlike John's blunt approach in France. Then he was engaged in a temporary assignment; now he urged an idea that he had made his own. He realized that his only hope for success was a proposal that did not threaten the property—or self-interest—of his fellow revolutionaries and their desire to maintain control over their own slaves. The House postponed deliberations until the next day.

The official journal of the House, which provided only a bare outline of the daily proceedings, merely recorded that "after some debate thereupon, The Question being put. It passed in the Negative."[46] Much is implied in those words, "after some debate thereupon." The discussion was heated. To opponents of the proposal, it appeared at first that Laurens had won over a sizable number of representatives. David Ramsay seconded Laurens's efforts, and this time he received support from Thomas Ferguson, a former member of the Privy Council. In the end, however, the measure was rejected decisively. As Nathanael Greene observed, the legislature spurned the plan "Not because they objected to the expence for they give a most enormous bounty to white Men . . . but from an apprehension of the consequences." Laurens's conclusion was even more pointed: "The single voice of reason was drowned by the howlings of a triple-headed monster in which prejudice Avarice & pusillamimity were united."[47]

Comments from opponents were especially revealing. Resistance again hinged on two essential points: white fears of arming and then emancipating a large number of blacks. Edward Rutledge, brother of John Rutledge and an influential political figure in his own right, found Laurens's proposal deeply upsetting, even though it won few adherents. To Arthur Middleton, a South Carolina delegate to the Continental Congress, Rutledge described the debate in martial terms: "We have had another hard Battle on the Subject of arming the Blacks. . . . About 12 or 15 were for it & about 100 against it—I now hope it will rest for ever & a day. But I do assure you I was very much alarmed on the Occasion. I was repeatedly told that a large party was made & I believe it was; but upon a fair full Argument, people in general returned to their Senses, & the Business ended as I have told you."[48]

Outside of his concern over arming slaves, Rutledge did not explicitly state what about Laurens's proposal alarmed him. A clue to the mindset of Rutledge and other opponents is provided by the testimony of the jurist Aedanus Burke, who also wrote a letter to Middleton. After mentioning that General Greene, a Rhode Island native, had supported Laurens's "favorite scheme," Burke launched into a discussion of northern views on slavery and race relations. "The northern people I have observed, regard the condition in which we hold our slaves in a light different from us," he commented. "I am much deceived indeed, if they do not secretly *wish* for a general Emancipation, if the present struggle was over—A very sensible m[a]n whom you well know in Philade[phi]a once mentioned seriously to me, that our Country w[oul]d be a fine one, if our whites & blacks inter-married—the breed w[oul]d be a hardy excellent race, he said, fit to bear our climate."[49] Burke's juxtaposition of miscegenation with the black regiment plan speaks volumes on the fears that John Laurens's proposal aroused. It mattered little that John offered to draw his regiment from confiscated loyalist estates, thereby depriving no revolutionary of his property. For all the talk of the sanctity of property and the inability to work low-country swamps without slave labor, what frightened many white males was an alarming and irrational image of a lower South without slavery, of unrestrained sexual relations between blacks and whites tainting the blood of the master race.[50]

While arming bondsmen was inconceivable, using them as military laborers was not. In response to a report from the committee on furnishing laborers for the army, the legislature resolved to recruit slaves from the confiscated estates to serve Greene's army as artisans, wagoners, pioneers, sappers, and as servants to gentlemen officers.[51]

The Jacksonborough assembly's decisions on slaves mirrored those of the British. Lured by promises of emancipation, thousands of slaves had escaped to the British lines. Though freed blacks were a powerful psychological weapon against southern revolutionaries, British military authorities rarely utilzed them as soldiers and at best granted them ostensible freedom. To do otherwise, the British feared, was to risk losing the allegiance of loyalist slaveholders. Thus blacks usually served as laborers and artisans and, in conditions akin to slavery, grew crops on sequestered rebel plantations under the supervision of white overseers. Respect for property rights and the frightening image of freed blacks bearing arms produced an ambivalent and hypocritical policy on both sides.[52]

In addition to a conclusive political defeat, John faced more unpleasantness. As chairman of the committee that determined which loyalists would lose their estates, he had to judge several old friends and relatives, including his old benefactor Alexander Garden. Though Laurens could not help Garden, his influence helped protect the estate of Alexander Garden, son of the worthy physician and naturalist. Young Garden had recently returned to America after years of study in England. Rather than follow in the footsteps of his loyalist parents, he volunteered his services to Greene's army. On the basis of Laurens's recommendation, Garden received a ready welcome and later joined Greene's staff as aide-de-camp. When Garden petitioned the legislature to preserve his property, he produced an affidavit from John that vouched for his fidelity to the American cause. Thus he escaped the fate of his father, whose estate was among those confiscated.[53]

The committee on confiscation faced a perplexing task. After Laurens made an initial report, the House enlarged the committee, and added twenty-four members so each parish and district would be represented. The committee, according to Aedanus Burke, started with a list of about seven hundred loyalists, but promptly began paring. Burke, an opponent of confiscation and hardly an unbiased observer, contended that greed was the dominant motive, but the committee's final report showed restraint. On 7 February Laurens presented to the House a list of 118 persons and merchant houses whose property was subject to confiscation. Besides Garden the list included John's cousin Elias Ball, and John Hopton, who had been one of Henry Laurens's clerks. For the remainder of the session, the House and Senate worked out the final details of the punitive acts, adding some names and subtracting others.[54]

When the legislature adjourned on 26 February, it had passed confiscation and amercement acts. Under the confiscation law, 237 persons were divided into six categories, including British citizens who were mostly nonresidents, people who had congratulated the redcoats after their victories, men who applied to join the royal militia or who held British commissions, and the severest classification, "inveterate enemies of this State." The amercement law dealt with 47 persons whose actions were "not considered Sufficiently criminal to merit Confiscation." The state fined them 12 percent of the assessed value of their estates. The legislature made an attempt at conciliation: an act of pardon compelled loyalists who did not submit before Rutledge's deadline but had since served in the American military to pay a 10 percent fine, either with money or with slaves.[55]

Among the representatives opinions on the confiscation issue varied. Opponents considered confiscation an arbitrary abuse of power. The proponents included men motivated by revenge and those who saw an opportunity to raise revenue for an indigent state; others, realizing that improved property would be made available, had their eyes on potential profits. In general, however, most assemblymen who favored confiscation probably held less sordid motives. Some retribution against the unfortunate losers was an essential concomitant of such a deleterious conflict. At the very least the penalties enacted by the legislature partially satisfied public clamors for vengeance and forestalled vigilante justice.[56] John Laurens's views are difficult to assess. Based on loyalist testimony and his subsequent actions, one could conclude that he was among the small minority who opposed the penalties. Because he chaired the committee that submitted names to be considered for confiscation, it was more likely that he merely advocated leniency whenever possible. Like several of his colleagues, Laurens probably viewed confiscation as a necessary evil.[57]

John departed Jacksonborough more than a week before the session ended and returned to his post. Before leaving, he again turned his attention to a personal concern. While at Jacksonborough, he received from his father's secretary, Moses Young, a letter dated 28 September. As of that date, Henry remained in the Tower of London, despite Congress's resolution that he be exchanged for John Burgoyne. John transmitted Young's letter to Congress and again urged the delegates to authorize an exchange involving his father and Cornwallis. He also solicited the personal intervention of Washington: "I entreat Your Excellencys pardon for troubling you . . . but my distress for a parent whom I love almost to adoration, and Your Excellency's goodness will form an excuse for me."[58] What John did not know was that Henry had been released on bond on New Year's Eve. In late April he finally received his freedom.[59]

Doubtless John rejoined the army with mixed emotions, relieved to be back where he was most comfortable yet disappointed by the irrevocable failure of a plan that had consumed his thoughts for four years. Whatever his mood, he soon faced a new, stimulating, and potentially rewarding challenge. Henry Lee had retired from the army. Greene decided to award Laurens the command of the army's light troops, which included Lee's Legion. Though he had commanded soldiers in actions before—at Newport, Savannah, Charleston, Yorktown, and Johns Island—those assignments had been temporary, tied to a particular siege or operation. This appointment was the most prestigious yet. "The ambition of serving my Country and desire of gaining Fame," he once said, "leads me to wish for the command of men."[60] Laurens wished to be measured as a gentlemen officer, a leader of men. He had lived and prepared for such a moment. It was potentially the pinnacle of his military career.

Chapter 11

"The Campaign is become perfectly insipid"

The South Carolina Low Country
February–August 1782

John Laurens appeared an ideal choice as commander of the light troops. A low-country native, he was familiar with the terrain and intimately acquainted with many inhabitants from both ends of the political spectrum. From these contacts, he could obtain accurate intelligence, which was one of the light corps's functions and an essential ingredient of its success. As a subsidiary of the main army, light troops were more adept at raiding and harassing the enemy than they were in set battles. Their triumphs depended on rapid mobility and deception. Greene placed under Laurens's command Lee's Legion, the Third Regiment of light dragoons, and the Delaware Regiment of light infantry. Laurens proved a controversial choice, largely because Henry Lee departed from the army under a cloud of recriminations.[1]

Even before the debacle at Johns Island, Lee had been dissatisfied. He contended that Greene slighted him in the official reports of the Southern campaign. In reality Lee's chagrin was sparked by Continental and militia officers who resented him as commander of an elite corps that received special attention. Haughty and petulant, he was sensitive to any snub to his honor. After years of active duty, he was also physically and emotionally drained and suffered from battle fatigue. Laurens's arrival and assumption of command at Johns Island only exacerbated Lee's discontent.[2]

Rumors abounded in camp that Laurens was the root of the problem. Greene planned to award Laurens a command, so the stories went, in order to placate Washington, who wanted his aide-de-camp to receive honors commensurate with his service. Lee did little to help matters. In a thinly veiled jab at Laurens's impulsiveness, he suggested that Greene "send an officer of great oeconomy to command" the Legion. "If he is an experimenter," concluded Lee, "he will waste the troops very fast." To no avail Greene attempted to assuage Lee's wounded honor and convince him to remain. "I wish to become truely obscure," Lee insisted. So he left.[3]

Laurens received his command when opportunities for military fame were few and far between. It was now a limited war, a concept he found intolerable. The American army kept watch on the British in Charleston and tried to prevent them from raiding the countryside for provisions. Outnumbered by the British garrison, Greene could do little else. "Every thing depends upon our holding our ground," he asserted. Typical of the operations of that period was Laurens's first assignment in late February, when a British detachment of 700 infantry and cavalry invaded St. Thomas Parish in search of forage. The redcoats routed a party of militia under General Francis Marion, although the celebrated "Swamp Fox" was absent at the time. Afraid that the enemy intended to pillage Georgetown, the only port open to the Americans, Greene promptly sent Laurens, with 170 infantry and 94 cavalry, to assist Marion. The British did not risk an encounter with the Continentals and returned to Charleston with their spoils. Laurens arrived too late to nab his prey.[4]

"The present is an insipid idle time," Laurens told Greene. He searched for action and found it. The British had stationed a galley on Ashley River whose crew made frequent incursions ashore "to plunder and distress the inhabitants." Laurens authorized Captain Michael Rudolph to plan a surprise attack. On the night of 20 March, Rudolph, along with a small party of the Legion infantry, ambushed and captured most of the galley's forty-man crew. After removing supplies, the Americans, who suffered no casualties, destroyed the vessel. "Their bravery & good conduct in surmounting a variety of difficulties entitle them to great applause," reported Laurens. Greene concurred: "No enterprise this war has exceeded it."[5]

Laurens spent much of his time performing an assignment that was essential to the army's security, a duty he was well qualified to discharge. He used personal connections, which as a prominent and respected Carolinian he had acquired, to recruit spies and gather intelligence of British plans. Greene believed that the "earliest intelligence of the Enemy's intentions" was vital "both to the People, protection of property, and Security of the Troops." Therefore, he later explained, "As Lt. Colo. Laurens was better acquainted with characters than I could be from being a Stranger in the Country, I prevailed on him to select such as he thought best calculated for this service."[6]

Laurens gathered intelligence from a variety of sources. Some informants, like Thomas Farr, were supporters of the revolutionary government who nonetheless had contact with inhabitants and refugees in Charleston. Laurens's position near the enemy lines placed him in position to receive deserters—both British regulars and loyalist militia eager to return to their homes—who invariably supplied the latest news. Loyalist informants from Charleston, a valuable source, frequently refused to give something for nothing. Laurens furnished them supplies in return for their testimony. More representative of his spies was Eliza Clitherall, the wife of Dr. James Clitherall, a loyalist whose estate had been confiscated. Hoping both to secure her husband's pardon and to obtain supplies from their plantation, Clitherall gave Laurens frequent reports of British activity in Charleston. Laurens regarded Clitherall as an irritant and even suggested to Greene that her services be discontinued. Still, she continued to provide intelligence, and her efforts proved at least partially successful. In 1784 the state legislature removed the Clitheralls from the confiscation list and amerced their estate.[7]

Considering the slowness of transatlantic communications, two important letters bearing bad tidings probably reached Laurens sometime in March. In November Benjamin Franklin wrote to inform him of the fallout from his hurried diplomatic mission. The fiasco in Holland, he told John, "cannot please you." In addition to the headaches caused by William Jackson, Alexander Gillon, and Jean de Neufville, there was the question of the ten-million-livre loan negotiated by Laurens. The French and Dutch finally approved the arrangement, wrote Franklin, "but as considerable Advances have already been made on the Faith of it, there will be great Deductions, and I would not have you expect too much of it to arrive in Cash."[8] Lauren's response, unfortunately, was not recorded. Whether or not he regretted the haste and naivete with which he had conducted arrangements with Gillon and de Neufville, it was now obvious that his mission had been less than a sterling success.

Of a personal and more melancholy nature was the news that Martha Manning Laurens had died the previous fall in Lisle, France. Upon learning that John was in France, it appears that Martha traveled there with Fanny, hoping to meet her husband and introduce him to his child. Doubtless the reunion never occurred, as his efforts to win additional French aid totally consumed his time and energies. It is likely, moreover, that Martha did not commence her journey until the mission was nearly completed. Once in France she apparently became ill and was compelled to stay. In death, as in life, Martha remained elusive. From Benjamin Vaughan, her brother-in-law, comes the only extant detail of her death: "Her clothes she bequeathed to her maid, to the amount only of some 20£ or 30£; & her watch & trinkets to a most lovely child, now in part the object of my cares."[9]

Even more frustrating, there is no record of John's reaction. Any pain he felt was perhaps dulled. After all, he had not seen his wife in over five years.

From his perspective, it was a marriage born of duty and honor, not deep and abiding love. Yet it would have been characteristic of John to reproach himself, to feel some responsibility. He had consistently put Martha off, telling her she could not come to America until travel was safer. To be sure, those admonitions contained more truth than disingenuousness. Yet Martha's desire to hazard all and take her child to America provides additional evidence that she at least viewed the marriage as more than an expedient. Now she had died alone in an alien country, bereft of loved ones, an ocean away from a husband who placed civic duty and military fame over any obligation to his family. Did Laurens feel guilt? Did he think of a five-year-old daughter he had never seen, who now became his charge? Did he reflect on his private foibles, such as the failure to resist sexual temptation, despite repeated warnings from his father, or his abandonment of his wife and child? The questions linger, the answers remain elusive.

On other occasions Laurens could have used military action as a catharsis, an escape from ennui and despair. This campaign, however, was different. Long periods of inactivity were punctuated by British incursions into the low country in search of provisions. A detachment of redcoats that raided St. Thomas Parish in late March had a different objective. Laurens, with his light infantry and cavalry, again went to aid Francis Marion. Greene hoped his troops could strike a decisive blow against the British and boost sagging American morale. At the very least Laurens wanted to "prevent their retiring with impunity."[10]

Their hopes were dashed. Unable to obtain intelligence of British movements from uncooperative slaves in the Santee River area, Laurens failed to block the redcoats' retreat to Charleston. Greene feared that the operation was merely a feint that had forced him to divide his force, whereupon the British would venture from Charleston and launch a major assault. He promptly recalled the light troops. Laurens knew better. "Their object was the capture of negroes," he told Greene.[11]

His assessment was confirmed by General Alexander Leslie, the commander at Charleston. The raid, he informed Greene, was retaliatory, a response to the confiscation acts passed by the Jacksonborough assembly. When the British captured Charleston, they sequestered the estates of prominent rebels such as Henry Laurens. According to Leslie, they carefully conserved, rather than squandered, sequestered property under their control. Unless the Carolinians retracted their punitive legislation against loyalists, Leslie resolved, his troops would continue to seize slaves belonging to supporters of the revolutionary government. Greene instructed Marion to warn slaves. "If the Negroes are advertized of the enemies intentions," Greene remarked, "I think they will get but few of them." Faced with the prospect of exchanging one master for another, slaves were truly caught between a rock and a hard place.[12]

Always respectful of civil authority, Greene forwarded Leslie's letter to Governor John Mathews, who had been elected at Jacksonborough to replace Rutledge. Mathews's response to Leslie was hot and direct. Contrary to Leslie's depiction of a benign British policy, Mathews charged the redcoats with commandeering from the sequestered estates "every species of property, Negroes, Plate, Household furniture, Horses, Carriages, Cattle, &c." On the other hand, when the state assembly implemented the confiscation legislation, it respected private contracts, such as marriages, and "left untouched" the debts owed to loyalists by state citizens. If Leslie persisted in seizing slaves, Mathews threatened to remove those safeguards. Each side appointed commissioners to deliberate their differences, but they could reach no settlement.[13]

So matters rested. The inaction was almost more than Laurens could bear. He searched for opportunities to strike the British light troops, he wrote Thomas Bee, "but their System is so strictly defensive that the Campaign is become perfectly insipid." Major Thomas Fraser, the British cavalry commander, avoided confrontation and always kept "a navigable River between" his troops and Laurens's men. Fraser's infrequent raids, Laurens complained, focused solely on "Stealing Negroes or poultry." Greene likewise wished to take the offensive, but the state legislature's refusal to sanction the enlistment of blacks prevented him from doing so.[14]

Laurens's frustration escalated when Greene temporarily sent the light troops to the rear of the army, a move made necessary because of the lack of forage. Not only was grain scarce but there were not enough wagons available to transport provisions. Compounding the problem, cavalry officers under Laurens's command irritated civil authorities when they allowed their sick horses to graze on confiscated plantations. The horses consumed what little rice that remained, depriving the slaves of their sustenance. After receiving a complaint from Governor Mathews, Greene issued a stern reprimand to two of Laurens's officers, Major John Rudulph of the Legion and Major Richard Call of the Third Regiment. Laurens, who always desired a position nearest the enemy, chafed over the limits placed on him. He reacted so strongly to the transfer of his troops that Greene became concerned. "This was little less than death to Laurens," Greene wrote, "who wishes to fight much more than I wish he should."[15]

Supply problems plagued both sides. According to Thomas Farr, one of Laurens's informants, the garrison at Charleston subsisted on reduced rations. For their part, the Americans lacked food, rum, and clothing, and many men were literally half-naked. The situation called for a temporary expedient. Governor Mathews and the Privy Council sanctioned commerce "by stealth" with the British garrison. Laurens helped organize the contraband trade, whereby the Americans furnished rice to the British in return for clothing and medical supplies. The arrangement served the needs of both sides and was renewed at intervals while the British held Charleston. There was, in addition, a substantial illicit trade conducted by self-interested civilians who were tempted because the British paid with hard money. That trade did not win Mathews's approval and he tried to stop it, but with limited success.[16]

Other expedients proved questionable. Several officers, resorting to a practice that had been common throughout the war, impressed supplies from civilians. Once officers appropriated private property for public use, they granted owners a receipt that could be used to receive payment from the state. Some plantation owners surrendered nearly all of their provisions, leaving little for their family's subsistence. Thomas Farr secured from Laurens written protection for his remaining stock, for without that safeguard, he believed, "my Family as well as my Slaves must inevitably Starve." The legislature had outlawed impressment, which was at best a necessary evil. Now Governor Mathews sought to enforce the new law, a statute Laurens considered too restrictive. He wondered how his troops would be supplied.[17]

In response Mathews appointed William Hort commissary general and the state assumed responsibility for supplying the army. Though Mathews continually expressed confidence in Hort, the new head of the commissary department failed to supply the army with choice beef. Greene protested, but in fairness to Hort the poor quality of beef was to a large extent a result of the war and not a reflection on his competence. Exhausted from two years of literal chaos, the state government alone simply could not meet the army's needs. While Greene appreciated Mathews's efforts, he believed that the problem stemmed from the low country's limited commitment to independence. Like Benjamin Lincoln before him, Greene contended that low-country Carolinians were selfish, that their "love of property" superseded "zeal for the service."[18]

The dearth of provisions spawned defiance among the troops, with Laurens's command being perhaps the chief offenders. Under Henry Lee's direction, the Legion had grown accustomed to being well fed. They expected and generally received special treatment. When it was not forthcoming, their officers took matters into their own hands and impressed cattle. Whether or not they had Laurens's endorsement is unclear. In any event, Mathews again objected to the violation of state law.

In civil-military disputes, Greene consistently and prudently submitted to civil authority. This case was no exception. He enjoined Laurens to put a stop to impressments, which were to be a last resort, utilized only "in cases of great necessity." While he considered the Legion an elite corps, on this occasion he found the soldiers' haughtiness oppressive. "The Governor says he has been informed that the light troops say they will not live as the Army does," Greene wrote Laurens. "This is a language so opposite to their general character that

I am persuaded there must be some mistake. . . . They will and shall live as the Army does. And I persuade my self they have too much pride and dignity to murmur at that fare which is common in the Army."[19]

Greene used a decidedly different tone with Mathews. He defended his light corps, assuring the governor that the soldiers' actions were impulsive, not premeditated. "The service of the light troops is a little peculiar," he informed Mathews, "and it is a rule in all Armies to grant them rather better fare than the line, because their service is harder and because they have greater opportunities for desertion as well as serve as a necessary check to the desertion of the Army. . . . The manner in which they move about the Country will afford greater opportunities for the Men to commit enormities than the line and this is unavoidable in some instances." Mathews agreed in theory, but he argued that this transgression was different. Members of the light corps had impressed beef while quartered with the main army, when they were encamped "within two miles of the magazine from which the army is supplyed."[20]

As a commander, Laurens found more frustration than rewards, albeit he proved attentive to the needs of his troops. His problems, to some extent, were a natural outgrowth of succeeding an almost legendary figure as leader of a corps already renowned in the war's annals. On the other hand, his temerity could not have endeared him to men who, while inured to danger, were also accustomed to Henry Lee's style of leadership, which had stressed detailed planning and prudent execution. In the hit-and-run warfare practiced by light troops, haste quite literally made waste.[21]

While Laurens's temperament made the transition of command difficult, he also inherited problems. A condescending air had prevailed among Legion officers, particularly Major John Rudulph, for some time. Rudulph had expected to be appointed Lee's replacement, but he lacked the requisite ability. "Major Rudolph wanted to personate you," Greene informed Lee, "but nature never formed him for it. He is a brave officer; but is too petulant and impatient at times." Rudulph often acted as if he, rather than Laurens, commanded the Legion. For example, on one occasion Rudulph imperiously demanded additional clothing for his troops, only to receive Greene's reminder that "some regard must be paid to the general condition of the army." Not a man who quieted down, Rudulph pressed Greene to shift horses from the state militia to the "*faithful gallant*" Legion. This time he had the support of Laurens, who went so far as to petition Governor Mathews and the Privy Council. Mathews concurred, but left the final decision to Greene. The general recognized the Legion's need for new horses and procured some from North Carolina, but he refused to deprive South Carolina's militia of their horses, which largely had been paid for by their own officers.[22]

While Henry Lee had instilled in his men a fierce, unswerving pride, he also demanded and received strict obedience to his orders. Under Lee, the Legion had won fame not only for heroic exploits but also for superior discipline. That reputation began to unravel after he departed. The soldiers did not respect Laurens and questioned his competency as a cavalry officer. "I am sorry to inform you that Col Laurens is by no means popular with the Legion," wrote Greene to Lee. Without Lee at the helm, the Legion became almost unruly, ceasing to pay attention to the small details he had emphasized. "Your absence from the Corps," one officer informed Lee, "has been too evident to escape even the unobserving."[23]

Complicating Laurens's headaches, "Great jealousies subsist[ed]" between the Legion cavalry and the light dragoons of the Third Regiment. Major Richard Call protested to Laurens when Greene gave to the Legion the post of honor. Under this arrangement, when the army marched, the Legion advanced in front, and in the order of battle the Legion assumed a position to the right of the Third Regiment. Laurens referred Call's complaint to Greene, who maintained his original stance. Call's irritation mounted when he determined that the Legion received favoritism in prisoner exchanges. "With the greatest emotion," Call informed Greene that his men were "being deprived of their usual post of honor & proper turn of exchange." Because the British appeared unwilling to risk a major battle, the frustrated Call requested a leave of absence.[24]

It was perhaps natural that inaction prompted the men to fight among themselves over questions of honor. "Nor can we hope for an agreeable change," observed Laurens. On 5 May, General Leslie, in response to orders from New York, dispatched thirteen hundred troops to Jamaica. Leslie parted with those soldiers reluctantly. Their departure, he feared, would force him to evacuate his advanced positions on Charleston Neck, from where raiding parties had sallied forth to harass the rebel army and obtain supplies. Despite the troop transfers, Leslie's garrison of almost four thousand still outnumbered the American force. So long as the redcoats continued to occupy Charleston and Savannah, Greene expected them to take the offensive. Laurens also reacted skeptically to reports that an evacuation was near and peace was at hand; he believed that the only reliable indicators would come from Parliament.[25]

In fact, in February the House of Commons had voted against further prosecution of the war. Upon receiving notification, Leslie forwarded the news to Greene and proposed a cease-fire. Without authorization from Congress, Greene responded that he could not terminate hostilities. "We all hope for peace," he said, "but only upon honorable and advantageous terms."[26] For the time being, the campaign continued as before, with each side warily eyeing the other, unable or unwilling to risk a costly engagement. And Laurens continued as before, brooding over the limited opportunities for action. "I wish the enemy would either withdraw or fight us," he said.[27]

If Laurens thought that insubordination and immoderate behavior among his troops could get no worse, he was sadly mistaken. The arrival of Lieutenant Colonel George Baylor at camp in early June prompted Greene to reorganize the light troops. He placed all the regiments under Brigadier General Mordecai Gist. Baylor, a cavalry officer, assumed command of the Legion cavalry and the light dragoons of the Third and Fourth Regiments. Laurens retained control over the Legion infantry, the Delaware Regiment, and dismounted troops from the Third Regiment.[28]

Major Rudulph, along with five captains of the Legion, issued an immediate protest. They argued that under no circumstance were their cavalry and infantry to be separated. That was one of the Legion's privileges. Greene disagreed, asserting that as commander he could rearrange the army as he saw fit, and on the present occasion he considered it necessary to combine his force. When the officers peremptorily submitted their resignations, Greene proved equally obdurate and accepted them. In calling their bluff, he cautioned them not "to suppose the public cannot do without you."[29]

Laurens was deeply embarrassed. His failure to win the respect of the Legion officers cut deeply and wounded his pride. Even before this controversy, there were rumors that he would resign his command. He was away from camp searching for a location to construct a bridge across the Ashley River and did not learn of this latest discord until 20 June. Laurens immediately informed Greene "that any considerations relative to me should be totally laid aside." The following day he expressed his wish for harmony above all else; to avoid dissension, he would have relinquished his command willingly. John offered to talk to the officers, though he considered their behavior inexplicable. He concluded his letter with a repetition of selflessness, in language that connoted resignation and defeat. "In any future discussion of it sh[oul]d the Gentlemen discover an inclination to return to their duty," he told Greene, "which I think if they know their own interest they must feel very strongly, beg that I may be considered totally out of the question."[30]

The Legion officers wanted anyone but Laurens as their leader. "They had taken a great dislike to poor Lawrens . . .," Greene wrote Lee, "and they were determined to be removed from under his command if possible, and would listen to nothing that opposed it." Though irritated by their arrogance, Greene remembered that in the past these officers had served with distinction. He thus settled the dispute in a manner that allowed them to preserve some semblance of their honor. He submitted the question to Congress, while Rudulph and the other officers returned to their posts. Not surprisingly, the delegates backed the general.[31]

As for Laurens, Greene sent him on a potentially hazardous assignment to gather intelligence. Greene still did not trust the British and needed accurate information about their plans. Because of the respect Laurens commanded in the low country, he was the best qualified man for the job, but Greene probably also wanted to spare the young officer further humiliation and remove him as far from the Legion officers as possible. John took a position between the two armies, beyond the protection offered by American sentries. It was imperative that his spies, a majority of whom were loyalists, be allowed free access to him. "I think there is a probability of the peoples being a little skitish who are employed in the channel of intelligence," acknowledged Greene. "One of them in particular who I know is very shy and who is most to be depended on." He ordered Mordecai Gist to supply a small number of guards to cover Laurens.[32]

At his new post, Laurens learned from spies that the British were removing cannon from Charleston but that a general evacuation would not occur until October at the earliest. The troops at the enemy's advanced post on Charleston Neck, known as the Quarter House, were unhealthy, and Leslie planned to relinquish that position. Laurens's sources, it turned out, proved essentially accurate and closely paralleled the particulars in Leslie's official correspondence.[33]

Laurens had always found inactivity grating and longed for some deviation from the monotony. Richard Howley, the former governor of Georgia, urged him to introduce his black regiment proposal to the state assembly, which was scheduled to convene that summer. Though Congress in 1779 had suggested that both South Carolina and Georgia form black regiments, the latter state had never debated the matter. The idea temporarily revived John, though by now he wisely realized that there was little hope for success. Still, he refused to let go—"my reputation is at stake," he had said earlier. He had immersed himself so deeply in his plan that each political defeat in a real sense became a personal failure.[34]

There are no extant reports from Laurens to Greene between mid-July and early August, so it is possible that John did go to Georgia. That period coincides with the meeting of Georgia's assembly, which convened from 13 July to 5 August. The evidence is circumstantial, for there is no record in the assembly's journal that a plan to employ slaves was introduced during the session. One thing is certain: the Georgians were no more interested in arming bondsmen than were their neighbors. Their primary concern, when the session opened, was to prevent the British who occupied Savannah from removing slaves, whose loss "wou'd be a manifest injury to this Country, and greatly impede the improvement thereof."[35]

If Laurens presented the plan in Georgia, his timing, to say the least, was poor. On 11 July the British evacuated Savannah, which appeared to obviate the need for additional American troops in Georgia. Greene soon confirmed this point. Fearing that the redcoats from Savannah would augment Leslie's force and allow him to mount an offensive, he ordered Anthony Wayne to return with his Continentals to South Carolina. Greene's apprehensions to the contrary, Leslie's force was in no condition to pose a threat, even if his superiors had authorized an offensive. Leslie did order ashore from the Savannah fleet over eight hundred provincial troops to reinforce his sickly garrison. The additional men allowed him to maintain his perimeter of defense. On 1 August he received orders from Sir Guy Carleton, the new British commander in chief, to prepare to evacuate Charleston.[36]

Despite the earlier authorized contraband trade, the Americans now attempted to prevent all supplies from reaching Charleston. To collect much-needed rice, Leslie sent a foraging expedition to raid plantations along the Santee River. The redcoats returned with over five hundred barrels of rice. With the evacuation imminent, Leslie asked that Greene agree to furnish rice, making future forays unnecessary. Greene forwarded the petition to Mathews and the Privy Council, who flatly refused. Like Greene, they reasoned that acquiescence in Leslie's request might prolong the British presence in Charleston. They preferred instead to chance additional foraging raids.[37]

While Carolina's leaders hoped to hasten the British evacuation of Charleston, their stance in this case was only partly influenced by strategic considerations. Another issue, one they deemed particularly critical, loomed in their minds. "The more scanty we can render their supplies of provisions," Greene observed, "the sooner it will happen, and the fewer negroes they will have in their power to take with them." Carolinians, like their neighbors in Georgia, worried frantically over the potentially ruinous loss of slave property—and with good reason. Leslie believed that blacks "who have voluntarily come in, under the faith of our protection, cannot in justice be abandoned to the merciless resentment of their former masters." He planned to remove as many as possible from Charleston.[38]

Laurens, meanwhile, continued to gather intelligence. One of his principal and most reliable sources was Andrew Williamson. From Williamson, he learned that lack of transport ships prevented the British from conducting a prompt withdrawal. Because of the inordinate delay, Greene had questioned British sincerity; this news provided evidence that forces beyond Leslie's control compelled him to remain.[39]

A backcountry planter, Williamson began the war as a prominent officer in the South Carolina militia. When the British subjugated the state, he switched sides and swore allegiance to George III. To many revolutionaries, Williamson's name became synonymous with treason. The Jacksonborough assembly branded him an enemy of the state, confiscated his estate, and ordered that he be exiled. He was understandably cautious about meeting Laurens. John preserved a veil of secrecy over Williamson and referred to him as "W" in correspondence with Greene. To facilitate their meetings, Laurens relocated near Thomas Fuller's Pierponts plantation on the Ashley River in St. Andrew Parish. This location provided improved access to both his spies and deserters from the loyalist militia.[40]

Eliza Clitherall remained part of Laurens's intelligence network, though he continued to view her as an irritant and pronounced one of her letters "as insignificant as all her preceeding epistles." Another loyalist whose estate had been confiscated, the merchant Edmund Petrie, informed Laurens that a party of armed blacks planned to raid Christ Church Parish. "This must be prevented," urged Petrie, "as they care not for Sex or Life of any thing they meet with." As the withdrawal neared, the British finally unleashed a force that fulfilled every Carolinian's worst nightmare.[41]

Loyalists such as Williamson, Clitherall, and Petrie played a dangerous game. They ran the risk of severe punishment if the British caught them. Their only hope lay in their service as spies, which was in effect an expiation for prior sins. Laurens's recommendation, coupled with Greene's, could sway the legislature to be merciful and restore their property and citizenship. If the gamble failed, they lost everything. Each of them exemplified a characteristic common among Americans during the war—the tendency to respond to brute strength, to align with the side that held the upper hand.

In early August Governor Mathews circulated a proclamation calling on loyalists to surrender to state authorities. While the exact details of the proclamation are unclear, apparently Mathews copied the earlier proclamation issued by Rutledge and required loyalists to serve in the state militia for six months or furnish a substitute.[42] Under the circumstances, with the evacuation only a matter of time, Laurens believed that Mathews should have been more conciliatory. "I am exceedingly sorry the Governors proclamation had not been dictated by a more liberal policy," he told Greene. "I think there w[oul]d have been such a sudden general defection from the british Interests as w[oul]d have ensured us great advantages."[43]

From his vantage point, Laurens had constant contact with loyalists. While the British contracted their defenses and loaded armaments on vessels, numerous loyal Carolinians desperately tried to avoid deportation from their native land. They faced an uncertain future. Laurens listened to them and proved sympathetic with their distress. "The exiles are in a State of despair," he observed, "my advice to them is to remonstrate in a body and sollicit leave to remain till the decision of a future Legislature can be had." In other words, there was more safety in numbers. Laurens thought that the revolutionary government should adopt a more lenient policy. "I wish that this State may even follow the example of Georgia," he mused, "in extending pardon to some of the least obnoxious exiles."[44]

Williamson, on the advice of friends, considered surrendering and accepting the terms offered by Mathews. "As he is likely to be of farther utility to us," explained Laurens to Greene, "I have discouraged it assuring him, of your protection & justification of his conduct to the Executive." Laurens's pledge was fulfilled. Greene later wrote to Mathews and recommended leniency toward Williamson. Greene informed the governor that Williamson had "run every risque to render his information useful" and he provided "generally the best information we have had, being much in the confidence of the enemy and a man of sense and observation." In response, the legislature removed Williamson from the confiscation list and amerced his estate. Greene also interceded for Petrie, who received a full pardon because he served as one of Laurens's spies.[45]

Although Laurens obtained valuable intelligence, he found his post exposed and isolated. Because he was positioned far from the main army, food often arrived late and was spoiled by the heat. Increasing the difficulties, Laurens and some of his troops became ill with fever. There were even implications that some of the men fretted over their monotonous duty. "The Detachment from the line on duty here, are rather sickly," Laurens informed Greene, "for this reason, and because they are not picked men, I request that they may be relieved." Greene promptly complied with Laurens's plea for reinforcements and augmented his small guard of one sergeant and twelve men with twenty troops and a dependable subordinate officer. The problems experienced by Laurens's small command were not unique. In 1782 the sickly season proved especially severe, and both armies were racked with illness. Despite a fever that occasionally confined him to his bed, Laurens continued to gather intelligence from his spies and, when possible, intervened on behalf of loyalist refugees.[46]

While John performed his duty in relative isolation, he maintained contact with his closest friend. Far away in Albany, New York, Alexander Hamilton lived with his wife and infant son and prepared for a law career. Earlier that year he penned two letters that, with his usual cynical bent, seemed to presage retirement from public service. John urged him to reconsider. A man of Hamilton's talents, he believed, could not withdraw when his country needed him. Laurens submitted himself so completely to the revolutionary cause that his wife and daughter had figured little in his public decisions, and he expected similar behavior from his friend. He could not imagine that the birth of a son could detain Hamilton from attending Congress: "Your private affairs cannot require such immediate and close attention; you speak like a pater familias surrounded with a numerous progeny." In previous campaigns in South Carolina, John had remained busy, consumed by his black regiment proposal or involved in military actions. Then he remained so absorbed in the affairs at hand that he neglected to write Hamilton. Now, frustrated by the limited opportunities for action and wounded by the dispute with the Legion officers, he longed for

Hamilton to write: "Adieu, my dear friend; while circumstances place so great a distance between us, I entreat you not to withdraw the *consolation* of your letters. You know the unalterable sentiments of your affectionate Laurens."[47]

On 15 August Hamilton replied, assuring Laurens that he would attend Congress. With peace at hand, he observed, it was now necessary to "secure our *union*." Forging a strong nation after a protracted war was indeed "an herculean task," and he longed for Laurens's assistance. "Quit your sword my friend," he urged, "put on the *toga*, come to Congress. We know each others sentiments, our views are the same: we have fought side by side to make America free, let us hand in hand struggle to make her happy." His wife and son aside, Laurens still occupied a prominent place in his heart. In closing the letter, Hamilton wrote, "Y[ou]rs for ever."[48]

At the same time, the British in Charleston proceeded with preparations for their departure. While they awaited sufficient transports, the paucity of provisions remained a pressing problem. On 21 August Leslie sent two detachments on foraging raids, one to St. Helena Parish, the other, under the command of Major William Brereton, to plantations along the Combahee River. After combing these areas, the two forces were to rendezvous at Barnwell's Island and forage near the Coosawhatchie River.[49]

Greene learned from his intelligence service that a small fleet consisting of a sloop of war, three galleys, three brigantines, and ten empty sloops and schooners, had departed Charleston. Not yet certain of their destination, he directed Francis Marion to be on the alert along the Santee River and ordered Mordecai Gist to march to the Combahee River with the light troops. "You should strike at them whenever you may meet them," Greene instructed Gist, "unless some particular circumstance should prohibit it." Stationed at Chehaw Neck, about twelve miles from Combahee Ferry, Captain William McKennan of the Delaware Regiment received frequent updates on Brereton's movements. The British, McKennan reported to Greene, probably aimed to procure corn and slaves from the plantations along the Combahee River.[50]

From his sickbed, Laurens learned of Gist's orders. He forwarded the latest news to headquarters and added a query: "Vague intelligence reached me of the march of the light troops—will you be so good as to inform me, whether any thing is likely to be done?" Aware of Greene's resolve to prevent the enemy from obtaining provisions, Laurens recognized the potential for action. Moving to counter a British foraging party hardly amounted to the decisive final battle he had dreamed of, but it would have to do. He hurried to the Combahee River, announcing "that he would return with all possible expedition" to his post.[51] Though his departure was a dereliction of his duty, it is unlikely that he vacillated. After all, he was still under Gist's command, and the light infantry remained his troops. Such rationalizations probably convinced him that he acted correctly.

Thus far it had been a year of repeated disappointments that fractured his self-esteem: a botched operation at Johns Island, a conclusive political defeat, a dormant military campaign, followed by another death that undoubtedly elicited ambivalent emotions, and all compounded by haughty officers whose insubordination reflected poorly on his ability to command. His aspirations in the public arena thwarted, Laurens desperately needed to prove himself again, at a time when opportunities to act were few. He sensed a last chance to demonstrate his public virtue and win military fame. It was a call he could not fail to heed.

Gist and his force reached the north side of the Combahee River on the evening of Sunday, 25 August. The British had arrived first and commandeered the ferry. The following morning Gist learned that about three hundred redcoats had crossed the river to Arthur Middleton's plantation and established separate camps. He sent Major Richard Call with the Third Regiment cavalry across the river to join the light infantry and militia already on the south side. At daybreak on 27 August, they were to attack the redcoats.

Gist also decided to construct a breastwork on Tar Bluff at Chehaw Neck in order to bombard the British vessels when they returned to sea. Laurens arrived on 26 August and asked for command of that post. Gist consented and sent with him a detachment of fifty troops, including infantry from the Delaware Regiment and artillerymen under Captain James Smith, who would man a howitzer.[52]

That evening, according to tradition, Laurens visited the Stock family plantation at the Combahee River. There, along with Captain Smith, he enjoyed the company of Mrs. Stock and her daughters. The conversation did not avoid the impending engagement. Instead, with characteristic gallantry, Laurens proposed that the ladies view the action from the safety of a scaffold. It was typical bravado from a man who had previously called combat a "game," and labeled one action "a frolicking skirmish."[53]

At 3:00 A.M. Laurens proceeded to Chehaw Neck, unaware that the British had already boarded their ships and "drop'd silently down the river with the Tide." Gist's lookouts did not detect their departure until 4:00 A.M., approximately two hours after they had slipped away. After dispatching a warning to Laurens, Gist hurried to Chehaw Neck with 150 infantry and cavalry, hoping to prevent the redcoats from going ashore. Laurens's tiny detachment, he realized, was extremely vulnerable.[54]

Prior to Laurens's arrival, about 150 redcoats had landed on the north bank of the river and deployed along the road leading to Chehaw Neck, behind a clump of underbrush. They outmaneuvered the Americans with such skill that it seems likely that spies informed them of Gist's plans. Shortly before dawn, Laurens's detachment arrived. When John discovered the enemy's position, he had two options: to attack or fall back and await help. The prudent alternative, with his troops outnumbered three to one, was to wait for Gist, who was only two miles away with reinforcements, "coming forward with Giantick Strides." John had faced similar choices before and always he responded in the same way. With Laurens was Captain William McKennan, who observed that his commander appeared "anxious to attack the enemy previous to the main body coming up." Laurens's "troops, although few in numbers, were as he supposed sufficient to enable him to gain a laurel for his brow previous to a cessation of arms, and . . . [he] could not wait until the main body of the detachment would arrive, but wanted to do all himself, and have all the honor." Giving little consideration to the enemy's superior numbers and strong position, John ordered an immediate assault. It was the only tactic he knew—act and force the enemy to react.[55]

When the Americans charged, the British immediately opened fire with deadly effect. Laurens collapsed to the ground mortally wounded. Before the volleys were completed, Captain Smith and several enlisted men also fell with wounds. The remainder of the detachment beat a hasty retreat, leaving the howitzer behind. Gist arrived with his cavalry in time to cover the withdrawal. He tried to dislodge the British from their position in the woods on his right flank, but his troops could not penetrate "a small work of Logs and Brush in which the enemy threw themselves." In this terrain Gist's cavalry was useless, and he found his infantry "dispirited and fatigued" from their forced march. He wisely refused to press further and allowed the British to retreat to their ships. Captain James Gunn made a final sally with a party of cavalry and managed to retrieve the artillery horses, but the howitzer remained a British prize. The brief affair proved costly for the Americans. They lost two killed—Laurens and a corporal of the Legion cavalry—and there were nineteen wounded and three missing. Captain Smith died later from his wounds. The British suffered "inconsiderable loss"—one dead and seven wounded.[56]

Gist dispatched to Greene a report of the skirmish and included a list of the medicine needed for the wounded. He decided to rest his weary detachment at the Stock plantation, "where the Corpse of Colo. Laurens shall be inter'd with every mark of distinction due to his Rank and Merit." After the burial ceremony, Gist remained along the Combahee River, maintaining a watchful eye on British movements. Facing no further opposition, Brereton consolidated his force with the other detachment of redcoats and continued to collect provisions. When the British returned to Charleston, they carried with them "a considerable number of cattle" and three hundred barrels of rice and corn.[57]

Chapter 12

"The loss is remediless"

The Family of John Laurens
1782–1860

When Nathanael Greene learned of the action at Chehaw Neck, he expressed sadness and annoyance. He had lost a valued officer and friend. At the same time, that officer had disobeyed orders, left his post of duty, and foolishly engaged an enemy that outnumbered his detachment three to one. The defeat came when American morale was shaky at best, and Greene remained unsure about British intentions. He could ill afford senseless losses.

Both emotions remained conspicuous in a letter he sent almost a month later to Otho Holland Williams, a brigadier general who had served in the Southern Department. Greene presented a portrait of a dispirited officer:

> Poor Laurens is fallen in a paltry little skirmish. You knew his temper, and I pre-dicted his fate. I wish his fall had been as glorious as his fate is much to be lamented. The love of military glory made him seek it upon occasions unworthy his rank. This state will feel his loss; and his father will hardly survive it. He ha[d] been rather unhappy in his command in the opposition he met with from the Offi-cers of the Legion. The pride of the Corps from long indulgence and from their great reputation made them not unlike the Pretorian guards difficult to govern and impatient of subordination.[1]

In Charleston both the British and loyalists mourned Laurens's untimely death. "The British lament the death of Colo Laurens very much," reported one woman, "and speak of him in terms unusually generous." A eulogy in the *Royal Gazette* could identify only one blemish on Laurens's character—his decision to rebel against his king. "His generosity of temper and liberality of opinion," observed the writer, "were as extensive as his abilities." According to confidential sources—most likely operatives in his spy network—Laurens criticized Governor Mathews's refusal to allow the British to purchase rice, the policy, ironically, that led to his death. It was heartless, Laurens had contended, to withhold provisions from the exiles and their slaves. "While we were thus marking the death of an enemy who was dangerous to our Cause from his abilities," concluded the paper, "we hope we shall stand excused for paying tribute . . . to the *moral* excellencies of his character—Happy would it be for the distressed families of those persons who are to leave this garrison with his Majesty's troops that another LAURENS could be found!"[2]

Throughout his life John Laurens, the man of feeling, showed compassion for the unfortunate—widows and orphans, slaves and loyalist refugees. Yet his actions also revealed curious anomalies. After Laurens's death, Colonel Thaddeus Kosciuszko, a Polish engineer serving under Greene, inquired about the dead officer's personal effects. John had left behind two slaves—presumably one of them was Shrewsberry—who lacked clothing, and Kosciuszko wanted them to receive some of their master's belongings. "They are nacked," he wrote Greene, "they want shirts, jackets Breeches and their skin can bear as well as ours good things."[3] At Valley Forge, John had been indifferent to Shrewsberry's clothing needs; in this final hot and humid summer he displayed similar indifference to the needs of those who served his needs. While he dealt in abstractions—blacks were of a similar human nature as whites, slavery was incompatible with natural rights—his own servants went around half-naked.

Despite this inconsistency between thought and behavior, John's persistence in pressing the black regiment issue revealed a desire to place the revolutionary cause on a higher plane, extending the promises of liberty to any man capable of bearing arms in his country's defense. Though John's immediate objective had been to procure reinforcements for the Continental ranks, his plan always offered the promise of emancipation. And he clearly hoped that the example of a few soldiers fighting for freedom would eventually lead to freedom for all slaves. An anonymous eulogist recognized this point in a tribute printed in the *Virginia Gazette:* "At several stages of this war he has solicited permission to embody the slaves against the enemy, and lately offered to present the State with 150 of his own property, upon condition they would make him up a regiment. . . . His object in this has been as well to emancipate that unhappy class of people as to raise a respectable force for the public service."[4]

By early fall news of Laurens's death reached the northern states. In the main army's camp at Verplanck Point, New York, his demise was "universally lamented," noted one observer, "more especially at this late period, when the contest is supposed to be near a termination." Obviously it was a needless death, which perhaps explains why Washington reacted with surprising equanimity, considering that Laurens was the first and only member of his staff to fall during the war. He knew well his aide's temperament; his words thus conveyed more bitterness than shock. "Poor Laurens is no more," he informed Lafayette. "He fell in a trifling skirmish in South Carolina, attempting to prevent the Enemy from plundering the Country of rice."[5]

Like Henry Laurens, Hamilton had repeatedly cautioned John not to endanger himself unnecessarily; now his closest friend and potential future political ally had thrown his life away. While he wrote eloquently of Laurens's virtues, to a limited extent Hamilton curbed his own feelings, a response characteristic of the man who once said that he endeavored to remain free of emotional attachments. "I feel a deepest affliction at the news we have just received of the loss of our dear and [inesti]mable friend Laurens," he wrote Greene. "His career of virtue is at an end. How strangely are human affairs conducted, that so many excellent qualities could not ensure a more happy fate? The world will feel the loss of a man who has left few like him behind, and America of a citizen whose heart realized that patriotism of which others only talk. I feel the loss of a friend I truly and most tenderly loved, and one of a very small number." Hamilton, a perceptive recent biographer has observed, "might more accurately have said the only such friend. Of admirers and close political associates he would have many, but none with whom he would be so intimate."[6]

Those who knew Laurens and had seen his recklessness in action seemed shocked only because he died at the close of the war in a skirmish over rice. They were perhaps baffled that it had not happened sooner. One French officer expressed no surprise, contending that Laurens had "fallen a victim to his too reckless valor . . . in a skirmish of little importance." To be sure, Laurens cheated death more than once, but for all his vitality, he always inspired others with foreboding. After the battle of Germantown, for example, John Wells Jr., a Charleston newspaper printer, wrote to Henry Laurens: "While I wish to congratulate you on the martial achievements of my old friend your Son, I fear there is more need for Condolance, as his active enterprising Spirit must occasion his Person being often in imminent danger. I hope my fears may not be ominous." The Chevalier de Mauduit Du Plessis, himself no stranger to foolhardiness, labeled Laurens a "Mad and rash fellow." Indeed, John conducted himself at Chehaw Neck as he always had. Except this time the outcome was different.[7]

An ocean away, the Laurens family remained unaware of the tragedy for several months. Well aware of John's intrepid temperament, they could not help feeling apprehensive. Ironically, in a letter to William Manning penned on 28 August, Henry clearly identified the motives that led John to the Combahee River: "He can't endure Idleness when there is scope for action." Toward the end of August, Martha, who may have possessed extrasensory gifts, ceased mentioning John in her prayers. She could not explain why she excluded him. In fact, on several occasions when she "resolved to retire for the purpose of praying for her brother . . . some sudden call or other unexpected event interposed to prevent her doing so."[8]

His health impaired from the long imprisonment, Henry initially declined to serve as a peace commissioner. Public service, however, again exerted a stronger hold than his private needs. On 12 November he received from John Adams a resolve from Congress that ordered all the commissioners to attend negotiations in Paris. In the same letter Adams transmitted the melancholy news of John's death and expressed his condolences. "Our Country has lost its most promising Character," he wrote.[9]

Despite his anguish, Henry obeyed the call of duty and left London for Paris. He arrived in time to participate in the final day of negotiations prior to the signing of the preliminary peace treaty. He insisted on the inclusion of an article prohibiting the British army from removing additional property from America, a clause that safeguarded the property of slaveholders.[10]

Laurens remained in France until mid-January 1783, when failing health forced a return to the warm waters at Bath, England. His bereavement had never been far from his mind. Work was at best a temporary palliative. "The loss is remediless," he said. It was a bitter irony, he thought, that he had been grieving for Jemmy at the outset of the war, and now at the end he "was in deep mourning for that brave honest man, that good soldier and good Citizen, that dutiful son and sincere friend, the dear object of my present woe." There remained some consolation. "Thank God I *had* such a Son," he reflected, "who dared to die for his Country."[11]

He longed for the assistance of his eldest daughter, who still resided in Vigan, France. Martha hesitated, not wanting to desert either the ailing James Laurens or his wife Mary, who spoke no French. None too subtly, Henry responded, "Take care of my Dear Brother, let me rather suffer than him." Ever the dutiful daughter, Martha needed no further prompting, and joined her father in Bath.[12]

Martha was shocked at Henry's appearance. Coming on the heels of the ordeal in the Tower of London, the shock of John's death had clearly aged him. No longer so robust, he had grown much thinner. Although they rarely alluded to John, Martha informed her aunt, "I can perceive his heart is bowed down, & he does indeed stand in need of some kind friend to soothe his Sorrows, I wish I were more adequate to the task, but notwithstanding my sincere desire to be his Comforter, my own heart is so heavy, that it is sometimes as much as I can do to appear tolerably chearful. You know how greatly I was affected by the late melancholy Event in our family. Time, instead of alleviating this Grief, makes me every day more and more feel my loss."[13]

Henry remained in England for another year and a half. During that
period, he attended to his personal affairs and occasionally acted as an unofficial American minister to Great Britain. He also corresponded frequently with
Thomas Day, the noted writer and man of feeling who had been John's antislavery compatriot.[14] While they differed on how best to attack the institution
of slavery, Laurens and Day nevertheless shared a common bond—their reverence for the young man's memory. When Day finally published his pamphlet
that denounced slavery in America, he included a moving tribute to a fallen
friend:

> In him, his country has lost one of its noblest and most useful citizens, his father
> the kindest and most affectionate friend; and all the wretched a generous and dis-
> interested patron. O my unfortunate country! must I add, that when I consider all
> the leaders of thy factions, all thy hereditary magistrates, all that are destined to
> engross thy dignities or share thy spoils, I seek in vain a colonel John Laurens![15]

By June 1784 Henry, accompanied by his remaining son Harry, was finally
able to return to America. Before his departure, he secured from William Manning permission to raise the orphaned Fanny in her father's homeland. Martha,
Polly (who was now fourteen years old), Fanny, and Aunt Mary stayed behind
in Bath, where they resided until arrangements were made for them to sail to
Charleston. James Laurens, after a long illness, had died the previous January.
The conscientious Martha assumed responsibility for the care and education of
both Polly and Fanny.[16]

After his arrival, Henry petitioned Congress to grant a pension to the
daughter of John Laurens. Although John had never demanded payment from
Congress for his military or diplomatic service, Congress concluded that some
provision should be made for the little orphan. The delegates resolved to pay
the balance of John's account to Henry, the executor of his estate; they also
agreed that compensation for John's diplomatic mission would be equivalent
to the salaries paid to other American ministers. Finally, they recommended
that Fanny receive her father's half-pay pension for a period of seven years.[17]

Laurens reached Charleston on 14 January 1785 and found his Ansonborough house in ruins and his plantations ravaged. Few Carolinians endured
the financial and personal woes he experienced during the war. He attempted
to bring some semblance of order to his property. On 11 May, the Laurens
women landed in Charleston. Mary Laurens died two months later, after
falling "on her side against a rude Vessel."[18]

Henry retired from public life and focused his energies on rebuilding his
property and on implementing agricultural innovations. In his later years his
statements on slavery centered on the complacency of his slaves and the corre-

lation between slave importations and the postwar debt crisis in South Carolina. Most Carolinians supported a prohibition on slave imports as a stopgap measure designed to relieve them of their indebtedness. A few others, including Laurens, made the connection between prohibition and gradual abolition. Yet he often blurred the distinctions, and it was unclear which issue concerned him most—that slavery be put on the road to extinction or merely that the debt crisis be resolved. On occasion he was still capable of bold pronouncements: "To recover and save the honor of the Country, an abolition of Slavery by wise and progressive measures is necessary." But when the state legislature finally imposed a three-year ban on slave importations in 1787, Laurens applauded the act not as a step toward emancipation but as a debtor relief bill.[19]

In April 1785 Henry received a letter from Alexander Hamilton concerning Frederic, one of his slaves, who had joined the British after they captured Charleston and, after a series of adventures, now found himself incarcerated in a New York City jail. Frederic declared that he was a free man and that John Laurens had emancipated him. Frederic's story, Henry told Hamilton, ran counter to John's character: "Our dear friend was too tenacious of propriety to have manumitted a Slave not his own; this is evinced by his conduct to the black Man who was actually with him and continues with me."

"Our dear friend and his father entertained but one opinion respecting Slavery," Henry wrote, "excepting that his generous Soul would have precipated a Work, which to make it glorious his father thought he saw could only be accomplished by gradual Steps. Haste would make havoc." At best Laurens could effect change on his own plantations. He thus had offered freedom to individual slaves, who, he claimed, had declined, preferring to remain under his humane rule. He paid wages to a few valued workers and was tolerant toward them all. "I will venture to say," he told Hamilton, "the whole are in more comfortable circumstances than any equal number of Peasantry in Europe." His slaves, he concluded, "are my Watchmen and my friends; never was an absolute Monarch more happy in his Subjects than at the present time I am." Yet Laurens had little patience with Frederic's aspirations for freedom. If possible, he desired Frederic's return, for "He is according to the Law of the Land my property."[20]

The letter starkly reveals another reason for the derision that had greeted John Laurens's proposals. Even a slaveholder like his father, who privately detested the institution, adhered to the Lockean tenet that private property was sacred. Henry Laurens depicted himself as a benign patriarch, yet his statements to Hamilton appear to have been at least partly calculated for effect. He was, after all, attempting to regain a runaway slave. And regain Frederic he did. By September 1785 Frederic was back among Laurens's slaves. "There he goes carrying a little dirt out of the Garden, not earning his Victuals," observed Laurens with derision. Not wanting to disrupt "a happy orderly family," he was reluctant to send Frederic back to his former position at Mepkin, the Laurens home plantation. On the other hand, he was "not less adverse from selling him, for I certainly wish not to increase the number of slaves."[21]

In the end Laurens spoke much but accomplished little. He formally manumitted one slave, George, a carpenter who had personally attended him during the Revolution. As for the others, he remained convinced that they were attached to him by common bonds of love and affection. Steadfast in his belief that in pressing the slavery issue he would do more harm than good, he acquiesced, consoling himself that his slaves at least were content, better off under his benevolent hand than they would be if they were thrust into the world. Yet nagging fears persisted. He dreaded the future, a future he would not live to see. "God forbid our conversion by too long a Delay," he wrote, "shall be the Effect of a direful Struggle."[22]

In late 1790 Henry again petitioned the national government on Fanny's behalf. Always lacking revenue, the Confederation Congress had failed to pay Fanny the compensation promised in 1785. The Constitution drafted in 1787, which Henry endorsed, gave Congress the power to tax, placing the new federal government on a firmer financial foundation and allowing it to pay old debts. Earlier, in August 1790, Congress passed a bill that finally awarded Fanny a sum equal to John's half-pay pension for a period of seven years. Henry now asked that the House of Representatives add interest to the amount owed for John's diplomatic service. Fearing that acquiescence in Henry's request would lead to other claims for interest payments, the House committee recommended that the petition be rejected. When Henry petitioned again the following year, he received another gentle rebuff.[23]

Henry spent most of his last years in retirement at Mepkin. From there he witnessed several family milestones. In 1787 Martha married David Ramsay, becoming the doctor's third wife. Polly wed Charles Pinckney in April 1788, one day after her eighteenth birthday. In 1792 Harry became the last to marry, cementing ties with the powerful Rutledge family by marrying Eliza, the daughter of John Rutledge.[24]

These diversions aside, Henry never fully recovered from the loss of his eldest and favorite child. On 8 December 1792, after a brief illness, he died at Mepkin. In his will he stipulated to Harry that his body be "burnt until it be entirely and totally consumed, and then collecting my bones, deposite them wherever he shall think proper." Martha, who was with her father when he died, departed Mepkin before "the awful ceremony was performed."[25]

Laurens's will divided his extensive property among his children. He bequeathed to Fanny his plantation at Long Canes in Ninety-Six District and his lots in the village of Hampstead outside Charleston. The Ramsays continued to act as her guardians. They took parenthood seriously, hoping to raise virtuous children who would make a positive contribution to republican society. In effect, Fanny was their first experiment. To prepare for the task, Martha read tracts, such as Benjamin Rush's *Thoughts upon Female Education*.[26]

David Ramsay launched a career as the young nation's premier historian. His writings, "a self-conscious effort to promote revolutionary republicanism and national unity," never failed to laud John Laurens as a model of republican virtue. In his *History of South Carolina*, he emphasized John's promotion of equality and his acts of benevolence on behalf of the downtrodden: "Though his fortune and family entitled him to pre-eminence, yet he was the warm friend of republican equality. Generous and liberal, his heart expanded with genuine philanthropy. Zealous for the right of humanity, he contended that personal liberty was the birthright of every human being, however diversified by country, color, or capacity."[27]

Tragic irony was never a stranger to the Laurenses. In 1794 Polly, like her mother before her, died from complications of childbirth. A year later Fanny, like her parents before her, married precipitately. Her elopement with Francis Henderson, a Scottish merchant, was inexplicable to observers. Described as a "little ugly" man, "shaped like a barrel," Henderson was not an appealing figure. The Ramsays did not approve the union. Shocked by Fanny's flight from home and disturbed by her husband's financial woes, Martha sank into an emotional crisis of deep intensity that lasted almost a year.[28]

For the rest of her life Martha remained a model of republican motherhood, constantly striving to inculcate virtuous habits in her eight children. When she died in 1811, her husband edited and published her letters and diary. The memoirs serve as a poignant tribute to her intellectual gifts and abiding religious faith.[29]

Of the Laurens children, Harry lived longest and prospered the most, even though his father had always doubted his abilities. At one point Harry's illustrious brother-in-law David Ramsay owed him $97,204. Harry died in 1821, leaving behind 459 slaves and an estate valued at $142,510. He bequeathed to his son John Ball the snuffbox his celebrated brother had received from Louis XVI in 1781 and then presented to Sarah Smith Bee. Thomas Bee had returned the token to Henry Laurens, and thus in the family it remained. In his will Harry stipulated that John's remains be removed from the Stock family plantation and buried beside his father in the Laurenses' plot at Mepkin.[30]

In the meantime, Fanny's marriage proved no more propitious than had her parents' union. By 1801 the Hendersons had separated, only a year after Fanny had given birth to a son, whom they named Francis Jr. There is no evidence that the couple obtained a divorce, but Francis Sr. apparently received custody of his son. He continued as administrator of the estate, including Fanny's inheritance, from which she received an annuity. According to tradition, Henderson left the child with relatives in Scotland and returned to America to oversee his financial affairs. Fanny lived in England for the remainder of her life.[31]

Henderson spent much time attempting to obtain money that he believed was owed to the heirs of John Laurens. On at least four occasions Henderson petitioned Congress unsuccessfully, requesting reimbursement for the out-of-pocket expenses John incurred in his military and diplomatic service and payment of the interest due on the balance of his diplomatic salary.[32] When Francis Jr. graduated from the University of Edinburgh in 1819, he journeyed to America and took possession of the family lands at Long Canes. He joined his father in an 1823 petition that included testimonials from such assorted personages as John Adams and John C. Hamilton, the son of Alexander Hamilton. This petition was referred to the Senate Committee on Foreign Relations. The committee's favorable report noted Laurens's indifference about keeping track of his expenditures and aptly described an important facet of his character: "A disinterestedness, even to carelessness, was a distinguished trait among his other qualities." In part because Fanny was not a participant, however, the U.S. Senate denied the petition, despite an eloquent appeal from Robert Y. Hayne, a senator from South Carolina.[33]

Standing before the Senate, Hayne called Laurens "the Bayard of America," a truly chivalrous hero. Hayne defended Laurens against charges of recklessness, imputations he believed had been propagated by contemporary revisionist historians. His "ardent enterprise and heroic courage," Hayne asserted, "had been mistaken for thoughtless desperation." The senator lauded Laurens's willingness to serve his country without pay. He had been, in short, "the purest and most disinterested of human beings."[34]

Hayne's oration illustrated why antebellum South Carolinians found John Laurens so appealing. Increasingly isolated, forced to defend the institution of slavery against outside attacks, and aware of the widening cultural gulf between them and the northern states, they found solace in their revolutionary forebears. Laurens served as a model of virtue for Carolinians who claimed that their society was superior, that they, unlike avaricious Yankees, were legitimate republican citizens, the possessors of the revolutionary birthright. In erecting Laurens as a paragon, Carolinians focused on aspects of his identity that comported with their own ideals—his public virtue and disdain for profits—and ignored his antislavery sentiments, which highlighted the wide gap between his values and theirs. If nothing else, Laurens's own life demonstrated that the pursuit of virtue was exacting, requiring moral and physical athleticism. Few antebellum Carolinians met the standard.[35]

Whatever one thought of the Hendersons, they were not quitters. They petitioned Congress in 1826, and again in 1831. John Laurens's slipshod management of his finances posed problems for his heirs. The Hendersons admitted that their financial statements were imprecise, but any ambiguity was "owing to the carelessness of the deceased about money transactions, his having kept no memorandums of his disbursements, either in public or private life."[36]

Two factors strengthened the petition that the 22nd Congress considered during its first session in 1832. First, Fanny was a participant, which eliminated an earlier objection. Second, the Hendersons's plea for relief coincided with Congress's move to award pensions to surviving Revolutionary War veterans. Still, the Hendersons met some opposition, largely because so many years had transpired since John's service and death. One opponent sarcastically called their claim "an old friend or rather an old acquaintance." This time, however, the family received the necessary votes. On 14 July 1832 Congress approved a payment to Laurens's heirs of $7,335.86.[37]

At this point Francis Henderson Sr. vanished from the historical record. Presumably he returned to Newport, Rhode Island, where he owned property. Francis Jr. spent the remainder of his days in Abbeville, South Carolina on the land his mother had inherited. Though he showed early promise as a lawyer, he never lived up to his potential. Instead, alcoholism sapped his will and his vigor. Henderson, who never married, died prematurely in 1847. "He seemed to be a fated man under a cloud," one friend observed, "and carried onward by a power and circumstances beyond his control."[38]

Like her mother, Fanny was a shadowy figure. Little is known of her life. Sometime after the death of Francis Sr., she remarried. This union, with James Cunnington of Gloucester Place, Kentish Town, at the very least provided companionship during her final years. For the remainder of her life, she received regular income from her property in South Carolina. On 25 April 1860 Frances Laurens Cunnington died at the age of eighty-three. With her death the line of John Laurens ended.[39]

Epilogue

In September 1779 Henry Laurens learned that John intended to obtain legislative sanction of the black regiment proposal, which had already been
rejected twice by the governor and his council. He tried to prepare the young
man for another defeat. From the beginning, he told John, the project had
faced "almost insurmountable difficulties," that impeded "the progress of your
liberal Ideas." "It is certainly a great task effectually to persuade Rich Men to
part willingly with the very source of their wealth, &, as they suppose, tranquility," he wrote. "You have encountred rooted habits and prejudices." Three
years earlier Henry had acknowledged that avarice stood in the way of change.
Now he brought up another obstacle. In referring to "tranquility" he perhaps
had in mind the genteel lifestyle planters enjoyed because of the labor of their
slaves. More likely he thought of the plan's social consequences, how it threatened the "tranquility" of a slave society. A large number of armed blacks
evoked white fears of slave insurrections producing a bloodbath; the emancipation of a black majority evoked white fears of miscegenation producing a
mongrel race.

Though John faced almost certain disappointment, Henry believed, there
remained some consolation. He reminded John that his grandfather foretold
slavery's eventual demise; now the grandson's plan promised to fulfill that
prophecy. "Your name will be honorably written & transmitted to posterity,"
Henry predicted, "but even the attempt without perfect success, will I know,
afford you unspeakable self satisfaction. The work will at a future day be effica-
ciously taken up & then it will be remembered who began it in South Carolina."[1]

To a young man consumed with the pursuit of virtue and fame, that prediction perhaps provided momentary reassurance. But the ensuing two hundred years have proven Henry Laurens a poor prophet. To be sure, John

Laurens largely played a secondary role in the important events of the American Revolution. One might label him quixotic, as his father did.[2] Yet in many respects he speaks more directly to the present than other figures of his time whose names are far more familiar. More clearly than any of his southern contemporaries, he realized that the ideals of the Revolution were incompatible with slavery.[3] He stood alone, both in his willingness to attack slavery directly and in his belief that blacks shared a similar nature with whites. Whereas southern leaders like his father considered property the basis of liberty, John believed liberty that rested on the sweat of slaves was not deserving of the name. There were obvious inconsistencies in his ideas, both in his opposition to slavery and in his advocacy of social leveling, the equalization of wealth. His conceptions bore the stamp of callow idealism. Yet he correctly perceived that political and social inequality threatened the fabric of the American republic. Today, when the Revolution's legacies of political equality and equality of opportunity seem so remote to many Americans, John Laurens's life and example remain vital and relevant.

But that example, and the man himself, are practically forgotten. Today Mepkin serves as a Trappist monastery. A roadside historic marker identifies the site as Henry Laurens's plantation, but there is no mention of John. On entering the grounds, one is struck by the tranquil beauty of the long avenue of stately live oaks, with Spanish moss lightly drooping from the branches. Yet it is beauty of a melancholy nature, the scene of Henry's retirement into grief. The Trappist monks' vow of silence seems fitting, as if somehow the stillness and quiet keep time at bay. With the exception of occasional interruptions from powerboats on the Cooper River, one can imagine the setting as it appeared in the eighteenth century—the Laurens children running along high bluffs overlooking the river, the slaves toiling in rice fields below. Henry Laurens wanted the best in life for his family, and he could afford it.

On the property are three bluffs separated by two narrow ravines. The southern bluff was the site of Henry's cremation. From the middle bluff, where the family home once stood, there is an impressive view of the river. A descent into a deep ravine along a path that crosses a tiny creek, followed by a steep climb on wooden planks, ends at the height of the northern bluff, where lies the Laurens family graveyard, enclosed by a brick wall with an iron gate.

To the left are the graves of Harry Laurens and his wife Eliza. On the far right a headstone marks the resting place of Mary Eleanor Laurens Pinckney, once the precocious child who wanted to wear breeches and enjoy the same privileges as men. Next to her lies Henry Laurens. Presumably, in accordance with Harry's will, John Laurens's remains were removed from the Stock family plantation and laid to rest beside his father. The stones of father and son are simple and unassuming, in keeping with republican modesty. The headstones display their names and dates of birth and death. John's headstone also contains a Latin inscription: "*Dulce et decorum est / pro patria mori* [sweet and proper it is to die for one's country]."

On the surface it seems a fitting epitaph. After openly expressing his willingness to die for his country, John seemed bent on making that pronouncement a self-fulfilling prophecy. Early in 1778, during the period when John fused the black regiment plan with his military career, Henry asked his son what limit he placed on service to his country. "Glorious Death, or the Triumph of the Cause in which I am engaged," he replied.[4]

To a great extent, John Laurens's ultimate fate belied those words. He did not live to see his country win independence, nor did his espousal of emancipation even dent an institution to which his fellow Carolinians were committed irrevocably. And his death, in an insignificant skirmish at an isolated point along an obscure river, was hardly glorious.

Yet his unremitting struggle to prove his virtue and significance, to put his stamp on the world and win eternal fame, merits admiration. It was his attempt to excel, rather than the final result, that most commands attention. Though his contemporaries viewed him as he wanted to be regarded—as a brave, virtuous officer, a model republican gentleman—in his own mind he never reached that lofty level of achievement. He constantly endeavored to reach greater heights, to perform nobler acts of heroism and benevolence. In the end his accomplishments never equaled his aspirations. Measured by his own standards, he failed.

Notes

Introduction

1. Royster, *Lee,* 39–54; Templin, "Lee," 198–201.
2. Garden, *Anecdotes,* 86–88; for O'Neal, see Heitman, *Historical Register,* 420.
3. Rogers, "South Carolina Federalists," 17–32; Garden, *Anecdotes,* 90.
4. The nineteenth-century South Carolina novelist and poet William Gilmore Simms published a small volume of letters written by JL to his father HL and prefaced the collection with a brief biography of JL. Simms, *Army Correspondence.* In 1915 historian David D. Wallace published a biography of HL, to which he appended a short account of JL's life. Wallace, *Life of Henry Laurens,* 463–94. For many years, Sara Bertha Townsend's *An American Soldier* has remained the only full-length biography. Townsend's work was overly laudatory and marred by frequent inaccuracies. In the late 1970s Robert M. Weir and Richard J. Hargrove produced separate scholarly essays that assessed JL's life and attempted to explain his early death. See Weir, "Portrait of a Hero," 16–19, 86–88; and Hargrove, "Portrait of a Southern Patriot," 182–202.
5. See, for example, Quarles, *Negro in the American Revolution,* 60–67; Robinson, *Slavery in the Structure of American Politics,* 118–22; Maslowski, "National Policy Toward the Use of Black Troops," 1–17; McDonough, "Christopher Gadsden and Henry Laurens," 463–75; and Chaplin, *An Anxious Pursuit,* 57–58, 364–65.
6. Massey, "Limits of Antislavery Thought in the Revolutionary Lower South," 495–530.
7. Greene, "Search for Identity," 143–73.
8. Much of the theoretical framework for this study's examination of JL's identity is drawn from the perspective of psychology, William James's essay "The Consciousness of the Self" in his *Principles of Psychology,* 1: 291–401; and moral philosophy, Charles Taylor's, *Sources of the Self;* supplemented by recent sociological findings, which are accessible in Stryker, "Identity Theory," and Felson, "Self-Concept." Daniel Walker Howe places the construction of identity in early America in its historical context; see Howe, *Making the American Self.* This subject is drawing

increasing attention from historians, and two recent anthologies provide convenient introductions to the literature. See the essays in *Rewriting the Self,* ed. Porter; and *Through a Glass Darkly,* eds. Hoffman, Sobel, and Teute.

9. On self-destructive behavior, consult Kushner, *American Suicide,* which makes a strong case for an interdisciplinary approach to the subject; a psychological viewpoint expressed in Shneidman, *Definitions of Suicide;* the essays on indirect self-destructive behavior in *The Many Faces of Suicide,* ed. Farberow; and an overview by a sociologist, Maris, *Pathways to Suicide.* Recent scientific research has uncovered evidence that genetic factors influence some people to be risk-takers. See, for example, Toufexis, "What Makes Them Do It." While scholars studying self-destructive behavior now utilize biological as well as psychological and sociological data, such evidence is infeasible for this study. See also Maris, "Suicide."

10. For an explicit statement by a historian that human behavior has remained constant over time, see Wyatt and Willcox, "Sir Henry Clinton," 3–26, particularly 19; but see also the caveats expressed in McDonald, *Novus Ordo Seclorum,* xii. For a similar debate among cultural anthropologists, see the different views of Geertz, "'From the Native's Point of View,'" Rosaldo, "Toward an Anthropology of Self and Feeling," and Spiro, "Some Reflections on Cultural Determinism and Relativism," in *Culture Theory,* eds. Shweder and LeVine, 123–36, 137–57, 323–46.

11. While Stephen Greenblatt's term "self-fashioning" is used here to describe JL's choice of social roles—lawyer, man of feeling, gentleman officer—each of which entailed training and preparation, I do not concur with his argument that individual autonomy is fictitious and human agency is strictly curbed by "relations of power." See Greenblatt, *Renaissance Self-Fashioning,* 8–9, 256 (quotation); for a trenchant critique of Greenblatt's position, see Martin, "Inventing Sincerity, Refashioning Prudence," 1309–42. On the individual as "historically and culturally contingent," see Mascuch, *Origins of the Individualist Self,* 13–24, especially 16.

12. Out of the vast literature on republicanism and virtue, most helpful for this study have been Edmund S. Morgan, "Puritan Ethic," 3–43; Gordon S. Wood, *Creation of the American Republic,* especially 46–70, 107–24; Weir, "'Harmony We Were Famous For,'" 473–501; and Greene, "Concept of Virtue," 208–35.

Chapter 1

1. Wallace, *Life of Henry Laurens,* 4–6; HL to Messieurs and Madame Laurence, 25 February 1774, in *Laurens Papers,* 9: 309; Butler, *Huguenots in America,* 91–143; Coclanis, *Shadow of a Dream,* 48–110.

2. HL to Messieurs and Madame Laurence, 25 February 1774, in *Laurens Papers,* 9: 309.

3. Wallace, *Life of Henry Laurens,* 7, 11–12; Hirsch, *Huguenots of Colonial South Carolina,* 90–102; Butler, *Huguenots in America,* 120–43; Inventory of John Laurens's Estate, 12 September 1747, in *Laurens Papers,* 1: 369. For the prediction about slavery, see HL to JL, 21 September 1779, Henry Laurens Papers, SCHS.

4. Ramsay, *History of South Carolina,* 2: 253.

5. Wallace, *Life of Henry Laurens,* 11–12.

6. HL to Messieurs and Madame Laurence, 25 February 1774, in *Laurens Papers,* 9: 309 (quotation); Wallace, *Life of Henry Laurens,* 15–16; *Laurens Papers,* 1: xiv–xv.

7. HL to James Crokatt, 3 June 1747, The Will of John Laurens, Recorded 19 June 1747, Inventory of John Laurens's Estate, Recorded 12 September 1747, ibid., 1: 3, 6–7, 369–81; Wallace, *Life of Henry Laurens,* 11.

8. Ibid., 17–19, 45; *Laurens Papers,* 2: xvii–xix; Rogers, *Charleston in the Age of the Pinckneys,* 34–35, 38; Ramsay, *History of South Carolina,* 2: 260–61 (quotation).

9. Wallace, *Life of Henry Laurens,* 57–58. For a succinct discussion of "companionate" marriages, see Taylor, *Sources of the Self,* 288–94.

10. Wallace, *Life of Henry Laurens,* 58–59, Appendix 3. JL's early artistic efforts are described in HL to Richard Clarke, 25 August 1770, in *Laurens Papers,* 7: 328.

11. Wallace, *Life of Henry Laurens,* 58–59, Appendix 3.

12. *Laurens Papers,* 2: xviii; Wallace, *Life of Henry Laurens,* 61. Regarding the economic diversification of South Carolina merchants in general and HL in particular, see Coclanis, "Hydra Head of Merchant Capital," 7, 16.

13. On the patrician class in the colonies, see Gordon S. Wood, *Radicalism of the American Revolution,* 24–42; for South Carolina's elite, see Weir, *Colonial South Carolina,* 229–64.

14. Greene, *Quest for Power,* 35–38, 361–62, 481; Sirmans, *Colonial South Carolina,* 223–24, 249–50.

15. Weir, "'Harmony We Were Famous For,'" 473–501. On slavery as a political abstraction in eighteenth-century America, see Bailyn, *Ideological Origins of the American Revolution,* 232–35.

16. *Laurens Papers,* 3: xviii, 100, 116; 4: xviii; Rogers, *Charleston in the Age of the Pinckneys,* 59–60. Gadsden and HL ended their friendship in 1761, when they argued over the prosecution of South Carolina's war with the Cherokees. See McDonough, "Christopher Gadsden and Henry Laurens," 33–54, 70–72.

17. HL to Isaac King, 20 May 1763, in *Laurens Papers,* 3: 457–59; HL to Thomas Mears, 22 December 1763, to John Ettwein, 13 March 1764, ibid., 4: 97–99, 209; HL to Benjamin Addison, 26 May 1768, ibid., 5: 702 (quotation); Wallace, *Life of Henry Laurens,* Appendix 3.

18. Diary of John Bartram, 7 July 1765, 12 July 1765, in *Laurens Papers,* 4: 647–48, 651, 669; James Laurens to JL, 5 December 1771, ibid., 8: 80–84; Bushman, *Refinement of America,* xii–xv, 100–138.

19. See the descriptions in Diary of Captain Ewald, Diary of Captain Hinrichs, in Uhlendorf, ed., *Siege of Charleston,* 91, 327–37 (quotation on 327); and Howe, ed., "Journal of Josiah Quincy, Junior," 441–57; Coclanis, *Shadow of a Dream,* 3–11.

20. Alexander Garden quoted in Hindle, *Pursuit of Science,* 50–51. See also the observations in Howe, ed., "Journal of Josiah Quincy, Junior," 441–57, especially 455; and the balanced appraisal in Weir, *Colonial South Carolina,* 260–61.

21. Rogers, *Charleston in the Age of the Pinckneys,* 26; Coclanis, *Shadow of a Dream,* 42–43; HL to George Appleby, 9 November 1764, in *Laurens Papers,* 4: 500.

22. HL to Bellamy Crawford, 26 May 1768, ibid., 5: 702; HL to James Habersham, 23 November 1773, ibid., 9: 157; Wallace, *Life of Henry Laurens,* 440, Appendix 3; Rogers, "Tribute to Henry Laurens," 276. On reactions to infant deaths among colonial Americans, see Norton, *Liberty's Daughters,* 87–89.

23. Ramsay, *History of South Carolina,* 2: 261; HL to James Grant, 13 October 1767, to James Habersham, 4 June 1768, in *Laurens Papers,* 5: 359, 717; for the argument that Carolinians were permissive fathers, see Zuckerman, "Penmanship Exer-

cises for Saucy Sons," 152–66; on the moderate approach to child rearing, see Greven, *Protestant Temperament,* 151–261; on the division of child rearing responsibilities by gender, consult Norton, *Liberty's Daughters,* 102.

24. HL to George Appleby, 9 November 1764, in *Laurens Papers,* 4: 499. For Eleanor's health during 1764, see HL to John Coming Ball, 6 October 1764, to Elias Ball Jr., 6 November 1764, to Joseph Brown, 17 November 1764, to James Grant, 13 December 1764, ibid., 4: 451, 493, 504, 530. Regarding her continuing health problems, see HL to Abraham Schad, 1 April 1765, to Joseph Brown, 19 August 1765, ibid., 4: 598, 664; HL to James Theodore Rossel, 8 April 1766, to Grant, 31 October 1766, 13 November 1766, 11 February 1767, to James Habersham, 4 June 1768, ibid., 5: 100, 207, 212, 232, 717. The two infant deaths are described in HL to James Penman, 13 October 1767, ibid., 5: 355; and HL to Grant, 1 October 1768, ibid., 6: 117–20.

25. Ramsay, *Memoirs of Martha Laurens Ramsay,* 12; HL to Joseph Brown, 21 August 1766, to John Lewis Gervais, 1 September 1766, in *Laurens Papers,* 5: 171, 171n, 184.

26. Ibid., 3: xvii; Weir, *Colonial South Carolina,* 250–51. HL to Benjamin Elliott, 9 September 1771, in *Laurens Papers,* 7: 586–87. For the efforts to establish a local college, see ibid., 7: xvii–xviii, 241–42n; the existing free school system is described in Rogers, *Charleston in the Age of the Pinckneys,* 97–98.

27. *Laurens Papers,* 4: xvii–xviii; ibid., 5: xx, 57–58.

28. HL to Richard Oswald, 27 April 1768, ibid., 5: 668.

29. HL to Lachlan McIntosh, 13 March 1773, ibid., 8: 618. The line between patriarchalism and paternalism is often blurred. For example, HL exhibited the traits and employed the language of both a patriarchal and paternalistic master. Because he was quick to punish or sell transgressors and little direct evidence exists of concern for his slaves' spiritual welfare, this study follows two recent essays that identify him as a patriarchal master. See Philip Morgan, "Three Planters and Their Slaves," 37–40 (distinctions between patriarchalism and paternalism), 54–68 (HL); and Olwell, "'Reckoning of Accounts,'" 33–52. See also Philip Morgan, *Slave Counterpoint,* 273–300, and especially 284–96, which stresses the late eighteenth-century development of an enlightened patriarchalism, a precursor to paternalism. On the development of a paternalistic ethos among some of HL's contemporaries, see Gallay, "Origins of Slaveholders' Paternalism," 369–94.

30. HL to Elias Ball, 1 April 1765, to Abraham Schad, 23 August 1765, in *Laurens Papers,* 4: 595–97 (second quotation), 665–66 (first quotation).

31. HL to Hinson Todd, 14 April 1769, ibid., 6: 437–38 (quotation). For an example of flogging, see HL to Abraham Schad, 30 April 1765, ibid., 4: 616; on the sale of a slave deemed lazy, see HL to Joseph Brown, 21 August 1766, ibid., 5: 170–71.

32. HL to Henry Bright & Co., 31 October 1769, ibid., 7: 192; on slaves as "refuse," see HL to Joseph Brown, 21 July 1764, to Arnold, Albert, & Alexander Nesbitt, 7 August 1764, to Samuel Wragg, 21 August 1764, to Lloyd & Barton, 24 December 1764, ibid., 4: 354, 360, 374, 558–59; for HL's continuing involvement in the slave trade, see HL to Smith & Baillies, 9 February 1764, ibid., 4: 167–68; Advertisement, 1 January 1768, HL to Smith & Baillies, 15 January 1768, ibid., 5: 537, 546–48.

33. John Ettwein to HL, 2 March 1763, HL to Ettwein, 19 March 1763, ibid., 3: 356–57, 373–74; Chaplin, "Slavery and the Principle of Humanity," 299–315.

34. Greene, "Seven Years' War and the American Revolution," 85–105, especially 95–99; Bullion, "'Ten Thousand in America,'" 647–54; for South Carolina's reaction to the Stamp Act, see Weir, *"A Most Important Epocha,"* 15–22.

35. Weir, *"A Most Important Epocha,"* 17–18; HL to Joseph Brown, 28 October 1765, to William Fisher, 27 February 1766, in *Laurens Papers,* 5: 29–32, 78.

36. Thomas, *British Politics and the Stamp Act Crisis,* 249, 361–62, 371; Jensen, *Founding of a Nation,* 264–73, 283–87, 301–12.

37. HL to Matthew Robinson, 19 October 1768, in *Laurens Papers,* 6: 139–40, 139–40n.

38. Calhoon and Weir, "'Scandalous History of Sir Egerton Leigh,'" 47–74.

39. HL to William Fisher, 1 March 1769, in *Laurens Papers,* 6: 390. On the cancellation of the trip to England, see HL to Fisher, 1 August 1768, to Andrew Turnbull, 17 August 1768, ibid., 6: 3–4, 73. The *Extracts* were published in two editions, one in Philadelphia in 1768, the other, with HL's critical comments on Leigh's conduct, in Charleston in 1769. Both editions are reprinted in *Laurens Papers,* 6, with JL's translation of Pufendorf on 36, 206, 350.

40. Egerton Leigh, *The Man Unmasked . . .,* in *Laurens Papers,* 6: 494; HL, *Appendix to the Extracts from the Proceedings of the High Court of Vice-Admiralty,* in *Laurens Papers,* 7: 9.

41. Leigh, *The Man Unmasked,* in *Laurens Papers,* 6: 528; HL, *Appendix to the Extracts,* in *Laurens Papers,* 7: 99–100; HL's religious views, in the context of this debate over slavery, are analyzed in Samuel C. Smith, "Henry Laurens: Christian Pietist"; on debates over slavery, see Chaplin, *An Anxious Pursuit,* 53–65.

42. HL to William Fisher, 24 August 1769, in *Laurens Papers,* 7: 127; HL to James Grant, 4 April 1769, ibid., 6: 425 (quotation); Berkeley and Berkeley, *Alexander Garden,* 229, 231. On JL as copyist, see, for example, HL to James Grant, 31 March 1768, to Alexander Gray, 26 May 1768, in *Laurens Papers,* 5: 643, 703–4.

43. HL to Charles Mill, 7 August 1769, to James Habersham, 15 August 1769, to James Grant, 27 October 1769, ibid., 7: 115–16, 125–26, 175; Alexander Garden to John Ellis, 13 July 1771, ibid., 7: 553–54 (quotation); Hindle, *Pursuit of Science,* 36–37, 52–56; Berkeley and Berkeley, *Alexander Garden,* 228–29; JL's drawings were printed in "An Account of two new Tortoises," 267–71.

44. HL to George Appleby, 26 September 1769, in *Laurens Papers,* 7: 150–51.

45. HL to James Grant, 3 April 1770, to Daniel Grant, 27 April 1770, to Matthew Robinson, 4 May 1770, to Richard Grubb, 8 May 1770, to Lachlan McIntosh, to Thomas Savage, to William Fisher, 10 May 1770, ibid., 7: 268, 286 (quotation), 287, 290–92.

46. HL to Matthew Robinson, 1 June 1770, ibid., 7: 300.

47. HL to Henry Humphreys, 19 May–8 June 1770, ibid., 7: 298. On the negative effects of incomplete mourning, see Kushner, *American Suicide,* 77–79, 126–32, 138–40, 162–65.

48. For HL's grief, see HL to Reeve, Son, & Hill, 21 June 1770, to Samuel Johnston, 13 August 1770, to John Baynton, 5 September 1770, to Henry Bright, 10 September 1770, in *Laurens Papers,* 7: 304–5, 321–22, 331–32, 350–51. Eleanor Laurens's dying statement is recorded in HL to Martha Laurens, 18 August 1782, Kendall Collection. For HL's reaction, see HL to John Polson, 13 November 1770, in *Laurens Papers,* 7: 401. His reasons for remaining single are expressed in HL to Messieurs and Madame Laurence, 25 February 1774, ibid., 9: 311.

49. HL to James Habersham, 1 October 1770, ibid., 7: 374–75.
50. HL to James Grant, 24 November 1770, ibid., 7: 407.
51. JL to James Grant, 22 October 1770, Grant to JL, 13 November 1770, JL to Grant, 10 December 1770, ibid., 7: 384, 402–3, 409–11.
52. Weir, *"A Most Important Epocha,"* 37–38; *Laurens Papers,* 7: 292, 411.
53. HL to Richard Clarke, 16 March 1771, to Edward Brice, 28 March 1771, to George Appleby, 2 April 1771, to Clarke, 6 April 1771, to Richard Baker, 6 April 1771, ibid., 7: 457–58, 463, 468–69 (second quotation), 480–83 (first quotation), 484–85.
54. HL to Richard Clarke, 25 August 1770, ibid., 7: 327–28; on the status of doctors in South Carolina, see Sydenham, "Practitioner and Patient," 36, 128–86, 243–54.
55. HL to Richard Clarke, 25 August 1770, *Laurens Papers,* 7: 327–28; Fliegelman, *Prodigals and Pilgrims,* 58–60, 66.
56. Alicia Hopton to JL, 17 June 1771, Kendall Collection. For additional information on Hopton and Kinloch, see *Laurens Papers,* 7: 431n, 446n.
57. Alexander Garden to John Ellis, 13 July 1771, ibid., 7: 553–54.
58. HL to John Moultrie, 27 June 1771, ibid., 7: 545–46; ibid., 8: xiii.
59. HL to John Hopton, 4 September 1771, to James Laurens, 9 September 1771, ibid., 7: 558–59, 580–83, the departure for Philadelphia is recorded on 555.

Chapter 2

1. HL to James Laurens, 10 October 1771, to William Fisher Jr., 24 October 1771, to George Appleby, 31 October 1771, to John Lewis Gervais, 7 November 1771, in *Laurens Papers,* 8: 3–4, 17–19, 27 (quotation), 37.
2. HL to James Laurens, 5 December 1771, ibid., 8: 68.
3. HL to Benjamin Elliot, 4 November 1771, to William Cowles, 19 November 1771, to James Laurens, 5 December 1771, to Thomas Savage, 5 December 1771, ibid., 8: 30–31 (first quotation), 44, 44n, 68, 75.
4. HL to James Laurens, 5 December 1771, to Peter Mazyck, 10 April 1772, ibid., 8: 68, 259.
5. On American views of Britain, see McCoy, *Elusive Republic,* 48–49, 51–61; Edmund S. Morgan, "Puritan Ethic," 14–16; Bailyn, *Ideological Origins of the American Revolution,* 86–93, 130–38.
6. HL to James Laurens, 1 April 1772, in *Laurens Papers,* 8: 238–39; JL to James Laurens, 17 April 1772, Kendall Collection.
7. HL to James Laurens, 12 December 1771, in *Laurens Papers,* 8: 86–87, 87n.
8. The mismanagement at Clarke's school is detailed in HL to James Laurens, 1 January 1772, ibid., 8: 147–49.
9. JL to James Laurens, 17 April 1772, Kendall Collection; HL to James Laurens, 13 May 1772, in *Laurens Papers,* 8: 305–6.
10. HL to William Cowles, 20 April 1772, to Alexander Garden, 24 May 1772, ibid., 8: 278–79, 325–27 (quotations).
11. Travel Journal, 30 May 1772, HL to Richard Oswald, 10 June 1772, ibid., 8: 359, 366–69.
12. HL to James Laurens, 22 June 1772, ibid., 8: 375–76, 375n.
13. Palmer, *Age of the Democratic Revolution,* 36, 116–19, 127–39; Durant and Durant, *Age of Voltaire,* 479–80.

14. Rogers, *Evolution of a Federalist*, 66; Keate, *Short Account of Geneva*, 125–36; Durant and Durant, *Age of Voltaire*, 481; Herbst, "First Three American Colleges," 29–35, 45.

15. Durant and Durant, *Age of Voltaire*, 479; Keate, *Short Account of Geneva*, 5–6, 108–9, 157–64.

16. HL to JL, 25 June 1772, 21 August 1772, to Jacques Prevost, 14 August 1772, in *Laurens Papers*, 8: 378n, 379, 412–13, 439; Durant and Durant, *Age of Voltaire*, 479. A year later, in part because of a personality conflict between Harry and the Chais's son, Charles, JL placed his brother in the home of David Chauvet, a local minister. Shortly thereafter, JL moved to a separate apartment owned by an unidentified landlord. HL to Jean-Antoine Chais, 5 March 1773, to JL, 9 March 1773, in *Laurens Papers*, 8: 595–97, 603–5, 604n; Chais to JL, [February 1773?], Kendall Collection; HL to Chais, 29 May 1773, to David Chauvet, 2 June 1773, in *Laurens Papers*, 9: 53–55, 58–59. For Chauvet, see ibid., 8: 405n.

17. HL to JL, 1 July 1772, ibid., 8: 388–89.

18. Puiz, "La Genève des Lumières," 225–54 (quotations on 245 and 246).

19. HL to James Laurens, 6 August 1772, to John Lewis Gervais, 8 August 1772, in *Laurens Papers*, 8: 397–98 (quotation), 401.

20. JL to James Laurens, 27 August 1772, Kendall Collection.

21. Watt, "Suicide in Early Modern Geneva," 63–86; Durant and Durant, *The Age of Voltaire*, 480–81.

22. JL to James Laurens, 19 December 1773, Kendall Collection.

23. For examples of this point, see Gordon S. Wood, *Radicalism of the American Revolution*, 158, 198, 330.

24. Crane, "Suggestions Toward a Genealogy of the 'Man of Feeling,'" 205–30 (second quotation on 221); Humphreys, "'Friend of Mankind,'" 203–18 (first quotation on 211); Sheriff, *Good-Natured Man*, 1–18; Barker-Benfield, *Culture of Sensibility*, 141–48; Langford, *A Polite and Commercial People*, 461–518; and Mullan, "Feelings and Novels," 119–31.

25. See HL to James Laurens, 18 December 1771, to Alexander Garden, 24 May 1772 (church services held at Fielding's asylum chapel), to William Cowles, 30 December 1771 (attendance at the play), in *Laurens Papers*, 8: 103, 103n, 142–43, 325. Originally published in 1688 as a novelette by Aphra Behn, *Oronooko* was adapted for the stage by Thomas Southerne. See Southerne, *Oronooko*, xix, xxxi.

26. Samuel C. Smith, "Henry Laurens: Christian Pietist"; Frech, "Republicanism of Henry Laurens," 71, 78–79; Dale Brown, *Understanding Pietism*, 112–15; on HL's use of the language of sentiment, employing such words as "sensibility" and "humanity," see HL to Mary Bremar, 2 June 1773, to George Austin Jr., 6 July 1774, to James Laurens, 7 July 1774, in *Laurens Papers*, 9: 60, 490, 493; HL to JL, 4 January 1776, ibid., 10: 618, as well as his views on the humanity of slaves, cited in chapter 1; for evidence of his religious tolerance, see HL to James Baillie, 9 February 1769, to William Fisher, 11 February 1769, in *Laurens Papers*, 6: 269, 273–74; and HL to JL, 1 July 1772, ibid., 8: 389; Leigh's description of HL's religiosity is in *The Man Unmasked*, in *Laurens Papers*, 6: 522–23.

27. Bellows, *Benevolence Among Slaveholders*, 1–20; on the spiritual and secular strains in the culture of sensibility, see Langford, *A Polite and Commercial People*, 467. Though South Carolinians were exposed to European works on humanity and

sympathy, they used those concepts to buttress slavery rather than question the institution. See Chaplin, "Slavery and the Principle of Humanity," 302–3.

28. JL to James Laurens, 17 April 1772, Kendall Collection; Langford, *A Polite and Commercial People*, 513–18.
29. JL to James Laurens, 17 April 1772, Kendall Collection.
30. For the importance of "orientation to the good" to one's identity and sense of self, see Taylor, *Sources of the Self*, 42–63.
31. Adair, "Fame and the Founding Fathers," 3–26; on "symbolic immortality," a corollary of the classical concept of fame, consult Lifton, *The Broken Connection*, 18–23.
32. JL's decision is recorded, with slight variations, in two letters that have been combined here to form one quotation: HL to James Laurens, 1 September 1773, to JL, 2 September 1773, in *Laurens Papers*, 8: 447–48, 450. In the transcription that James Laurens received, HL omitted JL's statement that he was "grieved to the Heart."
33. Canady, *Gentlemen of the Bar*, 215, 245–46, 257–58, 297–300, 327–28; Weir, *Colonial South Carolina*, 255–58; HL to James Laurens, 1 September 1772, in *Laurens Papers*, 8: 448.
34. HL to Richard Grubb, 1 September 1772, ibid., 8: 446.
35. HL to JL, 2 September 1772, 7 September 1772, ibid., 8: 450–51, 463.
36. HL to JL, 26 January 1773, ibid., 8: 548.
37. JL's remark is recorded in HL to John Lewis Gervais, 8 August 1772, ibid., 8: 401; see also HL's statement regarding Harry's ability in HL to James Laurens, 16 December 1773, ibid., 9: 201; the boy's timidity is described in HL to JL, 24 December 1773, 25 March 1774, 3 May 1774, ibid., 9: 208–9, 368, 423.
38. James Laurens to HL, 19 December 1772, HL to Egerton Leigh, 30 January 1773, to JL, 1 February 1773, ibid., 8: 506–9, 556–63, 567; Calhoon and Weir, "'Scandalous History of Sir Egerton Leigh,'" 63–64.
39. HL to James Laurens, 19 April 1773, in *Laurens Papers*, 8: 688; Travel Journal, [19 April 1773], 22 [April 1773], 23 [April 1773], HL to James Laurens, 24 April 1773, ibid., 9: 1, 9–10, 11, 12–13.
40. JL to James Laurens, 31 May 1773, Kendall Collection; HL to JL, 30 March 1773, to Alexander Garden, 8 April 1773, 19 April 1773, in *Laurens Papers*, 8: 652–53, 652–53n, 668–69, 694; Puiz, "La Genève des Lumières," 250.
41. HL to JL, 8 October 1773, in *Laurens Papers*, 9: 120–21; for Corbett, see Canady, *Gentlemen of the Bar*, 230, 281, 329.
42. *Laurens Papers*, 8: 356n; Himeli to JL, 15 May 1772, Kendall Collection; HL to JL, 8 October 1773, in *Laurens Papers*, 9: 120–21.
43. HL to JL, 1 February 1773, ibid., 8: 567; HL to JL, 14 January 1774, ibid., 9: 224–26; Greene, "Concept of Virtue," 208–25.
44. HL to Lachlan McIntosh, 13 March 1773, to Peter Nephew, to William Gambell, 15 March 1773, in *Laurens Papers*, 8: 617–18, 619–20, 621; HL to Mary Bremar, 2 June 1773, ibid., 9: 59; on duty as a synonym for obedience and industriousness as a "principal means of self-control," see Greven, *Protestant Temperament*, 159–180, 215–16.
45. On Locke's influence on American childrearing practices, see Fliegelman, *Prodigals and Pilgrims*, especially 12–15, 16, 57–60, 66; on the arguments regarding sympathy and reason, see Sheriff, *Good-Natured Man*, 81–91; and Radner, "Art of

Sympathy," 189–210. HL's concerns probably reflected the additional influence of moral philosophers of the Scottish Enlightenment; for their views on human faculties, consult Howe, *Making the American Self,* 63–66.

46. HL to JL, 15 December 1772, 22 March 1773, in *Laurens Papers,* 8: 500, 641; HL to James Laurens, 6 November 1774, ibid., 9: 633; Daniel Blake Smith, *Inside the Great House,* 82–125, particularly 87–89; and Weir, "Rebelliousness," 43.

47. HL to George Austin Sr., 26 September 1773, to JL, 25 May 1774, 4 June 1774, to George Austin Jr., 6 July 1774, in *Laurens Papers,* 9: 113–14, 461, 465–66, 489–90. On moderate parents' sense of "love and duty" toward their children, see Greven, *Protestant Temperament,* 180.

48. HL to JL, 15 February 1774, 21 February 1774, in *Laurens Papers,* 9: 275, 298–99; Himeli to JL, 2 December 1773, Kendall Collection.

49. L. de Vegobre to JL, 24 December 1774, 18 February 1775, 18 August 1775 (quotation), 7 June 1776, David Chauvet to JL, 1 November 1774, Kendall Collection; JL to Gabriel Manigault, 5 April 1776, Manigault Family Papers, South Caroliniana Library. On men and homosociality, see Kimmel, *Manhood in America,* 7–8, 26.

50. HL to Robert Smyth, to Robert Deans, 4 June 1773, to Etienne Bonnet, 5 June 1773, to David Chauvet, 6 June 1773, to JL, 22 March 1774, in *Laurens Papers,* 9: 68, 70–71, 363.

51. HL to JL, 15 February 1774, 21 February 1774, 22 March 1774, to Alexander Garden, 19 February 1774, to James Laurens, 13 April 1774, ibid., 9: 273–74, 294 (first quotation), 301, 363, 406 (second quotation).

52. On property and independence, see Weir, *Colonial South Carolina,* 252–53; and Daniel Blake Smith, *Inside the Great House,* 99. On the construction of masculinity, see Connell, *Masculinities,* 77–81, 189–91; and Kimmel, *Manhood in America,* 18. JL's use of prodigality and profligacy can be found in HL to JL, 8 March 1774, to James Laurens, 13 April 1774, in *Laurens Papers,* 9: 342, 406; definitions are taken from the *Oxford English Dictionary.*

53. HL to JL, 26 October 1773, 19 November 1773, 17 January 1774, 15 February 1774, 16 February 1774, 18 February 1774, 25 March 1774, 3 May 1774, in *Laurens Papers,* 9: 137, 137n, 153, 227–28, 275, 280–81, 290–92, 365 (quotation), 423; Rogers, *Evolution of a Federalist,* 17–22, 54, 62, 67–71. For Manning's family and the disciplinary problems with his son John, see Yorke, ed., *Diary of John Baker,* xi, 16–19, 239–40, 268, 271.

54. For references to JL's poor penmanship, see HL to JL, 7 March 1774, 22 March 1774, 8 April 1774, 19 April 1774, in *Laurens Papers,* 9: 342, 363, 379, 418–19, 420; on the importance of handwriting, see Bushman, *Refinement of America,* 92–96.

55. JL's reference to suicide and HL's response are both in HL to JL, 15 February 1774, in *Laurens Papers,* 9: 274.

56. HL to JL, 8 April 1774, ibid., 9: 379. Regarding changing attitudes toward suicide, see Rosen, "History," 3–29; and Fedden, *Suicide,* 222–41.

57. Goethe, *Sufferings of Young Werther.* By 1775 two French versions and a French dramatization of *Werther* had appeared. Nicholas Boyle, *Goethe,* 175. See also the discussion on Chatterton and Goethe in Alvarez, *Savage God,* 170–213.

58. Watt, "Suicide in Early Modern Geneva," 64.

59. The preceding discussion is drawn from Middlekauff, *Glorious Cause,* 219–31; and Jensen, *Founding of a Nation,* 483–507.

60. HL to George Appleby, 15 February 1774, to JL, 21 February 1774, to John Knight, 17 March 1774, in *Laurens Papers,* 9: 277–79, 300–301, 360 (quotation).
61. HL to JL, 25 May 1774, 21 June 1774, 5 July 1774, to George Appleby, 18 June 1774, to James Laurens, 6 July 1774, ibid., 9: 461–62 (first quotation), 471, 475 (second quotation), 479–81, 487.
62. HL to Gabriel Manigault, 6 July 1774, to John Petrie, 19 July 1774, to James Laurens, 21 July 1774, 27 August 1774, to George Appleby, 22 August 1774, ibid., 9: 485, 507–8, 516, 536 (quotation), 543; JL to Francis Kinloch, 23 August 1774, Manuscript Collection, Charleston Museum, S.C.
63. HL to John Petrie, 7 September 1774, to Richard Oswald, 22 September 1774, to James Laurens, 17 October 1774, in *Laurens Papers,* 9: 554, 572, 589–90.
64. JL to Francis Kinloch, 23 August 1774, Manuscript Collection, Charleston Museum.
65. HL to George Appleby, 5 September 1774, to Richard Oswald, 22 September 1774, in *Laurens Papers,* 9: 545, 572.
66. JL to James Laurens, 15 September 1774, Kendall Collection.
67. Canady, *Gentlemen of the Bar,* 338–43; James Laurens to JL, 24 January 1775, James Laurens Letterbook, Henry Laurens Papers, SCHS.
68. HL to James Laurens, 17 October 1774, in *Laurens Papers,* 9: 588.
69. HL to James Laurens, 15 September 1774, ibid., 9: 559–61; JL to James Laurens, 15 September 1774, Kendall Collection.
70. HL to JL, [31 October 1774], 7 November 1774, to William Stone, 7 November 1774, in *Laurens Papers,* 9: 611–12, 611–12n, 636, 642.

Chapter 3

1. HL to JL, 4 January 1775, in *Laurens Papers,* 10: 15–16.
2. JL to HL, 4 November 1774, 15 November 1774, ibid., 9: 622–23, 644; Lemmings, *Gentlemen and Barristers,* 22–23.
3. This discussion is based on Lemmings, *Gentlemen and Barristers,* 33–34, 48, 68, 75–109; Duman, *Judicial Bench in England,* 15–17; Canady, *Gentlemen of the Bar,* 206–50; and Rogers, *Evolution of a Federalist,* 90–92.
4. JL to HL, 20 January 1775, in *Laurens Papers,* 10: 34.
5. JL to Martha Laurens, 5 May 1775, Kendall Collection. Born in 1757, Martha Manning was the youngest of the sisters and therefore the closest in age to Martha Laurens. In his diary, Baker wrote: "N. B. Courtship J. L[aurens] c. P[atty] M[anning]." Yorke, ed., *Diary of John Baker,* 331–32.
6. JL to HL, 14 March 1775, in *Laurens Papers,* 10: 87; JL to Francis Kinloch, 10 March 1775, in "Original Letters 1775–89 Period," 345.
7. JL to HL, 3–4 December 1774, 5 December 1774, in *Laurens Papers,* 9: 646–50; HL to JL, 6 February 1775, ibid., 10: 60; *South-Carolina Gazette,* 6 February 1775.
8. JL to HL, 18 February 1775, in *Laurens Papers,* 10: 75.
9. JL to HL, 3–4 December 1774, ibid., 9: 647 (second quotation); JL to HL, 18 February 1775, ibid., 10: 75 (first quotation).
10. JL to Francis Kinloch, 10 March 1775, in "Original Letters 1775–89 Period," 345–46 (first quotation); JL to Kinloch, 6 November 1774, Myers Collection (MY 1362), NYPL (second quotation).

11. JL to HL, 15 November 1774, 3–4 December 1774, in *Laurens Papers*, 9: 643, 646–49 (quotation).
12. HL to JL, 6 February 1775, ibid., 10: 57–58.
13. HL to JL, 6 February 1775, ibid., 10: 58–59. For Jacob Read, see Edgar, et al., eds., *Biographical Directory*, 3: 597–99; for an account of a London escapade involving Read and Thomas Pinckney, see Rogers, *Evolution of a Federalist*, 69–70. Apparently HL later changed his mind about Read's character. See HL to Jacob Read, 16 August 1776, Henry Laurens Papers, South Caroliniana Library; and Read to HL, 16 July 1778, Gratz Collection, HSP.
14. JL to HL, 29 March 1775, in *Laurens Papers*, 10: 93–94. For the importance of others in forming self-appraisals, see Stryker, "Identity Theory," 874; and Felson, "Self-Concept," 1745.
15. HL to JL, 21 February 1774, in *Laurens Papers*, 302. On public and private virtue, consult Gordon S. Wood, *Creation of the American Republic*, 65–70; Edmund S. Morgan, "Puritan Ethic," 6–7; McCoy, *Elusive Republic*, 69; and Greene, "Concept of Virtue," 208–25. The "captive bird released from its gilded cage" was "a motif common in eighteenth-century literature and illustration." Fliegelman, *Prodigals and Pilgrims*, 115–16.
16. HL to JL, 26 January 1773, in *Laurens Papers*, 8: 548. On ideal identity see Rorty and Wong, "Aspects of Identity and Agency," 19–36; for a succinct sketch of John Mackenzie's life, see Weir, ed., *Letters of Freeman*, x–xiii.
17. JL to HL, 20 January 1775, 18 February 1775, HL to JL, 1 May 1775, in *Laurens Papers*, 10: 35–36, 76–77, 107. While JL remained in England, Mary Bremar continued to be a headache. She died in December 1777, an apparent suicide by an overdose of laudanum. JL to James Laurens, 12 June 1776, 9 November 1776, Kendall Collection; James Laurens to HL, 25 June 1778, Henry Laurens Papers, SCHS; HL to JL, 17 September 1778, in *Laurens Papers*, 14: 322; Yorke, ed., *Diary of John Baker*, 428.
18. Wallace, *Life of Henry Laurens*, 199–213; Weir, *"A Most Important Epocha,"* 58, 62–63; HL to JL, 18 January 1775, 22 January 1775, 8 June 1775, in *Laurens Papers*, 10: 27–31, 38–44, 164–79.
19. HL to JL, 15 May 1775, 27 May 1775, ibid., 10: 118–20 (quotation), 152–57.
20. JL to HL, 20 April 1775, HL to JL, 18 July 1775, ibid., 10: 99, 229–30; Lemmings, *Gentlemen and Barristers*, 23–25; Duman, *Judicial Bench in England*, 47–49; on the use of habits to master the passions, see Howe, *Making the American Self*, 26–32.
21. HL to JL, 27 May 1775, 30 May 1775, in *Laurens Papers*, 10: 152–61.
22. Ramsay, *Memoirs of Martha Laurens Ramsay*, 16–17; Barker-Benfield, *Culture of Sensibility*, 148–53, 324, 371.
23. HL to Martha Laurens, 18 May 1774, in *Laurens Papers*, 9: 458; James Laurens to HL, 2 August 1775, 12 August 1775, JL to HL, 4 September 1775, ibid., 10: 263–66, 294, 363; JL to James Laurens, 31 August 1775, to Martha Laurens, 31 August 1775, Kendall Collection; Gillespie, "Martha Laurens Ramsay's 'Dark Night of the Soul,'" 68–92.
24. HL to JL, 30 July 1775, 26 September 1775, JL to HL, 4 October 1775, in *Laurens Papers*, 10: 256–61, 259n, 427–28, 450. See also HL to JL, 6 March 1776, ibid., 11: 144–45.
25. HL to JL, 2 July 1775, ibid., 10: 205. On JL's correspondence with his uncle, see JL to James Laurens, October 1775, 31 October 1775, 2 February 1776 (quota-

tion), Kendall Collection; for James Laurens's lack of interest in politics, see HL to George Appleby, 16 July 1774, in *Laurens Papers,* 9: 506.

26. JL to HL, 20 August 1775, 4 September 1775, ibid., 10: 335–37 (first quotation), 361–62 (second quotation).

27. HL to James Laurens, 19 September 1775, 22 September 1775, to JL, 23 September 1775, ibid., 10: 403 (first quotation), 413 (second quotation), 421–23.

28. On the potential deleterious effects of withdrawing affection, consult Lifton, *The Broken Connection,* 123.

29. JL to HL, 24 November 1775, in *Laurens Papers,* 10: 512.

30. JL to James Laurens, 16 November 1775, 18 November 1775, [8 February 1776], Kendall Collection.

31. L. de Vegobre to JL, 18 February 1775, 18 August 1775 (quotation), Kendall Collection.

32. HL to JL, 18 July 1775, James Laurens to HL, 12 August 1775, in *Laurens Papers,* 10: 228, 295.

33. JL to HL, 4 September 1775, 4 October 1775, ibid., 10: 364–65, 452.

34. JL to James Laurens, 9 September 1775, Kendall Collection.

35. JL to James Laurens, 9 September 1775, Kendall Collection (first quotation); JL to HL, 4 October 1775, in *Laurens Papers,* 10: 451 (second quotation).

36. JL to HL, 4 October 1775, ibid., 10: 451–54. JL wrote two letters of condolence to HL, one on 9 September and another in early October. Because of the disruption of transatlantic communications after the outbreak of hostilities, HL often sent duplicates of letters, hoping at least one would get through. JL rarely followed this practice, but in this extraordinary circumstance he did. The *Laurens Papers* printed the second of these letters. See also JL to James Laurens, October 1775, Kendall Collection; HL to JL, 8 January 1776, in *Laurens Papers,* 11: 13.

37. On Manigault's role as intermediary, see JL to James Laurens, 9 September 1775, October 1775, Kendall Collection; for Manigault's character and position in Charleston, consult Edgar, et al., eds., *Biographical Directory,* 2: 428–31; for examples of HL's deference to Manigault, see HL to Gabriel Manigault, 27 May 1772, 30 September 1772, 8 March 1773, in *Laurens Papers,* 8: 332–33, 484–87, 599–602.

38. HL to JL, 4 January 1776, ibid., 10: 616–19.

39. The first quotation is from William Gilmore Simms, who in the mid–nineteenth century possessed numerous Laurens family letters and may have had access to more evidence than now survives. Simms, *Army Correspondence,* 20; and Francis Kinloch to JL, [November 1776], in private hands.

40. HL to JL, 8 January 1776, to William Manning, 27 February 1776, to Martha Laurens, 29 February 1776, to James Laurens, 1 March 1776, in *Laurens Papers,* 11: 12–13, 122–28, 129–32, 135–36.

41. HL to JL, 8 January 1776, JL to HL, 26 April 1776, ibid., 11: 13–14, 205.

42. HL to JL, 22 February 1776, ibid., 11: 114–15; for Paine and *Common Sense,* see Foner, ed., *Writings of Paine,* 1: ix–xv, 3–46.

43. JL to HL, 15 June 1776, Misc. Mss. Laurens, John, New-York Historical Society; JL to James Laurens, [20 June 1776?], Kendall Collection.

44. JL to Francis Kinloch, [12 April 1776], Miscellaneous Papers (John Laurens), NYPL; Edmund S. Morgan, "Puritan Ethic," 3–43.

45. Francis Kinloch to JL, 28 April 1776, Miscellaneous Manuscripts, NYPL.

46. JL to Francis Kinloch, 16 June [1776], Chamberlain Collection, Boston Public Library.

47. JL to Francis Kinloch, 16 June [1776], Chamberlain Collection, Boston Public Library; Kinloch to JL, 1 July 1776, in private hands.

48. On these points, see Pincus, "Neither Machiavellian Moment nor Possessive Individualism," 708–11.

49. JL to Francis Kinloch, 16 June [1776], Chamberlain Collection, Boston Public Library. On the sources of American political thought, consult Bailyn, *Ideological Origins of the American Revolution*, 22–54; and McDonald, *Novus Ordo Seclorum*, 57–96.

50. JL to Francis Kinloch, [12 April 1776], Miscellaneous Papers (John Laurens), NYPL.

51. JL to HL, 5 December 1774, in *Laurens Papers*, 9: 649.

52. Adam Smith, *Theory of Moral Sentiments*, 254–55; Greenblatt, *Renaissance Self-Fashioning*, 9.

53. Gignilliat, *Author of Sandford and Merton*, 102–10, 113–15, 122–32; Edgeworth and Edgeworth, *Memoirs of Richard Lovell Edgeworth*, 2: 110–11 (quotation). On the collaboration between Day and Bicknell, see Lonsdale, "Dr. Burney, 'Joel Collier,' and Sabrina," 281–308. For the connection between sensibility and the English antislavery movement, see Davis, *Problem of Slavery in Western Culture*, 348–64; and Langford, "Thomas Day and the Politics of Sentiment," 57–79.

54. Day, *Fragment of an original Letter*, 2–8.

55. JL to Francis Kinloch, [12 April 1776], Miscellaneous Papers (John Laurens), NYPL. For the argument that blacks adapted to hot climates better than whites, a common justification for slavery during the eighteenth century, see Jordan, *White over Black*, 260–64, 525–27.

56. Francis Kinloch to JL, 28 April 1776, Miscellaneous Manuscripts, NYPL.

57. JL to HL, 26 April 1776, in *Laurens Papers*, 11: 204–5; on deportment and conversation, see Bushman, *Refinement of America*, 63–69, 83–89.

58. JL to James Laurens, 19 August 1776, Kendall Collection; JL to HL, 20 March 1776, 26 April 1776, HL to JL, 3 February 1777, in *Laurens Papers*, 11: 184–85 (first quotation), 204 (second quotation), 292.

59. HL to Henry Laurens Jr., 24 March 1777, ibid., 11: 315–19. JL's failure to retain copies of correspondence occasionally caused problems when mail miscarried or when he was compelled to explain passages from previous letters. See, for example, JL to James Laurens, 19 August 1776, Kendall Collection; JL to Francis Kinloch, 30 September 1776 (EM 7981), Thomas Addis Emmet Collection, NYPL.

60. Ward, *War of the Revolution*, 2: 665–78; Tilley, *British Navy and the American Revolution*, 75–77; HL to JL, 14 August 1776, in *Laurens Papers*, 11: 225–26, 236–46.

61. HL to JL, 14 August 1776, ibid., 11: 228; JL to HL, 19 October 1775, ibid., 10: 475; JL to James Laurens, 19 August 1776, Kendall Collection.

62. HL to JL, 14 August 1776, in *Laurens Papers*, 11: 234; HL to JL, 17 August 1776, Henry Laurens Papers, SCHS; HL to Jacob Read, 16 August 1776, Henry Laurens Papers, South Caroliniana Library.

63. HL to JL, 20 August 1775 (Jeremiah plot and documentation), in *Laurens Papers*, 10: 319–35; HL to Stephen Bull, 16 March 1776 (draft for Council of Safety), to JL, 14 August 1776, ibid., 11: 171–73, 223–24 (quotation); on the Jeremiah plot

and Carolinian fears of slave insurrections, see Olwell, "'Domestick Enemies,'" 21–48; for early contacts between the Royal Navy and bondspeople, see Frey, *Water from the Rock,* 56–67; the connection between slave resistance and upheavals among whites is explored in Peter H. Wood, "'Liberty is Sweet,'" 149–84.

64. HL to JL, 14 August 1776, in *Laurens Papers,* 11: 223–25. HL's rationalizations, which were typical of many slaveholders, are placed in a larger context in MacLeod, *Slavery, Race and the American Revolution,* 31–47, 136–39.

65. JL to HL, 26 October 1776, in *Laurens Papers,* 11: 276–77.

66. HL to James Laurens, 23 August 1776, to JL, 16 September 1776, ibid., 11: 260–61, 268–69.

67. JL to HL, 29 September 1776, ibid., 11: 273–74; JL to Francis Kinloch, 30 September 1776 (EM 7981), Thomas Addis Emmet Collection, NYPL.

68. JL to James Laurens, 24 October 1776, Henry Laurens Papers, SCHS; HL to JL, 14 August 1776, in *Laurens Papers,* 11: 234.

69. JL to HL, 26 October 1776, HL to William Manning, 26 March 1777, ibid., 11: 277, 319–20.

70. JL to James Laurens, 25 October 1776, Kendall Collection.

71. JL to James Laurens, 9 November 1776, 26–27 December 1776, Kendall Collection; HL to Henry Laurens Jr., 24 March 1777, in *Laurens Papers,* 11: 317.

72. JL to James Laurens, 25 December 1776 (first quotation), 26–27 December 1776 (second quotation), Kendall Collection.

73. JL to James Laurens, 26–27 December 1776, Kendall Collection.

Chapter 4

1. Greenblatt, *Renaissance Self-Fashioning,* 9, 256.

2. JL to James Laurens, 11 January 1777, Kendall Collection; Dull, *Diplomatic History,* 50–56, 75–78.

3. JL to James Laurens, 27 January 1777, Kendall Collection; the information on White is from *Laurens Papers,* 11: 364n.

4. JL to James Laurens, 3 April 1777, Kendall Collection.

5. JL to James Laurens, 3 April 1777 (quotation), 16 April 1777, Kendall Collection; *The South-Carolina and American General Gazette,* 17 April 1777.

6. William Manning to JL, 12 July 1777, John Laurens Papers, SCHS. For the surgery, see Martha Manning Laurens to HL, 1 May 1777, in private hands. Frances Eleanor was baptized on 18 February. *Laurens Papers,* 11: 277n. In his diary John Baker recorded a 28 January visit to the Manning home at St. Mary Axe during which he ventured upstairs to see the mother and daughter. Yorke, ed., *Diary of John Baker,* 385.

7. JL to James Laurens, 16 April 1777 (two letters of the same date), Kendall Collection.

8. HL to William Manning, 26 March 1777, 7 June 1777, 16 August 1777, to James Laurens, 28 March 1777, in *Laurens Papers,* 11: 319–21, 322, 347–48, 459.

9. HL to William Manning, 7 June 1777, ibid., 11: 347–48.

10. HL to John Lewis Gervais, 21 June 1777, 26 June 1777, 25 July 1777, to William Brisbane, 14 August 1777, ibid., 11: 376–83, 389–91, 404, 453–54; for Custer and Shrewsberry, see HL to JL, 4 January 1775, 14 July 1775, ibid., 10: 17, 17n,

222. In the 25 July 1777 letter to Gervais cited above, HL mentioned that George was inoculated for smallpox.

11. George Washington to JL, 5 August 1777, in Fitzpatrick, ed., *Writings of Washington*, 9: 25. Washington officially announced JL's appointment as extra aide-de-camp on 6 September. General Orders, 6 September 1777, ibid., 9: 189. For Lafayette's arrival, see Gottschalk, *Lafayette Joins the American Army*, 14–39. In the eighteenth century, a high ranking military officer's staff was considered his "family." *Oxford English Dictionary*.

12. HL to John Lewis Gervais, 5 August 1777, to William Manning, 16 August 1777, in *Laurens Papers*, 11: 427–28 (first and second quotations), 459.

13. Middlekauff, *Glorious Cause*, 366–70; the Howes' plan to assault Philadelphia and the ensuing sea voyage are detailed in Gruber, *Howe Brothers*, 179–80, 183, 199–200, 207–8, 222–40.

14. Freeman, *Washington*, 4: 445–51; Flexner, *Washington*, 211–12, 215–16; HL to William Brisbane, 14 August 1777, JL to HL, 21 August 1777, in *Laurens Papers*, 11: 454–55, 466.

15. JL to HL, 13 August 1777, 21 August 1777, 30 August 1777, ibid., 11: 453 (second quotation), 466, 472 (first quotation); JL to HL, 17 August 1777, Henry Laurens Papers, Rare Book, Manuscript & Special Collections Library, Duke University, Durham, N.C.; for Washington's daily routine, see Ferling, *First of Men*, 258–59.

16. Freeman, *Washington*, 4: 459–60, 467–70; Flexner, *Washington*, 215–18.

17. Freeman, *Washington*, 4: 471; Flexner, *Washington*, 220; [JL to HL], 9 September 1777 in *South-Carolina and American General Gazette*, 16 October 1777. This letter, according to John Wells Jr., the publisher of the newspaper, was "an extract of a letter from a gentleman at Head Quarters, to his friend" in Philadelphia. It has been identified as a JL letter because its tone reflects his style when addressing his father about military operations. Moreover, during this period, HL transmitted much of JL's correspondence to John Lewis Gervais and allowed Gervais to show the letters to friends. Among those friends was Wells. See HL to John Lewis Gervais, 18 September 1777, 8 October 1777, in *Laurens Papers*, 11: 527, 527n, 546–47. On one occasion, when HL sent a JL letter to Gervais, he told his friend that "if you publish either abstract or extract I intreat you to avoid names & give Mr. Wells the same caution." See HL to Gervais, 13 December 1777, ibid., 12: 145.

18. This account of the battle of Brandywine was drawn from Freeman, *Washington*, 4: 473–89; Flexner, *Washington*, 221–26; and Middlekauff, *Glorious Cause*, 386–89. Lafayette's remark is recorded in HL to John Lewis Gervais, 8 October 1777, in *Laurens Papers*, 11: 547.

19. HL to John Lewis Gervais, 18 September 1777, 8 October 1777, ibid., 11: 527–29, 528n, 545–47; Middlekauff, *Glorious Cause*, 389–91.

20. Washington quoted in Middlekauff, *Glorious Cause*, 391; see also Ward, *War of the Revolution*, 1: 361–62; and Flexner, *Washington*, 230–31.

21. The account of the battle of Germantown was drawn from Freeman, *Washington*, 4: 505–19; and Middlekauff, *Glorious Cause*, 392–95; JL's role in the attack on the Chew House is described in Ward, *War of the Revolution*, 1: 366; and Chastellux, *Travels in North America*, 1: 138–40; JL's wounds are noted in an anonymous letter of 5 October, which was printed in the *South-Carolina and American General*

Gazette, 30 October 1777; and in Hastings, ed., *Public Papers of George Clinton,* 2: 367–73.

22. HL to JL, 8 October 1777, in *Laurens Papers,* 11: 548–49.
23. HL to John Lewis Gervais, 8 October 1777, ibid., 11: 547.
24. HL to JL, 30 September 1777, ibid., 11: 538–40.
25. Martha Manning Laurens to HL, 1 May 1777, in private hands.
26. William Manning to JL, 12 July 1777, John Laurens Papers, SCHS.
27. JL to Martha Manning Laurens, 9 November 1777, London, Public Record Office, HCA 32/392. This letter apparently was intercepted at sea, but the argument used by JL was probably reiterated in other letters written that fall. It is also the only JL-Martha letter that has been found.
28. JL to HL, 15 December 1777, HL to JL, 20 December 1777, in *Laurens Papers,* 12: 157, 166; Ralph Izard to HL, 6 October 1777, ibid., 11: 543; Edgar, et al., eds., *Biographical Directory,* 2: 82–83.
29. On the "heroism of renunciation," see Taylor, *Sources of the Self,* 295.
30. General Orders, 6 October 1777, in Fitzpatrick, ed., *Writings of Washington,* 9: 313.
31. George Washington to Joseph Reed, 23 January 1776, to John Hancock, 23 April 1776, ibid., 4: 269 (first quotation), 506 (second quotation).
32. For a description of Washington's official family, see Mitchell, *Hamilton,* 106–15; and, for the information on Meade, see Whiteley, *Washington and His Aides-De-Camp,* 46–47, an entertaining book marred by errors; for example, see 154–55, which contains an erroneous account of the JL-Martha Manning relationship. A list of the aides who served with Washington during the war is provided in Heitman, *Historical Register,* 13.
33. Miller, *Hamilton,* 3–23; Cooke, *Hamilton,* 13–18.
34. JL to Richard Kidder Meade, 22 October 1781, Alexander Hamilton Papers, LC; Alexander Hamilton to JL, [April 1779], in Syrett, ed., *Hamilton Papers,* 2: 34–35.
35. Pay Book of the State Company of Artillery, [1777], ibid., 1: 400; on the process of self-fashioning by transcribing quotations from other, printed sources, see Lockridge, *On the Sources of Patriarchal Rage,* especially 1–5.
36. The classic study remains Dover, *Greek Homosexuality;* on the Greeks in general as role models, see Sherrod, "The Bonds of Men," 229–31; and Crompton, "Byron and Male Love," 325–27; on the example of Damon and Pythias, see Miller, *Hamilton,* 22.
37. Heilbrun, *Writing a Woman's Life,* 98–103 (first quotation on 100); Durkheim, *Suicide,* 170 (second quotation); Aristotle, *Nicomachean Ethics,* Book 1, Chapter 5, in *Introduction to Aristotle,* 312; on men and homosociability, see Kimmel, *American Manhood,* 7–8, 26; for eighteenth-century warfare as an intimate theater, see Middlekauff, *Glorious Cause,* 500.
38. Royster, *Revolutionary People at War,* 83–96, 197–213; Middlekauff, *Glorious Cause,* 567–68.
39. Plutarch, "Lycurgus," in *Lives of the Noble Greeks,* 55–56; Ramsay, *Memoirs of Martha Laurens Ramsay,* 16–17; Alexander Hamilton to Elizabeth Schuyler, [August 1780], in Syrett, ed., *Hamilton Papers,* 2: 397.
40. JL to HL, 7 May 1777, in *Laurens Papers,* 13: 265–66; for penetrating character analyses of Washington, see Ferling, *First of Men,* 249–66; and Edmund S. Morgan, *The Meaning of Independence,* 29–55.

41. For the Saratoga campaign, see Middlekauff, *Glorious Cause,* 370–84; for HL's reaction to ongoing complaints about Washington in Congress, see HL to JL, 30 September 1777, 16 October 1777, in *Laurens Papers,* 11: 539, 554–55; on the value of JL's detailed letters, see HL to JL, 10 October 1777, ibid., 11: 550.

42. Ford, ed., *Journals of the Continental Congress,* 9: 852–54. On the political culture of HL's native Carolina, see Weir, "'Harmony We Were Famous For,'" 473–501.

43. For HL's reactions to other members of Congress, see HL to John Rutledge, 12 August 1777, to John Lewis Gervais, 5 September 1777, 18 September 1777, to JL, 10 October 1777, in *Laurens Papers,* 11: 443–52, 485–512, 527–29, 550–51; on his first months in Congress and the duties of the president, consult Frech, "Henry Laurens in the Continental Congress," 106–48, 150–57; JL to HL, 7 November 1777, HL to JL, 12 November 1777, in *Laurens Papers,* 12: 35, 48 (quotation).

44. JL to HL, 26 November 1777, ibid., 12: 91; for Wilkinson's promotion and the protest of other Continental colonels, see Nathaniel Folsom to Josiah Bartlett, 2 January 1778, in Paul H. Smith, ed., *Letters of Delegates,* 13: 517; HL to John Rutledge, 30 January 1778, in *Laurens Papers,* 12: 379; and Freeman, *Washington,* 4: 594–97.

45. HL to JL, 30 November 1777, in *Laurens Papers,* 12: 113; Henderson, *Party Politics,* 130–56; and Rakove, *Beginnings of National Politics,* 135–91.

46. JL to HL, 3 December 1777, in *Laurens Papers,* 12: 128–29; Henderson, *Party Politics,* 136, 157–58; Rakove, *Beginnings of National Politics,* 170–74.

47. JL to HL, 3 December 1777, in *Laurens Papers,* 12: 129–30; for the political factors behind the eventual decision to camp at Valley Forge, see Bodle, "Generals and 'Gentlemen,'" 59–89.

48. Freeman, *Washington,* 4: 561–63; JL to HL, 10 December 1777, in *Laurens Papers,* 12: 139.

Chapter 5

1. Ferling, *First of Men,* 221–22; JL to HL, 15 December 1777, 1 January 1778, in *Laurens Papers,* 12: 157, 231.

2. JL to HL, 23 December 1777, George Washington to HL, 23 December 1777, ibid., 12: 189–91, 192–97; Freeman, *Washington,* 4: 566–68.

3. JL to HL, 23 December 1777, George Washington to HL, 23 December 1777, in *Laurens Papers,* 12: 191, 192–97; Carp, *To Starve the Army,* 35–45.

4. HL to John Lewis Gervais, 30 December 1777/30 January 1778, to Isaac Motte, 26 January 1778, in *Laurens Papers,* 12: 220–26, 344–47 (quotation). For the departure of Heyward and Middleton, see ibid., 12: 19n.

5. JL to HL, 9 February 1778, 9 March 1778, ibid., 12: 429–30, 530 (quotation).

6. See HL to JL, 12 November 1777, 27 November 1777, 28 January 1778, 3 February 1778, 6 February 1778, JL to HL 20 November 1777, 15 December 1777, 9 February 1778, 15 February 1778, ibid., 12: 48, 89, 96–97, 158, 369, 393, 413–14 (quotation), 429–30, 446–47.

7. For JL's correspondence, see, for example, JL to Henry Lutterloh, 28 December 1777, 15 January 1778, George Washington Papers, Series 4, LC; JL to Clement Biddle, 12 January 1778, Washington-Biddle Correspondence, HSP; Henry Lutterloh to JL, 14 January 1778, 15 January 1778, Clement Biddle to JL, 5 March

1778, 14 June 1778, George Washington Papers, Series 4, LC; for the letters to Pulaski, see Fitzpatrick, ed., *Writings of Washington,* 10, 11; on Lutterloh and Pulaski, see Freeman, *Washington,* 4: 421n, 497–98, 615–16.

8. For JL's efforts to purchase additional military treatises, see Baron Holzendorff to HL, 8 February 1778, 10 February 1778, Misc. Mss. Holzendorff, Baron, New-York Historical Society; Chevalier Du Plessis to HL, 8 February 1778, JL to HL, 9 March 1778, HL to JL, 15 March 1778, in *Laurens Papers,* 12: 425, 535, 560; JL to HL, 22 March 1778, HL to JL, 29 March 1778, ibid., 13: 25, 52.

9. See Pay Book of the State Company of Artillery, [1777], in Syrett, ed., *Hamilton Papers,* 1: 373–411.

10. HL to John Lewis Gervais, 5 September 1777, in *Laurens Papers,* 11: 498; Bailyn, *Ideological Origins of the American Revolution,* 55–93; Hutson, "Origins of 'The Paranoid Style in American Politics,'" 332–72; Gordon S. Wood, "Conspiracy and the Paranoid Style," 401–41.

11. In addition to letters cited from the *Laurens Papers,* this account of the so-called Conway Cabal is drawn from Knollenberg, *Washington and the Revolution,* especially 37–92, 186–215; see also Higginbotham, *War of American Independence,* 216–22; and Henderson, *Party Politics,* 118–20.

12. JL to HL, 1 January 1778, 3 January 1778, in *Laurens Papers,* 12: 231 (second quotation), 245–46 (first quotation); Freeman, *Washington,* 4: 594–95; Ward, *War of the Revolution,* 1: 371.

13. JL to HL, 3 January 1778, in *Laurens Papers,* 12: 244–47.

14. HL to JL, 8 January 1778, ibid., 12: 269–73.

15. Lafayette to HL, 5 January 1778, HL to Lafayette, 12 January 1778, ibid., 12: 253–58, 283–87; for Carolinians's distaste for factional politics, see Weir, "'Harmony We Were Famous For,'" 473–501; for a succinct discussion of HL's attitude toward parties, see Higginbotham, *War of American Independence,* 221.

16. Royster, *Revolutionary People at War,* 178–89.

17. JL to HL, 28 January 1778, in *Laurens Papers,* 12: 369–71; HL to John Rutledge, 3 February 1778, in Paul H. Smith, ed., *Letters of Delegates,* 9: 18–20; Knollenberg, *Washington and the Revolution,* 78–92; Gottschalk, *Lafayette Joins the American Army,* 110–65.

18. Ford, ed., *Journals of the Continental Congress,* 10: 354; Freeman, *Washington,* 4: 628n; HL to JL, 3 February 1778, JL to HL, 9 February 1778, in *Laurens Papers,* 12: 393, 431; JL to HL, 14 June 1778, ibid., 13: 457.

19. Thomas Conway to HL, 22 April 1778, HL to JL, 5 June 1778, ibid., 13: 169–70, 407–8; HL to George Washington, 28 April 1778, in Paul H. Smith, ed., *Letters of Delegates,* 9: 516–17. Before leaving America, Conway fought a duel with John Cadwalader, a Pennsylvania militia general. In the exchange of fire, Conway was wounded in the mouth. Freeman, *Washington,* 5: 39, 55–56. Some studies have mistakenly identified JL as Conway's opponent in the duel. See, for example, Royster, *Revolutionary People at War,* 208–9; and Alden, *Washington,* 164.

20. James Laurens to HL, 16 December 1777, 5 February 1778, HL to JL, 8 January 1778, JL to HL, 23 January 1778, in *Laurens Papers,* 12: 158–60, 274–75, 330, 404–5.

21. See Haskell, "Capitalism and the Humanitarian Sensibility," 339–61, especially 357–58, wherein Haskell outlines four preconditions necessary for an individual to take steps to alleviate the suffering of another. The label "Conditional Terminator"

was applied first to Thomas Jefferson in Freehling, *Road to Disunion,* 121–43, especially 142.

22. Bartlett, ed., *Records of the State of Rhode Island,* 8: 358–60, 640–41.
23. JL to HL, 14 January 1778, in *Laurens Papers,* 12: 305–6; Haskell, "Capitalism and the Humanitarian Sensibility," 357–58; on the culture of sensibility's dependence on property, see Barker-Benfield, *Culture of Sensibility,* 228.
24. HL to JL, 28 January 1778, in *Laurens Papers,* 12: 367–68.
25. JL to HL, 2 February 1778, ibid., 12: 390–93; on the concept of an ideal self whose worth is measured only by a distant, ideal judge, see James, *Principles of Psychology,* 315–16; for the effects of environmentalism—the idea that man was shaped by his surroundings—on antislavery thought, see Jordan, *White over Black,* 281–89; on faculty psychology, an eighteenth-century theory that divided human faculties into separate components—involuntary reflexes, emotions, and rational powers—see Howe, *Making the American Self,* especially 5–8, 29, 63–66.
26. JL to HL, 2 February 1778, 15 February 1778, HL to JL, 6 February 1778, in *Laurens Papers,* 12: 391–92, 413, 447; Sheriff, *Good-Natured Man,* 6–10.
27. JL to HL, 10 March 1779, Henry Laurens Papers, SCHS. On the importance of disinterestedness to eighteenth-century gentlemen, see Gordon S. Wood, *Radicalism of the American Revolution,* 104–5, 205–12; for the use of symbolic gestures to display virtue, see Weir, "The South Carolinian as Extremist," 213–30; on symbolic immortality, consult Lifton, *The Broken Connection,* 18–23, 239–61.
28. JL to HL, 15 December 1777, in *Laurens Papers,* 12: 158; Martha H. Brown, "Clothing," 117–21.
29. JL to HL, 9 February 1778, in *Laurens Papers,* 12: 429–30.
30. HL to JL, 6 February 1778, ibid., 12: 412.
31. HL to JL, 6 February 1778, 18 February 1778, 1 March 1778, JL to HL, 15 February 1778, ibid., 12: 412–13 (first quotation), 446–47, 462, 494 (second quotation).
32. JL to HL, 9 March 1778, ibid., 12: 532.
33. Royster, *Revolutionary People at War,* 200–208; JL to "Lieutenant Hazard of the Light Dragoons," [n.d.], in *Joseph Rubinfine: Autographs-Manuscripts Historical Americana,* List 81, Item 36.
34. HL to George Washington, 5 May 1778, in *Laurens Papers,* 13: 255–59; Henderson, *Party Politics,* 120–24; Royster, *Revolutionary People at War,* 200–204.
35. The ensuing paragraphs, in addition to the letters cited from the *Laurens Papers,* draw on Peter Laslett's introduction to Locke, *Two Treatises of Government,* especially 92–120; Kramnick, *Republicanism and Bourgeois Radicalism,* 1–18; Zuckerman, "A Different Thermidor," 170–93; Pincus, "Neither Machiavellian Moment nor Possessive Individualism," 705–36; and Howe, *Making the American Self,* 10–16.
36. HL to James Marion, 31 August 1765, in *Laurens Papers,* 4: 672; JL to HL, 1 June 1778, ibid., 13: 388; on HL's support of JL, see also JL to HL, 23 October 1778, ibid., 14: 445; and Gordon S. Wood, *Radicalism of the American Revolution,* 210.
37. JL to HL, 11 April 1778, in *Laurens Papers,* 13: 100–103; Montesquieu, *The Spirit of the Laws,* book 7, chaps. 1, 2 (quotation), and 4.
38. See Gordon S. Wood, *Creation of the American Republic,* 70–75. For views on equality in JL's native South Carolina, see Greene, "'Slavery or Independence,'" 208–13.

39. JL to HL, 18 February 1775, in *Laurens Papers,* 10: 75–76 (first quotation); JL to James Laurens, 3 July 1776, Kendall Collection (second quotation); JL to Francis Kinloch, 16 June 1776, Chamberlain Collection, Boston Public Library; Gordon S. Wood, *Radicalism of the American Revolution,* 180–81; for a concise summary of South Carolina's 1776 constitution, see Haw, *John and Edmund Rutledge,* 79–82.

40. HL to JL, 18 February 1778, 1 March 1778, JL to HL, 24 February 1778, 9 March 1778, in *Laurens Papers,* 12: 462, 481 (first quotation), 491–92 (second and third quotations), 530; for an account of the fire, see John Wells Jr. to HL, 23 January 1778, ibid., 12: 331–36.

41. Henderson, *Party Politics,* 122–24.

42. JL to HL, 9 February 1778, in *Laurens Papers,* 12: 430–31; for examples of JL recommending foreign officers, see JL to HL, 14 January 1778, 3 February 1778, ibid., 12: 306–7, 398; JL to HL, 22 March 1778, 25 March 1778, ibid., 13: 25–26, 36–37; JL to HL, 27 May 1778, Gratz Collection, HSP.

43. John Rutledge to HL, 16 February 1778, HL to JL, 1 March 1778, 15 March 1778, JL to HL, 9 March 1778, in *Laurens Papers,* 12: 453–55, 495, 532, 558–61 (quotation); HL to JL, 22 March 1778, ibid., 13: 23–24.

44. JL to HL, 25 March 1778, 28 March 1778, ibid., 13: 34–37, 49–51.

45. HL to JL, 29 March 1778, to John Lewis Gervais, 3 May 1778, to John Rutledge, 4 May 1778, ibid., 13: 51–54, 239–40, 248 (quotation).

46. Carp, *To Starve the Army,* 48–51; Middlekauff, *Glorious Cause,* 415–17.

47. Palmer, *General Von Steuben,* 123–35; HL to JL, 18 February 1778, JL to HL, 28 February 1778, in *Laurens Papers,* 12: 462–63, 483–84.

48. Royster, *Revolutionary People at War,* 213–38; on relations between officers and their men, see also JL to HL, 15 June 1778, in *Laurens Papers,* 13: 461–62.

49. Palmer, *General Von Steuben,* 136–66; JL to HL, 25 March 1778, 1 April 1778, 18 April 1778, in *Laurens Papers,* 13: 35–37, 68 (quotation), 140.

50. Dull, *French Navy and American Independence,* 95–112; Dull, *Diplomatic History,* 89–99.

51. JL to HL, 1 May 1778, HL to John Rutledge, 4 May 1778, in *Laurens Papers,* 13: 237, 247–48.

52. JL to HL, 12 May 1778, HL to JL, 16 May 1778, ibid., 13: 294–95, 309.

53. Mackesy, *War for America,* 147–59, 212–15; Dull, *Diplomatic History,* 99–100.

54. For an account of Congress's dealings with the peace commission, see Frech, "Henry Laurens in the Continental Congress," 274–301.

55. George Johnstone's letter to JL is copied below Johnstone to HL, 10 June 1778, Wentworth Woodhouse Muniments (Correspondence of the 4th Earl Fitzwilliam), WWM F64/91, Sheffield Archives, Sheffield City Libraries, England; William Manning to JL, 11 April 1778, Kendall Collection; JL to HL, 7 June 1778, 9 June 1778, 11 June 1778, HL to JL, 13 June 1778, in *Laurens Papers,* 13: 416–18, 430–31 (quotation), 442–44, 453; Dull, *Diplomatic History,* 100; Frech, "Henry Laurens in the Continental Congress," 290–301.

56. Arthur Lee to HL, 4 April 1778, Henry Laurens Papers, SCHS; JL to HL, 7 November 1777, in *Laurens Papers,* 12: 35; JL to HL, 1 May 1778, 4 May 1778, 9 June 1778, 11 June 1778, ibid., 13: 237, 250, 430, 442.

57. Gabriel Manigault Diary, 21 June 1777, 24 July 1777, 29 July 1777, 2 August 1777, 7 August 1777, 9 August 1777, 11 August 1777, 13 August 1777, 25 October 1777, 5 July 1778, 19–20 July 1778, SCHS; JL to HL, 4 May 1778, in

Laurens Papers, 13: 250; Charles Bicknell to Gabriel Manigault, 16 January [1778], Manigault Family Papers, South Caroliniana Library.

58. JL to HL, 4 June 1778, 9 June 1778, 15 June 1778, in *Laurens Papers,* 13: 402–3, 430–31 (first quotation), 461 (second quotation).

59. Freeman, *Washington,* 5: 9–11; Middlekauff, *Glorious Cause,* 420–21.

Chapter 6

1. Middlekauff, *Glorious Cause,* 420–22; JL to George Washington, 23 June 1778, George Washington Papers, Series 4, LC.

2. Middlekauff, *Glorious Cause,* 422–23; for Charles Lee, see Alden, *Lee;* and Shy, "American Strategy," 133–62.

3. Thayer, *Making of a Scapegoat,* 33–39; Freeman, *Washington,* 5: 22–25.

4. JL to HL, 1 June 1778, in *Laurens Papers,* 13: 390; for Washington's plan to employ the militia against Clinton, see Kwasny, *Washington's Partisan War,* 196–97.

5. Middlekauff, *Glorious Cause,* 424; Willcox, *Portrait of a General,* 233–35; Alden, *Lee,* 213–19; JL to George Washington, 28 June 1778, George Washington Papers, Series 4, LC.

6. JL to HL, 2 July 1778, in *Laurens Papers,* 13: 545–46.

7. "Proceedings of a General Court Martial," in *Lee Papers,* 3: 51–53; Alden, *Lee,* 216–20; Thayer, *Making of a Scapegoat,* 39–51.

8. "Proceedings of a General Court Martial," in *Lee Papers,* 3: 53; JL to HL, 30 June 1778, in *Laurens Papers,* 13: 534.

9. "Proceedings of a General Court Martial," in *Lee Papers,* 3: 52; Thayer, *Making of a Scapegoat,* 49–51.

10. Ferling, *First of Men,* 245–46; Flexner, *Washington,* 303–5; JL to HL, 30 June 1778, in *Laurens Papers,* 13: 534.

11. Thayer, *Making of a Scapegoat,* 53–62; Alexander Hamilton to Elias Boudinot, 5 July 1778, in Syrett, ed., *Hamilton Papers,* 1: 513; James McHenry to Elias Boudinot, 2 July 1778, Thomas Addis Emmet Collection (EM 9294), NYPL (quotation).

12. Thayer, *Making of a Scapegoat,* 63–67; JL to HL, 30 June 1778, in *Laurens Papers,* 13: 536.

13. JL to HL, 30 June 1778, 2 July 1778, ibid., 13: 537 (second quotation) 545 (first quotation); Alexander Hamilton to Elias Boudinot, 5 July 1778, in Syrett, ed., *Hamilton Papers,* 1: 513–14.

14. JL to HL, 2 July 1778, in *Laurens Papers,* 13: 546; Willcox, *Portrait of a General,* 236–37; "Proceedings of a General Court Martial," in *Lee Papers,* 3: 98–101.

15. Alden, *Lee,* 235–36.

16. "Proceedings of a General Court Martial," in *Lee Papers,* 3: 51–57.

17. Ibid., 3: 8–10, 57–62, 200–201.

18. Ibid., 3: 40–42, 71 (Fitzgerald quotation), 83–94, 101–15, 126–43, 139 (Oswald quotation), 156–69; for Cumpston, who was called Captain Cumpiton in the trial record, see Heitman, *Historical Register,* 180.

19. "Proceedings of a General Court Martial," in *Lee Papers,* 3: 174–207 (quotation on 201).

20. Ibid., 3: 2, 208; Alden, *Lee,* 238–40; Shy, "American Strategy," 159.

21. Alden, *Lee*, 242–51; HL to JL, 6 July 1778, in *Laurens Papers*, 13: 552; John Penn to Richard Caswell, 15 July 1778, in Paul H. Smith, ed., *Letters of Delegates*, 10: 287–88.

22. HL to John Lewis Gervais, 15 July 1778, to JL, 26 July 1778, in *Laurens Papers*, 14: 30, 80.

23. JL to HL, 13 July 1778, ibid., 14: 24–25; George Washington to David Forman, 13 July 1778, to Count D'Estaing, 14 July 1778, to HL, 14 July 1778, in Fitzpatrick, ed., *Writings of Washington*, 12: 175, 178–81; Freeman, *Washington*, 5: 45–49; Lafayette to Count d'Estaing, 14 July 1778, in Idzerda, ed., *Lafayette Papers*, 2: 102–7.

24. Freeman, *Washington*, 5: 49; Count d'Estaing to HL, 26 August 1778, in *Laurens Papers*, 14: 223–24. JL translated this letter into English.

25. George Washington to John Sullivan, to Count d'Estaing, 17 July 1778, in Fitzpatrick, ed., *Writings of Washington*, 12: 184–87; Freeman, *Washington*, 5: 50–51.

26. George Washington to John Sullivan, to Lafayette, to JL, to Jonathan Trumbull, to Count d'Estaing, to HL, 22 July 1778, in Fitzpatrick, ed., *Writings of Washington*, 12: 201–13; Count d'Estaing to HL, 26 August 1778, in *Laurens Papers*, 14: 224–25.

27. JL to George Washington, 25 July 1778, George Washington Papers, Series 4, LC; JL to HL, 4 August 1778, in *Laurens Papers*, 14: 116 (quotation); Whittemore, *General of the Revolution*, 25–26, 82–84; Dearden, *Rhode Island Campaign*, 36.

28. JL to George Washington, 25 July 1778, George Washington Papers, Series 4, LC; JL to Washington, 4 August 1778, PCC, reel 187, item 169, vol. 4, p. 410, NA; JL to HL, 4 August 1778, in *Laurens Papers*, 14: 116.

29. JL to HL, 4 August 1778, ibid., 14: 116; JL to John Sullivan, 27 July 1778, in Hammond, ed., *Sullivan Papers*, 2: 128; JL to George Washington, 4 August 1778, PCC, reel 187, item 169, vol. 4, p. 410, NA (quotation); Whittemore, *General of the Revolution*, 90–91.

30. John Sullivan to Count d'Estaing, 25 July 1778, in Hammond, ed., *Sullivan Papers*, 3: 640–44. Greene was the cousin of Nathanael Greene; for the "colored regiment," see Dearden, *Rhode Island Campaign*, xiii, 23–24.

31. JL to George Washington, 4 August 1778, PCC, reel 187, item 169, vol. 4, p. 410, NA; Count d'Estaing to John Sullivan, 30 July 1778, 31 July 1778, 3 August 1778, in Hammond, ed., *Sullivan Papers*, 2: 151–53, 155, 170; Count d'Estaing to Washington, 3 August 1778, Henry Laurens Papers, SCHS (quotation); Lafayette to Washington, 6 August 1778, in Idzerda, ed., *Lafayette Papers*, 2: 133.

32. Count d'Estaing to John Sullivan, 3 August 1778, 4 August 1778, 7 August 1778, in Hammond, ed., *Sullivan Papers*, 2: 170, 172–74, 183–84; JL to HL, 22 August 1778, in *Laurens Papers*, 14: 200–201; JL to George Washington, 4 August 1778, PCC, reel 187, item 169, vol. 4, p. 410, NA; Lafayette to Count d'Estaing, 5 August 1778, in Idzerda, ed., *Lafayette Papers*, 2: 128–31; Dearden, *Rhode Island Campaign*, 46, 66–67, 73–74; Major Gibbes Orderly Book, 8 August 1778, 9 August 1778, SCHS.

33. Dearden, *Rhode Island Campaign*, 74–75; John Sullivan to HL, 10 August 1778, JL to HL, 22 August 1778, in *Laurens Papers*, 14: 145–46, 202. D'Estaing later admitted that Sullivan had acted correctly. See Count d'Estaing to HL, 26 August 1778, ibid., 14: 226–27.

34. Count d'Estaing to HL, 26 August 1778, ibid., 14: 227; Dearden, *Rhode Island Campaign,* 75.
35. John Sullivan to HL, 10 August 1778, Count d'Estaing to HL, 26 August 1778, in *Laurens Papers,* 14: 145–46, 227–29; Count d'Estaing to Sullivan, 21 August 1778, in Hammond, ed., *Sullivan Papers,* 2: 240–42; Dearden, *Rhode Island Campaign,* 49, 75–80.
36. John Sullivan to William Greene, to George Washington, 13 August 1778, in Hammond, ed., *Sullivan Papers,* 2: 202–7; JL to HL, 22 August 1778, Sullivan to HL, [23 August 1778], in *Laurens Papers,* 14: 203, 210–12; Whittemore, *General of the Revolution,* 97–99; Dearden, *Rhode Island Campaign,* 93–94.
37. Whittemore, *General of the Revolution,* 99–101; Dearden, *Rhode Island Campaign,* 95–98; John Sullivan to HL, 17 August 1778, JL to HL, 22 August 1778, HL to JL, 23 August 1778, in *Laurens Papers,* 14: 184–85, 203, 207.
38. Count de Cambis to John Sullivan, 20 August 1778, Count d'Estaing to Sullivan, 21 August 1778, in Hammond, ed., *Sullivan Papers,* 2: 237–38, 240–42; Lafayette to George Washington, 25 August 1778, in Idzerda, ed., *Lafayette Papers,* 2: 149–53.
39. JL to George Washington, 23 August 1778, George Washington Papers, Series 4, LC (first quotation); JL to HL, 22 August 1778, in *Laurens Papers,* 14: 204; John Sullivan to Washington, 23 August 1778, in Hammond, ed., *Sullivan Papers,* 2: 264–65; General Greene's Remonstrance to Count d'Estaing, 21 August 1778, A Protest of the General Officers on Rhode Island to Count d'Estaing, 22 August 1778, in Showman and Conrad, eds., *Greene Papers,* 2: 480–82, 487–91; Dearden, *Rhode Island Campaign,* 102–3.
40. JL to George Washington, 23 August 1778, George Washington Papers, Series 4, LC; Whittemore, *General of the Revolution,* 103–4; Dearden, *Rhode Island Campaign,* 118.
41. Dearden, *Rhode Island Campaign,* 118–20; Mackenzie, *Diary,* 2: 380–81.
42. This narrative of the battle of Rhode Island was drawn from John Sullivan to HL, 31 August 1778, in *Laurens Papers,* 14: 249–52; Nathanael Greene to George Washington, 28/31 August 1778, in Showman and Conrad, eds., *Greene Papers,* 2: 501–2 (concluding quotation); Mackenzie, *Diary,* 2: 381–85; and [JL to HL], 1 September 1778, in *South-Carolina & American General Gazette,* 8 October 1778. HL sent to John Lewis Gervais a letter from JL dated 1 September. He gave Gervais permission to publish the letter on the condition that JL's name was omitted. See HL to John Lewis Gervais, 6 September 1778, in *Laurens Papers,* 14: 271.
43. [JL to HL], 1 September 1778, in *South-Carolina & American General Gazette,* 8 October 1778; John Sullivan to HL, 31 August 1778, in *Laurens Papers,* 14: 252; Nathanael Greene to George Washington, 28/31 August 1778, in Showman and Conrad, eds., *Greene Papers,* 2: 502. Washington copied Greene's commendation for HL. Washington to HL, 4 September 1778, in *Laurens Papers,* 14: 265. For the overall casualty figures and the effectiveness of the black troops, see Dearden, *Rhode Island Campaign,* 124, 126–27.
44. George Washington to John Sullivan, 28 August 1778, in Hammond, ed., *Sullivan Papers,* 2: 270–71; Sullivan to HL, 31 August 1778, in *Laurens Papers,* 14: 252–53; Dearden, *Rhode Island Campaign,* 126–27.
45. Ibid., 118, 128.
46. JL to George Washington, 2 September 1778, George Washington Papers, Series

      4, LC; Count d'Estaing to John Sullivan, 30 August 1778, in Hammond, ed., *Sullivan Papers,* 2: 277–78.

47. JL to John Hancock, 17 September 1778, Etting Papers, 1: 103, HSP; JL to Hancock, 23 October 1778, William Jones Rhees Collection, RH 11, The Huntington Library; JL to HL, 24 September 1778, in *Laurens Papers,* 14: 357–58 (quotation); Count d'Estaing to George Washington, 5 September 1778, 8 September 1778 (two letters), George Washington Papers, Series 4, LC; Dearden, *Rhode Island Campaign,* 136–37.

48. HL to John Sullivan, 28 August 1778, in *Laurens Papers,* 14: 239–40; George Washington to Nathanael Greene, 1 September 1778, in Showman and Conrad, eds., *Greene Papers,* 2: 505–6; Stinchcombe, *American Revolution and the French Alliance,* 54–57; JL to Washington, 2 September 1778, George Washington Papers, Series 4, LC.

49. William Henry Drayton to JL, 7 September 1778, Thomas Addis Emmet Collection (EM 1213), NYPL.

50. HL to JL, 17 September 1778, JL to HL, 24 September 1778, in *Laurens Papers,* 14: 321, 355.

51. HL to JL, 13 September 1778, 17 September 1778, ibid., 14: 308 (second and third quotations), 322 (first quotation).

52. JL to HL, 24 September 1778, ibid., 14: 356–57; Ward, *War of the Revolution,* 2: 593–94.

53. JL to HL, 13 October 1778, 23 October 1778, in *Laurens Papers,* 14: 405, 445. Because the Articles of Confederation had not been ratified by each state, the delegates did not consider the stipulation of a one-year presidency binding in HL's case. See Frech, "Henry Laurens in the Continental Congress," 349–54.

54. Ford, ed., *Journals of the Continental Congress,* 12: 1105–6.

55. Adam Smith, *Theory of Moral Sentiments,* 203–31.

56. JL to HL, 13 October 1778, 6 November 1778, in *Laurens Papers,* 14: 406–7, 469–70; Ford, ed., *Journals of the Continental Congress,* 12: 1106–7.

57. HL to Rawlins Lowndes, 16 December 1778, Henry Laurens Papers, SCHS; on the Deane controversy and its impact on Congress, consult Rakove, *Beginnings of National Politics,* 249–74; for HL's resignation and an assessment of his performance as president, see Frech, "Henry Laurens in the Continental Congress," 355–77.

58. "General Lee's Vindication to the Public," 3 December 1778, JL to Alexander Hamilton, [December 1778], in *Lee Papers,* 3: 255–69, 273; for evidence that Hamilton accepted the challenge to rebut Lee, see HL to Rawlins Lowndes, 7 December 1778, in *Laurens Papers,* 14: 568; for Washington's reaction to Lee's publication, see George Washington to Joseph Reed, 12 December 1778, in Fitzpatrick, ed., *Writings of Washington,* 13: 383–84.

59. JL to Charles Lee, 3 December 1778, Special Collections, Tutt Library, Colorado College, Colorado Springs.

60. Alden, *Lee,* 260–62; Samuel Shaw to Reverend Eliot, 22 March 1779, in Quincy, ed., *Journals of Samuel Shaw,* 56. On dueling see Kiernan, *The Duel in European History,* 33–34, 137 (quotation).

61. JL to Charles Lee, 7 December 1778, Special Collections, Tutt Library, Colorado College, Colorado Springs; Lee to JL, [22 December 1778], in *Lee Papers,* 3: 283.

62. Graydon, *Memoirs,* 323.

63. Narrative of an Affair of Honor between General Lee and Col Laurens, [24 December 1778], in Syrett, ed., *Hamilton Papers,* 1: 602–4.

64. Alden, *Lee,* 263–64; Garden, *Anecdotes,* 86 (first quotation); Samuel Shaw to Reverend Eliot, 22 March 1779, in Quincy, ed., *Journals of Samuel Shaw,* 56 (second quotation).

65. Alden, *Lee,* 265–66; Charles Lee, "A Short History of the Treatment of Major General Conway, late in the service of America," 3 December 1778, in *Lee Papers,* 3: 265–69. On Hamilton's views of Washington, see Alexander Hamilton to Philip Schuyler, 18 February 1781, in Syrett, ed., *Hamilton Papers,* 2: 563–68; Hamilton to Tobias Lear, 2 January 1800, to Martha Washington, 12 January 1800, ibid., 24: 155, 184–85.

66. On making sense of one's identity through a narrative, see Taylor, *Sources of the Self,* especially 47–52, 288–89.

67. Coleman, *American Revolution in Georgia,* 120–21.

Chapter 7

1. Freeman, *Washington,* 5: 90–95; Tench Tilghman to James McHenry, 25 January 1779, in Steiner, ed., *Correspondence of James McHenry,* 25–26.

2. Frech, "Henry Laurens in the Continental Congress," 264–74, 383–91; the HL-John Penn encounter is mentioned in Samuel Shaw to Reverend Eliot, 22 March 1779, in Quincy ed., *Journals of Samuel Shaw,* 55; for the comments regarding dueling, see Paul H. Smith, ed., *Letters of Delegates,* 11: 440–41n.

3. See Frech, "Henry Laurens in the Continental Congress," 349–54, 378–83, for an account of this controversy that concludes that the statement given by "Philalethes" was probably accurate. Paine's version of HL's reelection appeared on 15 December 1778, and additional segments were printed on 2, 5, 7, and 9 January 1779. "Philalethes" published rebuttals to Paine on 20 and 23 January 1779. All letters appeared in the *Pennsylvania Packet.*

4. "Philopatros" to "Philalethes," 23 January 1779, Henry Laurens Papers, SCHS.

5. "Concerning the Publication by Philalethes," [April 1779?], Kendall Collection.

6. "Concerning the Publication by Philalethes," [April 1779?], John Parke to JL, 27 March 1779, Kendall Collection.

7. The preceding two paragraphs are drawn from "Concerning the Publication by Philalethes," [April 1779?], Kendall Collection.

8. Freeman, *Washington,* 5: 93–94; HL to Rawlins Lowndes, 29 January 1779, Henry Laurens Papers, SCHS; George Washington to John Rutledge, 15 March 1779, in Fitzpatrick, ed., *Writings of Washington,* 14: 245–46.

9. JL to HL, 17 February 1779, Henry Laurens Papers, SCHS.

10. JL to HL, 6 March 1779, Kendall Collection; Alexander Hamilton to John Jay, 14 March 1779, in Syrett, ed., *Hamilton Papers,* 2: 17–19.

11. JL to HL, 10 March 1779, Henry Laurens Papers, SCHS.

12. John Rutledge to South Carolina Delegates in Congress, 18 March 1779, Myers Collection (MY 1269), NYPL; Thomas Bee to William Henry Drayton, 5 April 1779, PCC, reel 86, item 72, p. 485, NA; for Huger's mission, see Haw, "A Broken Compact," 40–41.

13. Maslowski, "National Policy Toward the Use of Black Troops," 10; Ford, ed., *Journals of the Continental Congress,* 13: 336; Thomas Burke's Draft Committee Report, HL's Draft Committee Report, [ante 25 March 1779], in Paul H. Smith,

ed., *Letters of Delegates,* 12: 242–44 (quotations), 246–48; George Washington to HL, 20 March 1779, in Fitzpatrick, ed., *Writings of Washington,* 14: 266–67.

14. Ford, ed., *Journals of the Continental Congress,* 13: 384–88; on previous official policy regarding the enlistment of blacks, see Quarles, *Negro in the American Revolution,* 51–60; and Robinson, *Slavery in the Structure of American Politics,* 113–18.

15. Ford, ed., *Journals of the Continental Congress,* 13: 388–89; HL to JL, 3 April 1779, Kendall Collection; William Whipple to Josiah Bartlett, 27 April 1779, in Paul H. Smith, ed., *Letters of Delegates* 12: 398–99.

16. Alexander Hamilton to JL, [April 1779], in Syrett, ed., *Hamilton Papers,* 2: 34–38. The original letter is in the Alexander Hamilton Papers, LC.

17. Lennon, "'Graveyard of American Commanders,'" 133–58; Cavanagh, "American Military Leadership," 101–31; Shy, "A New Look at Colonial Militia," 175–85, especially 180–81.

18. Ramsay, *History of the Revolution of South-Carolina,* 2: 18–19; Cavanagh, "American Military Leadership," 108–9.

19. Ibid., 102, 109–10, 112–13; Council of General Officers, 19 August 1779, Benjamin Lincoln to William Moultrie, 22 April 1779, in Moultrie, *Memoirs,* 1: 374–75, 377–78.

20. Augustine Prevost to Sir Henry Clinton, 21 May 1779, London, Public Record Office, British Headquarters Papers (Sir Guy Carleton Papers), PRO 30/55/16, no. 2011; William Moultrie to Benjamin Lincoln, 30 April 1779, Benjamin Lincoln Papers, MHS.

21. Moultrie, *Memoirs,* 1: 401–2.

22. Ibid., 1: 402–3; William Moultrie to Benjamin Lincoln, 5 May 1779, Benjamin Lincoln Papers, MHS; Ramsay, *History of the Revolution of South-Carolina,* 2: 21; *South-Carolina & American General Gazette,* 29 May 1779; HL to JL, 30 May 1779, Kendall Collection; HL to Horatio Gates, 29 June 1779, Gates Papers, box 12, no. 98, New-York Historical Society. For Shubrick, see Edgar, et al., eds., *Biographical Directory,* 3: 642–44.

23. Moultrie, *Memoirs,* 1: 403–4.

24. William Moultrie to Benjamin Lincoln, 5 May 1779, Benjamin Lincoln Papers, MHS; Augustine Prevost to Sir Henry Clinton, 21 May 1779, British Headquarters Papers (Sir Guy Carleton Papers), PRO 30/55/16, no. 2011; *South-Carolina & American General Gazette,* 29 May 1779.

25. John Rutledge to Benjamin Lincoln, [4 May 1779], [4–5 May 1779], [6 May 1779], William Moultrie to Lincoln, 5 May 1779, 8 May 1779 (two letters), P[ierce] Butler to Rutledge, [5 May 1779], Council of Officers, 6 May 1779, Lincoln to Moultrie, 6 May 1779, Benjamin Lincoln Papers, MHS; Rutledge to Moultrie, [5 May 1779], [6 May 1779], in Moultrie, *Memoirs,* 1: 418–20.

26. Ramsay, *History of the Revolution of South-Carolina,* 23–27; for criticism of Moultrie's decision to enter Charleston, see McCrady, *South Carolina in the Revolution, 1775–1780,* 356–57, and for the estimates of troop strengths, 362–65.

27. JL to John Rutledge, [May 1779], Rutledge to JL, 26 May [1779], in *Dodd, Mead & Company's Catalogue of Autographs and Manuscripts,* 78 (November 1905), item 118, in American Antiquarian Society, Worcester, Massachusetts; William Moultrie to Augustine Prevost, 11 May 1779, 12 May 1779, James Mark Prevost to Moultrie, 11 May 1779, in Moultrie, *Memoirs,* 1: 426–28, 431–32;

"Account of the operations in South Carolina, respecting Capitulation," [May 1779], Henry Laurens Papers, SCHS.

28. Moultrie, *Memoirs*, 1: 432–33; "Account of the operations in South Carolina," [May 1779], and "Proposed surrender to General Prevost, 1779 (Minutes)," [May 1779], Henry Laurens Papers, SCHS. The latter document, of which only a fragment exists, was written by JL with his left hand because of his wound.

29. "Account of the operations in South Carolina," [May 1779], Henry Laurens Papers, SCHS; for a message with different wording, see Moultrie, *Memoirs*, 1: 433; for an analysis of the divergent surrender proposals, see McCrady, *South Carolina in the Revolution, 1775–1780*, 366–81; see also the account in "Intelligence from Georgia concerning Gen Prevost's March to & from Charles Town," *Georgia Royal Gazette*, 10 June 1779, extract in Henry Laurens Papers, SCHS.

30. Moultrie, *Memoirs*, 1: 432–33 (first quotation); "Proposed surrender to General Prevost," [May 1779], Henry Laurens Papers, SCHS (second quotation).

31. "Account of the operations in South Carolina," [May 1779], Henry Laurens Papers, SCHS.

32. "Account of the operations in South Carolina," [May 1779], Henry Laurens Papers, SCHS; Moultrie, *Memoirs*, 1: 434. While Moultrie wrote his account over twenty years after the event, the statement attributed to JL is in keeping with his temperament and probably captures the gist of his reaction.

33. Augustine Prevost to Sir Henry Clinton, 21 May 1779, British Headquarters Papers (Sir Guy Carleton Papers), PRO 30/55/16, no. 2011; McCrady, *South Carolina in the Revolution 1775–1780*, 376–78.

34. Cavanagh, "American Military Leadership," 111; John Rutledge to Benjamin Lincoln, 19 May 1779, Benjamin Lincoln Papers, MHS; HL to Horatio Gates, 14 July 1779, Gates Papers, New-York Historical Society.

35. HL to Jonathan Trumbull Sr., 8 July 1779, to William Livingston, 10 July 1779, Henry Laurens Papers, SCHS; *The Gazette of the State of South Carolina*, 4 August 1779; see also Ramsay, *History of the Revolution of South-Carolina*, 2: 27–28.

36. Warren, *History of the American Revolution*, 2: 173–74; "Intelligence from Georgia concerning Gen Prevosts March to & from Charles Town," *Georgia Royal Gazette*, 10 June 1779, extract in Henry Laurens Papers, SCHS. For an account that arrives at a similar conclusion but places little emphasis on the impact of JL's black regiment plan, see Haw, "A Broken Compact," 30–53.

37. JL to John Rutledge, [May 1779], *Dodd, Mead & Company's Catalogue of Autographs and Manuscripts*, 78 (November 1905), item 118, in American Antiquarian Society.

38. On slavery in early South Carolina, see Peter H. Wood, *Black Majority*, especially 124–30, 308–26. For free blacks serving in the colonial militia, see Weir, ed., "Muster Rolls of the Granville and Colleton County Regiments of Militia, 1756," 229, 232, 237. For the free black killed at Coosawhatchie River, see Petition of Malachi Hagins to the Mississippi General Assembly, ca. 1837, in Schweninger, ed., *Race, Slavery, and Free Blacks*, PAR (Petition Analysis Record) no. 11000016. In 1780 twelve blacks fought at Camden and were taken prisoner by the British. See Olwell, *Masters, Slaves, and Subjects*, 257–58.

39. John Rutledge to JL, 26 May [1779], *Dodd, Mead & Company's Catalogue of Autographs and Manuscripts*, 78 (November 1905), item 118, in American Anti-

quarian Society; Christopher Gadsden to Samuel Adams, 6 July 1779, in Walsh, ed., *Writings of Christopher Gadsden,* 166.

40. Benjamin Lincoln to George Washington, 5 June 1779, George Washington Papers, Series 4, LC; Ward, *War of the Revolution,* 2: 685–87; Cavanagh, "American Military Leadership," 113–14; David Ramsay to Benjamin Rush, 3 June 1779, in Brunhouse, ed., *David Ramsay,* 59–60; Frey, *Water from the Rock,* 91–93.

41. Benjamin Lincoln to John Rutledge, 24 July 1779, Benjamin Lincoln Papers, MHS; Hemphill, et al., eds., *Journals of the House of Representatives,* 317–18; JL to Alexander Hamilton, 14 July 1779, in Syrett, ed., *Hamilton Papers,* 2: 102–4.

42. Hemphill, et al., eds., *Journals of the House of Representatives,* 179–230; David Ramsay to William Henry Drayton, 1 September 1779, in Gibbes, ed., *Documentary History,* 2: 121.

43. HL to JL, 23 June 1775, in *Laurens Papers,* 10: 191; Christopher Gadsden quoted in Weir, ed., *Letters of Freeman,* 84; Olwell, "'Domestic Enemies,'" 23; Frey, *Water from the Rock,* 91–93; Menard, "Slavery, Economic Growth, and Revolutionary Ideology," 248. When the Rhode Island legislature debated the same issue in 1778, opponents argued that enlisting slaves would give the British "the idea of embodying black regiments against us." Bartlett, ed., *Records of the State of Rhode Island,* 8: 361; see also George Washington to HL, 20 March 1779, in Fitzpatrick, ed., *Writings of Washington,* 14: 266–67.

44. David Ramsay to Benjamin Rush, 21 March 1780, in Brunhouse, ed., *David Ramsay,* 66; Menard, "Slavery, Economic Growth, and Revolutionary Ideology," 244–74; Greene, "'Slavery or Independence,'" 193–214; Davis, *Problem of Slavery in the Age of Revolution,* 255–84; MacLeod, *Slavery, Race, and the American Revolution,* 79–80.

45. Jordan, *White over Black,* 546–69; Nash, *Race and Revolution,* 3–55 (quotation on 35); and MacLeod, *Slavery, Race, and the American Revolution,* 81–82. Similar to JL, the Virginia jurist George Wythe reasoned that blacks, as humans, possessed the same natural rights as whites. Yet Wythe, like his contemporaries, envisioned only a gradual emancipation followed by colonization, and he collaborated with Jefferson on such a plan. See McColley, *Slavery and Jeffersonian Virginia,* 35–36, 134–36; and Jefferson, *Notes on the State of Virginia,* 137–43.

46. David Ramsay to Benjamin Rush, 20 June 1779, in Brunhouse, ed., *David Ramsay,* 60–61.

47. HL to JL, 27 September 1779, Henry Laurens Papers, SCHS.

48. Alexander Hamilton to JL, 11 September 1779, in Syrett, ed., *Hamilton Papers,* 2: 165.

49. JL to Alexander Hamilton, 14 July 1779, ibid., 2: 102–3.

50. Benjamin Lincoln to Count d'Estaing, 1 September 1779, Benjamin Lincoln Papers, MHS; Commonplace Book of JL, 4 September 1779, HSP; Lawrence, *Storm over Savannah,* ix, 18; Dull, *French Navy and American Independence,* 159–61.

51. Commonplace Book of JL, 4 September 1779, HSP.

52. Count d'Estaing to JL, 6 September 1779, Thomas Addis Emmet Collection (EM 7509), NYPL; JL quoted in Lawrence, *Storm over Savannah,* 64.

53. Pechot: Journal of the Siege of Savannah, 16 September 1779, in Stevens, ed., *Facsimiles of Manuscripts in European Archives,* 23: no. 2010, 5; "Order Book of John Faucheraud Grimké," 180; JL quoted in HL to William Whipple, 28 Sep-

tember 1779, Gilmor Papers, MS 387.1, Manuscripts Department, Maryland Historical Society; Cavanagh, "American Military Leadership," 117.

54. Lawrence, *Storm over Savannah,* 31–51, 62–63.

55. Ibid., 41–43; Hough, ed., *Siege of Savannah,* 158–59.

56. The Fontanges-JL encounter is recorded in Lawrence, *Storm over Savannah,* 65, and is drawn from Count d'Estaing's notes on the Savannah siege.

57. Ibid., 54–55, 68–76; Ward, *War of the Revolution,* 2: 692.

58. Ibid., 2: 689, 692–93; Lawrence, *Storm over Savannah,* 49, 57–58, 82–88; Hough, ed., *Siege of Savannah,* 164–65; for slaves who served on the British side, see Frey, *Water from the Rock,* 96–98.

59. This account of the attack is drawn from Hough, ed., *Siege of Savannah,* 165–67; and Ward, *War of the Revolution,* 2: 693–94.

60. Hough, ed., *Siege of Savannah,* 167–68; Lawrence, *Storm over Savannah,* 107.

61. Weems, *Life of Francis Marion,* 61–65. Weems obtained documents from Peter Horry, one of Marion's subordinates, and wrote a highly embellished book. Outraged at the fabrications, Horry scribbled marginal comments on his copy of the volume. See Salley, ed., "Horry's Notes to Weems' *Life of Marion,*" 119–22. Horry did not specifically challenge this account of the conversation he had with JL at Savannah.

62. Hamilton, *Life of Alexander Hamilton,* 1: 390.

63. Benjamin Lincoln to Committee of Correspondence, 22 October 1779, Benjamin Lincoln Letterbook, Boston Public Library; Lawrence, *Storm over Savannah,* 104–6, 113–24; JL to HL, 23 October 1779, Thomas Addis Emmet Collection (EM 7519), NYPL; Dull, *French Navy and American Independence,* 162.

64. HL to JL, 2 October 1779, Henry Laurens Papers, SCHS; HL to Richard Henry Lee, 12 October 1779, Franklin Papers, APS (second quotation); HL to Jonathan Trumbull Sr., 19 October 1779, Trumbull Papers, Connecticut Historical Society (first quotation). For details on JL's nomination and approval, see James Lovell to John Adams, 28 September [1779], in Paul H. Smith, ed., *Letters of Delegates,* 13: 580–81; Samuel Huntington to JL, 2 October 1779, to Benjamin Franklin, 16 October 1779, ibid., 14: 12, 85; Ford, ed., *Journals of the Continental Congress,* 15: 1115, 1127–28; Congress: Commission to JL as Secretary to the Minister in France, 29 September 1779, PCC, reel 182, item 165, p. 5, NA.

65. JL to HL, 22 October 1779, Kendall Collection; HL to George Washington, 24 October 1779, BV Vail Collection, vol. 2, p. 85, New-York Historical Society.

66. Benjamin Lincoln to Committee of Correspondence, 22 October 1779 (first and second quotations), 24 October 1779 (third quotation), Benjamin Lincoln Letterbook, Boston Public Library; Peter Timothy to Lincoln, 13 October 1779, Benjamin Lincoln Papers, MHS.

67. Benjamin Lincoln to Committee of Correspondence, 24 October 1779, Benjamin Lincoln Letterbook, Boston Public Library; JL to HL, 23 October 1779, Thomas Addis Emmet Collection (EM 7519), NYPL; JL to [Lincoln], 28 October 1779, Charles Goddard Slack Collection, Marietta College Library; Commonplace Book of JL, 24 October–3 November 1779, HSP.

68. For HL's last months in Congress, see Frech, "Henry Laurens in the Continental Congress," 378–493.

69. These thoughts are contained in a draft written by JL, and are likely the arguments he used to convince Congress to act. See Commonplace Book of JL, [n.d.], HSP;

and JL to Benjamin Lincoln, 6 December 1779, Jared Sparks Collection, MS Sparks 12 (451–2), Houghton Library, Harvard University.

70. JL to Benjamin Lincoln, 6 December 1779, Sparks Collection, Houghton Library, Harvard University; George Washington to Samuel Huntington, 29 November 1779, 2 December 1779, 10 December 1779, to Henry Knox, 8 December 1779, to Lincoln, 12 December 1779, in Fitzpatrick, ed., *Writings of Washington*, 17: 206–8, 213, 237–38, 241–44, 247–49; JL to Alexander Hamilton, 12 December 1779, in Syrett, ed., *Hamilton Papers*, 2: 225–27. Rather than sailing to Chesapeake as ordered, de Grasse returned to the West Indies. Lawrence, *Storm over Savannah*, 124, 171.

71. JL to Samuel Huntington, 6 December 1779, PCC, reel 182, item 165, p. 7, NA; and Weir, "Portrait of a Hero," 87.

72. JL to Alexander Hamilton, 18 December 1779, in Syrett, ed., *Hamilton Papers*, 2: 230; Nathaniel Scudder to HL, 22 November 1779, Charles F. Jenkins Collection, HSP; James Lovell to HL, 15 December 1779, Henry Laurens Papers, SCHS; Nathaniel Peabody to HL, 17 December 1779, Sol Feinstone Collection, no. 1080, David Library of the American Revolution, on deposit at APS.

73. JL to Alexander Hamilton, 18 December 1779, in Syrett, ed., *Hamilton Papers*, 2: 230–31.

74. Ford, ed., *Journals of the Continental Congress*, 15: 1391; Robert R. Livingston to John Jay, 22 December 1779, 10 February 1780, in Paul H. Smith, ed., *Letters of Delegates*, 14: 295, 408–9. A fourth candidate, Colonel Walter Stewart, was nominated but apparently received no votes.

75. Alexander Hamilton to JL, 8 January 1780, in Syrett, ed., *Hamilton Papers*, 2: 254–55; Miller, *Hamilton*, 37–40; Cooke, *Hamilton*, 15.

76. JL to Samuel Huntington, 13 December 1779, PCC, reel 182, item 165, p. 10, NA; Ford, ed., *Journals of the Continental Congress*, 15: 1381; Committee Report regarding John Laurens, 23 February 1785, Veteran's Administration, Record Group 15, Revolutionary War Pension File, John Laurens, S.C., NA.

77. Samuel Holten to Benjamin Lincoln, 18 December 1779, in Paul H. Smith, ed., *Letters of Delegates*, 14: 279; JL to HL, 7 December 1779, Kendall Collection; Willcox, *Portrait of a General*, 293–301.

Chapter 8

1. *The South-Carolina and American General Gazette*, 19 January 1780; Hemphill, et al., eds., *Journals of the House of Representatives*, 261; HL to James Lovell, 24 January 1780, in *Laurens Papers*, 15:227.

2. JL to HL, 27 January 1780, Kendall Collection.

3. JL to Benjamin Lincoln, 26 January 1780 (two letters), J. S. H. Fogg Autograph Collection, vol. 55, Maine Historical Society; JL to Lincoln, 27 January 1780, John Laurens Papers, South Caroliniana Library; JL to HL, 27 January 1780, Kendall Collection.

4. Hemphill, et al., eds., *Journals of the House of Representatives*, 262, 268, 276–77, 299; JL to HL, 26 March 1780, Kendall Collection, (first and second quotations).

5. Middlekauff, *Glorious Cause*, 438–40; JL to George Washington, 14 February 1780, George Washington Papers, Series 4, LC.

6. Diary of Captain Ewald, in Uhlendorf, ed., *Siege of Charleston*, 91–93; JL to [?],

25 February 1780, in Moore, ed., *Correspondence of Henry Laurens,* 174.

7. HL to Nathaniel Peabody, 5 February 1780, Franklin Collection, Sterling Memorial Library, Yale University; HL to Committee for Foreign Affairs, 14 February 1780 (quotation), 24 February 1780, 1 July 1780, PCC, reel 117, item 89, pp. 185–193, NA; HL to Richard Henry Lee, 10 March 1780, Lee Collection, Manuscript Department and University Archives, University of Virginia; JL to HL, 1 March 1780, Kendall Collection.

8. JL to HL, 1 March 1780, Kendall Collection.

9. Tilley, *British Navy and the American Revolution,* 176–79; Benjamin Lincoln to George Washington, 4 March 1780, JL to Washington, 14 March 1780, George Washington Papers, Series 4, LC. The exchanges between Lincoln and the naval officers are reprinted in Lincoln to Washington, 17 July 1780, in "The Siege of Charleston," 364–71.

10. JL to HL, 25 March 1780, Kendall Collection.

11. JL to George Washington, 14 March 1780, George Washington Papers, Series 4, LC; Ward, *War of the Revolution,* 2: 698.

12. George Washington to JL, 26 April 1780, in Fitzpatrick, ed., *Writings of Washington,* 18: 298–300.

13. This account is drawn from JL to HL, 31 March 1780, John Lewis Gervais to HL, 31 March 1780, Kendall Collection; JL to HL, [31 March 1780], Peter Timothy to HL, 26 March–8 April 1780, Henry Laurens Papers, SCHS; JL to George Washington, 9 April 1780, George Washington Papers, Series 4, LC ("serious affair" quotation); McCrady, *South Carolina in the Revolution, 1775–1780,* 454–55 (quotation); Diary of Captain Ewald, Diary of Captain Hinrichs, in Uhlendorf, ed., *Siege of Charleston,* 35–37, 50–51, 223–29 (quotation on 227). The Hessian captains reported that the Americans suffered at least forty casualties, but Gervais's more plausible figures are accepted here.

14. Moses Young: Memorandum to HL, 31 March 1780, Kendall Collection; for a summary of siege warfare, see Duffy, *Military Experience,* 289–93.

15. Ward, *War of the Revolution,* 2: 698; JL to George Washington, 9 April 1780, Benjamin Lincoln to Washington, 9 April 1780, George Washington Papers, Series 4, LC.

16. Alexander Hamilton to JL, [30 March 1780], in Syrett, ed., *Hamilton Papers,* 2: 303–4.

17. John Lewis Gervais to HL, 17 April 1780, JL to HL, 25 May 1780 (quotation), James Custer to HL, June 1780, Kendall Collection; Ward, *War of the Revolution,* 2: 700–701; Cavanagh, "American Military Leadership," 125–27.

18. Joseph Johnson, *Traditions and Reminiscences,* 257–58.

19. Murdoch, trans., "A French Account of the Siege of Charleston," 147; McCrady, *South Carolina in the Revolution, 1775–1780,* 483.

20. Ibid., 483; Benjamin Lincoln to Sir Henry Clinton, 21 April 1780, Clinton to Lincoln, 21 April 1780, Articles of Capitulation proposed by Lincoln, 21 April 1780, Clinton and Marriot Arbuthnot to Lincoln, 21 April 1780, in "The Siege of Charleston," 380–83; Cavanagh, "American Military Leadership," 126–27; JL to Lincoln, 22 April 1780, Benjamin Lincoln Papers, MHS.

21. On the conclusion of the siege, see McCrady, *South Carolina in the Revolution, 1775–1780,* 482–93; Petition of Inhabitants of Charles Town to Benjamin Lincoln, 10 May 1780, Petitions of the Country Militia to Lincoln, 10 May 1780, 11

May 1780, Council of War, 11 May 1780, Benjamin Lincoln Papers, MHS; Mattern, *Benjamin Lincoln*, 103–8; Scheer and Rankin, *Rebels and Redcoats*, 568–69; for the 8 May council of officers and the negotiations with the British commanders, see "The Siege of Charleston," 349–51, 385–93.

22. Ward, *War of the Revolution*, 2: 703; JL to George Washington, 25 May 1780, George Washington Papers, Series 4, LC; JL to HL, 25 May 1780, Kendall Collection (second quotation).

23. HL to Committee for Foreign Affairs, 1 July 1780, PCC, reel 117, item 89, p. 193, NA; HL to South Carolina Delegates in Congress, 14 May 1780, Henry Laurens and John Laurens Collection, LC (quotation); and 23 May 1780, Etting Collection, HSP.

24. "Return of Servants belonging to General Lincoln's family and Attendants on the Gentlemen who embark in the Flag," 12 June 1780, Benjamin Lincoln Papers, MHS; HL to Committee for Foreign Affairs, 1 July 1780, PCC, reel 117, item 89, p. 193, NA; Paul H. Smith, *Loyalists and Redcoats*, 126–28, 134–42.

25. HL to Committee for Foreign Affairs, 1 July 1780, PCC, reel 117, item 89, p. 193, NA; Continental Congress: Resolution, 6 July 1780, London, Public Record Office, CO 5/43; Alexander Hamilton to JL, 30 June 1780, 12 September 1780, in Syrett, ed., *Hamilton Papers*, 2: 347 (first quotation), 427 (second quotation). On prisoner exchange policy, consult Knight, "Prisoner Exchange and Parole," 201–22.

26. Alexander Hamilton to JL, 30 June 1780, [16 September 1780], in Syrett, ed., *Hamilton Papers*, 2: 348, 431.

27. Alexander Hamilton to James Duane, 3 September 1780, to JL, 12 September 1780, ibid., 2: 400–418 (quotation on 410–11), 427–28; McDonald, *Hamilton*, 34–43.

28. See Taylor, *Sources of the Self*, 62–63, for the importance of "one highest good" to an individual's self-esteem.

29. Ford, ed., *Journals of the Continental Congress*, 17: 598–600.

30. Capture & Confinement in the Tower of London, 3 September 1780–31 December 1781, Kendall Collection (quotation); HL Diary, 1780–81, 13 August 1780, NYPL.

31. Capture & Confinement in the Tower of London, 3 September 1780–31 December 1781, Kendall Collection.

32. HL to JL, 14 September 1780, Kendall Collection, bracketed material from a copy in the Lloyd W. Smith Collection, Manuscript 3434–4, Morristown National Historical Park.

33. Capture & Confinement in the Tower of London, 3 September 1780–31 December 1781, Kendall Collection; Register of the Tower of London, 13 October 1780, 14 October 1780, 29 November 1780, 6 December 1780, London, Public Record Office, WO 94/11; HL Diary, 1780–81, 29 November 1780, NYPL.

34. Freeman, *Washington*, 5: 178–83, 187–88, 193–95; Lafayette to JL, 15 August 1780, Kendall Collection; Alexander Hamilton to JL, 12 September 1780, [16 September 1780], in Syrett, ed., *Hamilton Papers*, 2: 427 (first quotation), 431 (second quotation).

35. JL to Benjamin Lincoln, 28 August 1780, Jared Sparks Collection, MS Sparks 12 (397–400), Houghton Library, Harvard University.

36. Alexander Hamilton to JL, [16 September 1780], in Syrett, ed., *Hamilton Papers*, 2: 431. Hamilton responded to an 8 September letter from JL, which has not been

found. JL wrote the letter while awaiting a reply from Benjamin Lincoln concerning the negotiations for a prisoner exchange. See Lincoln to JL, 10 September 1780, Benjamin Lincoln Letterbook, Boston Public Library.
37. For Robert Merton's theory that a relationship exists between "blocked aspirations of major life goals" and suicide, see Maris, *Pathways to Suicide*, 156–64.
38. JL to George Washington, 25 May 1780, George Washington Papers, Series 4, LC; John Kilty to Nathanael Greene, 21 May 1782, Nathanael Greene Papers, WCL.
39. As a risk-taker in battle, JL demonstrated characteristics of what is now termed indirect self-destructive behavior, or subintentioned suicide. For indirect self-destructive behavior, see Farberow, "Indirect Self-Destructive Behavior," 15–27; and Litman, "Psychodynamics of Indirect Self-Destructive Behavior," 28–40. On subintentioned suicide, see Shneidman, *Definitions of Suicide*, 20–22, 52, 145, 178, 204.
40. Gordon S. Wood, *Creation of the American Republic*, 53–54, 65–70; on the "specific cultural and historical circumstances" that give shape to coping strategies, consult Kushner, *American Suicide*, 149–50; for the altruistic suicide, one who subordinates self to a cause or duty, see Durkheim, *Suicide*, 217–40, especially 221–23, 227–28.
41. Hamilton, *Life of Alexander Hamilton*, 1: 391. Presumably Hamilton heard his father reminisce about JL. George Washington to William Gordon, 8 March 1785, in Abbot, ed., *Papers of George Washington*, 2: 412.
42. James, *Principles of Psychology*, 310–11; Greenblatt, *Renaissance Self-Fashioning*, 9.
43. On incomplete mourning and suicidal behavior, see Kushner, *American Suicide*, 77–79, 126–32, 138–40, 162–65; on guilt and self-destructive behavior, consult Menninger, *Man against Himself*, 50–54, 119–20; Litman, "Psychodynamics of Indirect Self-Destructive Behavior," 29, 38–39; and Lifton, *The Broken Connection*, 135, 193–94, 198–99; on fame, see Adair, "Fame and the Founding Fathers," 3–26; on "man's tragic destiny," to "stand out, [and] be a hero," see Becker, *The Denial of Death*, 1–8 (quotation on 4).
44. James, *The Varieties of Religious Experience*, 356.
45. See Van Doren, *Secret History of the American Revolution*, 143–388; for eyewitness accounts of André's execution, see Scheer and Rankin, *Rebels and Redcoats*, 444–46; for JL's reaction to Arnold's treason, see JL to George Washington, 4 October 1780, George Washington Papers, Series 4, LC; Washington to JL, 13 October 1780, in Fitzpatrick, ed., *Writings of Washington*, 20: 173.
46. Alexander Hamilton to JL, [11 October 1780], in Syrett, ed., *Hamilton Papers*, 2: 460–70 (quotations on 467).
47. Charles Willson Peale Diary, 2 [October] 1780, 29 November 1788, in Miller, ed., *Papers of Charles Willson Peale*, 1: 352, 548. In a version done by Peale in 1784, JL appears softer and somewhat effeminate. This miniature is in the possession of Independence Hall, Philadelphia, and has been reprinted in Weir, "Portrait of a Hero," 16.
48. Abraham Skinner to Joshua Loring, 21 September 1780, PCC, reel 184, item 167, p. 65, NA; George Washington to Samuel Huntington, 7 November 1780, in Fitzpatrick, ed., *Writings of Washington*, 20: 314–15; Knight, "Prisoner Exchange and Parole," 208–14.
49. JL to George Washington, 6 [November] 1780, George Washington Papers, Series 4, LC; Washington to Nathanael Greene, 8 November 1780, to JL, 12 November 1780, in Fitzpatrick, ed., *Writings of Washington*, 20: 322, 340–41.

50. Dull, *Franklin the Diplomat,* 45–46, 65–67; for Palfrey's appointment, see Samuel Huntington to William Palfrey, 8 November 1780, in Paul H. Smith, ed., *Letters of Delegates,* 16: 314–15.
51. See Congress to Louis XVI: 22 November 1780, John Laurens Papers, SCHS; George Washington to Nathanael Greene, 8 November 1780, in Fitzpatrick, ed., *Writings of Washington,* 20: 320–21; Ferguson, *Power of the Purse,* 126.
52. Ford, ed., *Journals of the Continental Congress,* 18: 1138–40; JL to Samuel Huntington, [December 1780], John Laurens Papers, SCHS; JL to Huntington, 28 December 1780, Board of War: Report Regarding Arms and Supplies, 1 January 1781, PCC, reel 182, item 165, pp. 21, 25, NA; Lafayette to Prince de Poix, 30 January 1781, in Idzerda, ed., *Lafayette Papers,* 3: 302; Ford, ed., *Journals of the Continental Congress,* 19: 10. Once JL finally accepted the position, he needed to reserve his credit for the diplomatic mission. He asked Congress to assume payment for the supplies, which the delegates promptly did, voting to purchase the clothing and arms for public use. See the final three documents cited above.
53. Lafayette to Alexander Hamilton, 9 December 1780, to George Washington, 9 December 1780, 16 December 1780, in Idzerda, ed., *Lafayette Papers,* 3: 252, 254, 267; JL to Washington, 23 December 1780, George Washington Papers, Series 4, LC (first quotation); JL to Samuel Huntington, 21 December 1780, John Laurens Papers, SCHS.
54. Only Theodorick Bland of Virginia joined the South Carolina delegates in opposing the change. Ford, ed., *Journals of the Continental Congress,* 18: 1177–78; Thomas McKean to John Adams, 18 December 1780, Thomas McKean Papers, vol. 1, p. 38, HSP; Richard Bache to Benjamin Franklin, 26 December 1780, Franklin Papers, APS; for additional reservations concerning JL's appointment, see John Witherspoon to William Livingston, 16 December 1780 (which refers to JL's "Youth"), Oliver Wolcott to Jonathan Trumbull Sr., 18 December 1780, to Oliver Ellsworth, 2 January 1781, in Paul H. Smith, ed., *Letters of Delegates,* 16: 451–52, 461, 541–42; Lafayette to George Washington, 16 December 1780, in Idzerda, ed., *Lafayette Papers,* 3: 267.
55. JL to George Washington, 23 December 1780, George Washington Papers, Series 4, LC.

Chapter 9

1. Congress: Commission to JL, 23 December 1780, Instructions to JL, 23 December 1780, Additional Instructions to JL, 27 December 1780, John Laurens Papers, SCHS; Alexander Hamilton to JL, 4 February 1781, in Syrett, ed., *Hamilton Papers,* 2: 550; see also Samuel Cooper to Benjamin Franklin, 1 February 1781, Franklin Papers, APS.
2. Congress: Instructions to JL, 23 December 1780, John Laurens Papers, SCHS; Ford, ed., *Journals of the Continental Congress,* 18: 1198–99; Brant, *James Madison,* 66–67. For additional details provided to JL about the nation's finances and conditions in individual states, see Thomas Burke to JL, 26 December 1780, Oliver Wolcott to JL, 27 December 1780, James Duane's Memoranda, [2–3 January 1781], North Carolina Delegates to JL, 16 January 1781, in Paul H. Smith, ed., *Letters of Delegates,* 16: 499–501, 509–11, 530–34, 610–12.

3. JL to Samuel Huntington, 3 January 1781, PCC, reel 182, item 165, p. 37, NA; for American inexperience in diplomacy, see Dull, *Franklin the Diplomat,* 68. Documents relating to JL's diplomatic mission have been printed in Sparks, ed., *Diplomatic Correspondence,* 9; Wharton, ed., *Revolutionary Diplomatic Correspondence,* 4; and D. E. Huger Smith, ed., "The Mission of Col. John Laurens to Europe in 1781." Each compilation is marred by outdated editorial methods.

4. Fitzpatrick, "William Jackson," 559–61; for Paine's motives, see Thomas Paine to Robert Morris, 20 February 1782, to a Committee of the Continental Congress, [October 1783], in Foner, ed., *Writings of Paine,* 2: 1207–8, 1231–34; and Hawke, *Paine,* 105–6, 111–15.

5. On Paine's ideas on foreign relations, see Fitzsimons, "Tom Paine's New World Order," 569–82, a balanced article that at least partially rehabilitates the view that Americans injected new ideals into international relations, which was first stated forcefully in Gilbert, *To the Farewell Address.* For the contrary view, emphasizing that American diplomats conformed to the assumptions of traditional European power politics, see Hutson, "Intellectual Foundations of Early American Diplomacy," 1–19.

6. Chevalier de La Luzerne to Count de Vergennes, 15 December 1780, in Doniol, ed., *Histoire,* 4: 390n; La Luzerne to Vergennes, 28 December 1780, Correspondence Politique, États-Unis, 14: 452–61 (microfilm), Ministère des Affaires Etrangères, Paris (microfilm and transcripts in LC); Samuel Huntington to La Luzerne, 20 December 1780, in Paul H. Smith, ed., *Letters of Delegates,* 16: 473–74, 474n; Brant, *James Madison,* 66–67.

7. Van Doren, *Mutiny in January,* 27–81, 96–98; Lafayette to the Chevalier de La Luzerne, 4 January 1781, 7 January 1781, in Idzerda, ed., *Lafayette Papers,* 3: 276–81; Gottschalk, *Lafayette and the Close of the American Revolution,* 167–70.

8. JL to George Washington, 7 January 1781, George Washington Papers, Series 4, LC; JL to Anthony Wayne, 7 January 1781, Anthony Wayne Papers, HSP; Lafayette to Washington, Arthur St. Clair to Washington, 7 January 1781, in Idzerda, ed., *Lafayette Papers,* 3: 284–87.

9. Gottschalk, *Lafayette and the Close of the American Revolution,* 171; George Washington to William Heath, 12 January 1781, in Fitzpatrick, ed., *Writings of Washington,* 21: 90–91; Van Doren, *Mutiny in January,* 99–151, 194–203, 232–33; Freeman, *Washington,* 5: 239–44; and Higginbotham, *War of American Independence,* 404–5.

10. George Washington to Benjamin Franklin, to JL, 15 January 1781, to John Hancock, 19 January 1781, in Fitzpatrick, ed., *Writings of Washington,* 21: 100–101, 105–10, 115–16.

11. JL to Samuel Huntington, 4 February 1781, PCC, reel 182, item 165, p. 41, NA; JL to the Senate and House of Representatives of Massachusetts, 5 February 1781, Report of Joint Senate and House Committee on JL's 5 February Letter, 6–7 February 1781, Boston Public Library.

12. JL to George Washington, 4–7 February 1781, George Washington Papers, Series 4, LC; JL to Samuel Huntington, 4 February 1781, 7 February 1781, PCC, reel 182, item 165, pp. 41 (quotation), 49, NA; JL to Benjamin Lincoln, 5 February 1781, Benjamin Lincoln Papers, MHS; Washington to Lincoln, 27 February 1781, in Fitzpatrick, ed., *Writings of Washington,* 21: 307, 307n.

13. George Washington to JL, 30 January 1781, ibid., 21: 161–62; Van Doren, *Mutiny in January,* 204–27.

14. Lafayette to Marquis de Castries, to Prince de Poix, 30 January 1781, to Benjamin Franklin, to Count de Vergennes, 1 February 1781, to Adrienne de Noailles de Lafayette, 2 February 1781, to JL, 3 February 1781, in Idzerda, ed., *Lafayette Papers*, 3: 294–316. For the failure of the letters to arrive, see JL to George Washington, 24 March 1781, George Washington Papers, Series 4, LC; and Gottschalk, *Lafayette and the Close of the American Revolution*, 175–82.

15. Alexander Hamilton to JL, [4 February 1781], in Syrett, ed., *Hamilton Papers*, 26: 406–8.

16. Thomas Paine to James Hutchinson, 11 March 1781, in Foner, ed., *Writings of Paine*, 2: 1191–93.

17. JL to Benjamin Franklin, 9 March 1781, Franklin Papers, APS; JL to Samuel Huntington, 11 March 1781, PCC, reel 182, item 165, p. 53, NA; for Palfrey's death, see James Lovell to Elbridge Gerry, 14 June [1781], in Paul H. Smith, ed., *Letters of Delegates*, 17: 319.

18. JL to Benjamin Franklin, 9 March 1781, Franklin Papers, APS; JL to Samuel Huntington, 11 March 1781, PCC, reel 182, item 165, p. 53, NA; JL to Huntington, 23 March 1781, John Laurens Papers, SCHS; JL to George Washington, 24 March 1781, George Washington Papers, Series 4, LC; Marquis de Castries to Lafayette, 25 May 1781, in Idzerda, ed., *Lafayette Papers*, 4: 132 (quotation); Castries to Count de Vergennes, 11 March 1781, Correspondence Politique, États-Unis, 15: 356–58 (transcript), Ministère des Affaires Etrangères; Vergennes to Chevalier de La Luzerne, 14 May 1781, in Doniol, ed., *Histoire*, 4: 557n; Dull, *French Navy and American Independence*, 216–23, 223n; and Corwin, *French Policy and the American Alliance*, 292–94.

19. Benjamin Franklin to Samuel Huntington, 12 March 1781, PCC, reel 108, item 82, vol. 1, p. 301, NA; Francis Dana to Huntington, 24 March 1781, PCC, reel 117, item 89, p. 506, NA; Franklin to Count de Vergennes, 13 February 1781, in Wharton, ed., *Revolutionary Diplomatic Correspondence*, 4: 254–55.

20. Benjamin Franklin to Samuel Huntington, 12 March 1781, PCC, reel 108, item 82, vol. 1, p. 301, NA; Arthur Lee to Richard Henry Lee, 28 May 1781, Lee Collection, Manuscript Department and University Archives, University of Virginia Library; Daniel of St. Thomas Jenifer to Franklin, 20 June 1781, in Paul H. Smith, ed., *Letters of Delegates*, 17: 335.

21. Hutson, *Adams and Diplomacy*, 1–32.

22. Murphy, "Charles Gravier de Vergennes," 400–418; Murphy, "The View from Versailles," 107–49; Dull, *French Navy and American Independence*, 6–8; Corwin, *French Policy and the American Alliance*, 296–99.

23. For Necker's reforms, see Bosher, *French Finances*, 142–65.

24. JL to Samuel Huntington, 23 March 1781, John Laurens Papers, SCHS (quotation); Memorial to Count de Vergennes, 20 March 1781, JL to Thomas McKean, 2 September 1781, PCC, reel 182, item 165, pp. 123, 137, NA. Compare JL's memorial to Vergennes with George Washington to JL, 15 January 1781, in Fitzpatrick, ed., *Writings of Washington*, 21: 105–10.

25. Vergenne's reply is contained in JL to Samuel Huntington, 23 March 1781, John Laurens Papers, SCHS.

26. Richard Peters to JL, 2 January 1781, JL to Samuel Huntington, 23 March 1781 (first quotation), John Laurens Papers, SCHS; JL to Count de Vergennes, 19 March 1781, List of Supplies Requested from France, [March 1781], JL to

Thomas McKean, 2 September 1781, PCC, reel 182, item 165, pp. 57 (second and third quotations), 59, 137, NA.

27. JL to Samuel Huntington, 23 March 1781, John Laurens Papers, SCHS (first quotation); JL to Thomas McKean, 2 September 1781, PCC, reel 182, item 165, p. 137 (second quotation), NA; Hutson, "The American Negotiators," 52–69.

28. JL to Thomas McKean, 2 September 1781, PCC, reel 182, item 165, p. 137, NA; for the 18 March 1780 resolution, see Ford, ed., *Journals of the Continental Congress*, 16: 262–67; Samuel Huntington to the States, 20 March 1780, in Paul H. Smith, ed., *Letters of Delegates*, 14: 521–22, 522n; Ferguson, *Power of the Purse*, 46–52; for Vergennes's reaction, see Burnett, *The Continental Congress*, 425–27; and Hutson, *Adams and Diplomacy*, 60–66.

29. "Questions of which Col. Laurens is requested to give solutions," 29 March 1781, JL to Thomas McKean, 2 September 1781, PCC, reel 182, item 165, pp. 77, 137 (first quotation), NA; Memorial to Count de Vergennes, 18 April 1781, PCC, reel 134, item 109, p. 462 (second and third quotations), NA; Marquis de Castries to Lafayette, 25 May 1781, in Idzerda, ed., *Lafayette Papers*, 4: 132–33; for Castries's character, see Dull, *French Navy and American Independence*, 202.

30. Dull, *Diplomatic History*, 107–20; Dull, *French Navy and American Independence*, 110–18, 126–56.

31. Louis de Corny to JL, 1 April 1781, JL to Thomas McKean, 2 September 1781, PCC, reel 182, item 165, pp. 137, 185, NA.

32. Benjamin Franklin to John Jay, 12 April 1781, in Wharton, ed., *Revolutionary Diplomatic Correspondence*, 4: 359; JL to Samuel Huntington, 9 April 1781, PCC, reel 182, item 165, p. 99, NA.

33. Memorial to Count de Vergennes, 18 April 1781, PCC, reel 134, item 109, p. 462, NA. These arguments were first expressed orally after the announcement of the loan. Though JL presented this memorial more than a week later, it was merely a reiteration of his earlier statements. See JL to George Washington, 11 April 1781, George Washington Papers, Series 4, LC, for the comment about French finances.

34. JL to Thomas McKean, 2 September 1781, PCC, reel 182, item 165, p. 137, NA.

35. Count de Vergennes to Lafayette, 19 April 1781, in Idzerda, ed., *Lafayette Papers*, 4: 47.

36. See Stourzh, *Franklin and American Foreign Policy*, 154–66 (quotation on 159); Dull, *Franklin the Diplomat*, 11, 56, 65–69; and Hutson, *Adams and Diplomacy*, 70–72.

37. Jackson's account was first given at his address to the Society of the Cincinnati in Philadelphia on 4 July 1786. The timing of the oration, only five years after the mission to France, is the deciding factor in its inclusion here. See "Extract from the Diary of William Rawle," 253. As an old man, Jackson repeated this story with essentially the same dialogue, but he added dramatic embellishment of questionable accuracy. The later version had Laurens tell Vergennes, "The sword which I now wear in defence of France as well as my own country, unless the succour I solicit is immediately accorded, I may be compelled, within a short time, to draw against France, as a British subject." Garden, *Anecdotes*, 2nd ser., 14–15.

38. JL to George Washington, 11 April 1781, George Washington Papers, Series 4, LC.

39. Francis Wharton applied the term "militia diplomacy" to describe American defiance of the rules of European diplomacy. See Wharton, ed., *Revolutionary Diplo-*

matic Correspondence, 1: 511–14; and 2: 289–94. While Wharton's views have been largely discredited by modern diplomatic historians, part of his thesis, that American diplomats tended to violate norms calling for "delicacy" and spoke instead with "blunt simplicity," is reflected in JL's behavior. For modern appraisals of American diplomatic practice, see Hutson, *Adams and Diplomacy*, 144–45, 150–55; Dull, *Franklin the Diplomat*, 65–72; and Ferling, "John Adams, Diplomat," 227–52, especially 250–51.

40. JL to Thomas McKean, 2 September 1781, PCC, reel 182, item 165, p. 137, NA. Necker, in fact, resigned in May, prior to JL's departure, after a failed power play. See Dull, *French Navy and American Independence*, 199–201, 227; and Dull, *Franklin the Diplomat*, 67, for French court politics; and Benjamin Franklin to JL, 21 May 1781, JL to Franklin, 28 May 1781, Franklin Papers, APS, for Necker's resignation. On European diplomatic protocol, consult Dull, "Franklin and the Nature of American Diplomacy," 351–55.

41. JL to Samuel Huntington, 9 April 1781, 24 April 1781, PCC, reel 182, item 165, pp. 99 (second quotation), 103 (first quotation), NA.

42. Alexander Gillon to JL, 22 March 1781, 22 April 1781, John Laurens Papers, SCHS; JL to Samuel Huntington, 24 April 1781, PCC, reel 182, item 165, p. 103, NA; Stone, "'The *South Carolina* We've Lost,'" 159–65.

43. JL to Samuel Huntington, 24 April 1781, PCC, reel 182, item 165, p. 103, NA.

44. "Memorandum of agreement between lieutenant Colonel Laurens Special Minister from the United American States on the part of the said States, and Commodore Gillon on the part of the State of South Carolina," 28 April 1781, copies in Adams Papers, reel 355, MHS and John Laurens Papers, SCHS. For the goods Gillon sold to JL, see "Summary of Goods, the Property of the State of South Carolina sold in consequence of Commodore Gillons agreement with Colonel Laurens," [1781], PCC, reel 134, item 109, p. 510, NA.

45. JL to John Adams, 28 April 1781, Adams Papers, reel 354, MHS. For a description of de Neufville, who operated the merchant house with his son Leendert, see Van Winter, *American Finance and Dutch Investment*, 1: 29–34, 135, 150, 194; 2: 1014. On de Neufville's diplomatic activities, see Bemis, *Diplomacy of the American Revolution*, 157–61.

46. JL to John Adams, 28 April 1781, Adams to JL, 8 May 1781, Adams Papers, reel 354, MHS; for Adams's earlier contact with de Neufville, see Hutson, *Adams and Diplomacy*, 80–81.

47. JL to William Jackson, 28 April 1781, John Laurens Papers, SCHS; JL to Samuel Huntington, 24 April 1781, PCC, reel 182, item 165, p. 103, NA.

48. Stone, "'The *South Carolina* We've Lost,'" 161–65; Benjamin Franklin to JL, 8 November 1781, John Laurens Papers, SCHS; Franklin to John Adams, 5 June 1781, 7 November 1781, to Count de Vergennes, 10 June 1781, to William Jackson, 10 July 1781, in Wharton, ed., *Revolutionary Diplomatic Correspondence*, 4: 470, 485, 558, 835; Franklin to Jackson, 6 July 1781, to Thomas McKean, 5 November 1781, PCC, reel 108, item 82, vol. 2, pp. 9, 19, NA.

49. JL to Benjamin Franklin, 29 May 1781, Franklin Papers, APS (letter signed, in hand of Thomas Paine), John Laurens Papers, SCHS (draft that contains the reference to "unnecessary provision," which was deleted from the final copy). The ship *Lafayette* never made it to America. She lost contact with *Alliance* and was captured by the British. As a result, part of the funds obtained by Franklin and JL

in 1781 went toward replacing the cargo. See John Barry: Deposition regarding ship *Marquis de Lafayette*, 2 August 1782, PCC, reel 92, item 78, vol. 4, p. 325, NA; and Ford, ed., *Journals of the Continental Congress*, 21: 1004–6.

50. Memorial to Jacques Necker, 29 April 1781, PCC, reel 182, item 165, p. 119, NA.

51. Because of the holdup in molding howitzers and mortars of English caliber, JL decided to substitute some of French caliber. See JL to Samuel Huntington, 24 April 1781, PCC, reel 182, item 165, p. 103, NA; JL to Marquis de Ségur, 27 April 1781, John Laurens Papers, SCHS; Artillery Report, 17 April 1781, Franklin Papers, APS. For the efforts of Corny and Veimerange, see M. de Veimerange to JL, 24 April 1781, 27 April 1781, 28 April 1781, 29 April 1781, 7 May 1781, Louis Ethis de Corny to JL, [April? 1781], M. Cicogne to Veimerange, 8 May 1781, M. Gueret to Veimerange, 8 May 1781, Schweighauser & Dobrée to JL, 10 May 1781, John Laurens Papers, SCHS.

52. Sabatier Sons & Despres: Summary of Articles requested by JL, 26 April 1781, PCC, reel 182, item 165, p. 199, NA; JL to Benjamin Franklin, 28 May 1781, Franklin Papers, APS (quotation).

53. JL to Samuel Huntington, 15 May 1781, PCC, reel 182, item 165, p. 131, NA; Count de Vergennes to JL, 16 May 1781, PCC, reel 134, item 109, p. 479, NA; Vergennes to Chevalier de La Luzerne, 14 May 1781, in Doniol, ed., *Histoire*, 4: 557n.

54. JL to Thomas McKean, 2 September 1781, PCC, reel 182, item 165, p. 137, NA; Thomas McKean to Arthur Lee, 4 September 1781, in Paul H. Smith, ed., *Letters of Delegates*, 18: 9–10. The previous year Louis XVI presented a box to Arthur Lee, who departed France persona non grata. Potts, *Arthur Lee*, 240–41.

55. See Garden, *Anecdotes*, 2nd ser., 12–17; Count de Vergennes to the Chevalier de La Luzerne, 11 May 1781, in Doniol, ed., *Histoire*, 4: 560n. Among the other errors in Jackson's story was his assertion that Washington hand-picked JL for the mission. According to Jackson, JL finally lost his temper and approached Louis XVI in early May. Since by that time Jackson had already departed for Holland, his claims as an eyewitness are discredited.

56. Count de Vergennes to Lafayette, 11 May 1781, in Idzerda, ed., *Lafayette Papers*, 4: 92; Vergennes to the Chevalier de La Luzerne, 11 May 1781, 14 May 1781, in Doniol, ed., *Histoire*, 4: 560n, 562n (quotation).

57. JL to Thomas McKean, 6 September 1781, PCC, reel 182, item 165, p. 257, NA; JL to Benjamin Franklin, 29 May 1781, Franklin Papers, APS; Babut & Labouchere to JL, 15 May 1781, John Laurens Papers, SCHS; John Jay to JL, 2 May 1781, in Morris, ed., *John Jay*, 74.

58. HL Memoranda Book, 7 October 1780–31 December 1781, Kendall Collection; for HL's imprisonment and treatment in the Tower of London, see Clark, "Henry Laurens in the Anglo-American Peace Negotiations," 23–67.

59. Thomas Paine to Robert Morris, 20 February 1782, to a Committee of the Continental Congress, [October 1783], in Foner, ed., *Writings of Paine*, 2: 1208, 1234; Benjamin Franklin to John Adams, 29 April–8 May 1781, Adams Papers, reel 354, MHS. In a postscript Franklin informed Adams that "Col. Laurens set out yesterday for Brest on his Return." Adams docketed the postscript 8 May, as JL was in Paris as late as 15 May, apparently Adams mistakenly wrote 8 May instead of 18 May.

60. JL to Benjamin Franklin, 22 May 1781, 28 May 1781; Corban Barnes: Shipment Receipt on JL's Order, 25 May 1781; J. D. Schweighauser to JL, 29 May 1781, Franklin Papers, APS; JL to Marquis de Ségur, 28 May 1781, Jared Sparks Collection, Autograph File, Houghton Library, Harvard University; "Account of Supplies on the Frigate *Cibelle*," 27 May 1781, PCC, reel 182, item 165, p. 207, NA; M. Bertier to JL, 20 June 1781, PCC, reel 134, item 109, p. 515, NA; "Cloathing &ca transported from France," 3 September 1781, George Washington Papers, Series 4, LC; J. D. Schweighauser to JL, 28 April 1781, Schweighauser & Dobrée to JL, 10 May 1781, 12 May 1781, John Laurens Papers, SCHS.

61. JL to Benjamin Franklin, 22 May 1781, Franklin Papers, APS; JL to Count de Vergennes, 28 May 1781, Correspondence Politique, États-Unis, 16: 353–54 (microfilm), Ministère des Affaires Etrangères; JL to Marquis de Ségur, 28 May 1781, Jared Sparks Collection, Autograph File, Houghton Library, Harvard University.

62. Benjamin Franklin to JL, 17 May 1781, Thomas Addis Emmet Collection (EM 9464), NYPL; JL to Franklin, 22 May 1781, Franklin Papers, APS.

63. JL to Benjamin Franklin, 29 May 1781, 30 May 1781, Martha Laurens to Franklin, 28 April 1781, 14 November 1781, Franklin Papers, APS; JL to Martha Laurens, 29 May 1781, John Laurens Papers, South Caroliniana Library.

64. JL to Benjamin Franklin, 9 June 1781, Franklin Papers, APS; Franklin to JL, 8 November 1781, John Laurens Papers, SCHS. When Franklin attempted later to obtain remuneration for his grandson, he enclosed a copy of JL's letter to Congress as supporting evidence. See Franklin to Robert R. Livingston, 3 September 1782, in Wharton, ed., *Revolutionary Diplomatic Correspondence*, 5: 684–85.

65. Benjamin Franklin to President of Congress, 13 September 1781, ibid., 4: 709–10; Dull, *Diplomatic History*, 118–19.

66. Benjamin Franklin to John Adams, 29 April–8 May 1781, Adams Papers, reel 354, MHS; Franklin to Samuel Huntington, 14 May 1781, PCC, reel 108, item 82, vol. 1, p. 359, NA; Franklin to William Carmichael, 24 August 1781, in Wharton, ed., *Revolutionary Diplomatic Correspondence*, 4: 660.

67. Franklin quoted in Stourzh, *Franklin and American Foreign Policy*, 157.

68. Benjamin Franklin to William Jackson, 6 July 1781, PCC, reel 108, item 82, vol. 2, p. 9 (first quotation); John Adams to Robert R. Livingston, 21 February 1782, in Wharton, ed., *Revolutionary Diplomatic Correspondence*, 5: 197–98; for Adams's memorial, see Hutson, *Adams and Diplomacy*, 81–98. In two instances—on 92–93 and 95—Hutson maintains incorrectly that Franklin obtained the loan prior to JL's arrival. His source for this assertion is Stinchcombe, *American Revolution and the French Alliance*, 140–41. Stinchcombe apparently confused the gift obtained by Franklin with the Dutch loan acquired during JL's negotiations.

69. John Bradford to Charles Thomson, 28 August 1781, PCC, reel 92, item 78, vol. 4, p. 253, NA; Board of War to President of Congress, 28 August 1781, PCC, reel 123, item 95, vol. 1, p. 292, NA; JL to Thomas McKean, 2 September 1781, PCC, reel 182, item 165, p. 137, NA; Robert Morris to Benjamin Franklin, 28 August 1781, in Ferguson, et al., eds., *Morris Papers*, 2: 140–42. Carrying a cargo of medicines and tin, *Active* arrived in Boston in early September. Navy Board of the Eastern Department to Morris, 12 September 1781, ibid., 2: 264–66.

70. JL to Thomas McKean, 6 September 1781, PCC, reel 182, item 165, p. 257, NA; Thomas Paine to a Committee of the Continental Congress, [October 1783], in Foner, ed., *Writings of Paine*, 2: 1234–35.

71. Daniel Carroll to Thomas Sim Lee, 4 September 1781, in Paul H. Smith, ed., *Letters of Delegates*, 18: 6–7; JL to Thomas McKean, 2 September 1781, PCC, reel 182, item 165, p. 137, NA; Ford, ed., *Journals of the Continental Congress*, 21: 928–29, 932, 1004–6.

72. Robert Morris Diary, 7 September–9 September 1781, Morris to Tench Francis, 11 September 1781, in Ferguson, et al., eds., *Morris Papers*, 2: 207–9, 212–13, 221, 246–49; Ferguson, *Power of the Purse*, 126–27, 136–38.

73. Chevalier de La Luzerne to Count de Vergennes, 25 September 1781, Correspondence Politique, États-Unis, 18: 294–302 (transcript), Ministère des Affaires Etrangères.

74. Act of Congress, 5 September 1781, John Laurens Papers, SCHS; Thomas McKean to JL, 6 September 1781, Thomas McKean Papers, HSP.

75. JL to Thomas McKean, 6 September 1781, PCC, reel 182, item 165, p. 267, NA.

76. Thomas Paine to JL, 4 October 1781, to Robert Morris, 20 February 1782, in Foner, ed., *Writings of Paine*, 2: 1198–99, 1208. JL belatedly remembered his promise. See JL to Thomas Bee, 11 December 1781, Thomas Bee Papers, LC.

77. JL to Thomas McKean, 2 September 1781, PCC, reel 182, item 165, p. 137, NA; for the gift to Sarah Bee, see *Francis Henderson et al. v. Henry Laurens, Administrator of John Laurens*, 1 June 1804, Court of Equity, Charleston District Decree Book, 1795–1806, 262–265, South Carolina Department of Archives and History.

78. James Duane to George Washington, 9 September 1781, to Robert R. Livingston, 11 September 1781, in Paul H. Smith, ed., *Letters of Delegates*, 18: 26–27, 32–33.

79. John Rutledge to the Delegates of South Carolina in Congress, 4 October 1781, in Barnwell, ed., "Letters of John Rutledge," 160.

80. Van Winter, *American Finance and Dutch Investment*, 1: 39–40; John Adams to Samuel Huntington, 27 June 1781, Benjamin Franklin to William Jackson, 10 July 1781, to Thomas McKean, 5 November 1781, to John Adams, 7 November 1781, in Wharton, ed., *Revolutionary Diplomatic Correspondence*, 4: 522, 558, 827–28, 835–36; Jean de Neufville & Son to the President of Congress, 8 August 1781, PCC, reel 156, item 145, p. 71, NA.

81. Benjamin Franklin to JL, 8 November 1781, John Laurens Papers, SCHS; Franklin to Count de Vergennes, 4 June 1781, 10 June 1781, to William Jackson, 28 June 1781, 5 July 1781, 6 July 1781, 10 July 1781, to Samuel Huntington, 11 July 1781, to Thomas McKean, 5 November 1781, Vergennes to Franklin, 8 June 1781, in Wharton, ed., *Revolutionary Diplomatic Correspondence*, 4: 467–68, 484–87, 523, 544–46, 557–59, 827–28; Franklin to John Adams, 30 June 1781, Adams Papers, reel 355, MHS; Jackson to Franklin, 2 July 1781, Franklin to Jackson, 5 July 1781, 6 July 1781, PCC, reel 108, item 82, vol. 1, p. 391, vol. 2, pp. 1, 9, NA; Vergennes to Franklin, 17 June 1781, Jackson to Franklin, 2 July 1781 (two letters), 5 July 1781, Franklin Papers, APS; Silas Deane to William Duer, 14 June 1781, in *Deane Papers*, 4: 424–29.

82. Van Winter, *American Finance and Dutch Investment*, 1: 40–41; Grimball, "Alexander Gillon," 60–67; Stone, "'The *South Carolina* We've Lost,'" 165–67; William Jackson to Benjamin Franklin, 26 September 1781, enclosed in Franklin to John Adams, 12 October 1781, and Alexander Gillon to Franklin, 4 October 1781, enclosed in Franklin to Adams, 22 October 1781, copies in Adams Papers, reel 355, MHS; Jean de Neufville & Son to Franklin, 30 August 1781, Franklin

Papers, APS; Gillon to de Neufville & Son, 14 October 1781, de Neufville & Son to Gillon, 1 November 1781, to Thomas McKean, 28 December 1781, PCC, RG 360 (M332), reel 4, f528, 530, 624, NA.

83. Robert Morris Diary, 12 March 1782, in Ferguson, et al., eds., *Morris Papers*, 4: 393, 394n; Morris Diary, 19 September 1782, 7 October 1782, 21 October 1782, ibid., 6: 396, 397n, 515, 630; Stone, "'The *South Carolina* We've Lost,'" 167–72; Ford, ed., *Journals of the Continental Congress*, 22: 384; 23: 700–706; 27: 587–88; James Madison to Edmund Randolph, 15 October 1782, in Paul H. Smith, ed., *Letters of Delegates*, 19: 260–61 (quotation). The efforts of the de Neufvilles and the Chevalier de Luxembourg to obtain compensation from the state of South Carolina continued for many years; the latter case was not resolved until 1854. See Van Winter, *American Finance and Dutch Investment*, 1: 150, 194–95; and D. E. Huger Smith, "The Luxembourg Claims," 92–115. For Gillon's continuing legal troubles, which did not prevent him from becoming a prominent South Carolina politician, see Grimball, "Alexander Gillon," 83–85, 100–106, 108–9.

84. Van Winter, *American Finance and Dutch Investment*, 1: 42–43; Jean de Neufville to Robert R. Livingston, 5 August 1787, PCC, reel 156, item 145, p. 63, NA; John Adams to Benjamin Franklin, 22 October 1781, Franklin Papers, APS; Franklin to Adams, 7 November 1781, in Wharton, ed., *Revolutionary Diplomatic Correspondence*, 4: 835–36; Franklin to Adams, 26 November 1781, 14 December 1781, 17 December 1781, Adams to John Hanson, 4 December 1781, to Robert R. Livingston, 14 February 1782, ibid., 5: 8–9, 37 (first quotation), 46–48, 54, 163; Robert Morris to Hanson, 9 March 1782, in Ferguson, et al., eds., *Morris Papers*, 4: 376–77; Franklin to Morris, 25 June 1782, Morris to Franklin, 1 July 1782, ibid., 5: 477–78, 511 (second quotation); Morris Diary, 25 September 1782, Morris to Franklin, 30 September 1782, ibid., 6: 429, 464–65; Morris to Franklin, 11 January 1783, ibid., 7: 293.

85. In fact, JL's purchases of arms, ammunition, and clothing exceeded the gift of 6,000,000 livres by 686,109 livres. Robert Morris initially asserted that the United States was not accountable for JL's drafts that went beyond the 6,000,000 livres. See Count de Vergennes to Benjamin Franklin, 8 June 1781, in Wharton, ed., *Revolutionary Diplomatic Correspondence*, 4: 484; Circular to the Governors of the States, 19 October 1781, Robert Morris to Franklin, 27 November 1781, in Ferguson, et al., eds., *Morris Papers*, 3: 83–91, 272, 284, 288n.

86. Van Winter, *American Finance and Dutch Investment*, 1: 57–59; Benjamin Franklin to Robert Morris, 5 November 1781, in Ferguson, et al., eds., *Morris Papers*, 3: 150–51; Franklin to Morris, 4 March 1782, ibid., 4: 340; Franklin to Morris, 25 June 1782, ibid., 5: 479; Franklin to John Jay, 19 January 1782, Chevalier de La Luzerne to Thomas McKean, 28 January 1782, in Wharton, ed., *Revolutionary Diplomatic Correspondence*, 5: 119–20, 136; Charles Calonne to Count Vergennes, [undated], Calonne: Account of a Loan to the United States [undated], Sabatier Sons & Despres: Account of a Loan to the United States, [12 January 1783], PCC, RG 360 (M40), reel 1, item 120, vol. 1, pp. 107–12, NA; Ford, ed., *Journals of the Continental Congress*, 19: 599–606, 926; and 34: 619. Oliver Wolcott Jr. to Alexander Hamilton, 22 June 1792, in Syrett, ed., *Hamilton Papers*, 11: 546–49; Gouverneur Morris to the Commissaries of the French Treasury, 6 August 1792, Commissaries of the French Treasury to Morris, 9 August 1792, ibid., 12: 640–41.

87. Gouverneur Morris quoted in Stinchcombe, *American Revolution and the French Alliance,* 140. For similar assessments of JL's mission, see Dull, *Franklin the Diplomat,* 48–49; and Perkins, *France in the American Revolution,* 331–35, especially 335.

Chapter 10

1. For background to the siege of Yorktown, see Willcox, *Portrait of a General,* 376–429; Wickwire and Wickwire, *Cornwallis,* 249–364; Freeman, *Washington,* 5: 275–333; and Ward, *War of the Revolution,* 2: 866–85.
2. JL to Benjamin Lincoln, 9 September 1781, HM 20488, The Huntington Library; for JL's arrival, see Baron von Steuben to Nathanael Greene, 19 September 1781, in Zemensky, ed., *Steuben Papers,* 4: 298.
3. These figures are from Ward, *War of the Revolution,* 2: 886–87.
4. See Alexander Hamilton to Philip Schuyler, 18 February 1781, in Syrett, ed., *Hamilton Papers,* 2: 563–68; Miller, *Hamilton,* 71–76.
5. Alexander Hamilton to Philip Schuyler, 18 February 1781, to James McHenry, 18 February 1781, in Syrett, ed., *Hamilton Papers,* 2: 566–67, 569; for Hamilton's growing frustration with his duties as an aide, see Miller, *Hamilton,* 66–76.
6. Alexander Hamilton to Philip Schuyler, 18 February 1781, in Syrett, ed., *Hamilton Papers,* 2: 566–67; for Washington's temper, see Flexner, *Washington,* 413; on the JL-Washington correspondence, see especially JL to Washington, 11 April 1781, 19 May 1782, George Washington Papers, Series 4, LC; JL to Washington, 10 December 1781, Gratz Collection, HSP; and Washington to JL, 26 April 1780, in Fitzpatrick, ed., *Writings of Washington,* 18: 298–300; Washington to JL, 13 October 1780, ibid., 20: 173–74 (second quotation); Washington to JL, 9 April 1781, 21: 438–39 (first quotation); Washington to JL, 22 March 1782, Sol Feinstone Collection, no. 2198, David Library of the American Revolution, on deposit at APS.
7. Count de Grasse to George Washington, 23 September 1781, in Institut Français de Washington, ed., *Correspondence of Washington and De Grasse,* 45–48; Washington to Count de Grasse, 25 September 1781, in Fitzpatrick, ed., *Writings of Washington,* 23: 136–39, 137n.
8. Count de Grasse to George Washington, [25 September 1781], [26 September 1781], in Institut Français de Washington, ed., *Correspondence of Washington and De Grasse,* 51–54; Freeman, *Washington,* 5: 343–57; Middlekauff, *Glorious Cause,* 564–66; Duffy, *Military Experience,* 289–93.
9. Freeman, *Washington,* 5: 351; General Orders, 8 October 1781, in Fitzpatrick, ed., *Writings of Washington,* 23: 199.
10. Tilghman, ed., *Memoir of Tench Tilghman,* 105; Middlekauff, *Glorious Cause,* 568–69; Freeman, *Washington,* 5: 357–59; and Acomb, ed., *Journal of Closen,* 155.
11. Tilghman, ed., *Memoir of Tench Tilghman,* 105; Mitchell, *Hamilton,* 256–57; Freeman, *Washington,* 5: 365–69; Alexander Hamilton to Lafayette, 15 October 1781, in Syrett, ed., *Hamilton Papers,* 2: 679–80.
12. Alexander Hamilton to Lafayette, 15 October 1781, in Syrett, ed., *Hamilton Papers,* 2: 679–82 (quotation); Lafayette to the Chevalier de La Luzerne, 16 October 1781, in Idzerda, ed., *Lafayette Papers,* 4: 420–22; George Washington Diary,

14 October 1781, in Jackson and Twohig, eds., *Diaries of Washington*, 3: 426–28; Scheer and Rankin, *Rebels and Redcoats*, 561–63; Freeman, *Washington*, 5: 369–71.

13. Flexner, *Washington*, 453, 457–58; Freeman, *Washington*, 5: 372–77; George Washington Diary, 15–17 October 1781, in Jackson and Twohig, eds., *Diaries of Washington*, 3: 429–30.

14. George Washington Diary, 18 October 1781, in Jackson and Twohig, eds., *Diaries of Washington*, 3: 430; JL to Richard Kidder Meade, 22 October 1781, Alexander Hamilton Papers, LC; Earl Cornwallis to Washington, 17 October 1781, 18 October 1781, Washington to Cornwallis, 18 October 1781, Articles of Capitulation, 19 October 1781, in Institut Français de Washington, ed., *Correspondence of Washington and De Grasse*, 96, 98–101, 107–9.

15. Part of William Jackson's recollections of JL's career, this account was printed in Garden, *Anecdotes*, 2nd series, 17–18; for a slightly different version, see Observations on JL, [n.d.], William Jackson Papers, Manuscripts and Archives, Yale University Library. Because Jackson was not present at Yorktown, the details of the story are of doubtful veracity. Yet it has appeared in several studies; for example, see Scheer and Rankin, *Rebels and Redcoats*, 568–69.

16. George Washington Diary, 18–19 October 1781, in Jackson and Twohig, eds., *Diaries of Washington*, 3: 430; Tilghman, ed., *Memoir of Tench Tilghman*, 106–7; Freeman, *Washington*, 5: 383; Earl Cornwallis to Washington, 18 October 1781, Articles of Capitulation, 19 October 1781, in Institut Français de Washington, ed., *Correspondence of Washington and De Grasse*, 100, 104–11.

17. Acomb, ed., *Journal of Closen*, 153; Thatcher, *Military Journal*, 289 (quotation).

18. JL to Richard Kidder Meade, 22 October 1781, Alexander Hamilton Papers, LC.

19. Dull, *French Navy and American Independence*, 216–24, 238–49; Corwin, *French Policy and the American Alliance*, 291–94, 310–13.

20. JL to Richard Kidder Meade, 22 October 1781, Alexander Hamilton Papers, LC; Moses Young to HL, 10 April 1782, Dreer Manuscripts, Revolutionary Soldiers, HSP.

21. JL to Earl Cornwallis, 5 November 1781, in Ross, ed., *Correspondence of Cornwallis*, 1: 134; JL to Thomas Bee, 13 November 1781, Dreer Collection, HSP; Earl Cornwallis to JL, 25 November 1781, PCC, reel 182, item 165, p. 283, NA; Sir Henry Clinton to George Washington, 11 February 1782, Washington to John Hanson, 18 February 1782, PCC, reel 171, item 152, vol. 10, pp. 443, 447, NA; Washington to Clinton, 26 February 1782, in Fitzpatrick, ed., *Writings of Washington*, 24: 23.

22. Freeman, *Washington*, 5: 401–3; Miller, *Hamilton*, 79; for the last letters JL drafted as aide-de-camp, see George Washington to Count de Grasse, 5 November 1781 (two letters), in Fitzpatrick, ed., *Writings of Washington*, 23: 335–37; JL's reasons for returning to South Carolina are expressed in JL to Washington, 19 May 1782, George Washington Papers, Series 4, LC.

23. See Nadelhaft, *Disorders of War*, 52–69; Klein, *Unification of a Slave State*, 100–108; Weir, "'The Violent Spirit,'" 133–39; and Shy, "The American Revolution," 121–56.

24. JL to George Washington, 10 December 1781, Gratz Collection, HSP; for JL's optimism after meeting with Rutledge, see JL to Washington, 28 January 1782, Jared Sparks Collection, MS Sparks 49.3 (137), Houghton Library, Harvard University.

25. Nathanael Greene to John Rutledge, 9 December 1781, Nathanael Greene Papers, WCL.
26. John Rutledge to Nathanael Greene, 24 December 1781, Nathanael Greene Papers, WCL; Salley, ed., *Journal of the House of Representatives,* 3, 130; Nadelhaft, *Disorders of War,* 73–74.
27. For Lee and his Legion, see Templin, "Lee," 7–12, 53–54, 81, 97–98; Royster, *Lee,* 11–54; on his desire for a leave of absence, see Henry Lee to Nathanael Greene, 28 December 1781, Greene to Lee, 28 December 1781, Nathanael Greene Papers, WCL.
28. Henry Lee, *Memoirs,* 528–29 (quotation); Henry Lee to Nathanael Greene, 20 December 1781, JL to Greene, [20 December 1781] (quotation), Greene to John Rutledge, 16 January 178[2], Nathanael Greene Papers, WCL; JL to [Greene], 11 January 1782, Nathanael Greene Papers, Rare Book, Manuscript, & Special Collections Library, Duke University.
29. Nathanael Greene to Henry Lee, 21 December 1781, Sol Feinstone Collection, no. 430, David Library of the American Revolution, on deposit at APS; Lee to Greene, 28 December 1781 (first quotation), Greene to Lee, 28 December 1781 (second quotation), Nathanael Greene Papers, WCL. In his history of the Southern campaign, Lee claimed incorrectly—either because of disingenuousness or the passage of time and lapse of memory—that he was commander of the operation. See Henry Lee, *Memoirs,* 535.
30. JL to Henry Lee, 27 December 1781, Robert Alonzo Brock Collection, The Huntington Library.
31. Henry Lee to Nathanael Greene, 29 December 1781, HM 22697, Greene File, The Huntington Library; Lee to Greene, 28 December 1781, 31 December 1781, Greene to Lee, 1 January 178[2], Nathanael Greene Papers, WCL.
32. JL to [Nathanael Greene], 11 January 1782, Nathanael Greene Papers, Rare Book, Manuscript, & Special Collections Library, Duke University.
33. Henry Lee, *Memoirs,* 531–32; Nathanael Greene to John Hanson, 23 January 1782, Nathanael Greene Papers, WCL; "Extracts from the Journal of Lieutenant John Bell Tilden," 219.
34. See Middlekauff, *Glorious Cause,* 496–510.
35. JL: Draft of Message to his Troops before Battle, [January 1782], Charles F. Gunther Collection, Chicago Historical Society.
36. Henry Lee, *Memoirs,* 532.
37. Nathanael Greene to John Rutledge, 16 January 178[2], to John Hanson, 23 January 1782, Nathanael Greene Papers, WCL; Henry Lee, *Memoirs,* 533.
38. Nathanael Greene to John Hanson, 23 January 1782, Nathanael Greene Papers, WCL; Feltman, *Journal,* 35 (first quotation); Henry Lee, *Memoirs,* 533–34 (second quotation).
39. Nathanael Greene to John Rutledge, 16 January 178[2], to John Hanson, 23 January 1782 (quotation), JL to Greene, 15 January 1782, Nathanael Greene Papers, WCL.
40. Nathanael Greene to John Hanson, 23 January 1782, Nathanael Greene Papers, WCL; Henry Lee, *Memoirs,* 534; Templin, "Lee," 198; Royster, *Lee,* 46–48.
41. Feltman, *Journal,* 35 (quotation); McCrady, *South Carolina in the Revolution, 1780–1783,* 560; Salley, ed., *Journal of the House of Representatives,* 21.
42. JL to Nathanael Greene, 28 December 1781, Greene to John Rutledge, 21 January 1782, in Showman and Conrad, eds., *Greene Papers,* 10: 130–31, 228–30.

43. Nadelhaft, *Disorders of War,* 71–75; Salley, ed., *Journal of the House of Representatives,* 9–13; Aedanus Burke to Arthur Middleton, 25 January–5 February 1782, in Barnwell, ed., "Correspondence of Arthur Middleton [Part One]," 192–93.

44. Salley, ed., *Journal of the House of Representatives,* 17, 21–23 (quotation on 21), 26–27, 30–32, 34, 37, 41–42, 48–53, 56–62, 130.

45. Ibid., 42, 46–53, 62–63, 78–80; Cooper and McCord, eds., *Statutes at Large of South Carolina,* 4: 513–15; Weir, ed., *Letters of Freeman,* 83–84; on the general use of slaves as a bonus see Klein, *Unification of a Slave State,* 104–8; and Frey, *Water from the Rock,* 133–34.

46. Salley, ed., *Journal of the House of Representatives,* 56.

47. JL to George Washington, 19 May 1782, George Washington Papers, Series 4, LC; Nathanael Greene to Washington, 9 March 1782, Nathanael Greene Papers, WCL; Edward Rutledge to Arthur Middleton, 8 February 1782, in Barnwell, ed., "Correspondence of Arthur Middleton [Part Two]," 4.

48. Edward Rutledge to Arthur Middleton, 8 February 1782, in Barnwell, ed., "Correspondence of Middleton [Part Two]," 4. Rutledge and another opponent of the measure, Aedanus Burke, provided vote totals that corresponded with those given by David Ramsay in 1779. Thus JL's assertion that he received twice as much support in 1782 was obviously incorrect. See Burke to Arthur Middleton, 25 January–5 February 1782, in Barnwell, ed., "Correspondence of Arthur Middleton [Part One]," 194; JL to George Washington, 19 May 1782, George Washington Papers, Series 4, LC.

49. Aedanus Burke to Arthur Middleton, 25 January–5 February 1782, in Barnwell, ed., "Correspondence of Middleton [Part One]," 194. Bracketed material supplied by the author.

50. See Jordan, *White over Black,* 542–69; and Jefferson, *Notes on the State of Virginia,* 143. For HL's concerns about miscegenation, see HL to George Appleby, 28 February 1774, in *Laurens Papers,* 9: 316–317.

51. Salley, ed., *Journal of the House of Representatives,* 57–59, 75–76, 101; John Mathews to Nathanael Greene, 6 February 1782, Greene to Mathews, 7 February 1782, 11 February 1782, Nathanael Greene Papers, WCL; Cooper and McCord, eds., *Statutes at Large of South Carolina,* 4: 520.

52. For British policy toward slaves, see Frey, *Water from the Rock,* 113–42; the limited military use of blacks is detailed on 137–39.

53. JL to Nathanael Greene, 21 December 1781, Nathanael Greene Papers, WCL; Salley, ed., *Journal of the House of Representatives,* 96–99; Berkeley and Berkeley, *Alexander Garden,* 284–91; Garden, *Anecdotes,* 75; Heitman, *Historical Register,* 242. In 1784 the state legislature removed Garden the elder from the confiscation list and amerced his estate. Still, he remained an exile in England and never returned to South Carolina. See Coker, "Punishment of Loyalists in South Carolina," 157–68.

54. Salley, ed., *Journal of the House of Representatives,* 22–23, 61–62; Aedanus Burke to Arthur Middleton, 25 January–5 February 1782, in "Correspondence of Middleton [Part One]," 192–93; Lambert, *South Carolina Loyalists,* 238–39.

55. Cooper and McCord, eds., *Statutes at Large of South Carolina,* 4: 516–25, 526–28; 6: 629–33; Salley, ed., *Journal of the House of Representatives,* 62 (quotation); Lambert, *South Carolina Loyalists,* 239–40.

56. See the conclusions of Weir, "'The Violent Spirit,'" 141–58; and Nadelhaft, *Disorders of War,* 74–85.

57. See *Royal Gazette* (Charleston), 7 September 1782; and chapter 11 below.
58. Moses Young to JL, 28 September 1781, JL to John Hanson, 12 February 1782, PCC, reel 182, item 165, pp. 275, 279, NA; JL to George Washington, 12 February 1782, George Washington Papers, Series 4, LC.
59. The British freed HL after Benjamin Franklin approved an exchange involving Cornwallis. Ironically Congress, citing the earl's alleged atrocities in the South, refused to authorize his exchange. See Knight, "Prisoner Exchange and Parole," 212–14.
60. Nathanael Greene to Henry Lee, 12 February 1782, Nathanael Greene Papers, WCL; JL to HL, 9 March 1778, in *HL Papers,* 12: 532.

Chapter 11

1. Duffy, *Military Experience,* 268–79; Heitman, *Historical Register,* 27–28.
2. Templin, "Lee," 198–208; Royster, *Lee,* 39–54.
3. See Henry Lee to Nathanael Greene, 26 January 1782, quoted in William Johnson, *Sketches,* 321; Greene to Lee, 27 January 1782, in Gibbes, ed., *Documentary History,* 3: 242–43; Lee to Greene, 10 February 1782 (first quotation), HM 23426, 13 February 1782, HM 22704, 17 February 1782, HM 22773, [19 February 1782] (second quotation), HM 22708, Greene to Lee, 18 February 1782, HM 22706, Greene File, The Huntington Library; Greene to Lee, 6 June 1782, Nathanael Greene Papers, WCL; Henry Lee, *Memoirs,* 550–52.
4. JL to Nathanael Greene, 28 February 1782 (two letters), 1 March 1782, 6 March 1782, Francis Marion to JL, 4 March 1782, to Greene, 1 March 1782, 8 March 1782, Greene to Marion, 1 March 1782, to Anthony Wayne, 6 March 1782 (quotation), Nathanael Greene Papers, WCL; JL to Marion, 4 March 1782, in Gibbes, ed., *Documentary History,* 3: 263; McCrady, *South Carolina in the Revolution, 1780–83,* 600–606.
5. JL to Nathanael Greene, 9 March 1782 (first and second quotations), 11 March 1782, 18 March 1782, 20 March 1782 (third quotation), Nathanael Greene Papers, WCL; Greene to Henry Lee, 22 April 1782, BR Box 4, Robert Alonzo Brock Collection, The Huntington Library. In his memoirs Henry Lee claimed falsely that he had authorized Rudulph to assault the galley. Henry Lee, *Memoirs,* 537–38, 545–46. Two Rudulph brothers served in the Legion infantry: John was a major, Michael a captain. Heitman, *Historical Register,* 476.
6. Greene quoted in Coker, "Punishment of Loyalists in South Carolina," 315–16; on this point see also William Johnson, *Sketches,* 2: 269.
7. See JL to Nathanael Greene, 9 March 1782, 11 March 1782, 22 March 1782, 29 March 1782, 30 March 1782, 21 April 1782, 28 April 1782, 11 May 1782, 3 June 1782, Greene to Charles Cotesworth Pinckney, 16 May 1782, John Faucheraud Grimké to Greene, 22 May 1782, Eliza Clitherall to JL, 5 May 1782, 9 May 1782, 25 July 1782, Nathanael Greene Papers, WCL; Clitherall to JL, [1782], Lloyd. W. Smith Collection, Manuscript 1341–1, Morristown National Historical Park; Coker, "Punishment of Loyalists in South Carolina," 141–44; for the payment of spies, see the exchange between "Brutus" and "A Patriot" in *Gazette of the State of South-Carolina,* 6 August 1783, 27 August 1783; and *South-Carolina Gazette & General Advertiser,* 12 August 1783; as well as JL to Ichabod Burnet, 11 August 1782, Nathanael Greene Papers, WCL.

8. Benjamin Franklin to JL, 8 November 1781, John Laurens Papers, SCHS.

9. Benjamin Vaughan to Benjamin Franklin, [November? 1781], Franklin to Vaughan, 22 November 1781, Franklin Papers, APS. See also Moses Young to Henry Lee, [c. 1811], BR Box 4, Robert Alonzo Brock Collection, The Huntington Library.

10. Francis Marion to Nathanael Greene, 29 March 1782, Greene to Marion, 31 March 1782, JL to Greene, 30 March 1782 (quotation), 31 March 1782, Nathanael Greene Papers, WCL.

11. Ichabod Burnet to JL, 2 April 1782, Nathanael Greene to JL, 2 April 1782, in Gibbes, ed., *Documentary History*, 2: 150; JL to Greene, 2 April 1782, Nathanael Greene Papers, WCL.

12. Alexander Leslie to Nathanael Greene, 4 April 1782, Greene to Francis Marion, 6 April 1782, Nathanael Greene Papers, WCL; for a list of the sequestered estates, see McCowen, *British Occupation of Charleston*, 153–54.

13. John Mathews to Alexander Leslie, 12 April 1782, Nathanael Greene Papers, WCL; Horne, "Governorship of John Mathews," 63–65.

14. JL to Thomas Bee, 14 April 1782, Thomas Bee Papers, LC; Nathanael Greene to Robert R. Livingston, 13 April 1782, Nathanael Greene Papers, WCL.

15. John Mathews to Nathanael Greene, 20 March 1782, John Ewing Colhoun to [Mathews], 20 March 1782, William Pierce to John Rudulph and Richard Call, 21 March 1782, JL to Greene, 10 April 1782, 11 April 1782, Rudulph to Greene, 15 April 1782, Edward Dyer to Ichabod Burnet, 20 April 1782, Nathanael Greene Papers, WCL; Greene to Henry Lee, 22 April 1782, BR Box 4, Robert Alonzo Brock Collection, The Huntington Library.

16. Thomas Farr to JL, 17 May 1782, in Webber, ed., "Revolutionary Letters," 7–8; Farr to [JL?], 2 March 1782, Nathanael Greene to Benjamin Lincoln, 13 April 1782, John Wilson to JL, 26 August 1782, Nathanael Greene Papers, WCL; Greene to Henry Lee, 22 April 1782, BR Box 4, Robert Alonzo Brock Collection, The Huntington Library; Greene to Robert Morris, 9 March 1782, in Ferguson, et al., eds., *Morris Papers*, 4: 383; Greene to Morris, 13 August 1782, ibid., 6: 183–84 (quotation); John Mathews to Francis Marion, 14 August 1782, in Gibbes, ed., *Documentary History*, 2: 207; William Johnson, *Sketches*, 2: 317; McCowan, *British Occupation of Charleston*, 90–93; Horne, "Governorship of John Mathews," 53–55, 58–60; on the postwar controversy over the sanctioned trade with the British garrison at Charleston, see the arguments of "Brutus" in *The Gazette of the State of South-Carolina*, 6 August 1783, 27 August 1783; and the response of "A Patriot" in *South-Carolina Gazette & General Advertiser*, 12 August 1783.

17. Thomas Farr to JL, 17 May 1782, in Webber, ed., "Revolutionary Letters," 8–9; Farr to Nathanael Greene, 14 June 1782, Nathanael Greene Papers, LC; John Mathews to Greene, 7 March 1782, JL to Greene, 11 March 1782, Nathanael Greene Papers, WCL; Horne, "Governorship of John Mathews," 45–46; for a discussion of how impressment alienated civilians and eroded magisterial authority, see Carp, *To Starve the Army*, 96–98.

18. Horne, "Governorship of John Mathews," 52–53, 57–58; Nathanael Greene to John Mathews, 28 May 1782, 7 July 1782, to John Barnwell, 31 July 1782 (quotation), Mathews to Greene, 28 May 1782, 10 July 1782, John Meals to Ichabod Burnet, 7 July 1782, Nathanael Greene Papers, WCL.

19. Alexander Boxburgh to Mordecai Gist, 18 May 1782, Nathanael Greene to JL, 24 May 1782, to John Mathews, 28 May 1782, Nathanael Greene Papers, WCL; for the Legion under Lee and their special status, see Royster, *Lee,* 17–19; and Greene to John Hanson, 11 July 1782, Nathanael Greene Papers, WCL.

20. Nathanael Greene to John Mathews, 28 May 1782, Mathews to Greene, 29 May 1782, Nathanael Greene Papers, WCL.

21. See Royster, *Lee,* 12–54; and the introduction above.

22. William Johnson, *Sketches,* 2: 330; John Rudulph to Nathanael Greene, 21 March 1782, 26 March 1782, 22 April 1782 (quotation), to John Hamilton, 26 March 1782, Greene to Rudulph, 28 March 1782 (quotation), to Thomas Burke, 28 April 1782, to Henry Lee, 7 October 1782, Ichabod Burnet to Rudulph, 5 May 1782, JL to Greene, 26 April 1782, 6 May 1782, Alexander Martin to Greene, 24 May 1782, Nathanael Greene Papers, WCL; JL to Greene, 5 May 1782, Box 2, Folder 14, Andre de Coppet Collection, Manuscripts Division, Department of Rare Books & Special Collections, Princeton University Library.

23. Royster, *Lee,* 17–19; William Johnson, *Sketches,* 2: 328; Nathanael Greene to Henry Lee, 6 June 1782, Nathanael Greene Papers, WCL; Ichabod Burnet to Lee, 20 June 1782, Misc. Mss., New-York Historical Society. For the Legion's lack of discipline, see Ichabod Burnet to John Rudulph, 5 May 1782, Rudulph to Greene, [8 June 1782], Nathaniel Pendleton to Rudulph, 9 June 1782, John Meals to Greene, 13 June 1782, Nathanael Greene Papers, WCL.

24. Nathanael Greene to Benjamin Lincoln, 19 May 1782, to Henry Lee, 6 June 1782 (first quotation), Richard Call to Greene, 17 May 1782, 31 May 1782 (second quotation), Nathanael Greene Papers, WCL.

25. Because he was afraid to weaken his force, Leslie refused to send two thousand troops to Jamaica, as originally ordered. See Alexander Leslie to Sir Henry Clinton, 17 April 1782 (EM 15578, Leslie Letterbook), 28 April 1782 (EM 15583, Leslie Letterbook), to Lord George Germain, 23 April 1782 (EM 15580, Leslie Letterbook), 17 May 1782 (EM 15546, Leslie Letterbook), to James Robertson, 17 May 1782 (EM 15585, Leslie Letterbook), Board of General and Field Officers, 15 April 1782 (EM 15573, Leslie Letterbook), 27 April 1782 (EM 15579, Leslie Letterbook), Thomas Addis Emmet Collection, NYPL; Jones, "British Withdrawal from the South," 263–64. For the American reaction, see JL to Thomas Bee, 19 May 1782, Thomas Bee Papers, LC; Nathanael Greene to Alexander Martin, 18 May 1782, to Benjamin Lincoln, 19 May 1782, Nathanael Greene Papers, WCL.

26. Alexander Leslie to Nathanael Greene, 23 May 1782, Greene to Leslie, 25 May 1782, to John Hanson, 31 May 1782 (quotation), Nathanael Greene Papers, WCL.

27. JL to Alexander Hamilton, [July 1782], in Syrett, ed., *Hamilton Papers,* 3: 121.

28. General Orders, 13 June 1782, in Henry Lee, *Memoirs,* 552.

29. John Rudulph and the Captains of the Legion to Nathanael Greene, 18 June 1782, 19 June 1782, Nathanael Greene Papers, LC; Greene to Rudulph and the Captains, 18 June 1782, to John Hanson, 11 July 1782, Nathanael Greene Papers, WCL.

30. Thomas Farr to Nathanael Greene, 14 June 1782, JL to Greene, 20 June 1782, 21 June 1782, Nathanael Greene Papers, LC; JL to Mordecai Gist, 20 June 1782,

23 June 1782, Gist Papers, MS 390, Manuscripts Department, Maryland Historical Society.

31. William Pierce Jr. to John Rudulph and the Captains of the Legion, 23 June 1782,
in Gibbes, ed., *Documentary History*, 2: 195; Nathanael Greene to John Hanson,
11 July 1782, to Henry Lee, 12 July 1782, 7 October 1782 (quotation),
Nathanael Greene Papers, WCL; Lee to Greene, 17 August 1782, HM 22730,
Greene File, The Huntington Library; William Johnson, *Sketches*, 2: 329–31; Ford,
ed., *Journals of the Continental Congress*, 23: 529–30.

32. Mordecai Gist to Nathanael Greene, 11 July 1782, Greene to Gist, 11 July 1782,
Nathanael Greene Papers, WCL.

33. JL to Nathanael Greene, 5 July 1782, Nathanael Greene Papers, WCL; JL to
Mordecai Gist, 6 July 1782, John Laurens Papers, South Caroliniana Library;
Alexander Leslie to Earl of Shelburne, 8 July 1782 (EM 15607, Leslie Letter-
book), Thomas Addis Emmet Collection, NYPL.

34. JL to George Washington, 19 May 1782, 12 June 1782, George Washington
Papers, Series 4, LC; JL to HL, 10 March 1779, Henry Laurens Papers, SCHS
(quotation).

35. See Candler, ed., *Revolutionary Records of the State of Georgia*, 3: 118–88, especially
119 (quotation). On the eve of the assembly's session, Richard Howley, who had earlier encouraged JL to introduce his plan for a black regiment, was concerned primarily about conferences with the British over the return of slaves. Expecting General
Anthony Wayne to settle in Georgia after the war, Howley asked him to intervene in
the negotiations and exert his influence as a future citizen of the state. Richard Howley to Anthony Wayne, 4 July 1782, 10 July 1782, Anthony Wayne Papers, HSP.

36. Nathanael Greene to John Hanson, 13 July 1782, to James Habersham, 2 August
1782, Nathanael Greene Papers, WCL; Alexander Leslie to Sir Guy Carleton, 2
August 1782 (EM 15623, Leslie Letterbook), Thomas Addis Emmet Collection,
NYPL; Jones, "British Withdrawal from the South," 269.

37. Alexander Leslie to Sir Guy Carleton, 10 August 1782 (EM 15628, Leslie Letterbook), to Nathanael Greene, 13 August 1782 (EM 15631, Leslie Letterbook),
Thomas Addis Emmet Collection, NYPL; John Mathews to Greene, 14 August
1782, Greene to Leslie, 15 August 1782, Nathanael Greene Papers, WCL.

38. Nathanael Greene to Francis Marion, 9 August 1782, in Gibbes, ed., *Documentary History*, 2: 205; Alexander Leslie to Sir Guy Carleton, 10 August 1782 (EM
15628, Leslie Letterbook), Thomas Addis Emmet Collection, NYPL.

39. JL to Nathanael Greene, [5 August 1782], Greene to John Mathews, 22 December 1782, Nathanael Greene Papers, WCL; Jones, "British Withdrawal from the
South," 265–66. Though it was obvious that the British intended to withdraw,
Greene still distrusted their motives: "When the articles of peace are signed sealed
and delivered I shall beleive them in earnest and not before." See Greene to [?],
29 September 1782, Nathanael Greene Papers, WCL.

40. See JL to Nathanael Greene, 3 August 1782, [5 August 1782], to Ichabod Burnet, 10 August 1782, Nathanael Greene Papers, WCL; for biographical information on Williamson, see Coker, "Punishment of Loyalists in South Carolina,"
250–54; for Fuller and his plantation, see Edgar, et al., eds., *Biographical Directory*, 2: 257–58.

41. JL to Nathanael Greene, 8 August 1782, 14 August 1782, to Ichabod Burnet, 10
August 1782 (quotation), E[dmund] P[etrie] to JL, 12 August 1782, Nathanael

Greene Papers, WCL; for Petrie, see Coker, "Punishment of Loyalists in South Carolina," 314–17.

42. The details of Mathews's proclamation have been inferred from his statements to the General Assembly in January 1783. See Thompson and Lumpkin, eds., *Journals of the House of Representatives*, 32; and Cooper and McCord, eds., *Statutes at Large of South Carolina*, 4: 510–11.

43. JL to Nathanael Greene, 13 August 1782, Nathanael Greene Papers, WCL.

44. JL to Nathanael Greene, 14 August 1782 (first quotation), 22 August 1782 (second quotation), Nathanael Greene Papers, WCL.

45. JL to Nathanael Greene, 14 August 1782, Greene to John Mathews, 22 December 1782, Nathanael Greene Papers, WCL; Coker, "Punishment of Loyalists in South Carolina," 250–54, 314–17.

46. JL to Nathanael Greene, 3 August 1782, 21 August 1782 (including docket that mentions the unhealthiness of the British garrison), 22 August 1782 (quotation), to Ichabod Burnet, 11 August 1782, Nathanael Greene Papers, WCL; General Orders, 22 August 1782, Nathanael Greene Orderly Book, New-York Historical Society. On the general sickliness among the Americans, see William McKennan to Greene, 24 August 1782, Mordecai Gist to Burnet, 11 September 1782, John Gale to Greene, 15 September 1782, John Rudulph to Greene, 15 September 1782, Nathanael Greene Papers, WCL; Greene to Otho Holland Williams, 17 September 1782, Otho Holland Williams Papers, MS 908, Manuscripts Department, Maryland Historical Society; "Extracts from the Journal of Lieutenant John Bell Tilden," 228–229; and Seymour, "A Journal of the Southern Expedition," 392.

47. JL to Alexander Hamilton, [July 1782], in Syrett, ed., *Hamilton Papers*, 3: 120–22.

48. Alexander Hamilton to JL, 15 August 1782, ibid., 3: 144–45.

49. Alexander Leslie to Major Doyle, 21 August 1782 (EM 15636, Leslie Letterbook), to [William] Brereton, 21 August 1782 (EM 15637, Leslie Letterbook), to Sir Guy Carleton, 8 September 1782 (EM 15644, Leslie Letterbook), Thomas Addis Emmet Collection, NYPL.

50. Nathanael Greene to Francis Marion, 24 August 1782, in Gibbes, ed., *Documentary History*, 2: 212; William Pierce to Mordecai Gist, 23 August 1782, William McKennan to Greene, 24 August 1782, Ichabod Burnet to Richard Call, 24 August 1782, Nathanael Greene Papers, WCL.

51. JL quoted in William Johnson, *Sketches*, 2: 339.

52. Mordecai Gist to Nathanael Greene, 27 August 1782, Nathanael Greene Papers, WCL; Gist to Richard Call, 26 August 1782, Gist Papers, MS 390, Manuscripts Department, Maryland Historical Society; Edgar, et al., eds., *Biographical Directory*, 2: 457; Heitman, *Historical Register*, 503.

53. William Johnson, *Sketches*, 2: 340; see JL to Nathanael Greene, 1 June 1782, Nathanael Greene Papers, LC (first quotation); JL to HL, [31 March 1780], Henry Laurens Papers, SCHS (second quotation).

54. William Johnson, *Sketches*, 2: 341; Mordecai Gist to Nathanael Greene, 27 August 1782, Nathanael Greene Papers, WCL.

55. William Johnson, *Sketches*, 2: 340–41; Mordecai Gist to Nathanael Greene, 27 August 1782, Nathanael Greene Papers, WCL; Alexander Leslie to Sir Guy Carleton, 8 September 1782 (EM 15644, Leslie Letterbook), Thomas Addis Emmet

Collection, NYPL; "Extracts from the Journal of Lieutenant John Bell Tilden," 229; Joseph Lee Boyle, ed., "Revolutionary War Diaries of Captain Walter Finney," 144 (first quotation); Bennett, "Delaware Regiment in the Revolution," 461 (McKennan quotations).

56. Mordecai Gist to Nathanael Greene, 27 August 1782, "List of the Killed and wounded in the Action of 27th August," 27 August 1782, Nathanael Greene Papers, WCL; Alexander Leslie to Sir Guy Carleton, 8 September 1782 (EM 15644, Leslie Letterbook), Thomas Addis Emmet Collection, NYPL; Heitman, *Historical Register,* 503.

57. Mordecai Gist to Nathanael Greene, 27 August 1782, Nathanael Greene Papers, WCL; Gist to Greene, 30 August 1782, 31 August 1782, 2 September 1782, 4 September 1782, Greene to Gist, 3 September 1782, Gist Papers, MS 390, Manuscripts Department, Maryland Historical Society; Alexander Leslie to Sir Guy Carleton, 8 September 1782 (EM 15644, Leslie Letterbook), NYPL.

Chapter 12

1. Nathanael Greene to Otho Holland Williams, 17 September 1782, Otho Holland Williams Papers, MS 908, Manuscripts Department, Maryland Historical Society.
2. William Pierce to Nathanael Greene, 7 September 1782, Nathanael Greene Papers, WCL; *Royal Gazette* (Charleston), 7 September 1782.
3. Thaddeus Kosciuszko to Nathanael Greene, 2 September 1782, in Budka, ed., *Letters of Thaddeus Kosciuszko,* 77.
4. *The Virginia Gazette, or, the American Advertiser* (Richmond: James Mayes), 12 October 1782.
5. Thatcher, *Military Journal,* 323–24; George Washington to Lafayette, 20 October 1782, in Fitzpatrick, ed., *Writings of Washington,* 25: 281.
6. Alexander Hamilton to Nathanael Greene, 12 October 1782, in Syrett, ed., *Hamilton Papers,* 3: 183–84; Cooke, *Hamilton,* 17.
7. Chastellux, *Travels in North America,* 1: 304; John Wells Jr. to HL, 1 November 1777, Kendall Collection; Chevalier Du Plessis to HL, 8 February 1778, in *Laurens Papers,* 12: 425.
8. HL to William Manning, 28 August 1782, Kendall Collection; Ramsay, *Memoirs of Martha Laurens Ramsay,* 19, 29.
9. Clark, "Henry Laurens in the Anglo-American Peace Negotiations," 92–94, 113; John Adams to HL, 6 November 1782, Kendall Collection.
10. Morris, *The Peacemakers,* 376–82; John Adams Diary: 29–30 November 1782, in Butterfield, ed., *Diary and Autobiography of John Adams,* 3: 79–85, 82.
11. Clark, "Henry Laurens in the Anglo-American Peace Negotiations," 117–18; HL to Mary Laurens, 30 December 1782, to George Appleby, 28 January 1783 (first quotation), Henry Laurens Papers, SCHS.
12. HL to Martha Laurens, 7 January 1783, Henry Laurens Papers, SCHS. See also HL to Martha Laurens, 18 August 1782, Kendall Collection; HL to James Laurens, 17 December 1782, James Laurens to HL, 1 January 1783, Henry Laurens Papers, SCHS.
13. Martha Laurens to Mary Laurens, 15 February 1783, Henry Laurens Papers, SCHS.
14. Clark, "Henry Laurens in the Anglo-American Peace Negotiations," 121–46; Langford, "Thomas Day and the Politics of Sentiment," 71–72.

15. Day, *Fragment of an original Letter,* 3. Day's eulogy was reprinted in Gordon, *History,* 4: 302–3; see also George Washington to William Gordon, 8 March 1785, in Abbot, ed., *Papers of George Washington,* 2: 412.

16. HL to William Manning, 17 July 1783, Henry Laurens Papers, SCHS; HL to Martha Laurens, 13 June 1784, 19 June 1784, 20 June 1784, Kendall Collection; Clark, "Henry Laurens in the Anglo-American Peace Negotiations," 140–46.

17. Memorial & Petition to Congress, 8 November 1784, PCC, reel 117, item 89, p. 357, NA; Ford, ed., *Journals of the Continental Congress,* 18: 94–97, 111–12.

18. Wallace, *Life of Henry Laurens,* 420–30; HL to Manning & Vaughan, 20 July 1785, Henry Laurens Papers, SCHS.

19. HL to James Bourdieu, 6 May 1785 (quotation), 9 June 1785, 6 July 1785, Kendall Collection; HL to Catherine Futterel, 30 June 1787, Henry Laurens Papers, SCHS; for the postwar debt crisis, see Nadelhaft, *Disorders of War,* 155–72; on HL's agricultural experimentation, consult Chaplin, *An Anxious Pursuit,* 137, 150, 153, 249–50.

20. HL to Alexander Hamilton, 19 April 1785, in Syrett, ed., *Hamilton Papers,* 3: 605–8.

21. HL to James Cogswell & William Shotwell, 16 July 1785, to Jacob Read, 16 July 1785, 15 September 1785, Henry Laurens Papers, SCHS. The available documents do not reveal HL's final decision regarding Frederic.

22. HL to David Ramsay, 7 July 1790, Henry Laurens Papers, South Caroliniana Library; HL to Alexander Hamilton, 19 April 1785, in Syrett, ed., *Hamilton Papers,* 3: 607 (quotation).

23. Bowling, et al., eds., *Revolutionary War-Related Claims,* 7: 24–27, 262–70.

24. Wallace, *Life of Henry Laurens,* 430–31.

25. Martha Laurens Ramsay to David Ramsay, 17 December 1792, in Ramsay, *Memoirs of Martha Laurens Ramsay,* 207–10; for HL's will, see *In Equity. Charleston District. Jacob K. Sass, Executor of Wm. C. Gatewood v. Eliza R. Toomer, et al.* (Charleston, S.C.: A. J. Burke, 1861), 51–56, (quotation on 56), in Henry Laurens Papers, SCHS.

26. *Sass v. Toomer,* 51–56, in Henry Laurens Papers, SCHS; David Ramsay to Benjamin Rush, 29 September 1788, in Brunhouse, ed., *David Ramsay,* 122–23; Shaffer, *To Be an American,* 206–17.

27. Ramsay, *History of South Carolina,* 1: 250–51; on Ramsay as a historian, see Shaffer, *To Be an American,* 104–27 (quotation on 104).

28. Wallace, *Life of Henry Laurens,* 431, Appendix 3, Gillespie, "Martha Laurens Ramsay's 'Dark Night of the Soul,'" 68–92; the description of Francis Henderson was printed in *Abbeville Press and Banner* (Abbeville, S.C.), 19 April 1876; see also Affidavit of David Ramsay, 13 July 1813, Veterans' Administration, RG 15, Revolutionary War Pension File, John Laurens, S.C., NA.

29. Shaffer, *To Be an American,* 206–17; Gillespie, "Martha Laurens Ramsay's 'Dark Night of the Soul,'" 67–73; Ramsay, *Memoirs of Martha Laurens Ramsay.*

30. For Harry's estate, see Edgar, et al., eds., *Biographical Directory,* 3: 416; for his will, see *Sass v. Toomer,* 57–58, in Henry Laurens Papers, SCHS; regarding the snuffbox, see also *Francis Henderson, et al. v. Henry Laurens, Administrator of John Laurens,* 1 June 1804, Court of Equity, Charleston District Decree Book, 1795–1806, 262–65, South Carolina Department of Archives and History. On Ramsay's debt, see Shaffer, *To Be an American,* 248.

31. *Abbeville Press and Banner* (Abbeville, S.C.), 19 April 1876; Blanding and McCord, eds., *Carolina Law Journal*, 136, 139.

32. For the first of these efforts, see Joseph Nourse to William H. Crawford, 21 February 1817, 20 March 1818, William H. Crawford to Jonathan Roberts, 22 February 1817, 27 March 1818, Records of the U.S. Senate, RG 46, 15A-61, NA.

33. Simms, *Army Correspondence*, 41–44; Francis Henderson Sr. to John Adams, 3 January 1822, Adams to Henderson, 11 January 1822, Adams Papers, reel 454, reel 124, MHS; *Memorial and Petition of Francis Henderson and Francis Henderson, Jun.*, 7 (quotation); for the Senate debates, see *Debates and Proceedings in Congress*, 47, 77, 82, 85–87, 91–95, 97–100, 305–7.

34. Ibid., 92–94.

35. See Rogers, "South Carolina Federalists," 17–32; and Weir, "The South Carolinian as Extremist," 213–30.

36. *Memorial and Petition of Francis Henderson and Francis Henderson, Jun.*, 4.

37. *Register of Debates in Congress*, 8: 110–13, 939–43, 3867 (quotation on 110); Congress, House, 22d Cong., 1st sess., H.R. 386; R. Harrison to Mr. St. Clair Clarke, 20 August 1832, Records of the U.S. Senate, RG 46, NA; Congress, Senate, 23d Congress, 2d sess., S. 100.

38. *Abbeville Press and Banner* (Abbeville, S.C.), 19 April 1876. According to this narrative, Henderson, having been told that Fanny died in childbirth, started drinking after he discovered that she was alive. See also *In Equity. Charleston District. William C. Gatewood v. Eliza R. Toomer, et al.* (Charleston, S.C.: A. J. Burke, 1860), 2, in Henry Laurens Papers, SCHS.

39. *Gatewood v. Toomer*, 2; and *Sass v. Toomer*, 5–6, both in Henry Laurens Papers, SCHS.

Epilogue

1. HL to JL, 21 September 1779, Henry Laurens Papers, SCHS.

2. HL to JL, 28 January 1778, in *Laurens Papers*, 12: 368.

3. In the eighteenth century slavery paradoxically buttressed republicanism and freedom. See Edmund S. Morgan, *American Slavery—American Freedom*, especially 363–87.

4. JL to HL, 23 January 1778, in *Laurens Papers*, 12: 330.

Bibliography

Unpublished Manuscripts

American Philosophical Society, Philadelphia, Pennsylvania. Franklin Papers.

Boston Public Library, Boston, Massachusetts. Chamberlain Collection. Benjamin Lincoln Letterbook.

Charleston Museum, Charleston, S.C. Manuscript Collection.

Chicago Historical Society, Chicago, Illinois. Charles F. Gunther Collection.

Tutt Library, Colorado College, Colorado Springs. Special Collections.

Connecticut Historical Society, Hartford. Jonathan Trumbull Sr. Papers.

David Library of the American Revolution, Washington Crossing, Pennsylvania. Sol Feinstone Collection (on deposit at American Philosophical Society).

Rare Book, Manuscript, & Special Collections Library, Duke University, Durham, North Carolina. Nathanael Greene Papers. Henry Laurens Papers.

The Houghton Library, Harvard University, Cambridge, Massachusetts. Jared Sparks Collection.

Historical Society of Pennsylvania, Philadelphia. Commonplace Book of John Laurens. Dreer Collection. Etting Collection. Gratz Collection. Charles F. Jenkins Collection. Thomas McKean Papers. Washington-Biddle Correspondence. Anthony Wayne Papers.

Henry E. Huntington Library, San Marino, California. Greene File. Robert Alonzo Brock Collection. William Jones Rhees Collection.

Kendall Whaling Museum, Sharon, Massachusetts. Henry W. Kendall Collection of Laurens Papers.

Library of Congress (Manuscript Division), Washington, D.C. Thomas Bee Papers. Nathanael Greene Papers. Alexander Hamilton Papers. Henry Laurens and John Laurens Collection. George Washington Papers (microfilm).

Maine Historical Society, Portland. J. S. H. Fogg Autograph Collection.

Marietta College Library, Marietta, Ohio. Charles Goddard Slack Collection.

Maryland Historical Society, Baltimore. Gilmor Papers, MS 387.1. Gist Papers (microfilm), MS 390. Otho Holland Williams Papers, MS 908.

Massachusetts Historical Society, Boston. Adams Papers (microfilm). Benjamin Lincoln Papers (microfilm).

William L. Clements Library, University of Michigan, Ann Arbor. Nathanael Greene Papers (microfilm).

Ministère des Affaires Étrangères, Paris. Correspondence Politique, États-Unis (microfilm and transcripts at Library of Congress).

Morristown National Historical Park, Morristown, New Jersey. Lloyd W. Smith Collection.

National Archives, Washington, D.C. Papers of the Continental Congress (microfilm). Records of the U.S. Senate. Veteran's Administration (Revolutionary War Pension File).

New-York Historical Society, New York. Gates Papers. Nathanael Greene Orderly Book. Misc. MSS Holzendorrf, Baron. Misc. MSS Laurens, John. Vail Collection.

Manuscript Division, The New York Public Library, Astor, Lenox and Tilden Foundations. Thomas Addis Emmet Collection. Henry Laurens Diary, 1780–81. Miscellaneous Manuscripts. Miscellaneous Papers (John Laurens). Myers Collection.

New York State Library, Albany, New York. Philip Schuyler Papers.

Princeton University Library, (Manuscripts Division, Department of Rare Books & Special Collections), Princeton, New Jersey. Andre de Coppet Collection.

Public Record Office, London, England. British Headquarters Papers (Sir Guy Carleton Papers) (microfilm). Colonial Office. High Court of Admiralty. War Office.

Sheffield Archives, Sheffield City Libraries, England. Wentworth Woodhouse Muniments (4th Earl Fitzwilliam's Correspondence).

South Carolina Department of Archives and History, Columbia. Court of Equity, Charleston District Decree Book, 1795–1806.

South Carolina Historical Society, Charleston. Major Gibbes Orderly Book. Henry Laurens Papers. John Laurens Papers. Gabriel Manigault Diary.

South Caroliniana Library, University of South Carolina, Columbia. Henry Laurens Papers. John Laurens Papers. Manigault Family Papers.

University of Virginia Library (Manuscript Department and University Archives), Charlottesville. Lee Collection.

Beinecke Rare Book and Manuscript Library, Yale University, New Haven, Connecticut. Franklin Collection.

Manuscripts and Archives, Yale University Library, New Haven, Connecticut. William Jackson Papers.

Contemporary Publications, Published Documents, and Memoirs

Abbot, W. W., ed. *The Papers of George Washington: Confederation Series.* 6 vols. Charlottesville: University Press of Virginia, 1992–97.

Acomb, Evelyn M., ed. *The Revolutionary Journal of Baron Ludwig Von Closen, 1780–1783.* Chapel Hill: University of North Carolina Press, 1958.

"An Account of two new Tortoises; in a Letter to Matthew Maty, Sec. R.S.: By Thomas Pennant, Esq., F.R.S." *Philosophical Transactions of the Royal Society* 61 (1771): 267–71.

Barnwell, Joseph W., ed. "Correspondence of Hon. Arthur Middleton, Signer of the Declaration of Independence." Parts 1 and 2. *South Carolina Historical Magazine* 26 (October 1925): 183–213; 27 (January 1926): 1–29.

———. "Letters of John Rutledge." *South Carolina Historical Magazine* 18 (October 1917): 155–67.

Bartlett, John Russell, ed. *Records of the State of Rhode Island and Providence Plantations in New England.* 10 vols. Providence, R.I.: Cooke, Jackson, 1856–63.

Bennett, Major C. P. "The Delaware Regiment in the Revolution." *Pennsylvania Magazine of History and Biography* 9 (October 1885): 451–62.

Blanding, A., and D. J. McCord, eds. *Carolina Law Journal.* Columbia, S.C.: Times and Gazette Office, 1831.

Bowling, Kenneth R., William Charles diGiacomantonio, and Charlene Bangs Bickford, eds. *Documentary History of the First Federal Congress, 1789–1791.* Volume 7, *Petition Histories: Revolutionary War-Related Claims.* Baltimore: Johns Hopkins University Press, 1997.

Boyle, Joseph Lee, ed. "The Revolutionary War Diaries of Captain Walter Finney." *South Carolina Historical Magazine* 98 (April 1997): 126–52.

Brunhouse, Robert L., ed. *David Ramsay, 1749–1815: Selections from his Writings. Transactions of the American Philosophical Society.* New ser. 55. Philadelphia: American Philosophical Society, 1965.

Budka, Metchie J. E., ed. *Autograph Letters of Thaddeus Kosciuszko in the American Revolution.* Chicago: Polish Museum of America, 1977.

Butterfield, L. H., ed. *Diary and Autobiography of John Adams.* 4 vols. Cambridge: Harvard University Press, 1961.

Candler, Allen D., ed. *The Revolutionary Records of the State of Georgia.* 3 vols. Atlanta: Franklin-Turner, 1908.

Chastellux, Marquis de. *Travels in North America in the Years 1780, 1781, and 1782.* Edited by Howard C. Rice Jr. 2 vols. Chapel Hill: University of North Carolina Press, 1963.

Cooper, Thomas, and David J. McCord, eds. *The Statutes at Large of South Carolina.* 10 vols. Columbia, S.C.: A. S. Johnston, 1836–41.

Day, Thomas. *Fragment of an Original Letter on the Slavery of the Negroes Written in the Year 1776.* Philadelphia: Francis Bailey, 1784.

Deane Papers, The. 5 vols. New-York Historical Society Collections. New York: n.p., 1887–91.

Debates and Proceedings in the Congress of the United States. 18th Cong. Washington, D.C.: Gales & Seaton, 1856.

Dodd, Mead, & Company's Catalogue of Autographs and Manuscripts (November 1905). Held in American Antiquarian Society, Worcester, Massachusetts.

Doniol, Henri, ed. *Histoire de la participation de la France à L'etablishment Des Etats-Unis D'Amerique.* 5 vols. Paris: Imprimerie Nationale, 1888.

Edgeworth, R. L., and Maria Edgeworth. *Memoirs of Richard Lovell Edgeworth, Esq. Begun by Himself and Concluded by his Daughter, Maria Edgeworth.* 2 vols. London: Hunter, 1820.

"Extract from the Diary of William Rawle, Esq." *Pennsylvania Magazine of History and Biography* 22 (April 1898): 253.

"Extracts from the Journal of Lieutenant John Bell Tilden, Second Pennsylvania Line, 1781–1782." *Pennsylvania Magazine of History and Biography* 19 (April 1895): 208–33.

Feltman, William. *The Journal of Lieut. William Feltman, of the First Pennsylvania Regiment, 1781–82.* 1853. Reprint, New York: Arno Press, 1969.

Ferguson, E. James, John Catanzariti, Elizabeth M. Nuxoll, and Mary A. Gallagher, eds. *The Papers of Robert Morris.* 9 vols. to date. Pittsburgh: University of Pittsburgh Press, 1973– .

Fitzpatrick, John C., ed. *The Writings of George Washington from the Original Manuscript Sources 1745–1799.* 39 vols. Washington, D.C.: Government Printing Office, 1931–44.

Foner, Philip S., ed. *The Complete Writings of Thomas Paine.* 2 vols. New York: Citadel Press, 1945.

Ford, Worthington C., ed. *Journals of the Continental Congress, 1774–1789.* 34 vols. Washington, D.C.: Government Printing Office, 1904–37.

Garden, Alexander. *Anecdotes of the American Revolution.* 2d ser. Charleston: A. E. Miller, 1828.

———. *Anecdotes of the Revolutionary War in America.* 1822. Reprint, Spartanburg, S.C.: Reprint Company, 1972.

Gibbes, R. W., ed. *Documentary History of the American Revolution.* 3 vols. New York: D. Appleton, 1857.

Goethe, Johann Wolfgang von. *The Sufferings of Young Werther.* Translated by Bayard Quincy Morgan. New York: Frederick Unger, 1957.

Gordon, William. *The History of the Rise, Progress, and Establishment of the Independence of the United States of America.* 4 vols. London: n.p., 1788.

Graydon, Alexander. *Memoirs of His Own Times: with Reminiscences of the Men and Events of the Revolution.* Edited by John Stockton Littell. Philadelphia: Lindsay & Blakiston, 1846.

Hamer, Philip M., George C. Rogers Jr., David R. Chesnutt, C. James Taylor, and Peggy J. Clark, eds. *The Papers of Henry Laurens.* 15 vols. to date. Columbia: University of South Carolina Press, 1968– .

Hamilton, John C. *The Life of Alexander Hamilton.* 2d ed. 2 vols. New York: D. Appleton, 1840–41.

Hammond, Otis G., ed. *Letters and Papers of Major-General John Sullivan.* 3 vols. *Collections* of the New Hampshire Historical Society, vols. 13–15. Concord, N.H.: New Hampshire Historical Society, 1930–39.

Hastings, Hugh, ed. *Public Papers of George Clinton, First Governor of New York.* 10 vols. Albany, N.Y.: State Printer, 1899–1914.

Hemphill, William Edwin, Wylma Anne Wates, and R. Nicholas Olsberg, eds. *Journals of the General Assembly and House of Representatives 1776–1780.* Columbia: University of South Carolina Press, 1970.

Hough, Franklin Benjamin, ed. *The Siege of Savannah.* 1866. Reprint, New York: De Capo Press, 1974.

Howe, Mark Antony De Wolfe, ed. "Journal of Josiah Quincy, Junior, 1773." Massachusetts Historical Society *Proceedings* 49 (June 1916): 424–81.

Idzerda, Stanley J., ed. *Lafayette in the Age of the American Revoluton: Letters and Papers, 1776–1790.* 5 vols. Ithaca, N.Y.: Cornell University Press, 1979–83.

Institut Français de Washington, ed. *Correspondence of General Washington and Comte De Grasse.* Washington, D.C.: Government Printing Office, 1931.

Jackson, Donald, and Dorothy Twohig, eds. *The Diaries of George Washington.* 6 vols. Charlottesville: University Press of Virginia, 1976–79.

Jefferson, Thomas. *Notes on the State of Virginia.* Edited by William Peden. Chapel Hill: University of North Carolina Press, 1955.

Johnson, Joseph. *Traditions and Reminiscences Chiefly of the American Revolution in the South.* 1851. Reprint, Spartanburg, S.C.: Reprint Company, 1972.

Johnson, William. *Sketches of the Life and Correspondence of Nathanael Greene, Major General of the Armies of the United States, in the War of the Revolution.* 2 vols. 1822. Reprint, New York: De Capo Press, 1973.

Keate, George. *A Short Account of the Ancient History, Present Government, and Laws of the Republic of Geneva.* London: R. & J. Dodsley, 1761.

Lee Papers, The. 4 vols. New-York Historical Society *Collections.* New York: n.p., 1871–74.

Lee, Henry. *Memoirs of the War in the Southern Department of the United States.* New York: University Publishing Company, 1869.

Locke, John. *Two Treatises of Government.* Edited by Peter Laslett. 2d ed. Cambridge: Cambridge University Press, 1970.

Mackenzie, Frederick. *The Diary of Frederick Mackenzie.* 2 vols. Cambridge: Harvard University Press, 1930. Reprint, New York: Arno Press, 1968.

Memorial and Petition of Francis Henderson and Francis Henderson, Jun. On Behalf of Themselves and Family, Heirs and Representatives of John Laurens, Deceased. 20th Cong. Washington, D.C.: Gales & Seaton, 1827.

Miller, Lillian B., ed. *The Selected Papers of Charles Willson Peale and His Family.* 4 vols. to date. New Haven: Yale University Press, 1983– .

Montesquieu, Charles Louis de Secondat, Baron de. *The Spirit of the Laws.* Translated by Thomas Nugent. New York: Hafner Press, 1949.

Moore, Frank, ed. *Correspondence of Henry Laurens, of South Carolina, 1776–1782.* New York: Zenger Club, 1861.

Morris, Richard B., ed. *John Jay, The Winning of the Peace: Unpublished Papers, 1780–1784.* New York: Harper & Row, 1980.

Moultrie, William. *Memoirs of the American Revolution.* 2 vols. 1802. Reprint, New York: Arno Press, 1968.

Murdoch, Richard K., trans. "A French Account of the Siege of Charleston, 1780." *South Carolina Historical Magazine* 67 (July 1966): 138–54.

"Order Book of John Faucheraud Grimké." *South Carolina Historical Magazine* 16 (October 1915): 178–83.

"Original Letters 1775–89 Period." In *Yearbook of the City of Charleston.* Charleston, S.C.: 1882.

Quincy, Josiah, ed. *The Journals of Samuel Shaw, the First American Consul at Canton. With a Life of the Author.* Boston: Wm. Crosby & H. P. Nichols, 1847.

Ramsay, David. *History of South Carolina, From Its First Settlement in 1670 to the Year 1808.* 2 vols. Newberry, S.C.: W. J. Duffie, 1858.

———. *The History of the Revolution of South-Carolina, from a British Province to an Independent State.* 2 vols. Trenton, N.J.: Isaac Collins, 1785.

———. *Memoirs of the Life of Martha Laurens Ramsay.* 2d ed. Charleston, S.C.: Samuel Etheridge, 1812.

Register of Debates in Congress. 14 vols. Washington, D.C.: Gales & Seaton, 1825–37.

Ross, Charles, ed. *Correspondence of Charles, First Marquis Cornwallis.* 2d ed. 3 vols. London: John Murray, 1859.

Rubinfine, Joseph. *Joseph Rubinfine: Autographs-Manuscripts Historical Americana.* List 81.

Salley, Alexander S., ed. "Horry's Notes to Weems' *Life of Marion.*" *South Carolina Historical Magazine* 60 (July 1959): 119–22.

———. *Journal of the House of Representatives of South Carolina: January 8, 1782–February 26, 1782.* Columbia, S.C.: The State, 1916.

Seymour, William. "A Journal of the Southern Expedition, 1780–1783." *Pennsylvania Magazine of History and Biography* 17 (October 1893): 377–94.

Showman, Richard K., and Dennis R. Conrad, eds. *The Papers of General Nathanael Greene.* 10 vols. to date. Chapel Hill: University of North Carolina Press, 1976– .

"Siege of Charleston—1780, The." In *Yearbook of the City of Charleston.* Charleston, S.C.: 1897.

Simms, William Gilmore. *The Army Correspondence of Colonel John Laurens in the Years 1777–8.* 1867. Reprint, New York: Arno Press, 1969.

Smith, Adam. *The Theory of Moral Sentiments.* 1759. Reprint, Indianapolis, Ind.: Liberty Classics, 1976.

Smith, D. E. Huger, ed. "The Mission of Col. John Laurens to Europe in 1781." *South Carolina Historical Magazine* 1 (January–October 1900): 13–41, 136–51, 213–22, 311–22; 2 (January–April 1901): 27–43, 108–25.

Smith, Paul H., ed. *Letters of Delegates to Congress, 1774–1789.* 25 vols. Washington, D.C.: Library of Congress, 1976–98.

Southerne, Thomas. *Oronooko.* Edited by Maxmillian E. Novak and David S. Rodes. Lincoln: University of Nebraska Press, 1976.

Sparks, Jared, ed. *The Diplomatic Correspondence of the American Revolution.* 12 vols. Boston: Nathan Hale and Gray & Bowen, 1829–30.

Steiner, Bernard C., ed. *The Life and Correspondence of James McHenry.* Cleveland: Burrows Brothers, 1907.

Stevens, B. F., ed. *Facsimiles of Manuscripts in European Archives Relating to America 1775–1783.* 25 vols. 1889–95. Reprint, Wilmington, Del.: Mellifont Press, 1970.

Syrett, Harold C., ed. *The Papers of Alexander Hamilton.* 27 vols. New York: Columbia University Press, 1961–87.

Thatcher, James. *Military Journal of the American Revolution.* 1862. Reprint, New York: Arno Press, 1969.

Tilghman, Oswald, ed. *Memoir of Lieut. Col. Tench Tilghman, Secretary and Aid to Washington.* Albany, N.Y.: J. Munsell, 1876.

Thompson, Theodora J., and Rosa S. Lumpkin, eds. *Journals of the House of Representatives, 1783–1784.* Columbia: University of South Carolina Press, 1977.

Uhlendorf, Bernhard A, ed. *The Siege of Charleston.* Ann Arbor: University of Michigan Press, 1938.

Walsh, Richard, ed. *The Writings of Christopher Gadsden.* Columbia: University of South Carolina Press, 1966.

Warren, Mercy Otis. *History of the Rise, Progress and Termination of the American Revolution.* 3 vols. Boston: Manning & Loring, 1805.

Webber, Mabel Louise, ed. "Revolutionary Letters." *South Carolina Historical Magazine* 38 (January 1937): 1–10.

Weems, Mason Locke. *The Life of Gen. Francis Marion.* 2d ed. Baltimore: W. F. Bell & J. F. Cook, 1814.

Weir, Robert M., ed. *The Letters of Freeman, Etc.: Essays on the Nonimportation Movement in South Carolina.* Columbia: University of South Carolina Press, 1977.

————. "Muster Rolls of the South Carolina Granville and Colleton County Regiments of Militia, 1756." *South Carolina Historical Magazine* 70 (October 1969): 226–39.

Wharton, Francis, ed. *The Revolutionary Diplomatic Correspondence of the United States.* 6 vols. Washington, D.C.: Government Printing Office, 1889.

Yorke, Philip C., ed. *The Diary of John Baker.* London: Hutchinson & Co., 1931.

Microform Editions

Schweninger, Loren, ed. *Race, Slavery, and Free Blacks: Petitions to Southern Legislatures, 1777–1867.* Bethesda, Md.: University Publications of America, 1998. Microfilm.

Zemensky, Edith von, ed. *The Papers of General Friedrich Wilhelm von Steuben, 1777–1794.* Millwood, N.Y.: Kraus International Publications, 1982. Microfilm.

Classical Literature

Aristotle. *Introduction to Aristotle.* Edited by Richard McKean. New York: Modern Library, 1947.

Plutarch. *Lives of the Noble Greeks.* Edited by Edmund Fuller. New York: Dell Publishing Co., 1972.

Newspapers

Abbeville Press and Banner (Abbeville, S.C.)
Pennsylvania Packet (Philadelphia)
Royal Gazette (Charleston)
South-Carolina Gazette (Charleston)
South-Carolina Gazette & General Advertiser (Charleston)
The Gazette of the State of South Carolina (Charleston)
South-Carolina and American General Gazette (Charleston)
The Virginia Gazette, or, the American Advertiser (Richmond: James Mayes)

Books

Alden, John R. *General Charles Lee: Traitor or Patriot?* Baton Rouge: Louisiana State University Press, 1951.

————. *George Washington: A Biography.* Baton Rouge: Louisiana State University Press, 1984.

Alvarez, A. *The Savage God: A Study of Suicide.* New York: Random House, 1972.

Bailyn, Bernard. *The Ideological Origins of the American Revolution.* Cambridge: Harvard University Press, 1967.

Barker-Benfield, G. J. *The Culture of Sensibility: Sex and Society in Eighteenth-Century Britain.* Chicago and London: University of Chicago Press, 1992.

Becker, Ernest. *The Denial of Death.* New York: The Free Press, 1973.

Bellows, Barbara L. *Benevolence among Slaveholders: Assisting the Poor in Charleston 1670–1860.* Baton Rouge: Louisiana State University Press, 1993.

Bemis, Samuel Flagg. *The Diplomacy of the American Revolution.* New York: D. Appleton-Century, 1935. Reprint, Bloomington: Indiana University Press, 1957.

Berkeley, Edmund, and Dorothy Smith Berkeley. *Dr. Alexander Garden of Charles Town*. Chapel Hill: University of North Carolina Press, 1969.

Bosher, J. F. *French Finances, 1770–1795: From Business to Bureaucracy*. Cambridge: Cambridge University Press, 1970.

Boyle, Nicholas. *Goethe: The Poet and the Age*. Vol. 1, *The Poetry of Desire, 1749–1790*. Oxford: Clarendon Press, 1991.

Brant, Irving. *James Madison: The Nationalist, 1780–1787*. New York: Bobbs-Merrill, 1948.

Brown, Dale. *Understanding Pietism*. Grand Rapids, Mich.: William B. Eerdmans, 1978.

Burnett, Edmund Cody. *The Continental Congress*. New York: The Macmillan Company, 1941.

Bushman, Richard L. *The Refinement of America: Persons, Houses, Cities*. New York: Alfred A. Knopf, 1992.

Butler, Jon. *The Huguenots in America: A Refugee People in New World Society*. Cambridge: Harvard University Press, 1983.

Canady, Hoyt P. *Gentleman of the Bar: Lawyers in Colonial South Carolina*. New York: Garland Publishing, Inc., 1987.

Carp, E. Wayne. *To Starve the Army at Pleasure: Continental Army Administration and American Political Culture 1775–1783*. Chapel Hill: University of North Carolina Press, 1984.

Chaplin, Joyce E. *An Anxious Pursuit: Agricultural Innovation and Modernity in the Lower South, 1730–1815*. Chapel Hill: University of North Carolina Press, 1993.

Coclanis, Peter A. *The Shadow of a Dream: Economic Life and Death in the South Carolina Low Country, 1670–1920*. New York: Oxford University Press, 1989.

Coleman, Kenneth. *The American Revolution in Georgia, 1763–1789*. Athens: University of Georgia Press, 1958.

Connell, R. W. *Masculinities*. Berkeley and Los Angeles: University of California Press, 1995.

Cooke, Jacob Ernest. *Alexander Hamilton*. New York: Charles Scribner's Sons, 1982.

Corwin, Edward S. *French Policy and the American Alliance of 1778*. Princeton: Princeton University Press, 1916.

Davis, David Brion. *The Problem of Slavery in the Age of Revolution 1770–1823*. Ithaca, N.Y.: Cornell University Press, 1975.

———. *The Problem of Slavery in Western Culture*. Ithaca, N.Y.: Cornell University Press, 1966.

Dearden, Paul F. *The Rhode Island Campaign of 1778: Inauspicious Dawn of Alliance*. Providence: Rhode Island Bicentennial Foundation, 1980.

Dover, K. J. *Greek Homosexuality*. New York: Vintage Books, 1980.

Duffy, Christopher. *The Military Experience in the Age of Reason*. New York: Atheneum, 1988.

Dull, Jonathan R. *A Diplomatic History of the American Revolution*. New Haven: Yale University Press, 1985.

———. *Franklin the Diplomat: The French Mission. Transactions of the American Philosophical Society*. New ser., pt. 1, 72. Philadelphia: American Philosophical Society, 1982.

———. *The French Navy and American Independence: A Study of Arms and Diplomacy, 1774–1787*. Princeton: Princeton University Press, 1975.

Duman, Daniel. *The Judicial Bench in England 1737–1875: The Reshaping of a Professional Elite*. London: Royal Historical Society, 1982.

Durant, Will, and Ariel Durant. *The Story of Civilization*. Vol. 9, *The Age of Voltaire*. New York: Simon and Schuster, 1965.

Durkheim, Emile. *Suicide: A Study in Sociology*. Translated by John A. Spaulding and George Simpson. New York: The Free Press, 1951.

Edgar, Walter B., N. Louise Bailey, Elizabeth Ivey Cooper, and Alexander Moore, eds. *Biographical Directory of the South Carolina House of Representatives*, 5 vols. to date. Columbia: University of South Carolina Press, 1974– .

Fedden, Henry Romilly. *Suicide: A Social and Historical Study*. London: Peter Davies, 1938. Reprint, New York: Benjamin Blom, Inc., 1972.

Ferguson, E. James. *The Power of the Purse: A History of American Public Finance, 1776–1790*. Chapel Hill: University of North Carolina Press, 1961.

Ferling, John. *The First of Men: A Life of George Washington*. Knoxville: University of Tennessee Press, 1988.

Flexner, James Thomas. *George Washington in the American Revolution (1775–1783)*. Boston: Little, Brown, 1967.

Fliegelman, Jay. *Prodigals and Pilgrims: The American Revolution against Patriarchal Authority, 1750–1800*. Cambridge: Cambridge University Press, 1982.

Freehling, William W. *The Road to Disunion: Secessionists at Bay, 1776–1854*. New York: Oxford University Press, 1990.

Freeman, Douglas Southall. *George Washington: A Biography*. Vol. 4, *Leader of the Revolution*. New York: Charles Scribner's Sons, 1951.

———. *George Washington: A Biography*. Vol. 5, *Victory with the Help of France*. New York: Charles Scribner's Sons, 1952.

Frey, Sylvia R. *Water from the Rock: Black Resistance in a Revolutionary Age*. Princeton: Princeton University Press, 1991.

Gignilliat, George Warren Jr. *The Author of Sandford and Merton: A Life of Thomas Day, Esq*. New York: Columbia University Press, 1932.

Gilbert, Felix. *To the Farewell Address: Ideas of Early American Foreign Policy*. Princeton: Princeton University Press, 1961.

Gottschalk, Louis. *Lafayette and the Close of the American Revolution*. Chicago: University of Chicago Press, 1942.

———. *Lafayette Joins the American Army*. Chicago: University of Chicago Press, 1937.

Greenblatt, Stephen. *Renaissance Self-Fashioning: From More to Shakespeare*. Chicago and London: University of Chicago Press, 1980.

Greene, Jack P. *The Quest for Power: The Lower Houses of Assembly in the Southern Royal Colonies, 1689–1776*. Chapel Hill: University of North Carolina Press, 1963.

Greven, Philip. *The Protestant Temperament: Patterns of Child-Rearing, Religious Experience, and the Self in Early America*. New York: Alfred A. Knopf, 1977.

Gruber, Ira D. *The Howe Brothers and the American Revolution*. New York: Atheneum, 1972.

Haw, James. *John and Edward Rutledge of South Carolina*. Athens and London: University of Georgia Press, 1997.

Hawke, David Freeman, *Paine*. New York: Harper & Row, 1974.

Heilbrun, Carolyn G. *Writing a Woman's Life*. New York: W. W. Norton, 1988.

Heitman, Francis B. *Historical Register of Officers of the Continental Army During the War of the Revolution.* Washington, D.C.: Rare Book Shop, 1914.

Henderson, H. James. *Party Politics in the Continental Congress.* New York: McGraw-Hill, 1974.

Higginbotham, Don. *The War of American Independence: Military Attitudes, Policies, and Practice, 1763–1789.* New York: Macmillan, 1971.

Hindle, Brooke. *The Pursuit of Science in Revolutionary America.* Chapel Hill: University of North Carolina Press, 1956.

Hirsch, Arthur Henry. *The Huguenots of Colonial South Carolina.* Durham, N.C.: Duke University Press, 1928.

Hoffman, Ronald, Mechal Sobel, and Fredrika J. Teute, eds. *Through a Glass Darkly: Reflections on Personal Identity in Early America.* Chapel Hill and London: University of North Carolina Press, 1997.

Howe, Daniel Walker. *Making the American Self: Jonathan Edwards to Abraham Lincoln.* Cambridge and London: Harvard University Press, 1997.

Hutson, James H. *John Adams and the Diplomacy of the American Revolution.* Lexington: University Press of Kentucky, 1980.

James, William. *The Principles of Psychology.* 2 vols. New York: Henry Holt & Co., 1890. Reprint, New York: Dover Publications, 1950.

———. *The Varieties of Religious Experience: A Study in Human Nature.* New York: Longmans, Green, 1902.

Jensen, Merrill. *The Founding of a Nation: A History of the American Revolution, 1763–1776.* New York: Oxford University Press, 1968.

Jordan, Winthrop D. *White over Black: American Attitudes Toward the Negro, 1550–1812.* Chapel Hill: University of North Carolina Press, 1968.

Kiernan, V. G. *The Duel in European History: Honour and the Reign of Aristocracy.* Oxford: Oxford University Press, 1988.

Kimmel, Michael. *Manhood in America.* New York: The Free Press, 1996.

Klein, Rachel N. *Unification of a Slave State: The Rise of the Planter Class in the South Carolina Backcountry, 1760–1808.* Chapel Hill: University of North Carolina Press, 1990.

Knollenberg, Bernhard. *Washington and the Revolution: A Reappraisal.* New York: Macmillan, 1940.

Kramnick, Isaac. *Republicanism and Bourgeois Radicalism: Political Ideology in Late Eighteenth-Century England and America.* Ithaca, N.Y. and London: Cornell University Press, 1990.

Kushner, Howard I. *American Suicide: A Psychocultural Exploration.* New Brunswick, N.J.: Rutgers University Press, 1989.

Kwasny, Mark V. *Washington's Partisan War, 1775–1783.* Kent, Ohio and London: Kent State University Press, 1996.

Lambert, Robert Stansbury. *South Carolina Loyalists in the American Revolution.* Columbia: University of South Carolina Press, 1987.

Langford, Paul. *A Polite and Commercial People: England, 1727–1783.* Oxford: Clarendon Press, 1989.

Lawrence, Alexander A. *Storm over Savannah: The Story of Count d'Estaing and the Siege of the Town in 1779.* 2d ed. Athens: University of Georgia Press, 1968.

Lemmings, David. *Gentlemen and Barristers: The Inns of Court and the English Bar, 1680–1730.* Oxford: Clarendon Press, 1990.

Lifton, Robert Jay. *The Broken Connection: On Death and the Continuity of Life.* New York: Simon and Schuster, 1979.

Lockridge, Kenneth. *On the Sources of Patriarchal Rage: The Commonplace Books of William Byrd and Thomas Jefferson and the Gendering of Power in the Eighteenth Century.* New York and London: New York University Press, 1992.

McColley, Robert. *Slavery and Jeffersonian Virginia.* Urbana: University of Illinois Press, 1964.

McCowen, George Smith Jr. *The British Occupation of Charleston, 1780–82.* Columbia: University of South Carolina Press, 1972.

McCoy, Drew R. *The Elusive Republic: Political Economy in Jeffersonian America.* Chapel Hill: University of North Carolina Press, 1980.

McCrady, Edward. *The History of South Carolina in the Revolution, 1775–1780.* New York: Macmillan, 1901.

———. *The History of South Carolina in the Revolution, 1780–1783.* New York: Macmillan, 1902.

McDonald, Forrest. *Alexander Hamilton: A Biography.* New York: W. W. Norton, 1979.

———. *Novus Ordo Seclorum: The Intellectual Origins of the Constitution.* Lawrence: University Press of Kansas, 1985.

Mackesy, Piers. *The War for America 1775–1783.* Cambridge: Harvard University Press, 1964.

MacLeod, Duncan. *Slavery, Race and the American Revolution.* London: Cambridge University Press, 1974.

Maris, Ronald W. *Pathways to Suicide: A Survey of Self-Destructive Behaviors.* Baltimore: Johns Hopkins University Press, 1981.

Mascuch, Michael. *Origins of the Individualist Self: Autobiography and Self-Identity in England, 1591–1791.* Stanford, Calif.: Stanford University Press, 1996.

Mattern, David B. *Benjamin Lincoln and the American Revolution.* Colombia: University of South Carolina Press, 1995.

Menninger, Karl A. *Man against Himself.* New York: Harcourt, Brace, 1938.

Middlekauff, Robert. *The Glorious Cause: The American Revolution, 1763–1789.* New York: Oxford University Press, 1982.

Miller, John C. *Alexander Hamilton: Portrait in Paradox.* New York: Harper & Brothers, 1959.

Mitchell, Broadus. *Alexander Hamilton: Youth to Maturity 1755–1788.* New York: Macmillan, 1957.

Morgan, Edmund S. *American Slavery—American Freedom: The Ordeal of Colonial Virginia.* New York: W. W. Norton, 1975.

———. *The Meaning of Independence: John Adams, George Washington, and Thomas Jefferson.* New York: W. W. Norton, 1976.

Morgan, Philip D. *Slave Counterpoint: Black Culture in the Eighteenth-Century Chesapeake and Lowcountry.* Chapel Hill and London: University of North Carolina Press, 1998.

Morris, Richard B. *The Peacemakers: The Great Powers and American Independence.* New York: Harper & Row, 1965.

Nadelhaft, Jerome J. *The Disorders of War: The Revolution in South Carolina.* Orono, Maine: University of Maine at Orono Press, 1981.

Nash, Gary B. *Race and Revolution.* Madison, Wis.: Madison House, 1990.

Norton, Mary Beth. *Liberty's Daughters: The Revolutionary Experience of American Women, 1750–1800*. Boston: Little, Brown, 1980.

Olwell, Robert. *Masters, Slaves, and Subjects: The Culture of Power in the South Carolina Low Country, 1740–1790*. Ithaca, N.Y. and London: Cornell University Press, 1998.

Palmer, John McAuley. *General Von Steuben*. New Haven: Yale University Press, 1937. Reprint, Port Washington, N.Y.: Kennikat Press, 1966.

Palmer, R. R. *The Age of Democratic Revolution, A Political History of Europe and America, 1760–1800: The Challenge*. Princeton: Princeton University Press, 1959.

Perkins, James Breck. *France in the American Revolution*. 1911. Reprint, Williamstown, Mass.: Corner House Publishers, 1970.

Porter, Roy, ed. *Rewriting the Self: Histories from the Renaissance to the Present*. London and New York: Routledge, 1997.

Potts, Louis W. *Arthur Lee: A Virtuous Revolutionary*. Baton Rouge: Louisiana State University Press, 1981.

Quarles, Benjamin. *The Negro in the American Revolution*. Chapel Hill: University of North Carolina Press, 1961.

Rakove, Jack N. *The Beginnings of National Politics: An Interpretive History of the Continental Congress*. New York: Alfred A. Knopf, 1979.

Robinson, Donald L. *Slavery in the Structure of American Politics, 1765–1820*. New York: Harcourt Brace Jovanovich, 1971.

Rogers, George C. Jr. *Charleston in the Age of the Pinckneys*. Norman: University of Oklahoma Press, 1969. Reprint, Columbia: University of South Carolina Press, 1980.

———. *Evolution of a Federalist: William Loughton Smith of Charleston (1758–1812)*. Columbia: University of South Carolina Press, 1962.

Royster, Charles. *A Revolutionary People at War: The Continental Army and American Character, 1775–1783*. Chapel Hill: University of North Carolina Press, 1979.

———. *Light-Horse Harry Lee and the Legacy of the American Revolution*. New York: Alfred A. Knopf, 1981.

Scheer, George F., and Hugh F. Rankin. *Rebels and Redcoats*. New York: World, 1957.

Shaffer, Arthur. *To Be an American: David Ramsay and the Making of the American Consciousness*. Columbia: University of South Carolina Press, 1991.

Sheriff, John K. *The Good-Natured Man: The Evolution of a Moral Ideal, 1660–1800*. University, Ala.: University of Alabama Press, 1982.

Shneidman, Edwin. *Definitions of Suicide*. New York: John Wiley & Sons, 1985.

Sirmans, M. Eugene. *Colonial South Carolina: A Political History*. Chapel Hill: University of North Carolina Press, 1966.

Smith, Daniel Blake. *Inside the Great House: Planter Family Life in Eighteenth-Century Chesapeake Society*. Ithaca, N.Y.: Cornell University Press, 1980.

Smith, Paul H. *Loyalists and Redcoats: A Study in British Revolutionary Policy*. Chapel Hill: University of North Carolina Press, 1964.

Stinchcombe, William C. *The American Revolution and the French Alliance*. Syracuse, N.Y.: Syracuse University Press, 1969.

Stourzh, Gerald. *Benjamin Franklin and American Foreign Policy*. Chicago: University of Chicago Press, 1954.

Taylor, Charles. *Sources of the Self: The Making of the Modern Identity*. Cambridge: Harvard University Press, 1989.

Thayer, Theodore. *The Making of a Scapegoat: Washington and Lee at Monmouth*. Port Washington, N.Y.: Kennikat Press, 1976.

Thomas, Peter D. G. *British Politics and the Stamp Act Crisis: The First Phase of the American Revolution, 1763–1767.* Oxford: Clarendon Press, 1975.

Tilley, John A. *The British Navy and the American Revolution.* Columbia: University of South Carolina Press, 1987.

Townsend, Sara Bertha. *An American Soldier: The Life of John Laurens.* Raleigh, N.C.: Edwards & Broughton, 1958.

Van Doren, Carl. *Mutiny in January.* New York: Viking, 1943.

———. *Secret History of the American Revolution.* New York: Viking, 1941.

Van Winter, Pieter J. *American Finance and Dutch Investment, 1780–1805.* Translated by James C. Riley. 2 vols. New York: Arno Press, 1977.

Wallace, David Duncan. *The Life of Henry Laurens, with a Sketch of the Life of Lieutenant-Colonel John Laurens.* New York: G. P. Putnam's Sons, 1915.

Ward, Christopher. *The War of the Revolution.* Edited by John Richard Alden. 2 vols. New York: Macmillan, 1952.

Weir, Robert M. *"A Most Important Epocha": The Coming of the Revolution in South Carolina.* Columbia: University of South Carolina Press, 1970.

———. *Colonial South Carolina: A History.* Millwood, N.Y.: KTO Press, 1983.

Whiteley, Emily Stone. *Washington and His Aides-De-Camp.* New York: Macmillan, 1936.

Whittemore, Charles P. *A General of the Revolution: John Sullivan of New Hampshire.* New York: Columbia University Press, 1961.

Wickwire, Franklin, and Mary Wickwire. *Cornwallis: The American Adventure.* Boston: Houghton Mifflin, 1970.

Willcox, William B. *Portrait of a General: Sir Henry Clinton in the War of Independence.* New York: Alfred A. Knopf, 1964.

Wood, Gordon S. *The Creation of the American Republic, 1776–1787.* Chapel Hill: University of North Carolina Press, 1969.

———. *The Radicalism of the American Revolution.* New York: Alfred A. Knopf, 1992.

Wood, Peter H. *Black Majority: Negroes in Colonial South Carolina from 1670 through the Stono Rebellion.* New York: Alfred A. Knopf, 1974.

Articles and Essays

Adair, Douglass. "Fame and the Founding Fathers." In *Fame and the Founding Fathers: Essays by Douglass Adair,* edited by Trevor Colbourn, 3–26. New York: W. W. Norton, 1974.

Bodle, Wayne. "Generals and 'Gentlemen': Pennsylvania Politics and the Decision for Valley Forge." *Pennsylvania History* 62 (Winter 1995): 59–89.

Brown, Martha H. "Clothing." In *Dictionary of Afro-American Slavery,* edited by Randall M. Miller and John David Smith, 117–21. Westport, Conn.: Greenwood Press, 1988.

Bullion, John L. "'The Ten Thousand in America': More Light on the Decision on the American Army, 1762–1763." *William and Mary Quarterly,* 3rd ser., 43 (October 1986): 647–54.

Calhoon Robert M., and Robert M. Weir. "'The Scandalous History of Sir Egerton Leigh.'" *William and Mary Quarterly,* 3rd ser., 26 (January 1969): 47–74.

Cavanagh, John C. "American Military Leadership in the Southern Campaign: Benjamin Lincoln." In *The Revolutionary War in the South: Power, Conflict, and Lead-*

ership. Essays in Honor of John Richard Alden, edited by W. Robert Higgins, 101–31. Durham, N.C.: Duke University Press, 1979.

Chaplin, Joyce E. "Slavery and the Principle of Humanity: A Modern Idea in the Early Lower South." *Journal of Social History* 24 (Winter 1990): 299–315.

Coclanis, Peter A. "The Hydra Head of Merchant Capital: Markets and Merchants in Early South Carolina." In *The Meaning of South Carolina History: Essays in Honor of George C. Rogers Jr.,* edited by Clyde N. Wilson and David R. Chesnutt, 1–18. Columbia: University of South Carolina Press, 1991.

Crane, R. S. "Suggestions Toward a Genealogy of the 'Man of Feeling.'" *ELH: A Journal of English Literary History* 1 (December 1934): 205–30.

Crompton, Louis. "Byron and Male Love: The Classical Tradition." In *The Making of Masculinities: The New Men's Studies,* edited by Harry Brod, 325–32. Boston: Allen & Unwin, 1987.

Dull, Jonathan R. "Benjamin Franklin and the Nature of American Diplomacy." *International History Review* 3 (August 1983): 346–63.

Farberow, Norman L. "Indirect Self-Destructive Behavior: Classification and Characteristics." In *The Many Faces of Suicide: Indirect Self-Destructive Behavior,* edited by Norman L. Farberow, 15–27. New York: McGraw-Hill, 1980.

Felson, Richard B. "Self-Concept." In *Encyclopedia of Sociology,* edited by Edgar F. Borgatta and Marie L. Borgatta, vol. 4, 1743–49. New York: Macmillan, 1992.

Ferling, John. "John Adams, Diplomat." *William and Mary Quarterly,* 3rd ser., 51 (April 1994): 227–52.

Fitzpatrick, John. "William Jackson." In *Dictionary of American Biography,* edited by Allen Johnson and Dumas Malone, vol. 9, 559–61. New York: Charles Scribner's Sons, 1928–58.

Fitzsimons, David M. "Tom Paine's New World Order: Idealistic Internationalism in the Ideology of Early American Foreign Relations." *Diplomatic History* 19 (Fall 1995): 569–82.

Frech, Laura P. "The Republicanism of Henry Laurens." *South Carolina Historical Magazine* 76 (April 1975): 68–79.

Gallay, Alan. "The Origins of Slaveholders' Paternalism: George Whitefield, the Bryan Family, and the Great Awakening in the South." *Journal of Southern History* 52 (August 1987): 369–94.

Geertz, Clifford. "'From the Native's Point of View': On the Nature of Anthropological Understanding." In *Culture Theory: Essays on Mind, Self, and Emotion,* edited by Richard A. Shweder and Robert A. LeVine, 123–36. Cambridge: Cambridge University Press, 1984.

Gillespie, Joanna Bowen. "Martha Laurens Ramsay's 'Dark Night of the Soul.'" *William and Mary Quarterly,* 3rd ser., 48 (January 1991): 68–92.

Greene, Jack P. "The Concept of Virtue in Late Colonial British America." In *Imperatives, Behaviors, and Identities: Essays in Early American Cultural History,* 208–35. Charlottesville: University Press of Virginia, 1992.

———. "Search for Identity: An Interpretation of the Meaning of Selected Patterns of Social Response in Eighteenth-Century America." In *Imperatives, Behaviors, and Identities: Essays in Early American Cultural History,* 143–73. Charlottesville: University Press of Virginia, 1992.

———. "'Slavery or Independence': Some Reflections on the Relationship among Liberty, Black Bondage and Equality in Revolutionary South Carolina." *South Carolina Historical Magazine* 80 (July 1979): 193–214.

———. "The Seven Years' War and the American Revolution: The Causal Relationship Reconsidered." *Journal of Imperial and Commonwealth History* 8 (January 1980): 85–105.

Hargrove, Richard J. "Portrait of a Southern Patriot: The Life and Death of John Laurens." In *The Revolutionary War in the South: Power, Conflict, and Leadership. Essays in Honor of John Richard Alden,* edited by W. Robert Higgins, 182–202. Durham, N.C.: Duke University Press, 1979.

Haskell, Thomas L. "Capitalism and the Humanitarian Sensibility, Part I." *American Historical Review* 90 (April 1985): 339–61.

Haw, James. "A Broken Compact: Insecurity, Union, and the Proposed Surrender of Charleston, 1779." *South Carolina Historical Magazine* 96 (January 1995): 30–53.

Herbst, Jurgen. "The First Three American Colleges: Schools of the Reformation." *Perspectives in American History* 8 (1974): 7–52.

Humphreys, A. R. "'The Friend of Mankind' (1700–60)—An Aspect of Eighteenth-Century Sensibility." *Review of English Studies* 24 (July 1948): 203–18.

Hutson, James H. "The American Negotiators: The Diplomacy of Jealousy." In *Peace and the Peacemakers: The Treaty of 1783,* edited by Ronald Hoffman and Peter J. Albert, 52–69. Charlottesville: University Press of Virginia, 1986.

———. "Intellectual Foundations of Early American Diplomacy." *Diplomatic History* 1 (Winter 1977): 1–19.

———. "The Origins of 'The Paranoid Style in American Politics': Public Jealousy from the Age of Walpole to the Age of Jackson." In *Saints & Revolutionaries: Essays on Early American History,* edited by David D. Hall, John M. Murrin, and Thad W. Tate, 332–72. New York: W. W. Norton, 1984.

Jones, Eldon. "The British Withdrawal from the South, 1781–85." In *The Revolutionary War in the South: Power, Conflict, and Leadership. Essays in Honor of John Richard Alden,* edited by W. Robert Higgins, 259–85. Durham, N.C.: Duke University Press, 1979.

Knight, Betsy. "Prisoner Exchange and Parole in the American Revolution." *William and Mary Quarterly,* 3rd ser., 48 (April 1991): 201–22.

Langford, Paul. "Thomas Day and the Politics of Sentiment." In *Perspectives on Imperialism and Decolonization: Essays in Honor of A. F. Madden,* edited by P. Holland and G. Rizvi, 57–79. London: Cass, 1984.

Lennon, Donald R. "'The Graveyard of American Commanders': The Continental Army's Southern Department, 1776–1778." *North Carolina Historical Review* 67 (April 1990): 133–58.

Litman, Robert E. "Psychodynamics of Indirect Self-Destructive Behavior." In *The Many Faces of Suicide: Indirect Self-Destructive Behavior,* edited by Norman L. Farberow, 28–40. New York: McGraw-Hill, 1980.

Lonsdale, Roger. "Dr. Burney, 'Joel Collier,' and Sabrina." In *Evidence in Literary Scholarship: Essays in Memory of James Marshall Osborn,* edited by René Wellek and Alvaro Ribeiro, 281–308. Oxford: Clarendon Press, 1979.

Maris, Ronald W. "Suicide," in *Encyclopedia of Human Biology,* edited by Renato Dulbecco, vol. 7, 327–35. New York: Academic Press, 1991.

Martin, John. "Inventing Sincerity, Refashioning Prudence: The Discovery of the Individual in Renaissance Europe." *American Historical Review* 102 (December 1997): 1309–42.

Maslowski, Pete. "National Policy Toward the Use of Black Troops in the Revolution." *South Carolina Historical Magazine* 73 (January 1972): 1–17.

Massey, Gregory D. "The Limits of Antislavery Thought in the Revolutionary Lower South: John Laurens and Henry Laurens." *Journal of Southern History* 63 (August 1997): 495–530.

Menard, Russell R. "Slavery, Economic Growth, and Revolutionary Ideology in the South Carolina Lowcountry." In *The Economy of Early America: The Revolutionary Period, 1763–1790*, edited by Ronald Hoffman, John J. McCusker, Russell R. Menard, and Peter J. Albert, 244–74. Charlottesville: University Press of Virginia, 1988.

Morgan, Edmund S. "The Puritan Ethic and the American Revolution." *William and Mary Quarterly*, 3rd ser., 24 (January 1967): 3–43.

Morgan, Philip. "Three Planters and Their Slaves: Perspectives on Slavery in Virginia, South Carolina, and Jamaica, 1750–1790." In *Race and Family in the Colonial South*, edited by Winthrop D. Jordan and Sheila L. Skemp, 37–79. Jackson: University Press of Mississippi, 1987.

Mullan, John. "Feelings and Novels." In *Rewriting the Self: Histories from the Renaissance to the Present*, edited by Roy Porter, 119–31. London and New York: Routledge, 1997.

Murphy, Orville T. "Charles Gravier de Vergennes: Profile of an Old Regime Diplomat." *Political Science Quarterly* 83 (September 1968): 400–418.

———. "The View from Versailles: Charles Gravier Comte de Vergennes's Perceptions of the American Revolution." In *Diplomacy and Revolution: The Franco-American Alliance of 1778*, edited by Ronald Hoffman and Peter J. Albert, 107–49. Charlottesville: University Press of Virginia, 1981.

Olwell, Robert A. "'A Reckoning of Accounts': Patriarchy, Market Relations, and Control on Henry Laurens's Lowcountry Plantations, 1762–1785." In *Working Toward Freedom: Slave Society and Domestic Economy in the American South*, edited by Larry E. Hudson, 33–52. Rochester, N.Y.: University of Rochester Press, 1994.

———. "'Domestick Enemies': Slavery and Political Independence in South Carolina, May 1775–March 1776." *Journal of Southern History* 55 (February 1989): 21–48.

Pincus, Steve. "Neither Machiavellian Moment nor Possessive Individualism: Commercial Society and the Defenders of the English Commonwealth." *American Historical Review* 103 (June 1998): 705–36.

Puiz, Anne-Marie. "La Genève des Lumières." In *Histoire de Genéve*, edited by Paul Guichonnet, 225–54. Toulouse: Edouard Privat, 1974.

Radner, John B. "The Art of Sympathy in Eighteenth-Century British Moral Thought." In *Studies in Eighteenth-Century Culture*, edited by Roseann Runte, vol. 9, 189–210. Madison: University of Wisconsin Press, 1979.

Rogers, George C. Jr. "South Carolina Federalists and the Origins of the Nullification Movement." *South Carolina Historical Magazine* 71 (January 1970): 17–32.

———. "A Tribute to Henry Laurens." *South Carolina Historical Magazine* 92 (October 1991): 269–76.

Rorty, Amélie Oksenberg, and David Wong, "Aspects of Identity and Agency." In *Identity, Character and Morality: Essays in Moral Psychology*, edited by Owen

Flanagan and Amélie Oksenberg Rorty, 19–36. Cambridge, Mass. and London: MIT Press, 1990.

Rosaldo, Michelle Z. "Toward an Anthropology of Self and Feeling." In *Culture Theory: Essays on Mind, Self, and Emotion,* edited by Richard A. Shweder and Robert A. LeVine, 137–57. Cambridge: Cambridge University Press, 1984.

Rosen, George. "History." In *A Handbook for the Study of Suicide,* edited by Seymour Perlin, 3–29. New York: Oxford University Press, 1975.

Sherrod, Drury. "The Bonds of Men: Problems and Possibilities in Close Male Relationships." In *The Making of Masculinities: The New Men's Studies,* edited by Harry Brod, 213–39. Boston: Allen & Unwin, 1987.

Shy, John. "A New Look at Colonial Militia." *William and Mary Quarterly,* 3rd ser., 20 (April 1963): 175–85.

———. "American Strategy: Charles Lee and the Radical Alternative." In *A People Numerous and Armed: Reflections on the Military Struggle for American Independence,* 133–62. New York: Oxford University Press, 1976.

———. "The American Revolution: The Military Conflict Considered as a Revolutionary War." In *Essays on the American Revolution,* edited by Stephen G. Kurtz and James H. Hutson, 121–56. Chapel Hill: University of North Carolina Press, 1973.

Smith, D. E. Huger. "The Luxembourg Claims." *South Carolina Historical Magazine* 10 (April 1909): 92–115.

Spiro, Melford E. "Some Reflections on Cultural Determinism and Relativism with Special Reference to Emotion and Reason." In *Culture Theory: Essays on Mind, Self, and Emotion,* edited by Richard A. Shweder and Robert A. LeVine, 323–46. Cambridge: Cambridge University Press, 1984.

Stone, Richard G. Jr. "'The *South Carolina* We've Lost': The Bizarre Saga of Alexander Gillon and His Frigate." *The American Neptune* 39 (July 1979): 159–72.

Stryker, Sheldon. "Identity Theory." In *Encyclopedia of Sociology,* edited by Edgar F. Borgatta and Marie L. Borgatta, vol. 2, 871–76. New York: Macmillan, 1992.

Toufexis, Anastasia. "What Makes Them Do It." *Time,* 15 January 1996, 60.

Watt, Jeffrey R. "The Family, Love, and Suicide in Early Modern Geneva." *Journal of Family History* 21 (January 1996): 63–86.

Weir, Robert M. "'The Harmony We Were Famous For': An Interpretation of Pre-Revolutionary South Carolina Politics." *William and Mary Quarterly,* 3rd ser., 26 (October 1969): 473–501.

———. "John Laurens: Portrait of a Hero." *American Heritage,* April 1976.

———. "Rebelliousness: Personality Development and the American Revolution in the Southern Colonies." In *The Southern Experience in the American Revolution,* edited by Jeffrey J. Crow and Larry E. Tise, 25–54. Chapel Hill: University of North Carolina Press, 1978.

———. "The South Carolinian as Extremist." In *"The Last of American Freemen": Studies in the Political Culture of the Colonial and Revolutionary South,* 213–30. Macon, Ga.: Mercer University Press, 1986.

———. "'The Violent Spirit,' the Reestablishment of Order, and the Continuity of Leadership in Postrevolutionary South Carolina." In *"The Last of American Freemen": Studies in the Political Culture of the Colonial and Revolutionary South,* 133–58. Macon, Ga.: Mercer University Press, 1986.

Wood, Gordon S. "Conspiracy and the Paranoid Style: Causality and Deceit in the Eighteenth Century." *William and Mary Quarterly,* 3rd ser., 39 (December 1982): 401–41.

Wood, Peter H. "'Liberty is Sweet': African-American Freedom Struggles in the Years before White Independence." In *Beyond the American Revolution: Explorations in the History of American Radicalism,* edited by Alfred F. Young, 149–84. DeKalb: Northern Illinois Press, 1993.

Wyatt, Frederick, and William B. Willcox. "Sir Henry Clinton: A Psychological Exploration in History." *William and Mary Quarterly,* 3rd ser., 16 (January 1959): 3–26.

Zuckerman, Michael. "A Different Thermidor: The Revolution Beyond the American Revolution." In *The Transformation of Early American History: Society, Authority, and Ideology,* edited by James A. Henretta, Michael Kammen, and Stanley N. Katz, 170–93. New York: Alfred A. Knopf, 1991.

————. "Penmanship Exercises for Saucy Sons: Some Thoughts on the Colonial Southern Family." *South Carolina Historical Magazine* 84 (July 1983): 152–66.

Theses, Dissertations, and Unpublished Conference Papers

Clark, Peggy J. "Henry Laurens's Role in the Anglo-American Peace Negotiations." Master's thesis, University of South Carolina, 1991.

Coker, Kathy Roe. "The Punishment of Revolutionary War Loyalists in South Carolina." Ph.D. diss., University of South Carolina, 1987.

Frech, Laura Page. "The Career of Henry Laurens in the Continental Congress, 1777–1779." Ph.D. diss., University of North Carolina, 1972.

Grimball, Berkeley. "Commodore Alexander Gillon of South Carolina, 1741–1794." Master's thesis, Duke University, 1951.

Horne, Paul Adams Jr. "The Governorship of John Mathews, 1782–1783." Master's thesis, University of South Carolina, 1982.

McDonough, Daniel Joseph. "Christopher Gadsden and Henry Laurens: The Parallel Lives of Two American Patriots." Ph.D. diss., University of Illinois at Urbana-Champaign, 1990.

Smith, Samuel C. "Henry Laurens: Christian Pietist." Paper presented at the conference "New Directions in Carolina Lowcountry Studies: From the Revolution to the Civil War, 1775–1860," College of Charleston, 9–11 May 1996.

Sydenham, Diane Meredith, "Practitioner and Patient: The Practice of Medicine in Eighteenth-Century South Carolina." Ph.D. diss., Johns Hopkins University, 1979.

Templin, Thomas E. "Henry 'Light Horse Harry' Lee: A Biography." Ph.D. diss., University of Kentucky, 1975.

Index

Abbeville, S.C., 237

Active (ship), 188, 280n. 69

Adams, John: appointed peace commissioner, 189; diplomatic style of, 183, 190; and goods purchased in the Netherlands, 194; informs HL of JL's death, 231; and de Neufville and Gillon, 184–85; on JL, 190; and petition by JL's heirs, 236

Albany, N.Y., 74, 224

Alliance (Continental Navy frigate), 175, 177, 185, 278n. 49

Altamaha River, 14, 71

Amsterdam, Netherlands, 184–85

André, John, 169–70

Anglican church, 8, 32

Ansonborough, HL's house at, 11–12, 24, 137, 160, 232

Appendix to the Extracts (Henry Laurens), 19

Appleby, George, 9, 14, 22, 27–28, 36

Arbuthnot, Marriot, 157, 160, 162

Aristotle, 82

army, British: deserters from, 116, 214; evacuation preparations in Charleston, 221, 225; foraging expeditions of, 87, 213, 222, 225–27; harshness of, 140, 202; Hessians serving with, 118, 120, 140, 158–59, 196, 199; and military use

of blacks, 209, 223; officers of, 82, 204; performance in battle, 75, 76–77, 109–10, 120, 147; in Philadelphia, 85, 92; reaction to JL's death, 228; seizure of slaves by, 215; and sequestered American estates, 215–16; and siege of Charleston, 156, 159, 160, 162; and siege of Yorktown, 196, 198–99; supply shortages, 216–17, 222

army, Continental: black troops enlisted in, 132; description of, 69; foreign officers in, 80, 101, 123; and impressments, 202, 217–18; lack of, in South Carolina, 134, 207; mutinies, 174–75, 176; officers of, 4, 81–82, 97–98, 101–2, 123–24, 164, 167; performance in battle, 77, 110, 120, 147, 198–99; promotions in, 84, 89–90, 101–2, 123–24, 152–53; reinforcements sent to Charleston, 150; and siege of Yorktown, 196, 200; soldiers of, 87, 97, 103, 164; supply shortages, 87, 159, 164, 171, 174; at Valley Forge, 85, 86–87, 102, 103, 106

army, Continental, regiments in: Delaware Regiment of light infantry, 212, 220, 225, 226; Fifth South Carolina Regiment, 147; First